The Art of Living

SATHER CLASSICAL LECTURES

Volume Sixty-one

THE ART OF LIVING

The Art of Living

Socratic Reflections
from Plato to Foucault

Alexander Nehamas

UNIVERSITY OF CALIFORNIA PRESS

Berkeley / Los Angeles / London

University of California Press
Berkeley and Los Angeles, California

University of California Press, Ltd.
London, England

© 1998 by
The Regents of the University of California

Library of Congress Cataloging-in-Publication Data

Nehamas, Alexander, 1946–
    The art of living : Socratic reflections from Plato to Foucault /
Alexander Nehamas.
        p.   cm. — (Sather classical lectures; v. 61)
    Includes bibliographic references and index.
    ISBN 0-520-21173-1 (cloth : alk. paper)
        1. Conduct of life.   2. Socrates.   3. Philosophers — Conduct of
    life.   I. Title.   II. Series.
BJ1595.N37   1998
190 — dc21   97-25834
                                                                  CIP

Printed in the United States of America
9   8   7   6   5   4   3

The paper used in this publication meets the minimum requirements of
American National Standards for Information Sciences — Permanence
of Paper for Printed Library Materials, ANSI Z39.48-1984.

*For Susan Glimcher
and Nicholas Nehamas*

Contents

Preface

The invitation to deliver the Sather Classical Lectures is perhaps the greatest honor that can be bestowed on a classical scholar. When the scholar in question is not really a classicist, as I am not, the honor is even greater, but the responsibility it imposes is very heavy indeed. The honor the Department of Classics at the University of California at Berkeley did me by their invitation to be the Sather Professor of Classical Literature in 1992–93 filled me with joy. The sense of responsibility that came along with it filled me with terror. The terror soon outstripped the joy, and for a long time I was not at all sure that I would really be able to discharge my obligations in a reasonable manner. The lectures finally having been delivered in the Spring Term of 1993, I am now faced with the same sentiment of joy subdued by terror as I contemplate the book I have produced as a result. I am acutely aware of the book's inadequacies, and I realize in addition that some classical scholars may find that many of its concerns do not fit squarely with their own professional interests. Though that is something I am sorry for, it is an unavoidable feature of this work. A central part of the book's argument is that the effort to combine diverse and sometimes conflicting features into a unity is an activity crucial both to philosophy and to life and that its model—the model of the most extreme and alluring unity—is the Socrates of Plato's early dialogues. In that way, I combine my own philosophical interests with the little I know about classics and literary criticism, in the hope that the final combination can form a unity of its own.

It is impossible to imagine how I can thank my colleagues at Berkeley enough without at the same time repeating what so many others before me have already said. The department as a whole demonstrated an exquis-ite combination of tact and hospitality—tact in leaving me to myself while I was madly at work on those lectures that were still not finished by the time I arrived in California, and hospitality in welcoming me as one of their own once the series began. Mark Griffith was a constant source of good cheer and reassurance. I was particularly happy to renew my friend-ship with Tony Long, who also presented a set of very valuable comments on the first three lectures. Giovanni Ferrari and Kate Toll were intellec-tually interesting and socially elegant companions. My interactions with William Anderson, Stephen Miller, Charles Murgia, Ronald Stroud, and Thomas Rosenmeyer were consistently pleasant and profitable.

Hans Sluga, whose comments on the second set of three lectures were particularly helpful, Judith Stacey, Bernard Williams, and Richard Wollheim were kind enough to discuss various aspects of my ideas with me while I was in California. John Cooper—a real model of what a friend and col-league should be, and to whom I owe so much over so many years and for so many different reasons, personal as well as intellectual—and Jerry Schneewind interrupted their own research at the Center for Advanced Study in the Behavioral Sciences in Stanford to come to Berkeley and offer me their company and encouragement. Froma Zeitlin gave me invaluable guidance while I was preparing my lectures: I hope I was able to return part of the favor while she was herself preparing and delivering her own Sather Lectures in 1995–96. Paul Guyer, despite our vastly dif-ferent approaches to philosophy, has always helped me formulate and hone many of my views over many years and in various places, and I am grate-ful to him for his generosity. Myles Burnyeat heard me out on a number of occasions, and a particular suggestion he once made proved crucial to my final conception of Socrates' version of what this book calls the art of living. Vassilis Lambropoulos provoked me to think about some very difficult issues on the basis of his extraordinary reading of my introduction.

The influence of Gregory Vlastos, who died before the lectures were delivered and with whose views on Socrates this book engages in a run-ning dialogue, will be too obvious to every reader of this book for me to have to do anything but mention it here. I disagree with him on many important issues. I wish he could have been there and that I could have had the benefit of his stern but always considerate advice. I did not, by contrast, seek to benefit from Sarah Kofman's *Socrate* (Paris: Galilée, 1989). Her book discusses many of the authors I too address, but her approach differs so much from mine that to engage with her work, for which I have the deepest admiration, would have forced my argument to become even more convoluted than it already is. I hope to be able to write about her ideas on a separate occasion. I must also express my thanks to James Miller, who generously provided me with a transcript of the lectures of Michel Foucault that constitute the main subject of chapter 6, and for his interest in the main subject of this book.

Rachel Barney, Philip Robbins, and Mika Provata provided me with efficient and cheerful research assistance. I am grateful to them for their efforts.

I owe a deeper and more intimate debt to Thomas Laqueur, who participated in the conception, preparation, delivery, and revision of these lectures, from the very beginning to the very end. Considerate in listening, quick in understanding, thoughtful in advising, he has influenced every aspect of my work. Along with Gail Saliterman, he took the most generous practical care of me while I was living in Berkeley: I don't know what I would have done without him. He has shown me why Horace was right to say that a friend is one half of one's own soul.

Susan Glimcher and Nicholas Nehamas, in their vastly different ways, put up with behavior on my part which I sincerely doubt I would have been able to forgive in them. A family makes what this book calls a philosophical life much more complex and difficult than it might otherwise be. But that complexity is worth accepting and integrating with the rest of one's life and work. My own family, who even agreed with all the good will in the world to cancel a long-planned trip to Greece on the eve of our departure so that this book could be finished in time, has proved to me that Nietzsche's quip, "A married philosopher belongs to comedy," is not simply wrong but a comically shallow and ignorant joke. There are no constraints on the materials of which a philosophic life can consist: I am grateful to have learned that lesson and I offer them my thanks for having taught it to me.

When will you begin to live virtuously, Plato
asked an old man who was telling him that
he was attending a series of lectures on virtue.
One must not just speculate for ever; one must
one day also think about actual practice. But
today we think that those who live as they
teach are dreamers.

Immanuel Kant,
The Philosophical Encyclopaedia

When one has no character one has to apply
a method.

Albert Camus, *The Fall*

Introduction

Philosophy is a theoretical discipline. It has few practical implications for everyday life. The various fields of "applied" philosophy that have emerged in recent years—medical or business ethics, for example—have been quickly absorbed by the professions they concern. To the extent that they really are practical, these fields belong more to medicine or business than to philosophy itself. Philosophy also has few implications for the life of those who practice it. What philosophers study makes no more claim to affecting their personal lives than the work of physicists, mathematicians, or economists is expected to affect theirs. And yet there is a lingering sense in most people as well as in a few philosophers that somehow that is not how matters should be, a sense of puzzlement and even of disappointment that the lives of philosophers do not reflect their convictions.

"Philosophy is a theoretical discipline." Like many general statements, this one too conceals a perfect tense in its apparently timeless "is." The truth is that philosophy *has become* a theoretical discipline over time and as a result of many complex historical developments. The "fact" that its "nature" is theoretical is nothing but the historically given reality that philosophy has mainly been practiced as a theoretical discipline for as long as the knowledge and memory of most philosophers extend. Since we generally tend to consider what is true near us to be true everywhere else as well and to identify the products of history with the facts of nature, we also believe that our current practice displays the unchanging essence of philosophy. Which is not to say that philosophy "really" is a practical discipline after all: that would simply be to confuse another one of its historical phases with its nature; it would betray the same lack of historical sense.

During the period that began with classical Greece and ended in late pagan antiquity, philosophy was more than a merely theoretical discipline. Even when Aristotle identified philosophy with "theory," his purpose was to argue, as he does in the tenth and last book of the *Nicomachean Ethics*, that a *life* of theoretical activity, the life of philosophy, was the best life that human beings could lead. One could not lead such a life unless one acquired not only a number of philosophical views but also, over time and through serious effort, the very particular sort of character whose elements and presuppositions Aristotle described and justified in the previous nine books of the *Ethics*. The theoretical life, in turn, affects the character of those who lead it. Theory and practice, discourse and life, affect one another; people become philosophers because they are able and willing to be the best human type and to live as well as a human being possibly can.[1] What one believes and how one lives have a direct bearing on one another.

Since my own view is that no single mode of life exists that is best for all people and that the philosophical life is only one among many praiseworthy ways of living, I do not urge a "return" to a conception of philosophy as a way of life, or, as I shall often call it in this book, the art of living. But I do believe that we should recognize that such a conception exists, study how it survives in some major modern philosophers, and see that it is what some of us are still doing today. This book aims at opening a space for a way of doing philosophy that constitutes an alternative, though not necessarily a competitor, to the manner in which philosophy is generally practiced in our time. Some philosophers want to find the answers to general and important questions, including questions about ethics and the nature of the good life, without believing that their answers have much to do with the kind of person they themselves turn out to be. Others believe that general views, when organized in the right manner and adhered to in everyday life, create a right sort of person—perhaps really good, perhaps simply unforgettable and, to that extent, admirable. In the case of pure theory, the only issue that matters is whether the answers to one's questions are or are not correct. In the case of theory that affects life, the truth of one's views is still an issue, but what also matters is the kind of person, the sort of self, one manages to construct as a result of accepting them.

The sort of self one constructs as a result of adopting certain theories is not simply a biographical matter. It is, much more importantly, a literary and philosophical accomplishment. The self presented by the philosophers I discuss here is to be found in their writings. It can function as an example that others, depending on their own views and preferences, can either imitate or avoid. It is a sort of blueprint that others with a similar purpose can follow, ignore, or deny as they form their own selves. It is a philosophical accomplishment because the content and nature of the self created in the process I will try to describe in what follows depends on holding views on issues that have traditionally been considered philosophical and not on anything one pleases. It is literary because the connection between those philosophical views is not only a matter of systematic logical interrelations but also, more centrally, a matter of style. It is a question of putting those views together so that, even when the connections between them are not strictly logical, it makes psychological and interpretative sense to attribute them to a single, coherent character. It is reasonable to say that a single person can hold them all. That is another way of saying that holding such views creates a character in the way that literary characters are created by and consist of everything they say and do within the works in which they appear. Philosophers of the art of living, however, usually play a double and more complex role. With the notable exception of Socrates, with whom their tradition originates, and a few others (the skeptic Pyrrho comes immediately to mind)[2] who did not compose any works of their own, they are both the characters their writings generate and the authors of the writings in which their characters exist. They are creators and creatures in one.

We are therefore faced with at least two conceptions of philosophy. One avoids personal style and idiosyncrasy as much as possible. Its aim is to deface the particular personality that offers answers to philosophical questions, since all that matters is the quality of the answers and not the nature of the character who offers them. The other requires style and idiosyncrasy because its readers must never forget that the views that confront them are the views of a particular type of person and of no one else. That is why it is composed in a self-conscious literary manner; and that is one of the reasons the modern philosophers I consider in this book— Montaigne, Nietzsche, and Foucault—have by and large belonged to literature, history, or anthropology departments and not to the traditional canon of analytical philosophy as it has been practiced so far. To theoretical philosophers, the construction of character appears to be merely a literary enterprise. And if we think, as we do, of philosophy in impersonal terms, it will be, as it has been, difficult to think of such authors as philosophers at all. The same is true, I believe, of other figures whom I do not discuss here: they include (this is a partial list) Pascal, Schopenhauer, Kierkegaard, Emerson, Thoreau, and, on one reading at least, Wittgenstein as well.

For a long time, each side has been suspicious of the other. Systematic philosophers think of the philosophers of the art of living at best as "poets" or literary figures, at worst as charlatans writing for precocious teenagers or, what for many amounts to the same thing, for professors of literature. The philosophers of the art of living accuse systematic philosophy of being a misguided and self-deceived way of doing what they consider true philosophy to be. They think that its adherents are cowardly, dry pedants who desire scientific objectivity because they are unable to create a work that is truly their own and use disinterestedness and detachment to mask their own sterility. Both are wrong, for the same reason. They both overlook the fact that each approach is a legitimate historical development of philosophy as it began in classical Greece; neither of these approaches has an exclusive hold on the essence of philosophy (which does not, in any case, exist).

The philosophers of the art of living I discuss in this book all consider the self to be not a given but a constructed unity. The materials for that construction are supplied, at least in the beginning, by accident — by the views and events that are due to the particular circumstances in which one finds oneself and that, in the nature of the case, are different for each particular individual. One, as I will say, acquires or creates a self, one becomes an individual, by integrating those materials with others acquired and constructed on the way. When the work is finished (if it ever is) few "accidents" remain, since the elements that constitute the individual produced are all part of an orderly, organized whole. Each element makes a specific contribution to that whole, which would be different without it. Each element is therefore to that extent significant, essential to the whole of which it has become a part, and it is no longer accidental.

Expressions like "creating" or "fashioning" a self sound paradoxical. How can one not already have, or be, a self if one is to engage in any activity whatever? How can one not already have, or be, a self if one is even to be conscious of the experiences and views one is supposed to integrate? That paradox may be mitigated if we distinguish this notion of the self from the strict philosophical idea presupposed by the very fact that I am and must be conscious of my experiences as mine. It is not what Kant called the "transcendental unity of apperception," the "I think" that in principle accompanies all my experiences and is required for me to be an agent, a person, in the first place. It is a homelier notion. To create a self

is to succeed in becoming *someone*, in becoming a *character*, that is, someone unusual and distinctive. It is to become an individual, but again not
in the strict sense in which an individual is anything we can point out and
reidentify, anything that, like human beings and material things, exists
independently in space and time. To become an individual is to acquire
an uncommon and idiosyncratic character, a set of features and a mode
of life that set one apart from the rest of the world and make one memorable not only for what one did or said but also for who one was.

It might seem that I am urging that we use philosophical terms in a
nonphilosophical sense. Nietzsche has often been thought to do that: to
place the philosophical sense of a term, which he generally rejects, within
quotation marks and to continue using it in a nonphilosophical sense,
without quotation marks, in his own thought and writing. So, for example, he is supposed to deny the existence of "truth" (which many
philosophers understand as the "correspondence" of our views to the facts
of the world) while he uses his own notion of truth (a nonphilosophical
idea that has not been easy to explicate) without contradiction. I find the
distinction between philosophical and nonphilosophical senses of terms,
especially within the writing of philosophers themselves, very unclear. I
prefer to think that in many such cases we are faced with two different,
though equally "philosophical" uses of the same term. The distinction
between them, especially in the case of terms like "self" or "individual,"
is a matter of generality. In the general, weaker sense of the term, every
person has a self and is an individual, to begin with. In the narrower,
stronger sense, which will occupy me in what follows, only some people
create themselves or become individuals, over time.

These are people we remember for themselves, people we can admire
even if we reject many of their views, much in the way that we accept,
admire, and even love our friends despite their weaknesses and faults. As
we say, we know our friends as individuals. We are interested in their character as a whole, not in each and every one of their features separately and
in its own right. Even their weaknesses are essential to their being the
people we are happy to be close to. However, it is hard to believe that we
can really keep as a friend someone who never thinks anything true and
never does anything right. Similarly, it is hard to believe that philosophers
can practice the art of living successfully, that they can become individuals, if each and every one of their views, however artfully it is has been
woven together with the rest, is obviously or trivially mistaken. In both
cases, we must have some respect for the content of what is organized
into the whole we love or admire. But just as we can be wrong in choos-

ing our friends, so we can admire the wrong philosophers. And just as our choice of friends shows something about our own character, so the philosophers we admire reveal something about our own personality as well. The study of philosophy as the art of living discloses our own ethical preferences and compels us to reveal part of ourselves. This personal type of philosophy reflects on our own person, and it is personal in that additional sense as well. To study it is also to practice it.

Not everyone who has constructed an unusual life has been a philosopher. Great literary authors, visual artists, scientists, public figures, and even generals have often left similar legacies. What distinguishes the philosophers from those others? To begin with, we must realize that the distinction is fluid: at its edges, the project of constructing a philosophical life is not easily separated from the activities or the goals of literary figures like Proust, Rimbaud, or Oscar Wilde. And that is as it should be. The boundaries of philosophy have never been absolutely clear: just as, at one end, philosophy comes close to mathematics, psychology, and even physics, it slides over into literature at the other. But differences still remain.

Those who practice philosophy as the art of living construct their personalities through the investigation, the criticism, and the production of philosophical views—views, that is, that belong to the repertoire of philosophy as we have come to understand it. The connection is historical: even though the philosophers of the art of living often introduce new questions, their inspiration always comes from the tradition that we already accept as the tradition of philosophy. More important, the philosophers of the art of living make the articulation of a mode of life their central topic: it is by reflecting on the problems of constructing a philosophical life that they construct the life their work constitutes. The body of work that reflects on the philosophical life is the very content of the life it composes. The project of establishing a philosophical life is largely self-referential. Philosophical lives differ from others, to the extent that they do, because they proceed from a concern with issues that have traditionally been considered philosophical and because those issues provide the material out of which they are fashioned.

Philosophy as the art of living began with Socrates. Two features separate Socrates from those who have followed in his footsteps, especially in modern times. One is the fact that, as we have already remarked, Socrates wrote nothing himself. The Socrates who first practiced living as an art is the figure we find in Plato's Socratic dialogues.[3] And though, for reasons I explain in chapter 3, we now find it difficult to believe that

Plato's Socrates is not the Socrates of history, the fact is that to all effects and purposes Plato's literary figure is a fictional character. Even if we could isolate those elements in Plato's representation that correspond to his historical original, it is the whole character who confronts us in those works, not some smaller cluster of his features, that has fired the imagination of the tradition he created. And that, of course, raises the question whether it was in fact Socrates and not Plato himself who originates that tradition: the Platonic Socrates is also the Socratic Plato. Goethe once wrote, "He who would explain to us when men like Plato spoke in earnest, when in jest or half-jest, what they wrote from conviction and what merely for the sake of the argument, would certainly render us an extraordinary service and contribute greatly to our education."[4] That is one case no one will ever explain.

The second feature that distinguishes Socrates from the rest of his followers is that we know much less about his life than we do about theirs. We know many of the views and events that Montaigne, Nietzsche, and Foucault had to face and arrange as they tried to combine their many tendencies into one. We can follow them, more or less, in their effort to create themselves. But when Socrates appears in Plato's dialogues, he appears ready-made: he is already one; he never makes an effort. His own unity is so extreme that he even believes that the human soul, the self, is itself in principle indivisible and that it is therefore impossible for us to do anything other than what we consider to be the good. Apart from our judgment that something is a good thing to do, Socrates believes that there is no other source of motivation, no conflicting set of values or desires, that can ever push us in a different direction: there is no room for multiplicity in his view of the soul. That is a view that Socrates consistently exemplifies in his own life as Plato depicts it: he always does only what he considers the right thing to do; he never wavers in the slightest way from the course of action he has chosen as best, even at the hour of his death. There is no Garden of Gethsemane, no Mount of Olives in his story.

Does the fact that our Socrates is a literary character distinguish him from philosophers like Montaigne, Nietzsche, and Foucault, whose biographies are available to us? The difference is less decisive than it appears. For the most important accomplishments of these modern thinkers are the self-portraits that confront us in their writings. Their biographers have been disputing even the most basic facts concerning their lives and personalities. Their readers, however, can find in their writings convincing models of how a unified, meaningful life can be constructed out of the chance events that constitute it. Perhaps these people succeeded in applying their models to themselves; perhaps they did not. Whether they did is a matter of biography, and it will most likely remain a matter of contention as well. But the image of life contained in their writings is a philosophical matter, and though it too will remain a matter of contention, the contention will be over whether that image is or is not coherent or admirable. That is a different question altogether. It concerns the nature of the character constructed in their writings, the question whether life can be lived, and whether it is worth living, as they claim. It is a question about us and not primarily about them. The same is true of Plato's Socrates. Is it possible and desirable that someone might live as Socrates is shown to have lived? Is it worth living that way? That is the question that matters, not the question whether Plato's character actually led the life Plato attributes to him, whether he corresponds to a historical figure whose life is now beyond our reach and who, if we learned a lot more about him than we now know, would probably become even more controversial than he already is.

The art of living, though a practical art, is therefore practiced in writing. The question whether its practitioners applied it successfully to themselves is secondary and in most cases impossible to answer. We want a philosophy that consists of views in harmony with the actions, with the mode of life of those who hold them. But the main question still is not whether, as a matter of historical fact, someone else succeeded in living that way but whether one can construct such a life oneself. That can be done in two ways. One can either try to apply someone else's conception to one's own life, and to that extent live well, perhaps, but derivatively; or one can formulate one's own art of living. But it is difficult to imagine that one can formulate one's own art of living without writing about it because it is difficult to imagine that the complex views that such an art requires can be expressed in any other way. Further, unless one writes about it, one's art will not be able to constitute a model for others in the longer run. And the moment one writes about the art of living, the question for others again becomes not whether its originator succeeded in practicing it but whether they can in turn practice it on their own. Socrates himself wrote nothing. But had not Plato created an art of living in his name—and in writing—there would be nothing for us to think about, no art and no model to accept, reject, manipulate, or even pass by indifferently. The same is true of Montaigne, Nietzsche, and Foucault. The purpose of philosophy as the art of living is, of course, living. But the life it requires is a life in great part devoted to writing. The monument one leaves behind is in the end the permanent work, not the transient life.

It is, then, Socrates' second peculiar feature that separates him from his followers: the fact that he appears ready-made, that we have no idea how he came to be who he was. One of the most vivid characters in world literature, Socrates is also the least understood. He is a mystery because of his irony, his persistent silence about himself, which has given rise to a swirl of voices surrounding it and trying to speak for him, to explain who he was and how he came to be that way. But no interpretation, no other voice, has filled the silence that remains Socrates' main legacy.

The first of these voices is Plato's own. In the works that follow his Socratic dialogues, Plato offers a hypothesis about what enabled Socrates to lead the good life his own early dialogues attribute to him. The Socratic dialogues reflect Socrates without reflecting on him. In his later works, Plato, followed by Montaigne, Nietzsche, and Foucault, offers further reflections of that reflection as well as reflections about it. The philosophers of the art of living keep returning to Plato's Socratic works because they contain both the most coherent and the least explicable model of a philosophical life that we possess. Like a blank sheet, Socrates invites us to write; like a vast stillness, he provokes us into shouting. But he remains untouched, staring back with an ironic gaze, both beyond his reflections and nothing above their sum total.

The art of living comes in three varieties, three genres. One is that of Socrates in Plato's early dialogues. Practicing his art in public, and to that extent committed to his interlocutors' welfare, Socrates still cannot show that his mode of life is right for all. Convinced that it is, Socrates has no arguments to persuade others that his conviction is correct. He urges people to join him in the examined life he considers the only life worth living for a human being, but he has nothing to say when someone like Euthyphro simply walks away from their confrontation. His ideal may be universalist, but he has no means by which to prove that is right. He remains tentative and protreptic.

A second genre is found in Plato's middle works, especially the *Phaedo* and the *Republic*. There Plato claims that a mode of life inspired by (though not absolutely identical with) the life of Socrates, the life of philosophy as he defines it in detail in these works, is best for all, and he offers a series of controversial arguments in order to convince those who can do so to choose that life for themselves and those who can't to try to approximate it as closely as their abilities allow.[5] In other words, Plato (and in that he is followed by other great philosophers who, like Aristotle and perhaps Kant, also belong to this version of the tradition of the art of living) tries to prove that a single type of life is best for all people. Both his ideal, which he shares with Socrates, and his method, which he does not, are universalist.

The third and final genre of the art of living is the subject of this book. It is the least universalist of all. According to it, human life takes many forms and no single mode of life is best for all. Philosophers like Montaigne, Nietzsche, and Foucault articulate a way of living that only they and perhaps a few others can follow. They do not insist that their life is a model for the world at large. They do not want to be imitated, at least not directly. That is, they believe that those who want to imitate them must develop their own art of living, their own self, perhaps to exhibit it for others but not so that others imitate them directly. Imitation, in this context, is to become someone on one's own; but the someone one becomes must be different from one's model.

This last genre of the art of living is aestheticist. As in the acknowledged arts, there are no rules for producing new and exciting works. As in the acknowledged arts, there is no best work—no best life—by which all others can be judged. As in the acknowledged arts, that does not imply that judgment is impossible, that every work is as good as every other. As in the acknowledged arts, the aim is to produce as many new and different types of works—as many different modes of life—as possible, since the proliferation of aesthetic difference and multiplicity, even though it is not often in the service of morality, enriches and improves human life.

It is within this third genre that the notion of the individual finds its central place. Those who practice the individualist art of living need to be unforgettable. Like great artists, they must avoid imitation, backward and forward. They must not imitate others: if they do, they are no longer original but derivative and forgettable, leaving the field to those they imitate. They must not be imitated by too many others: if they are, their own work will cease to be remembered as such and will appear as the normal way of doing things, as a fact of nature rather than as an individual accomplishment. We will see in chapter 5 how Nietzsche in particular was tyrannized by that problem.

This aestheticist genre of the art of living forbids the direct imitation of models. Why is it, then, that Montaigne, Nietzsche, and Foucault all have a model? And why is their model always Socrates? What makes him capable of playing that role? The answer is again provided by Socrates' irony, by the silence that envelops his life and character. The central participant in innumerable conversations, "a lover of talking" as he describes himself in the *Phaedrus*, Socrates remains persistently silent about himself throughout Plato's early works. In him we see a person who created himself without ever showing anyone how he did it. These philosophers care more about the fact that Socrates made something new out of himself, that he constituted himself as an unprecedented type of person, than about the particular type of person he became. What they take from him is not the specific mode of life, the particular self, he fashioned for himself but his self-fashioning in general. Socrates is the prototypical artist of living because, by leaving the process he followed absolutely indeterminate, he also presents its final product as nonbinding: a different procedure, with different materials, can create another life and still be part of his project. To imitate Socrates is therefore to create oneself, as Socrates did; but it is also to make oneself different from anyone else so far, and since that includes Socrates himself, it is to make oneself different from Socrates as well. That is why he can function as the model for the individualist, aestheticist artists of living whose main purpose is to be like no one else, before them or after.

Since Socrates' irony is so important to my conception of the art of living, I devote the first half of this book to an examination of its various aspects. Chapter 1 begins abruptly with a discussion of a seemingly irrelevant subject—Thomas Mann's use of irony in *The Magic Mountain*. As Mann places his readers in the apparently superior situation of observing Hans Castorp, his young hero, deceive himself, he causes them to deceive themselves in exactly the same way. Plato, I argue, places the readers of his early dialogues in that situation as well. As Socrates demolishes his various opponents, we join him against them; but Plato forces us to occupy unwittingly the very position on account of which we feel such contempt for them and deprives us of any reason to think ourselves—as we do—superior to them. In addition, Hans Castorp is an essentially ambiguous figure; it is impossible to tell whether he is perfectly ordinary or totally extraordinary. That, too, is a feature of Plato's Socrates, who is fully part of his world and yet totally outside it. Both features—inducing self-deception in one's readers as one is depicting it in one's characters and constructing a hero whom it is impossible to understand once and for all—constitute a deeply ironical relationship between author and audience. Mann furnishes a clear contemporary case of a practice originating in Plato and an instance of the irony that surrounds Socrates, without once mentioning Socrates' name. That is the most distant Socratic reflection, the weakest echo, discussed in the book. From it, I turn, in the rest of the chapter, to one of the closest reflections and loudest echoes, in Plato's *Euthyphro*, and to the manner in which Plato's irony is directed toward his readers.

Plato is able to be ironic toward his readers because he beguiles them into identifying their point of view with Socrates' own. Since Socrates' attitude toward his interlocutors is ironic, so is ours. And our irony proves our undoing, since, although ironists always make an implicit claim to be superior to their victims, Plato shows us that we have no grounds for making it. Chapter 2, then, turns to the structure of Socrates' irony toward the other participants in Plato's dialogues. I argue—against the common view, exemplified in Gregory Vlastos' own reflection of Socrates—that irony does not consist in saying the contrary of, but only something different from, what one means. In the former case, if we know that we are faced with irony we also know what the ironist means: all we need to do is to negate the words we hear in order to understand what the ironist has in mind. In the latter, even when we know that we are confronted with irony, we have no sure way of knowing the ironist's meaning: all we know is that it is not quite what we have heard. Irony therefore does not allow us to peer into the ironist's mind, which remains concealed and inscrutable. Socratic irony is of that kind. It does not ever indicate what he thinks: it leaves us with his words, and a doubt that they express his meaning. That is why I think of Socratic irony as a form of silence.

In chapter 3, I argue that Socrates' goal was essentially individualist. He pursued the knowledge of "virtue," which he considered necessary for living well and happily, primarily for his own sake. Though he invited others to join him in his search, his ultimate purpose was his own improvement. That is another reason he has been able to function as a model for the artists of living whose own goal was equally individualist though not for that reason egoistic or oblivious of others. One can care for oneself without disregarding others: one can be a good human being without *devoting* oneself to them. I also claim that Socrates' silence is not limited to his interlocutors and to Plato's readers. I argue, not without realizing how strange that claim must sound, that he is also ironic—silent—toward Plato himself, despite the fact that he is the latter's creature. In one of the greatest literary feats of which I am aware, Plato implicitly admits (since he never appears in his dialogues, he could have done so in no other way) that he does not understand the character he has constructed. In his early dialogues, Plato presents Socrates as a paradoxical character in his own right: convinced that the knowledge of "virtue" is necessary for the good life, Socrates admits that he lacks it, and yet he leads as good a life as Plato has ever known. Plato does not resolve that paradox. His Socrates is completely opaque, and his opacity explains why, ever since Romanticism brought irony into the center of our literary consciousness, Plato's early works and not, as before, Xenophon's writings have been our main source for the historical figure. Opacity, a character's being beyond the reach of his author and not subject to his will, has become one of the central grounds of verisimilitude. Verisimilitude, in turn, appears as a mark of the real.

Plato, however, did not long remain satisfied with his early portrait of Socrates. In his later works, he began a series of efforts to explain how Socrates became who he was. In the process, he also produced a reflection of Socrates that differed from what he had done before and initiated a whole tradition of such reflections. In chapter 4, I examine Montaigne's reliance on Socrates in his own effort to create himself as he composed the *Essays*, particularly in connection with the essay "Of physiognomy." Montaigne, who claimed to turn away from worldly affairs in order to think only of "Michel," appeals explicitly to Socrates as a model of what a nearly perfect human being can be. "Of physiognomy" contains the core of his confrontation with, and appropriation of, Socrates. Montaigne wants to emulate Socrates, but he claims that Socrates' ugly, sensual physical appearance, so different from his beautiful and self-controlled nature, is totally different from his own open and honest countenance, which perfectly reflects his inner self. I argue that in fact Montaigne denies that "the physiognomic principle," according to which a thing's external appearance should reflect its inner reality, applies to Socrates, to himself, or to his own writing, including "Of physiognomy" itself: none of them can be taken at face value. Montaigne's effort to emulate Socrates, when the essay is read with that point in mind, turns out to be his effort to displace him and to accomplish something that is truly his own. What Montaigne learns from Socrates is that to follow him is to be different from him. To practice the Socratic art of living turns out, once again, to be the creation of a self that is as different from Socrates as Socrates was different from the rest of his world.

No one tried to be more different from Socrates than Nietzsche, who fought consistently against everything Socrates represented, which, for him, often meant everything that was wrong with the world as he understood it. Chapter 5 examines Nietzsche's lifelong involvement with Socrates. I ask why Nietzsche, who was uncannily capable of seeing everything from many sides and who remained grateful even to Schopenhauer and Wagner after he denounced their views in the most poisonous terms, never showed the same generosity toward Socrates. Everything about Nietzsche suggests that he tried to fashion himself into a character who denied everything he took Socrates to have stood for, especially the view that a single mode of life, the life of reason, was best for all. And yet his unmitigated hatred of Socrates, on closer inspection, turns out to be caused by the deep and not at all implausible suspicion that the two of them, despite the immense specific differences that separate them, were after all engaged in the very same project of self-fashioning. If so, Nietzsche was faced with two serious problems. First, he turned out to be less original than he wanted to think he was: he was more of an imitator than his view allowed him to be. Second, the fact that Socrates' private project of self-creation could have been taken as a universalist praise of the life of reason as best for all suggested that Nietzsche's own effort to "become who he was" might one day be taken in a similar way. Perhaps, then, the fate of successful efforts at self-creation is that they cease to appear as personal accomplishments. But in that case, Socrates and Nietzsche, despite the differences that separate them, might turn out to be allies after all. What would that say about Nietzsche's effort to escape the "dogmatist," universalist philosophy he believed Socrates to have originated? Escaping Socrates might prove for him as impossible as escaping himself.

Nietzsche's abhorrence of Socrates was not reflected in the attitude of his greatest twentieth-century disciple. In chapter 6, I examine Michel Foucault's final lectures at the Collège de France. Foucault refuses to accept Nietzsche's view that Socrates' final words in the *Phaedo* revealed that he had always thought of life as a disease and that he was relieved to be dying. On the contrary, Foucault claims that Socrates loved life, Athens, and the world and that he had devoted himself to the improvement of his fellow citizens. Foucault, who identifies with Socrates to the extent of mixing his own voice with his in a manner that seems designed to eliminate the distinction between them, insists on the usefulness of Socrates to Athens and to the world at large. I claim, on the basis of the argument that runs through the whole book, that Socrates' project was more private than Foucault allows. Socrates was primarily concerned with the care of his own self, and he urged his fellow citizens to undertake a similar private project for themselves. I offer an overview of Foucault's intellectual development, from the forbidding, detached historical thinker of his early works to the compassionate advocate of "an aesthetics of existence" of his late writings. And I argue that he insisted on Socrates' usefulness because he had come to believe that he himself could be of use to the people for whom he cared. Foucault took himself to have created a self and a life that could be important for others like him. And though he did not address himself to the broad audience, the whole state, as he believed Socrates had done, he was convinced that his project of self-creation, of "the care of the self," could serve as a model for groups, particularly homosexuals and other oppressed minorities who, repressed in today's world, find themselves unable to speak with a voice of their own.

My overview of how Socrates was treated by various philosophers who were concerned more with establishing new modes of life than with answering independently given philosophical questions finally turns out to contain its own version of who Socrates was. The historical objectivity I took to be my aim when I first began thinking about the lectures from which this book emerged gradually gave way—only partially, I hope—to a more personal involvement with the figure who stands at the head of that tradition and with the other philosophers I examined. I slowly realized that I too tried to find in Socrates a model for my own approach to the things that are important to me. My own interest has turned from the study of the art of living to its practice; or, rather, I have come to realize that to study the art of living is to engage in one of its forms. That is an interest I discovered only recently, and I am not sure where it is likely to lead me. And though, like all such projects, mine too is, and is bound to remain, unfinished, I hope that is not also true of the part of the project this book constitutes.

PART ONE

Silence

I

Platonic Irony
Author and Audience

Isn't it grand, isn't it good, that language has only one *word for everything we associate with love—from utter sanctity to the most fleshly lust? The result is perfect clarity in ambiguity, for love cannot be disembodied even in its most sanctified forms, nor is it without sanctity even in its most fleshly . . .* Caritas *is assuredly found in the most admirable and most depraved passions. Irresolute? But in God's name, leave the meaning of love unresolved! unresolved—that is life and humanity, and it would betray a dreary lack of subtlety to worry about it.*

Thomas Mann, *The Magic Mountain*

No novel can match the irreducible ambivalence that permeates *The Magic Mountain*. No passage can sum up that ambivalence better than this short discourse on the double nature of love, both "utter sanctity" and "fleshly lust," elegantly and irresolubly poised between these two seemingly inconsonant poles. Thomas Mann's irony deprives his readers of any final ground. Mann makes self-deceivers of all those who try to determine once and for all the nature of Hans Castorp, the novel's unassuming and unusual hero, and of the illness that brings him to a sanatorium for a stay that goes from three weeks to seven years. Mann's irony induces self-deception in the novel's readers in the very process of exposing them to a set of characters whose lives are filled with constant self-deception and to whom he makes these readers feel, for no good reason, superior. "Its questioning smile," a critic has written, "embraces impartially the author and its subject alike."[1] But this smile, as we shall see, also embraces the reader, and it is neither purely genial nor wholly benevolent.

I will begin with Thomas Mann in order to illustrate a kind of irony that goes all the way down: it does not reveal the ironist's real state of mind, and it intimates that such a state may not exist at all. It makes a mystery of its author as well as of his characters, and it often turns its readers into fools. It originates in Plato, who remains perhaps its most disturbing practitioner. My goal is to examine the peculiar, almost paradoxical phenomenon that out of the irony of Plato and Socrates, the character Plato created and to whom he gave a stronger foothold on reality than he gave himself, a whole tradition according to which life can be lived eventually came to grow.

That tradition has been constantly reinterpreted and directed at the most disparate ends by Socrates' enemies as well as by his admirers. It has now become a whole family of traditions, a whole approach to philosophy not as a theoretical discipline but as an art of living. It has produced the most diverse pictures of Socrates as well as the most different conceptions of life itself. In particular, it has inspired a particular approach that takes a human life to be at its most worthwhile when it is at its most individual and most inimitable. Yet all these various individual lives, three of which we shall address in the second part of this book, go back explicitly to Socrates, who persistently presents a silent, impenetrable appearance to them, refusing to let them see how he managed to live as he did. Which makes one wonder whether all his followers—friends and foes alike—are not, in a way, Socrates' fools. But before we turn to Socrates, we begin with a humbler, much less imposing and admirable but perhaps equally enigmatic character, who also, in his own phlegmatic, middle-class way, tried to make a life for himself.

On his first morning at the International Haus Berghof, where he had gone on a three-week visit to rest and to entertain his tubercular cousin, Hans Castorp woke up earlier than usual despite his deep exhaustion the night before. While, with characteristic fastidiousness, he devoted himself to his morning toilet before going down to breakfast, thoughts about his troubled sleep rose in his mind. "He recalled his confused dreams and shook his head complacently over so much nonsense, with the superior feeling a man has shaving himself in the clear light of reason. He did not feel precisely rested, but he had a sense of morning freshness" (38/56).[2]

Sounds of music drifted up from the valley below the Berghof as Hans

Castorp stood on his balcony on the magic mountain. Hans, who loved music deeply, "from his heart," gave himself to it. "He listened, well pleased, his head on one side, his eyes a little bloodshot" (38/56). First-time readers of Mann's novel cannot yet know that Hans always listens to music, drinks his beer, and confronts death, either manifest or merely intimated, with his head on one side. The pose is throughout the work one way of expressing that he understands, appreciates, or sympathizes with a particular situation from which he is also keeping his distance, that he remains at least superficially unaffected by it, as is proper for a man of his station and temperament.[3] And whether the readers do or do not realize it, Hans's early sense of "morning freshness" is already tainted with intimations of death. Soon after his arrival the night before he had learned that the bodies from another sanatorium, higher up on the slopes than the Berghof, had to be transported down to the village on bobsleds during the winter. But even as Hans's hysterical laughter at the gruesome idea—"a violent, irrepressible laugh, which shook him all over and distorted his face" (9/17)—turned that grim fact into a comic outlandishness, death had already intruded into the young man's visit and into his life. Superficially organized as a playground for the idle rich, the mountain is really a place of death. But death can still provoke laughter.

Confused dreams, bloodshot eyes, a feeling of not having rested, a posture associated with the contemplation of death (though Hans is no more aware of that connection than the novel's first-time reader): something is not quite right with the young engineer. But the official story that both he and the readers have been told is that he has come to the sanatorium primarily to provide a distraction for his sick cousin. And with that idea foremost in his mind, Hans is still pleased, complacent, and at ease. The symptoms of his unease, which turn out to be the symptoms of his disease, are muted and understated. They pass unnoticed, or almost so. They slip in just below the threshold of the consciousness of character and reader alike. They (and others, as we shall soon see) are there, but they still mean little or nothing.[4]

Still on his balcony, Castorp finds himself watching a black-clad woman walking about alone in the sanatorium garden. Again, though neither hero nor reader knows this yet, this connects him further with death, since the woman, known to the Berghof patients as Tous-les-deux, is there to tend her two dying sons.[5] And while he is watching her, Castorp begins to hear "certain noises" in the room of the Russian couple who live directly next to him. Still immersed in the pure beauty of his surroundings, Hans feels that these sounds "no more suited the blithe freshness of the morning than had the sad sight in the garden below" (39/56–57).[6] He now recalls that he had heard similar sounds coming from the same room the night before, as he was preparing himself for bed, "though his weariness had prevented him from heeding them: a struggling, a panting and giggling, the offensive nature of which could not long remain hidden to the young man, try as he good-naturedly might to put a harmless construction on them" (39/57).

Castorp, then, knows how to defend himself—up to a point—against embarrassing or unpleasant events. Even this morning, as he hears the sounds once more and begins to form a clear idea of their nature, he resists them. And his resistance is not innocent: "Perhaps something more or other than good nature was in play." His attitude, Mann writes, is what we sometimes call "purity of soul," sometimes "chastity," sometimes "hypocrisy," and sometimes "an obscure sense of awe and piety." As is his practice throughout the novel, Mann does not try to decide among those alternatives: "In truth, something of all these was in Hans Castorp's face and bearing as he listened. He seemed to be practicing a seemly obscurantism; to be mentally drawing the veil over these sounds that he heard; to be telling himself that honour forbade his taking any cognizance of them, or even hearing them at all—it gave him an air of propriety which was not quite native, though he knew how to assume it on occasion" (39/57).[7]

We are told clearly that such an air of propriety is definitely not natural to the young engineer. He must have acquired both the facial expression and the self-deceptive strategy it manifests at some specific point in his life. And, in fact, we have already been told when that was. When Castorp's paternal grandfather, in whose house he had spent part of his childhood, died, he lay in state dressed not in his everyday black clothes but in an old-fashioned uniform that Hans had always felt expressed "the genuine, the authentic grandfather" (25/39). While the old man reposed in his coffin, resplendent in his uniform, Hans noted that "a fly had settled on the quiet brow, and began to move its proboscis up and down" (27–28/42). The grandfather's manservant tried to remove it without drawing attention to the situation: "Old Fiete shooed it cautiously away, taking care not to touch the forehead of the dead, putting on a seemly air of absent-mindedness—of obscurantism, as it were—as though he neither might nor would take notice of what he was doing" (28/43).[8] Fiete's lesson is not lost on the boy. Hans Castorp has learned to be good at denying the obvious; his treatment of his neighbors' lovemaking is a perfect case in point.[9]

In order not to have to listen to what is becoming more and more difficult to explain away, Hans leaves the balcony for his room. But that is a total failure, since the sounds of his Russian neighbors are even louder as they come through the thin wall that separates their room from his. He is shocked. He blushes. He tries to excuse them: "Well, at least they are married. . . . But in broad daylight—it's a bit thick! And last night too, I'm sure. But of course they're ill, or at least one of them, or they wouldn't be here" (40/57–58).

It is hard to imagine at this point that a man like Hans, who cannot admit in good conscience that such behavior even exists, could ever engage in it himself. For one thing, unlike his neighbors, he is not sick. He is a visitor at the Berghof. He is not there on account of his health: his family doctor's prescription of a few weeks on the mountains has been presented so casually and without fanfare that it slips by without being noticed (36/53). And, to the extent that the episode is noticed, the reason given for the prescription is that Hans is simply a little tired after his examinations and needs a short rest before he joins his firm and starts work in earnest. Even more to the point, his cousin Joachim, who is a patient at the sanatorium on account of a very real case of tuberculosis, could do with a little company. And yet Hans's unthinking comment that at least one of the Russians must be ill "or they wouldn't be there" casts his own presence at the sanatorium in an ambiguous light. Since he, too, is there, why should he be different from them? But before we can even raise that question, the narrative moves on and its brisk pace prevents us from focusing seriously on such an apparently incidental point. Good readers will remember this little incident later on, but it is hard to turn it into a topic in its own right at this time.

There is also a second reason Castorp would never dream of behaving like his neighbors, who take their meals at what is known as the "bad" Russian table. We already know that he is a supremely proper and particular German young man, and he knows, as we have just seen, that the Berghof's walls are so thin that everyone can hear whatever goes on in its rooms. He would never expose himself to the danger of becoming the target of the sanatorium's many gossips. And yet eventually he does behave just like his coarse neighbors. On carnival night, he tries long, and perhaps successfully, to convince Clawdia Chauchat, the Russian woman with whom he has fallen in love in the meantime, that he really is ill— "one of us"—and not just an impostor from the "flat-land." Clawdia, whose own demeanor is far from proper,[10] invites him to her bedroom, and he spends part of the night with her. Like many of the patients he so disdains, Hans too ends up having what, at least from the outside, looks like a sordid little affair. But that too is something we do not yet know.

What we do know at this early point is that the behavior of his neighbors has upset Castorp immensely:

> The flush which had mounted in his freshly shaven cheek [*die frisch rasierten Wangen*] did not subside, nor its accompanying warmth: his face glowed with the same dry heat as on the evening before. He had got free of it in sleep, but the blush had made it set in again. He did not feel the friendlier for this discovery towards the wretched pair next door; in fact he stuck out his lips and muttered a derogatory word in their direction, as he tried to cool his hot face by bathing it in cold water—and only made it glow the more. He felt put out; his voice vibrated with ill humour as he answered to his cousin's knock on the wall; and he appeared to Joachim on his entrance like anything but a man refreshed [*erfrischt*] and invigorated by a good night's sleep. (40/58)

Hans Castorp practices this "seemly obscurantism" quite frequently in the course of the novel. It is a form—perhaps mild, perhaps not—of self-deception. The particular section devoted to his first morning at the sanatorium exhibits, and makes a topic of, Hans's ability to ignore, at least up to a point, subjects that upset or threaten him—in this case, the tactless lovemaking of his neighbors, who he believes are coarser and less healthy than himself.

The veil Hans draws is at best tullelike, semitransparent, incapable of finally hiding the doings of the Russian couple. Yet, in the same motion, Hans also draws another set of curtains, more substantial, heavier, velvetlike. As we observe Hans formulate and manipulate his feelings about his neighbors, as we see him first deny and then excuse their behavior on account of their illness, we miss—we *should* miss, I think, as Hans himself misses—a number of indications of his own state of health, which is a subject of much greater importance to the novel as a whole.

Those indications are presented subtly. I have cited them already: "He did not feel precisely rested, yet he had a sense of morning freshness"; "he listened well pleased, his head on one side, his eyes a little bloodshot"; "his face glowed with the same dry heat as on the evening before." But Mann counterbalances those allusions to Hans's discomfort by his references to the good feelings that are only to be expected when a man wakes up in the pure mountain air and shaves himself "in the clear light of reason." At the very end of the section, when Joachim arrives to take his cousin to breakfast, Mann allows us to see Hans's irritable voice and flushed face, more objectively so to speak, from Joachim's point of view.

Joachim has no excuses for his cousin's appearance. But Hans's mounting anger over his neighbors' behavior, to which most of the paragraph leading to Joachim's entrance has been devoted, has come so much to the forefront of our attention that it provides a convincing psychological explanation of his unsettled appearance: Hans is flushed because he is shocked, dismayed, and angry. It is difficult to interpret his red face as the first symptom of the consumption that keeps him on the mountain and ultimately makes him, from one point of view, just like the rest of the patients from whom, even at the end of the book, we will still be trying to distinguish him.

This tiny part of this very long novel exhibits the workings of self-deception. Mann does not explain how self-deception works; he has no "theory" of it. But his mere depiction of the phenomenon creates a chilling effect. Throughout most of the narrative, though progressively less in its later stages, Mann identifies the points of view of Hans, the narrator, and the reader.[11] That strategy enables Mann to produce in his readers the same incomplete awareness of Hans's state that Hans himself possesses. We, too, are deceived for a long time about Hans's illness. We, too, choose to ignore the information that, in retrospect, should have convinced us that Hans had been sick (however sickness is to be understood in this questionable book) for some time—perhaps since childhood and certainly before he was told, as we are told, that it would be nice to visit his cousin and relax before he took up his first professional position. We remain deceived about this character who, because our point of view is so close to his, becomes for a long time our own second self. His errors are also errors of our own. And they are not only errors about Hans. They are errors about ourselves as well. We overlook the fact that we have at our disposal all the evidence that is necessary to decide that Hans is indeed sick; we refuse, or are simply unwilling, to confront that evidence directly and to interpret it as we should. As we attend to Hans trying to deceive himself about his neighbors, we disregard his much more successful disregard of his tubercular symptoms. Our ignorance regarding Hans's illness is also ignorance regarding ourselves as well. In depicting self-deception in his character, Mann induces it in his readers. The effect is chilling indeed.

Indications that Hans Castorp is and has been ill for a long time are strewn all over *The Magic Mountain*. We know, very early on, that both Hans's young father and his paternal grandfather, with whom Hans shares so many characteristics—physical, psychological, and even spiritual—died of an inflammation of the lungs (19/30; 26/39).[12] "Inflammation of the lungs" ("Lungenentzündung") does not call tuberculosis immediately to mind,[13] especially because at this early stage of the work the disease has not yet become a central theme. That is surely the reason Mann uses that more neutral expression, but in retrospect its significance is unmistakable. And though it is true that Hans's mother died not of lung problems but of cardiac arrest, Joachim is her half-sister's son. Her family, too, was therefore in all probability predisposed to the disease.

Hans, then, is in the midst of a serious tubercular episode.[14] But both he and the narrator and, by means of the identification of the points of view we have already mentioned, the readers of the novel as well wave its symptoms away. Hans's flushed face, for example, is, we shall come to understand, a classic symptom of the disease: the sanatorium's chief physician, Hofrat Behrens, who is not untainted by the disease he fights, is always blotched and red-faced.[15] But when Hans brings up "this damned heat I feel all the time in my face" during his very first walk with Joachim, his cousin tells him that that was exactly what happened to him when he first came to the Berghof: "I was rather queer at first. Don't think too much about it. I told you it is not easy to accustom oneself to the life up here. But you will get right again after a bit" (52/74). In that way, the flush is dismissed. But if we were to change our point of view to the slightest extent, we would have realized that since Joachim is actually ill, the parallel between the two cousins is actually evidence for the presence of the disease rather than evidence against it.[16]

However, such a change of point of view is difficult to accomplish because every indication that Hans is ill is counterbalanced by an explanation that minimizes each symptom's significance and accounts for it in a different way. On the evening of Hans's arrival at the sanatorium, for example, his state is peculiar indeed: he laughs without measure, his face is flushed and yet he feels cold, he is unable to enjoy his cigar, he is short of breath and unusually sleepy. But all that is explained away the next morning, and Hans's condition is made to seem different from that of the (rest of the) Berghof patients, by Behrens's pronouncement that the young man is obviously anemic (46/67).[17] It is only much later, when Consul James Tienappel, Hans's uncle, comes to reclaim him and bring him back to the "flat-land" (425/580) that the real function of Behrens's diagnosis of anemia becomes apparent. On the evening of his arrival, James exhibits, and continues to display throughout his visit, all the symptoms that Hans had experienced during his first days at the Berghof.[18] But next morning, exactly as it had happened with Hans, James runs into Behrens, who applauds his idea of coming for a visit but adds that James "has served his own interest even better in so coming, for that he was totally anaemic was plain to any eye." Behrens even suggests, as he had suggested to Hans, that James follow the sanatorium's regimen (434/592). The diagnosis of anemia, in other words, is the sanatorium's way of "breaking in" new patients. But until we are able to see through that stratagem, the fact that Hans seems to be suffering from anemia appears to distinguish him from the rest of the patients of the Berghof and to place him in a class by himself.

For a long time, everyone refers to Hans as a "visitor" to the sanatorium, or as a "vacationer," despite the fact that both his state of health and his mode of life are indistinguishable from those of everyone else. Not only does Hans suffer from consumption, as surely as they all do; in addition, his behavior, which in its propriety and fastidiousness placed him apart from them at the beginning of his visit, gradually becomes identical to theirs. We have already said that his distaste at his neighbors' behavior is eventually belied by his own visit to Clawdia's room after their long conversation during carnival.[19] Much more important, Hans Castorp's propriety gives way to a willingness to see the sexual affairs that spice the life of the Berghof patients in an equivocal light. The narrator sometimes describes those affairs in contemptuous, sarcastic terms (236/326–27), intimating that Hans's own attitude toward them is equally negative. And yet Hans also begins to feel that on the magic mountain sexuality acquired "an entirely altered emphasis. It was weighty with a new weight; it had an accent, a value, and a significance which were utterly novel" (237/326). One is left wondering whether Hans's bourgeois attitudes have really changed or whether his new insight is just his way of excusing his mounting passion for Clawdia, or perhaps both. What is certain is that less than five weeks after his arrival, Hans has become so accustomed to the Russians in the next room that he no longer pays any attention to them. Taking the evening cure like everyone else, "Hans Castorp too took his temperature for the last time, while soft music, near or far, stole up from the dark valley. The cure ended at ten. He heard Joachim, he heard the pair from the 'bad' Russian table; he turned on his side and invited slumber" (202/279).[20]

The Magic Mountain depicts a character who deceives himself, with varying success, about his health as well as about his differences—physical, moral, and spiritual—from the people among whom he happens to find himself. In the process, Mann replicates his character's self-deception in his readers, mostly by identifying their point of view with that of the narrator and thus with the point of view of his character as well. We have spent a considerable amount of time examining that procedure; we must now address another aspect of the novel, which, we shall see, also finds its origins in Plato.

The novel establishes beyond a doubt that Hans Castorp, like the rest of the Berghof patients, is suffering from tuberculosis: he is nothing but a patient himself. Not even his general demeanor can be distinguished from theirs. For example, the lawyer Paravant at one point abandons sex for the sake of dedicating himself to squaring the circle (or perhaps it is the other way around; 417/569). His maniacal commitment to his absurd project is not so different from the ardor of Hans Castorp's devotion to playing the same game of solitaire over and over again. He is so preoccupied with it that he is not even capable of holding a reasonable conversation about the coming war with his self-appointed mentor, Lodovico Settembrini. When Settembrini raises for the first time the topic of Europe's headlong rush to destruction, Castorp can only reply: "Seven and four. . . . Eight and three, Knave, queen and king. It is coming out. You have brought me luck, Herr Settembrini" (632–33/867–68).

On his first day at the sanatorium, Hans had listened with deep distaste to the loud banter of Herr Albin as he was trying to impress the ladies on the Berghof veranda (78–81/110–13). Two months later, the distaste is forgotten as Hans, in a manner obvious to everyone and extremely embarrassing to Joachim, acts in a similar way in order to attract the attention of Clawdia Chauchat (232–33/320–21). By that time, Hans's infatuation with Clawdia has turned him into an object of derision and gossip. When he crosses the dining room in order to draw a curtain that allowed the sun to disturb Clawdia's conversation, he fancies himself a gallant, heroic figure: "Only after the whole thing was over . . . did he become conscious that Joachim had kept his eyes directed upon his place. Afterwards, too, he realized that Frau Stöhr had nudged Dr. Blumenkohl in the side, and then looked about at their own and other tables, trying to catch people's eyes" (231/319).

And yet, despite all that, one still wants to say that Hans really *is* different from the rest of these people. After all, his case of consumption is not a mere mindless physiological phenomenon like theirs. Hans's disease, as Mann suggests throughout the novel, is the physical expression of his spiritual inability to fit into the bourgeois world of the flat-land. Hans, we are told, never really belonged to everyday life; he never saw the point of the efforts made by everyone around him: "He positively saw no reason, or, more precisely, saw no positive reason, for exertion." That is why, the narrator claims, Hans is not like the rest of the Berghof clientele, why "we may not call him mediocre: . . . somehow or other, he was aware of the lack of such a reason" (32/47). Hans's disease, unlike perhaps the commonplace complaints of vulgar Frau Stöhr, seems spiritual in origin. By the end of the narrative, he is able to leave the sanatorium behind, return to the world, and join the ranks of the German army, unlike Joachim, whose dream of joining the colors died with him on the slopes of the magic mountain.

But is it really so clear that the other patients' illness is as purely physiological (or "stupid") as the narrative often tempts us to think? Consider, as only one instance among many, the case of Joachim. No one among the Berghof patients is more eager than he to return to the world below. Joachim's only purpose in life is to get cured so that he can resume his military career. No one thinks of the disease as a purely physical indisposition to be set aside so he can go about the serious business of life more than Joachim does. And yet it is clear that Joachim is also attracted to the mountain because, despite his efforts to hide it, he is deeply in love with his tablemate, another Russian, the giggling Marusja. He does once try to renounce her and the mountain, and leaves the Berghof to return to the "flat-land" without the doctors' permission. But his effort is a complete failure. He soon returns, more seriously ill than before. And, on the night before he finally takes to his bed never to rise again, he approaches Marusja and addresses her for the first and last time, though, in contrast to Hans's long talk with Clawdia, Joachim's conversation remains completely private. Is Joachim's illness physical or spiritual? The novel will not let us decide. Hans is aware of its irreducibly double nature — as much a physiological phenomenon as a desire to give up the commonplace life of the flat-land — and he muses when he learns that his cousin is returning to the sanatorium soon after his unauthorized departure:

> And directly before the maneuvers he has been so on fire to go to. . . . The body triumphs, it wants something different from the soul, and puts it through — a slap in the face of all those lofty-minded people who teach that the body is subordinate to the soul. . . . The question I raise is how far they were right when they set the two over against each other; and whether they aren't rather in collusion, playing the same game. . . . Is it possible that you have not been able to forget a certain refreshing perfume, a tendency to giggle, a swelling bosom, all waiting for you at Frau Stöhr's table? (500/682)[21]

Everyone on the magic mountain is sick, but everyone's disease is as much a physiological as it is a spiritual phenomenon. That is why even to decide that Hans's, or anyone else's, case is purely one or the other is to fall into a trap that Mann has constructed with the greatest care and is difficult to avoid. Any unqualified judgment of this sort requires an almost intentional overlooking of clear, though subtle, evidence and is therefore one more episode of self-deception. The novel relentlessly undermines our ability to make unconditional judgments in the same process that it tempts us to keep doing so.

Mann's irony, "not the 'classic,' didactic device valued by Settembrini [but] the ambiguous kind the humanist sternly warns his pupil against . . . is irony that goes both ways."[22] As we shall see in the next chapter, it is an irony that goes back to the very origins of the concept. It undercuts every effort to determine once and for all whether, say, Hans's disease is due to love or any other psychological or spiritual factor or to stark physiological reasons. The same is true of the disease of all the other protagonists and of the minor characters as well. The novel simply does not give us enough information to decide. More correctly, it gives us too much, enough to support both interpretations, and in large measure its irony consists in such abundance.[23] As Hermann Weigand has observed, though Mann's irony includes "in its range the most passionate intensity of experience, it refuses to yield the clarity of its vision for any price."[24]

Is Hans's illness different from or the same as that of the other patients? It is and it isn't. The factors that cause it seem to be similar to those responsible for the illness of his companions, both physiological and spiritual: all of them suffer from genuine cases of tuberculosis and all of them are also in one way or another unable to cope with life "below." But Hans seems to be able to use his illness to accomplish something that the others cannot: he finally accepts that life really occurs in the flat-land and returns there of his own free will.[25] Those who, following Mann himself, find the essence of the novel distilled in the chapter entitled "Snow" generally accept this optimistic interpretation. Its climax occurs when Hans, having had a miraculous vision during a snowstorm he runs into while on a skiing expedition, exclaims, "For the sake of goodness and love, man shall let death have no sovereignty over his thoughts." That is his great insight, the idea that distinguishes him from the rest of the Berghof's world.[26] But Hans beholds that vision only after he has had a healthy dose of the port he has carried with him on his excursion. The port has muddled his head, and he knows it: " 'The port was not at all the right thing; just the few sips of it have made my head so heavy I cannot hold it up, and my thoughts are all just confused, stupid quibbling with words. I can't depend on them—not only the first thought that comes into my head, but even the second one, the correction which my reason tries to make upon the first—more's the pity" (489/667). But this casts doubt on both the seriousness and the clarity of his vision, as well as on the message he receives from it. And though he says that his dream has given him that insight "in utter clearness," so that he "may know it for ever," his state changes rather quickly once he finds his way back to the sanatorium. The chapter ends with these words: "An hour later the highly civilized atmosphere of the Berghof caressed him. He ate enormously at dinner. What he had dreamed was already fading from his mind. What he had thought—even that selfsame evening it was no longer so clear as it had been at first" (498/679). We do not need to discount this extraordinary episode completely[27] or to argue that Mann actually portrays Castorp in a purely negative light[28] to sense that here, too, we cannot make an unequivocal judgment of Hans's qualities and accomplishments.[29] His vision in the snow is as significant as his disease is purely physical.

It is certainly true that Hans finally returns to the flat-land, leaving some other characters, particularly Settembrini, his self-appointed "pedagogue" who has been urging him to leave the sanatorium from the day they met, behind. That is, of course, the central reason Hans does seem so different from the rest of the Berghof world. But even in this case, his behavior is not as unusual as it seems. Or, rather, it is—like Hans himself, who is both an ordinary young man ("ein einfacher junger Mensch") and "Life's problem-child" ("ein Sorgenkind des Lebens")—both common and unusual at the same time. Hans does indeed leave the mountain, but then so does almost everybody else. When the war begins, the "Berghof was the picture of an anthill in a panic: its little population was flinging itself, heels over head, five thousand feet downwards to the catastrophe-smitten flat-land. They stormed the little trains, they crowded them to the footboard . . . and Hans Castorp stormed with them" (712/975). But where does Hans go, after his seven years of "sympathy with death" on the mountain? Not where many of the weak former patients of the sanatorium would have ventured. He goes directly into the trenches, exchanging his effort to understand death on the heights for a march toward it on the plains where we take our final leave of him.

Does Hans Castorp accomplish anything remarkable on the magic mountain? The answer, again, is yes and no. From one point of view, he learns a lot from his seven teachers during his seven years: he learns about love, friendship, and courage; about the body, the spirit, and feeling; about life and death—and perhaps he even comes to terms with them. He liberates himself from both his fear of ordinariness and his dependence on a set of questionable influences; he marches, obedient to his duty, to a hero's death. From another point of view, however, he idles away some of the best years of his life: he eats and drinks like an animal; he listens to and utters a lot of philosophical gibberish; he has a sordid secret one-night affair; he becomes a companion of people he detested when he first arrived and would have abhorred had he met them anywhere else (660/904–5); and he leaves only to die a meaningless death on a horrible battlefield before his life ever really begins.

Mann simply does not allow us to take sides on these questions: he forces both points of view equally on us. Hans Castorp is as ordinary, as much a part of the world, as anyone else in the novel. But he is also, at the same time, an extraordinary character, who cannot fit into a commonplace mold. We could perhaps hold his self-deception against him, but then we would also have to hold the same self-deception against ourselves. One thing that distinguishes him is that he does become aware that taking sides is a very complicated affair, that expressing one's "real," final view of things is far more complex than we generally tend to think: " 'You have to take humanity as it is— but even so I find it magnificent' " (370/506). In Hans Castorp, Mann has created a character who, despite all we know about him, remains a mystery, a blank. His endless conversations ultimately yield an impenetrable silence. We simply don't know who he is, what exactly he has accomplished, and how he accomplished whatever that was. By tempting his readers to think they understand Castorp, and to believe that they are either superior like him or superior to him, Mann reveals the self-deception involved in the attempt to take a moral stand on characters and issues that are irresolubly ambiguous. Most centrally, *The Magic Mountain* shows that the attribution of self-deception to others is one of the surest paths to the deception of oneself.

There are no irresoluble moral ambiguities in Plato's Socratic dialogues. But these works revolve around a character who remains completely mysterious to the other figures that share his fictional world, to the dialogues' readers, and finally, like Hans Castorp, to his own author as well. And though Castorp and Socrates are vastly different characters, Mann's novel and Plato's Socratic dialogues are two of the most scornful displays of the weakness of readers who assume they are morally superior to various characters while they are in fact revealing that they are made of the same stuff as those they deride.[30]

That has been my main reason for beginning this discussion of issues drawn from classical literature and philosophy with a consideration of an author who is neither a philosopher nor part of the classical canon. Another reason, perhaps as central, is the fact that this book concerns what I call Socratic "reflections," that is, both images of that original character and ways of thinking that are shaped by considering his character and accomplishment as well as the strategies that have constituted him as the character he has become. But the original cannot be separated from its reflections. Socrates, through whom Plato introduced the philosophical distinctions between original and image, reality and appearance, the authentic and the fake, is himself an original that is nothing over and above his images, reflections, and the distant echoes we hear in works like *The Magic Mountain*. Just as the historical origins of Socrates may now be beyond our reach, his reflections often outrun the treatments that contain his name. A Socratic reflection, a Platonic way of writing and treating one's audience, may confront us even when the name "Socrates" does not appear in a particular work, as it does not appear in Mann's novel. A third reason is that considering Mann's literary strategy enables me to begin my discussion of Plato by discussing his own literary practice. That is not to say that I propose to read Plato as a "literary" and not as a "philosophical" figure. On the contrary, I hope to show that just as literary authors often raise and illuminate philosophical issues, philosophers, too, reach philosophical conclusions by means of features we tend to associate mainly with literary authors. That is true neither of all literary authors nor of all philosophers. But it is true enough in the case of our main subject here.

None of this implies that philosophy and literature collapse into one another. Even if philosophy is in the end "a kind of writing," it still has characteristics that are specifically its own.[31] One's aims for philosophy can be more modest than Arthur Danto's, who claims that in contrast to literature "philosophy wants to be more than universal: it wants necessity as well: truth for all the worlds that are possible,"[32] and still believe that the two are distinct institutions and practices. Literary ideas, however "philosophical," remain tied to the texts in which they appear. Mann's speculations about the mixture of the sensual and the intellectual in the human soul, for example, are not—and cannot—be discussed without being constantly illustrated by the affair between Hans and Clawdia. By contrast, Plato's distinction between the appetitive and the rational part of the soul, despite the fact that it is in great part motivated by his specific desire to account for, justify, and systematize Socrates' way of life, also has a life of its own. It can and must be discussed without any reference to Socrates; its connection to Socrates could even be unknown—as, unfortunately, it is—to many who reflect upon it. Philosophical ideas are in that sense abstract, capable of living independently of their original manifestations. Even authors who long for particularity and individuality—Montaigne, Nietzsche, Foucault—construct ideas that can be detached from their texts in a way that the most abstruse speculations of Mann's Settembrini and Naptha cannot. But many of the problems literary authors address belong as surely to philosophy as many of the practices philosophical authors pursue are drawn from literature.

Consider now Plato's *Euthyphro*. It is one of his shorter, livelier, philosophically more complex and most widely read earlier works.[33] Socrates has come to the King Archon's stoa to respond to Meletus' writ of impiety, which is eventually to send him to his death. At the entrance, he meets Euthyphro, who has come to press a suit against his father for murdering one of his own day laborers.[34] Euthyphro's action is at least shocking if not downright impious, and Socrates, like Euthyphro's own relatives, expresses his amazement that Euthyphro has decided to pursue it:[35] sons are not to prosecute their fathers according to classical Greek moral and religious tradition. Since Euthyphro's action is controversial enough to seem obviously impious, Socrates infers, reasonably enough, that Euthyphro must have a clear and articulate view of what piety is: otherwise he could not have pressed such a suit (4eff.; cf. 15d–e). Euthyphro, who has been eager for a talk with Socrates anyway, agrees that he does indeed know the nature of piety, and that is all Socrates needs. He asks Euthyphro to define piety for him, and the dialectical portion of the dialogue gets under way.

I say "the dialectical portion" because only part and not the whole of the dialogue, as one might think on the basis of most of the commentaries written about it, is devoted to the definition of piety. Though it is inaccurate and misleading to refer to the work as "a play,"[36] it is equally unjustified to claim that literary analysis is useless in the case of the *Euthyphro*: "*Formgeschichte* . . . cannot be mechanically applied. So far as the *Euthyphro* is concerned, its relevance is slight: no substantive issue in the interpretation of the dialogue turns on it."[37] The author who holds this latter view is forced to conclude that the work's real business begins only after "a lengthy introduction—lengthy in relation to the total bulk of the dialogue," and to consider that the "introduction," which actually occupies a full quarter of the dialogue, is irrelevant to his interpretation.[38]

That is not at all to say that the arguments by which Socrates refutes Euthyphro's four definitions of piety are not crucial to our understanding of the dialogue. But it is to say that the work is in fact a *dialogue*, that it belongs to a genre that allows Plato to pursue strategies, both philosophical and literary, that another genre (say, a treatise) would not have permitted. Those strategies need to be investigated in their own right.

A great deal has been written recently about Plato's use of the dialogue form, and whole schools of thought revolve around the issue whether Plato's choice of genre is or is not relevant to the interpretation of his works.[39] My own view is that, to a great extent, Plato wrote dialogues not for any deep reason but simply because that was the established form of Socratic literature at the end of the fifth and the beginning of the fourth century BC. Whoever wanted to commemorate Socrates mostly wrote dialogues, doubtless because that had been Socrates' favorite mode of discourse. Many authors composed Socratic dialogues,[40] and there is no reason to believe that Plato was the first among them.[41] I am therefore suspicious of interpretations that take the dialogue form as an end in itself, which Plato chose freely and intentionally among other possible genres in order to exploit some particular features he discerned in it. But I also believe that Plato, like any other author, could and did use the genre for purposes of his own.

One of these purposes, obviously enough, is the characterization of Socrates and his interlocutors. Some people think that Plato uses characterization to advance a doctrinal point that the actual discussion of the dialogue does not articulate. So, for example, one interpreter has argued that Plato stresses Euthyphro's gross ignorance to allow himself to make "the suggestion, only partly revealed to Euthyphro [who, this author believes, wouldn't understand it], that justice, not piety, connects the human and the divine."[42] It is somewhat ironic that such readings, which are often identified with the approach of Leo Strauss and his students, despite their emphasis on the literary character of Plato's dialogues, presuppose an absolute distinction between the literary and the philosophical and rigidly subordinate the former to the latter. The main idea is that Plato holds a number of explicit philosophical views that, for a number of reasons, he does not want to make public. Accordingly, he uses the structure and characterization of his works to undermine their obvious meaning and to suggest his real intentions to those who can follow the secret thread of his thought. The most famous of these cases, of course, is that of the *Republic,* the true message of which — according to this approach — is not that philosophers should rule the city, as Plato seems to argue (473cff.), but that they should leave the government to the types represented by Socrates' interlocutors, "gentlemen" like Glaucon and

Adeimantus.[43] The details of the case are not important; I am not even concerned at this point with the question whether Strauss's interpretation of Plato is correct. What concerns me is the more general idea that Plato uses the dialogue form to encode his real position and reveal it only to those of his readers who are capable of reading his code. For that idea actually subordinates literature to philosophy and transforms it into a supplementary carrier of a detachable philosophical message.[44]

We must leave the immense complications of the *Republic* aside, since it is not clear that the doctrinal points even of a short work like the *Euthyphro* can be articulated clearly enough for us to be able to say what the dramatic structure of the work reveals about them.[45] More important, we must realize that Plato's characterization plays a role that is not connected to the illustration of some independent doctrine. Such a role is one we might in good conscience consider philosophical: the characterization turns out to be itself part of the philosophical point of the dialogue. In Plato's case, at least, the easy distinction between literature and philosophy does not even begin to capture his complex practice.

What do we know about the character of Euthyphro? Nothing apart from what this dialogue and a few scattered references in Plato's *Cratylus* tell us.[46] But the *Euthyphro* itself gives us a lot of information about its protagonist, and though some of that has already been discussed in the secondary literature more remains to be said about it.

The first thing to note is that, as in most of Plato's Socratic dialogues, it is the interlocutor of Socrates, Euthyphro himself, and not Socrates who makes a point of initiating their discussion. Contrary to what most people think, it is not Socrates who stops people in the street and, out of the blue, asks them to define virtue and to justify their lives but someone else who draws him into conversation.[47] So it is in this case as well. Euthyphro seems to know Socrates: he is certainly familiar with his habits and is therefore surprised to find him at the King Archon's portico instead of his "usual haunts in the Lyceum."[48] He finds it impossible to believe that Socrates, whom he knows to be a just and peaceful man, is himself the instigator of a suit: he is sure that Socrates must be a defendant (2b1–2). Euthyphro is also familiar with Socrates' *daimonion*, the voice that prevented Socrates from engaging in certain courses of action from time to time; he is convinced that that must be the reason Meletus has accused Socrates of impiety (3b5–8).[49] The impression we get is that Socrates and Euthyphro know each other relatively well, even though Euthyphro does not understand the first thing about Socrates' complexity.

Because of the *daimonion*, Euthyphro thinks that Socrates shares with him the special knowledge of the divine he believes himself to possess. That makes him eager to try to speak for both of them in a single voice: the Athenians, he says, are "envious of everyone who is like *us*" (3c2–3) — an identification Socrates is quick to reject: "How all this will turn out," he says about his impending trial, "is unclear except to *you* seers" (3e2–3). Euthyphro's own religious views are a matter of controversy. There is in general no agreement whether Euthyphro is represented as a "sectary" and religious innovator[50] or as an expert in traditional theology[51] — whether he is part of the Athenian religious establishment or its enemy. But his confidence in the accuracy of his theology and in the correctness of his legal position is so extreme and absolute that it destroys from the very first any confidence we might have had in the soundness of his judgment: "Religious accusations," he claims, "are easy to make in the presence of the crowd. Even at me—even at me they laugh as if I were mad when I discuss the divine at the assembly, predicting the future for them; and yet nothing I have predicted has not turned out true" (3b8–c3).[52] He preens himself on his wisdom concerning the gods and contrasts his own knowledge to the ignorance of the crowd (4e1–3). He self-confidently tells Socrates, missing the ironic overtones of the latter's question, that he does in fact understand the religious complications of his case perfectly well (4e4–8). He asserts that what makes him different from the rest of the world is precisely the fact that his knowledge of these matters is so exquisitely precise ($\dot{\alpha}\kappa\rho\iota\beta\dot{\eta}\varsigma$, 4e9–5a2). He is proud of his knowledge of the various traditional stories concerning the gods (6b3–c7), and he predicts that he will easily win his case if only the judges are able to listen to him impartially (9b9–10).[53]

Plato's portrait of Euthyphro—a portrait he goes to great lengths to construct—is one of a prodigiously conceited character: so conceited that he remains totally impervious to the incredibly heavy-handed irony with which Socrates treats him throughout the dialogue. Again and again, in a manner that is as obvious to the work's readers as it is invisible to its target, Socrates begs Euthyphro to take him on as his student ($\mu\alpha\theta\eta\tau\dot{\eta}\varsigma$) and to teach him ($\delta\iota\delta\dot{\alpha}\sigma\kappa\epsilon\iota\nu$) his wisdom ($\sigma o\phi\dot{\iota}\alpha$) about piety so that when he goes to court himself he will be able to mount a successful defense against Meletus' suit. Socrates uses these three terms and their derivatives twenty-four times in the course of the work.[54] Seldom has Plato, in my opinion, portrayed Socrates being so transparently nasty with one of his interlocutors. Socrates' irony is so extreme that it soon ceases to be humorous. It is much less humorous here, for example, than it is in the *Protagoras*, in which the sophist, who knows how to take care of himself, actually fights back successfully on a number of occasions during his conversation with Socrates. Euthyphro, by contrast, is made to seem like nothing but a pompous fool.

Plato's Euthyphro, in short, is unusually stupid. Even his name, in the context of the dialogue, is an obvious joke and in stark contrast to the structure of his conversation with Socrates. This "straight thinker," which is what "Euthyphro" means in Greek, is led again and again in a circle, made to formulate new definitions of piety that are continually reduced to his original, easily refuted account of piety as what is pleasing to the gods.[55] And as if that was not obvious enough, Plato makes an explicit point of the image of going about in a circle: "You call me a Daedalus," Socrates tells Euthyphro. "You say I make [words] walk. But in fact it is you who are a good deal more skillful than Daedalus, for you make them walk in circles. Or aren't you aware that our discussion has gone round and come back to the very same place?" (15b7–c1).

Plato's disdain for Euthyphro is reflected in the attitude of his readers and is replicated by his interpreters. Paul Friedländer described Euthyphro simply as a "bigoted nature."[56] Gregory Vlastos, as usual, did not mince words: Euthyphro, he wrote, "is as good as told that his failure to make his confident claim to know exactly . . . what piety is, means not just that he is intellectually hard up, but that he is morally corrupt."[57] According to Laszlo Versenyi, "Euthyphro is essentially a comic figure. . . . His pretended elevation above [his contemporaries] is pure imposture and alazony; a boastful pretense to being different, an ignorant claim to know what they ignore, a holier-than-thou attitude that has no basis in reality."[58] "In his fanaticism," writes another commentator, "Euthyphro has gotten everything backward,"[59] while yet another claims that the dialogue's unsuccessful, aporetic ending is at least in part due to Euthyphro's "conceit, lack of prior philosophical reflection in an area in which he claims to be an expert, and to his general dullness."[60]

That is all doubtless true of the character in Plato's dialogue. But that is just the point: Euthyphro is a literary character and not a real person. Euthyphro is not responsible for his stupidity; Plato is. Yet the exceptional verisimilitude of Plato's writing overcomes our staunchest precautions and seduces us into taking his dialogues not as works of literature and imagination but, instead, as transcriptions of actual conversations. We feel, therefore, that Euthyphro is stupid because some historical person of that name happened to be an intellectual simpleton. His stupidity thus seems to be a brute fact that needs no further explanation: a witless man cannot possibly appreciate the importance of the questions Socrates puts to him.

But that is a delusion. There is no such fact. The actual fact is that Euthyphro is stupid only because Plato decided to create a character with those features. And that is a fact that any interpretation of the dialogue must explain.

Why, then, did Plato make Euthyphro such a fool? So much contempt does not sit well with the further fact that he represents him as a friend of Socrates, familiar (as we have seen) with his character and habits, well disposed toward him, and even unwilling to lose his temper in the face of Socrates' relentless and far from gentle questioning.[61]

Perhaps Plato wants to use Euthyphro to caricature the complacency of traditional religious attitudes in Athens.[62] But we have already seen that Euthyphro's relationship to traditional religious practices in Athens is difficult to determine. The dialogue also shows him to be a literal believer in Hesiod's tales about the quarrels of the gods (6b–c, 7bff.), which does not correspond with the little we know about the skepticism with which such stories were generally regarded at the very end of the fifth century BC; that does not make Euthyphro a good representative of traditionalism in Athenian religion.[63] By contrast, then, we might think that Plato wanted to expose the silliness of religious innovators ("sectaries"). But this does not help very much either. For the question both alternatives fail to answer is what Plato would have to gain by such a strategy. Whatever Euthyphro's relation to religious traditionalism, the fact remains that the Athenians, as he himself explicitly complains, refuse to take him seriously. And if they don't, Socrates' outwitting him as he does cannot serve either "to reveal Athenian religious orthodoxy in all its absurdity"[64] or to display the folly of its religious radicalism. If Plato intends to satirize either religious conformity or religious deviance, his choice of its representative is quite unfortunate. He would have done much better to show how a highly intelligent and respected religious figure was unable to articulate his beliefs—not how a foolish fanatic was apt to botch them.

Why then is Euthyphro so stupid, and why is Socrates' irony toward him so heavy handed? The beginning of an answer to these questions can be found in the fact that, as James Arieti has also noticed, the *Euthyphro* is "about self-delusion so intense that it thrives even when the hollowness of its foundation is absolutely manifest."[65] All the elements of Euthyphro's character that we have listed so far—his supreme confidence, his arrogance, his sense that the people cannot understand him—seem perfectly chosen to constitute a person who, quite as conceited as he is dull, can remain painlessly unaware of Socrates' personal and dialectical pressure.[66]

Given how silly, how slow, and how self-confident Euthyphro is, it is only to be expected that he would miss the main points Socrates has been trying to make throughout their conversation. For Socrates has claimed that an action as disputable as Euthyphro's own cannot be undertaken without a secure understanding of the nature of piety: if you tell me that it is just to steal from the poor and to give to the rich, you had better have a clear conception of what you think justice is and a number of good reasons to support it; Euthyphro's action falls into a similar category. But Socrates makes it perfectly clear that Euthyphro, despite his grand claims, has no idea regarding what piety is and no idea that he lacks all knowledge concerning it. Most important, he suggests that in remaining unaware of his ignorance, Euthyphro exhibits the lack of self-knowledge that Socrates considers the most serious human failing. And it is precisely such truths about himself that Euthyphro's personality is designed to prevent him from being able to see. His self-assurance is a form of blindness, of self-deception.

Plato has prepared the ground perfectly for the dialogue's completely negative end. At the beginning, Euthyphro took great pains to engage Socrates in conversation. He was eager to "teach" him what piety is and also to tell him all sorts of shocking stories about the gods which only he knew. He was therefore ready to engage in what would have been a traditional *epideixis* — a formal exhibition of one's talents and abilities, often associated with orators and sophists (cf. *G.* 447b8; *Pr.* 317e3ff.). And yet, at the end of the work, after yet another failed effort to say what piety is and confronted with Socrates' invitation to begin again at the beginning, he suddenly remembers a pressing appointment: "Some other time, Socrates," he says, as he has clearly already started on his way; "just now I need to hurry to get somewhere, and I am already late" (15e3–4). The excuse is transparently lame, but the character who makes it has been drawn appropriately: this self-satisfied, overconfident man has just had enough of Socrates and his tricks. He may have lost the argument, but that means nothing to him: he departs undaunted and unchanged.

Given Euthyphro's character, it is natural for us, as the dialogue's imaginary audience, to believe that he could have missed Socrates' point so completely. How *could* he have seen it given how dull, how ignorant, and how self-satisfied he is? Euthyphro's personality explains why Socrates fails to have any effect on him. And that in turns explains why Plato chose to compose his dialogue around him. Despite all Socrates' efforts, Euthyphro's supreme self-confidence allows him to remain quite unshaken in his conviction that his legal action is correct and that no one can match his knowledge of the gods' desires. No argument can move him from his Olympian assurance.

But we know better. We can see through his self-deception. We look on as Euthyphro, blind in his self-assurance, misses Socrates' point again and again, and we manage to avoid the traps into which he falls. We realize, as generations of Plato's readers have realized, that self-delusion of the kind Euthyphro manifests is Socrates' greatest enemy. Detecting self-deception in others is not such a difficult thing to do, after all; as Lionel Trilling remarked, the "deception we best understand and most willingly give our attention to is that which a person works upon himself."[67] And we are not like this grotesquely silly, conceited, and inane man: how could we be like this gross caricature, whose only reason for being is simply to misunderstand what Socrates believes? But we understand; we are on Socrates' side; we know better.

And knowing better, what do we do? Mostly, we read this little dialogue and then we close the book, in a gesture that is an exact replica of Euthyphro's sudden remembering of the appointment that ends his conversation with Socrates. We too go about our usual business, just as he proposes to do. And our usual business does not normally center on becoming conscious of and fighting against the self-delusion that characterizes Euthyphro and that, as we turn away from the dialogue, we demonstrate to be ruling our own lives as well — *which is really the aim of this whole mechanism*. Socrates' irony is directed at Euthyphro only as a means; its real goal are the readers of Plato's dialogue.

The *Euthyphro* is not alone among Plato's works in taking such an insultingly ironical approach to its audience. Though the *Charmides*, unlike the *Euthyphro*, ends on a positive note, with Charmides accepting Critias' advice to stay close to Socrates and to continue his search for temperance with him (176a6–d5), its effect is similar. For Critias excludes himself from that project even though it has been shown that his own understanding of temperance is anything but satisfactory (175a8–11). We also know that Charmides eventually became one of the vicious Thirty Tyrants who ruled Athens at the end of the Peloponnesian War, under the brutal leadership of Critias himself. So we know that, despite the dialogue's promising end, neither ever learned Socrates' lesson. But we are able to explain their lack of understanding, and to distinguish ourselves from them, because we know as a matter of historical fact that they were depraved, evil characters. That, however, is an easy and unsatisfactory way out. Are Critias and Charmides oblivious to Socrates because they are evil, or do they become evil because they do not take him seriously? Plato does not answer that question directly. But this gives reason to pause and ask whether avoiding Socrates, as we ourselves so often do, may be the reason for depravity and not its effect. If Charmides, who is portrayed as a particularly admirable character in the dialogue, and Critias, who does not seem to be at all corrupt at that time, eventually became evil because they paid no attention to Socrates, and not the other way around, why should we suppose that we are so different from them after all?

The *Laches*—to take one more example—ends with an expression of warm fellow-feeling on the part of all its participants. But Nicias and Laches, the generals who have been shown to know nothing about the nature of courage, bow out of the continued investigation of the nature of virtue (200c7–d8) and turn the matter over to Socrates and the fathers of the two young boys their conversation originally concerned. Even someone who, like Nicias, is perfectly aware of the point of the Socratic elenchus (187e6–c3) finds it easy to shrug it off and return to his everyday life. Being Socrates' friend is not the same as joining him in the life he advocates as the only life appropriate for human beings (*Ap.* 38a5). And though we, too, think of ourselves as his friends, we are very like Nicias: we go our own way.

Some people do, it is true, spend a reasonably large part of their lives examining Socrates' arguments and reading Plato's works again and again—I myself am one of them. But though a direct examination of the dialogues' doctrines and arguments is absolutely necessary to come to terms with Socrates, it is simply not enough. The Socratic dialogues demand of their audience what Socrates asks of his interlocutors: to examine their beliefs on any subject of importance to them, to determine to what other beliefs they are logically related, to accept only those that are compatible with one another, and to live their lives accordingly. That is a question we are as good at ignoring as any of Socrates' simple interlocutors.

The close study of Plato's texts is mostly a logical exercise; its apparent dryness may disappoint those who expect more of philosophy. But when it comes to justice, wisdom, courage, or temperance—when it comes to the virtues that were Socrates' central concern—our beliefs about them are central to our whole life, to who we are. To examine the logical consistency of those beliefs, when undertaken correctly, is to examine and mold the shape of our self. It is personal, hard exercise, a whole mode of life. As Michael Frede has written, "to revise beliefs which are so deeply interwoven with the fabric of our life in such a way as to achieve and maintain consistency is extremely difficult, in part because it means, or at least might mean, a basic change of life."[68] The logical examination of belief is a part—but only a part—of the examined life.

The dialogues ask their readers, as Socrates asks Euthyphro, to make their life harmonize with their views. Is there, as Plato's Socrates seems to think, a consistent set of beliefs in accordance with which life can be lived? Can we have the harmony he is after? I am not sure. And even if we can, I am almost certain that there isn't a single set of beliefs that supports a single mode of life that is good for everyone. But that is not directly the issue that faces us here. That issue, in Frede's words again, is that "to know, we learn from the early dialogues, is not just a matter of having an argument, however good it may be, for a thesis. Knowledge also involves that the rest of one's beliefs, and hence, at least in some cases, one's whole life, be in line with one's argument. . . . In this way, knowledge, or at least a certain kind of knowledge Plato is particularly interested in, is a highly personal kind of achievement."[69] Philosophy is not here a matter only of reading books: it is a whole way of life, even if, as I believe, it does not dictate a single manner of living that all should follow.

The simple investigation of the structure of Socrates' arguments is not enough to enable us to live a philosophical life. Nor is that accomplished by a more "dialogical" interaction with Plato's works, by an investigation of their dramatic form as well as of their arguments.[70] The enterprise is personal as well as intellectual; and it may even proceed in part, as I shall argue in the second part of this book, independently of the detailed study of Plato's works, though never without attention to Socrates himself. To the extent that most of us do not engage in a project of that sort—and we don't—we end up, despite our dedication to his study, as Plato's *casual* readers. And that is the result of a deliberate strategy on Plato's part. The *Charmides* prompts us to look down on its characters because of our knowledge of their depraved nature. The *Laches* allows us to excuse the generals because of their age, complacency, and general good nature. The *Euthyphro* makes it easy for us to take Socrates' side and to feel a contempt for Euthyphro that, in reality, we should also feel for ourselves. In each case, Plato provides a different reason for the incomprehension with which Socrates' interlocutors react to him. One of these reasons is bound to become our own excuse.

In fact, our situation is in some ways worse than Euthyphro's. For Plato puts us in the position of believing that we know what is better and of doing what is worse: we tell ourselves and our students that Socrates is right and Euthyphro wrong, and yet we refuse the kind of life our agreement with Socrates demands. But as Plato has Socrates argue throughout his early dialogues, there is no such thing as knowing the better and doing the worse: there is only ignorance of the better.[71] Euthyphro, at least, does not agree with Socrates: we do, or say that we do. The *Euthyphro* shows us that in our positive, enthusiastic reaction to it, we are simply displaying our ignorance of our own ignorance—the same self-delusion that generations of commentators have discerned in Euthyphro but overlooked in themselves; the same self-delusion we found in Hans Castorp and ignored in ourselves.

Plato's irony is more disturbing than Socrates'. It uses Socratic irony as a means for lulling the dialogues' readers into the very self-complacency it makes them denounce. It is deep, dark, and disdainful. It is at least as arrogant a challenge to Plato's readers as Socrates' irony was to his interlocutors and perhaps even more so. Plato's irony, if I am right, is as easy for his readers to miss as Socrates's irony, sometimes to our shocked surprise, is easy to miss for the characters he addresses. But by inducing the same structure of self-deception in Plato's readers, Platonic irony explains why Socrates was so unsuccessful in convincing his interlocutors of his view and way of life. For in the process of producing in us a disdain for Socrates' interlocutors, the dialogues turn us into characters just like them. In observing Euthyphro deceive himself in Plato's fiction, we deceive ourselves in our own life.

It is in this sense that Mann's irony constitutes an echo or reflection of the Socrates of Plato's early works. Though the characters they construct are deeply different from one another, Mann's and Plato's strategies are similar and their purposes identical. They both produce or replicate self-deception in their readers as they exhibit it in their characters. Plato's dialogues, however, involve an additional, more troubling element. Being works of philosophy, they require a philosophical, ethical response. We may decide Socrates is wrong and try to refute him; we may perhaps even try to show that Euthyphro was not so bad after all.[72] We may consciously decide to ignore Socrates' approach, freely choosing another sort of life for ourselves. We may agree with him and, in no uncertain terms, live a life like his with all its attendant difficulties, dangers, and risks. Or we may, as the authors we shall examine in the second part of this book all did, interpret his activity on a more abstract level and imitate not the content but the form of his life—not necessarily his dedication to reason but his creation of and devotion to his own inimitable voice. What we cannot do, even though that is just what we usually do, is to agree with Socrates on the one hand and turn away from Plato's work, as Euthyphro turns away from his difficult interlocutor, on the other.

In the next two chapters, we shall turn from the irony of the author to the irony of his character, from Plato to Socrates. First, for the simple reason that Socratic irony is a necessary element of the Platonic irony we have been discussing so far. Second, because Socratic irony is the product of a literary strategy the effect of which has been to convince modern readers that the "real" Socrates is to be found in Plato's texts and not in the works of Xenophon, whose own literary strategy created a sense of verisimilitude for an earlier era. We shall ask, among other things, why it has become so natural to believe that in Plato's work we can confront Socrates himself, why we think that Plato's Socratic reflection is not a reflection at all but a direct view of its original. Finally, we shall examine Socratic irony because, as I will argue in the second part of this book, it provides in large measure an explanation of two strange and important facts. First, the fact that a number of modern philosophers have imitated Socrates in taking philosophy to be, as he thought it was, the art of living. Second, the fact that the lives they describe and exemplify in practicing his art are radically different from, perhaps even contrary to, his own. Socrates' irony, his silence, is the reason he created a tradition that manifests itself in the most diverse ways of life and of which even some of his most vicious opponents, like Nietzsche, sometimes, to their own horror, find themselves to be a part. The art of living is a Socratic art. Even those who reject him are bound to perpetuate him.

2

Socratic Irony
Character and Interlocutors

---

*The typical victim of an ironic situation is essentially an innocent.
Irony regards assumptions as presumption and therefore innocence
as guilt. Simple ignorance is safe from irony, but ignorance
compounded with the least degree of confidence counts as intellectual
hubris and is a punishable offense.*

D. C. Muecke, *The Compass of Irony*

     Plato lures the readers of his early dialogues into a cunningly induced state of confident ignorance. He instills confidence by lulling us into believing that we know better than Socrates' interlocutors. He makes us presume that, unlike them, we see Socrates' point; he makes us imagine that we agree, if not with every single one of Socrates' views, at least with his general outlook on life. And he displays our ignorance by showing that in fact we do nothing of the sort. He forces us to see that although we claim to agree with Socrates' uncompromising demand to devote our life to the pursuit of reason and virtue, we remain ultimately indifferent to it. In the second part of this book, we shall see that "the pursuit of reason and virtue" is not the only appropriate description of Socrates' philosophical project: the Socratic art of living can take many forms. But those who claim to agree with Socrates that the rational pursuit of the knowledge of virtue is the right way to live face a hard test the moment they turn away from Plato's early works to face the rest of their lives.

Plato therefore places his readers—he places us—in a particularly difficult situation. Moreover, our situation is just that in which Socrates' own victims find themselves in the course of the dialogues. As we read those works, Plato creates a fictional physical distance that separates us from the action of the works: he allows us to imagine that we are part of the audience observing Socrates practicing the elenchus—the devastating question-and-answer method by means of which he tries to puncture his interlocutors' self-confidence. Sometimes, the distance is even greater: Plato then allows us to imagine that we stand a little further back; that we are a second group, observing Socrates' own, immediate audience as well. And while we watch Socrates engage others in the elenchus, the elenchus is being practiced on us all the while. In convincing us that we are his ultimate audience, Plato turns us into participants in his dialogues, almost into characters of his own fictions. The dialogues' final audience, watching all watchers, is Plato himself, who stands behind the most distant observers of Socrates' dialectic and follows ironically the dramatic action he has created. His gaze is one we cannot see. For, as Montaigne wrote, "Our eyes see nothing behind us. A hundred times a day we make fun of ourselves in the person of our neighbor and detest in others the defects that are more clearly in ourselves, and wonder at them with prodigious impudence and heedlessness."[1] Platonic irony forms the ultimate background of the dialogues.

That shows how difficult it is to recognize when the elenchus is being practiced on us, when it is that we are being shown that we know less than we think. And if that is so difficult for us, there is no reason it should have been easy for Socrates' own interlocutors. We must therefore not be so hard on them. It seems perfectly reasonable to us to brush Socrates aside and to go on with our lives as before even while we are agreeing with him that we shouldn't. Just so, it appears natural to them to refuse to take him seriously even if they sometimes suspect they have failed to answer his questions. As a matter of fact, those who think of Socrates as a bore or a cheat may be less objectionable than those who claim to be convinced that he is right but do not act on their conviction. The former are wrong; the latter are hypocrites. And those who choose to ignore Socrates may not even be wrong, since it is not at all obvious that we should accept Socratic dialectic as the best guide to life. Not everyone values it as much as Socrates and his direct followers do. One can even be a Socratic, as I hope to show in the course of my argument, without such an unquestioning commitment to a life of pure reason. Nietzsche, who was himself such a Socratic but insisted on identifying Socrates with rationality "at any price," was not exaggerating when he wrote that "Before Socrates, dialectic manners were repudiated in good society. . . . Honest things, like honest men, do not carry their reasons like that. . . . Wherever authority still forms part of good bearing, where one does not give reasons but commands, the dialectician is a kind of buffoon: one laughs at him, one does not take him seriously."[2] Socrates' interlocutors do not miss his point simply because they are stupid like Euthyphro, naive like Ion, corrupt like Charmides or Critias, or self-important like Protagoras—not unless we ourselves miss it because we are equally stupid, naive, corrupt, or self-important.

Plato, whose disdain for people is matched only by his passion for improving them, may well have thought that stupid, naive, corrupt, and self-important is just what most of us are. But at least in order to salvage some of our self-esteem, we would do better to think that arrogant innocence is not found only in caricatures like Euthyphro or Ion. It is a very common state, difficult to notice and to overcome—a general human state that characterizes many of us even if we are not particularly stupid, naive, corrupt, or self-important.

Plato populates his works with arrogant innocents—each one of them, of course, arrogant and innocent in his own way and for his own reasons. He then places us next to Socrates and his interlocutors, as part of the dialogues' notional audience, and encourages us to think that by and large our point of view is the same as Socrates'. He encourages us to assume a superior, ironic attitude toward Socrates' dialectical partners. And in so doing, he turns us into arrogant innocents like them. As we treat Socrates' victims ironically, unaware of our own misplaced confidence, we become ourselves the objects of Plato's own, higher-order irony.

What allows us to be ironic toward Socrates' interlocutors? Obviously enough, the fact that Socrates' attitude toward them is itself almost unfailingly ironic. Socratic irony, therefore, plays a double role in Plato's work. It is part of the dialogues' subject matter; it is represented within them and plays a specific role in characterizing Socrates and his relations to others. But it is also a formal structure, a mechanism for creating one of the dialogues' most powerful effects. As we watch Socrates manipulate his interlocutors, we ourselves are being manipulated by Plato. The character's irony is indispensable to his author's; the creature is essential to its creator. Plato's later works, which seldom give Socrates reason to be ironic, do not make life as difficult for their readers as his early dialogues so often do.

Being ironical is therefore a dangerous affair: "The only shield against irony . . . is absolute circumspection, a shield no man can lift. If this seems to put the ironist at an altogether unfair advantage it has to be observed that the ironist is equally vulnerable, for the very act of being ironical implies an assumption of superiority." Ironists themselves are particularly vulnerable to irony: the tables can always be turned, and one can never quite know whether one is not also a victim, as well as an agent, of irony. "The ironist is therefore faced with the same need to be universally circumspect and with the same chance of success."[3]

Ironists are vulnerable to their own tactics because their assumption that they are superior to their victims proves to be their fatal weakness. That assumption is essential to irony in all its forms, from its simplest rhetorical cases to its most cosmic and ethereal romantic versions. Irony always implies that the ironist knows something that someone else does not and, at least for the present, cannot know. In all irony, therefore, there is an element of boastfulness, which is part of the reason irony has always been met with such suspicion.

Socrates himself connects irony with boastfulness and anticipates the suspicion it provokes on the one occasion when he uses that term in connection with himself. In Plato's *Apology* (37e3–38a1), he tells the court that they should not spare his life in the hope that he will change his ways. That can never happen: as long as he is alive, he will continue to ask his fellow citizens the very same disquieting questions that have brought him to court in the first place. But why should he refuse, he now imagines someone might ask, to live in peace and quiet (σιγῶν καὶ ἡσυχίαν ἄγων)? That, he continues, is the most difficult thing for him to explain. For if he told the court—which, of course, is exactly what he goes on to do—that if he were to stop doing philosophy he would be disobeying the god's command (τῷ θεῷ . . . ἀπειθεῖν), they "would not listen to him, thinking that he was engaged in *eirôneia* (ὡς εἰρωνευομένῳ)."[4]

What exactly does Socrates mean by *eirôneia*? Where would the irony be in his claim that his philosophical activity constitutes a divine mission? John Burnet relies on the original sense of *eirôneia* as "shirking responsibility by sly excuses" (among which he counts "the Socratic profession of ignorance"), and he translates the last phrase of Plato's Greek as "regarding this pretext as a sly evasion."[5] But this interpretation misses an important aspect of what Socrates says here. He is not offering just *any* "sly evasion." He is saying that he has a special connection to the god, whose desires he is carrying out by engaging in philosophy. Whether his judges believe that Socrates is sincerely convinced of his divine connection or is making fun of them, they will think that his claim is also a claim that he is superior to them. Socrates' "evasion," whether truthful or dishonest, would be taken to involve a boast, and that is why he finds it so difficult to make it.[6]

Let us keep the connection between *eirôneia* and boasting in mind as we review, in the roughest terms, the general outlines of the sense of *eirôneia* in classical Greek.[7] The history of the word is relatively well known. Originally terms of abuse, *eirôneia* and its derivatives, which first appear in the works of Aristophanes, carried the sense of dissembling, shamming, and deceiving.[8] The same sense is sometimes found in Plato,[9] and in a form slightly more complex than that of its original Aristophanic uses it survives as late as Demosthenes.[10]

But in some other cases in Plato, a radically new sense of *eirôneia* emerges for the first time.[11] The *eirôn* — the person who uses *eirôneia* — is now no longer simply a cunning, dissembling hypocrite, an outright deceiver who intends and needs to escape completely undetected. The *eirôn* is now transformed into a much more subtle character who lets part of his audience know that his words do not obviously or necessarily express his considered opinion, that he does not always mean what he says, and who does not mind if some people are aware of his dissembling. The dissembling is no longer secret, at least not from all of one's audience. This new understanding of the term, which I intend to articulate in what follows, is made concrete and personified in Socrates.

The first ancient author to offer a systematic discussion of irony is, not surprisingly, Aristotle. In the *Rhetoric*, he offers a rather traditional and negative view of *eirôneia*.[12] In the *Nicomachean Ethics*, however, Aristotle contrasts *eirôneia* with boastfulness, writes positively of it, and establishes once and for all its connection with Socrates: in contrast to the boastful, ironists, "who understate things, seem more attractive in character; for they are thought to speak not for gain but to avoid parade; and here too it is qualities which bring reputation that they disclaim, as Socrates used to do."[13] Interestingly enough, Theophrastus followed the *Rhetoric* and gave a purely negative portrait of the *eirôn* in his *Characters*, returning to the term's original, Aristophanic sense.[14] But equally interestingly, the rhetorical tradition, which derived essentially from Aristotle's school,[15] bypassed the *Rhetoric* and approached irony in the affirmative manner of the *Ethics*. Irony is listed as a common trope in Anaximenes of Lampsacus' *Rhetoric to Alexander*[16] as well as in the *Letter to Alexander*. And the concept was finally codified — with an important qualification we will soon discuss — by Cicero and Quintilian.

The most common ancient understanding of irony is what Cicero calls "refined dissembling" (*urbana . . . dissimulatio*), of which Socrates is the greatest example.[17] Its most familiar contemporary sense—saying something but meaning its contrary—is derived from that understanding. In particular, it can be traced back to one (though, as we shall see, not the only one) of Quintilian's formulations. Irony, according to Quintilian, is a trope that belongs to the genus allegory and "in which something contrary to what is said is to be understood."[18]

This, then, is the traditional picture of the development from Aristophanes' *eirôneia* to Cicero's irony—from coarse lying to the avowed, elegant pretense of hiding what one really thinks, which Dr. Johnson described as "a mode of speech in which the meaning is contrary to the words."[19] The general outlines of that picture are beyond dispute. But we need to pay closer attention than we have done so far to the implicit claim of superiority that is, I am convinced, inherent to irony. Irony and boastfulness are never far apart, and we cannot understand one without the other. In particular, to force them apart leads us into mistaking Dr. Johnson's formulation, which at best applies to one of its minor and least interesting variations, for irony's central sense. The stark contrast between the term's Aristophanic and Ciceronian uses, between pure deception on the one hand and refined honesty on the other is much too simple. Boastfulness complicates the clear, elegant, and forceful story Gregory Vlastos has recently told about the development of irony from its early Greek to its later Roman version and to which I now turn: "The image of Socrates as the paradigmatic *eirôn* effected a change in the previous connotations of the word. Through the eventual influence of the after-image of its Socratic incarnation, the use which had been marginal in the classical period became its central, its normal and normative use: *eirôneia* became *ironia*" (29). Though Socrates is indeed crucial to that story, his character is both darker and more complex than Vlastos supposes. And so is his most characteristic practice.

We have already found a connection between irony and presumed superiority in Plato's *Apology*. More clearly, in the *Nicomachean Ethics* Aristotle distinguishes between *eirôneia*, the mock modesty that makes people pretend they lack valuable qualities they actually possess, from *alazoneia*, the boastfulness that causes them to brag of possessing valuable qualities they in fact lack. Aristotle thinks that both are vices, extremes between which lies the virtue of truthfulness,[20] though he thinks *eirôneia*, the best instance of which is represented by Socrates, is preferable to *alazoneia*. But—what is most important for us here—he goes on to point out that understatement itself can be overstated. The Spartans' clothing, for example, was so exaggeratedly simple that it turned into its opposite and became a form of bragging: "Both great excess and great deficiency are boastful."[21] Montaigne also noticed the same point: to Aristotle, he wrote, "self-appreciation and self-depreciation often spring from the same kind of arrogance."[22] Irony does not only insinuate superiority: it can actually assert it. It then turns into its own contrary, exactly as Philodemus eventually claimed during the first century BC: "The ironist," he wrote, confirming beyond the shadow of a doubt the connection on which I have been insisting, "is for the most part a species of the boastful."[23] In putting themselves down, ironists, sometimes secretly and sometimes not, express disdain for their victims and draw themselves above them.[24]

That irony always presumes the speaker's superiority shows that the relationship between irony and shamming or dissembling is more complicated than the traditional picture of irony, which Vlastos endorses, allows. Even if we grant that in its early uses *eirôneia* was almost synonymous with dissimulation and deceitfulness, does it follow that irony, perhaps as transformed by Socrates, eventually becomes totally innocent of deceit? That it does, that irony and deceit absolutely exclude one another, is the keystone of Vlastos's extremely influential interpretation of the concept, which in turn supports his own grand Socratic construct. But the keystone needs to be reshaped and the construct must be rebuilt.

Vlastos's Socrates is overwhelmingly sincere, uncompromisingly honest.[25] Truth is his only goal, and truthfulness his sole means to it. Vlastos's image of Socrates would disintegrate if Kierkegaard was right to claim that "one can deceive a person about the truth and (remembering old Socrates) one can deceive a person into the truth. Indeed when a person is under an illusion, it is only by deceiving him that he can be brought into the truth."[26] Vlastos cannot possibly accept Kierkegaard's position, and in this strong version, neither can I. Truth is much more important to Socrates than Kierkegaard allows, both as a means and as a goal.

In the *Gorgias*, for example, Socrates says that he would rather lose than win an argument for a wrong conclusion:

> What kind of man am I? One of those who would be pleased to be refuted if I say something untrue, who would be pleased to refute anyone who says something untrue, and who would be even more pleased to be refuted than to refute. For I consider that to be much better—as much better, in fact, as avoiding the greatest evil oneself is better than helping someone else avoid it. And nothing, I believe, is a greater evil for a human being than to have false opinions about the subjects we are now discussing. (458a2–b1)

Vlastos asks: "What could he stand to gain by slipping in a false premiss or a sophistical inference?" (43). It is essential to his image of a Socrates who is absolutely and in all ways committed to truth that his irony be completely unconnected with deception, dissimulation, dissembling, or duplicity. For that reason, Vlastos insists that Socrates' irony must be absolutely transparent. Even if his interlocutor, like Euthyphro, cannot see it, we must always be aware of it and understand the point he is making by its means. For if it is not transparent, if Socratic irony has anything in common with the lying Aristophanic *eirôneia* with which Vlastos contrasts it, then Socrates cheats. And, for Vlastos, a cheating Socrates is no better than his sophistic opponents.

Irony, therefore, Vlastos writes, "is simply expressing what we mean by saying something contrary to it. This is something we do all the time — even children do it — and if we choose to do it we forfeit in that very choice the option of speaking deceitfully" (43).[27] Irony makes itself immediately understood: if it is missed, either the speaker botched it or the listener was not careful enough. Successful irony is honesty that is accompanied by a slightly mocking smile. But the mockery, in the form of deprecation, is directed primarily at oneself.

There is no question that the version of irony Vlastos describes surely exists — even children, as he writes, do it. But his general interpretation of irony, which is in that respect representative of a number of recent discussions, overlooks one of its major features. Vlastos believes that successful irony, as Kierkegaard would have put it, ultimately cancels itself: the listener listens to the soul, not to the voice, of the speaker. Wayne Booth makes exactly that point in his discussion of what he calls "stable irony," which he considers the central species of the trope. When we decipher an ironic statement, "we can finally choose a new meaning . . . in harmony with the unspoken beliefs" we attribute to its author. "Even the most simple-minded irony, when it succeeds, reveals in both participants a kind of meeting with other minds."[28] Faced with irony, we perform the simple operation of establishing the contrary of what is said, and that allows us to know precisely what we are really being told. The puzzles of irony have a simple solution.

But "the primary use" or the "stable form" of irony — saying the contrary of what you mean — is primary only in the sense that it is the *simplest* case of irony. Even then, it is the simplest case only of the rhetorical understanding of the term. Rhetoric, in turn, involves only one species of this all-pervasive figure. Its other species — dramatic irony, the irony of fate or circumstance, romantic irony — have little to do with Dr. Johnson's pithy formulation.[29] And even rhetorical irony, we shall now see, often involves a considerably more complex relationship between what one says and what one means.[30]

Cicero himself, for example, does not separate irony from indirectness. He thinks, of course, of irony in positive terms. But when he writes that "of the Greeks, we are told that a pleasant and humorous and genial conversationalist, who put up a pretence whenever he spoke, was Socrates (the Greeks called him an *eirôn*)," his reference to pretending (*simulare*) leaves the question of transparency open.[31] One might object, as Vlastos does, that "pretense" here does not have its "basic use" of "deceiving" or "alleging falsely." Instead, "pretending" must be understood in its "subsidiary use," as it is applied for example to "children 'pretending' that their coloured chips are money . . . or that their dolls are sick or die or go to school." This "subsidiary" use, "altogether innocent of intentional deceit," allows us to understand *eirôneia* as a figure of speech totally devoid of "willful misrepresentation" (27).

But many activities that go under the name of "pretending" cannot be reduced to either of these two starkly defined opposites. The children who pretend that some colored chips are money may not intend to deceive anyone by their pretense, but that does not mean that to them the chips clearly are *not* money, either: children have a much more complex relation to toys than the dichotomy between the primary and the subsidiary use of "pretending" can possibly capture. To take another sort of case, I may pretend to be—I may act like—a classical scholar, all the while leaving my audience (and perhaps myself as well) in doubt as to whether I really am one or not. Sometimes we pretend in order to eventually become what we pretend to be. Sometimes we pretend in order to find out whether we already are something or not. To call someone a pretender, a *simulator* (as Cicero calls Socrates), shows neither that we know their mind nor even that they know it themselves.

Cicero's best-known statement about irony, on which Vlastos bases his interpretation, occurs in *De oratore*:[32] "Urbane is the dissimulation when what you say is quite other than what you understand. . . . In this irony and dissimulation Socrates, in my opinion, far excelled all others in charm and humanity. Most elegant is this form and seasoned in seriousness." Vlastos, whose translation of Cicero I used here, insists that even if *dissimulatio* is translated as "dissembling," "*deceitful* concealment . . . is absent from the figure of speech Cicero has in view" (28 n. 24). But the matter is much more complex.

To begin with, it is not obvious that Vlastos's translation of Cicero's "alia dicuntur ac sentias" as "what you say is *quite* other than what you understand" is correct. The addition of "quite" suggests something much closer to "contrary" than the simple term *alium* ("other," "different") does by itself and makes Cicero appear as if he is anticipating Dr. Johnson's definition. But Cicero has just that simpler term in mind, as we can see by looking at the passage that Vlastos surprisingly elides in his citation. For Cicero praises this form of *urbana dissimulatio*, in which what you say is different from what you understand, and explicitly contrasts it, in the elided passage, with "another kind, of which I spoke earlier, in which you say *the contrary*, as Crassus did to Lamia." He then returns to the case he is now discussing, which involves not the contrary of what is in your mind but a case "where the whole tenor of your speech shows that you are gravely jesting in speaking *differently* from what you think."[33] Cicero does not describe the irony he finds in Socrates as saying the contrary of what one means. And if what you mean when you speak ironically is simply different from what you say, then your words do not make your meaning clear. That is not deceit, but neither is it revelation.

Even Cicero, therefore, believes that apart from the very simplest cases of irony the words you use when speaking ironically do not make your meaning obvious. In general, he is saying, irony gives the impression that you are saying something different from (*alium, aliter*), not contrary (*contrarium*) to, what you are thinking. But what it is that you are thinking is thereby left unclear. Of course, Cicero doesn't seem to think — and he certainly doesn't say — that irony involves "*deceitful* concealment"; but we have seen that the simple contrast between deceit and truthfulness cannot begin to capture the complexities of irony. Irony allows you simply to refuse to let your audience know what you think and to suggest simply that it is not what you say. And though that may not amount to deceit as we most commonly understand it, preventing your audience from knowing what you actually think is far from constituting "a meeting with other minds."[34]

Quintilian's two references to irony are no less complex than Cicero's.[35] He first makes some vague and general comments about it as an expression of a speaker's character (*êthos*) and claims that "it requires that something *different* from that which is said be understood."[36] In his second discussion, however, Quintilian distinguishes between irony as a simple trope (*tropos*) and irony as a complex figure (*schema* or *figura*). Here we must be very careful. For, though Quintilian claims that the trope doesn't differ much from the figure, "since in both the contrary of what is said is to be understood,"[37] a closer look shows that they are after all distinct.

Quintilian's theory does not seem to reflect his practice. The trope, he writes, is more revealing (*apertior*) than the figure: though it expresses something different from what it means, it doesn't really make any effort to hide it. That, Quintilian says, was Cicero's point when he described Catiline's accomplice, Metellus, as a "most excellent man" (*vir optimus*): you hear *optimus*, and knowing Cicero's views, you immediately understand *pessimus* ("most awful"). This example shows that irony as trope applies to words and that its meaning is clear.[38] But irony as figure, which involves not just words but phrases and whole sentences, makes it much more difficult to know what meaning is being expressed. Here, "the whole intention is disguised, more a matter of suggestion than avowal." While in the trope a word or two are different (*diversa*) from their real meaning, the figure puts the whole sense of a passage in question.[39] Despite Quintilian's remark on the similarities between trope and figure, it is difficult to say that the latter allows us to know a speaker's mind as readily as the former. And when finally Quintilian claims that "a whole life," like Socrates', may be characterized by irony, it becomes very difficult to see how the simple formula of saying something by uttering its contrary is to be applied at all: this most complex case of irony does not even depend on words, and it is not clear what the contrary is for which we should be looking.[40] Even though Quintilian writes that Socrates was called an *eirôn* because of his pretended ignorance and feigned admiration of those who seemed to be wise, the fact remains—as I shall argue in what follows—that this rather simple explanation cannot do justice to the phenomenon it is intended to capture.[41] Quintilian's theory and practice, to repeat, do not go together.

Cicero and Quintilian, then, do not believe that irony always points to the contrary of what it says. And if it does not, then it is difficult to believe that Socrates' irony always allows us to know exactly what he means. The rhetorical texts are not committed to such a general interpretation of irony, even if Quintilian believes that as a matter of fact Socrates' irony consists in falsely pretending not to know the answers to his own questions. If we took Quintilian's explanation of Socratic irony too seriously, we would have to conclude that Socrates did after all know what justice, or courage, or virtue really was and that his claims of ignorance were never serious. That would be a wrong interpretation of Socrates. In addition, neither Cicero's nor Quintilian's general view of irony entails that Socrates knew the nature of the virtues, nor do we have any independent reason for thinking that he did.

If we cannot move transparently from what Socrates says to what he means, if irony does not make one mind so readily accessible to another, if it involves saying something other than, and not just contrary to, what one means, then Vlastos cannot be right when he defines Socratic irony simply as "the perfect medium for mockery innocent of deceit" (28). Lying is not the only mode of deception. You can hide the truth (assuming that you know what it is) even when you are not lying. And sometimes you may yourself not be sure what the truth is even if you are convinced that it is not what your words mean.

One element in the traditional picture of irony is not affected by the criticisms I have made of it so far. Kierkegaard, whose admiration of Socrates paled before his love of Jesus,[42] did not mind thinking of the Greek thinker as a sophist using sophistry against sophists. I cannot. Even though Socrates was part and parcel of "the Sophistic movement,"[43] our image of Socrates makes it impossible to attribute to him outright, intentional deceptiveness.[44] And as long as we think that we can only choose between honesty and fraud, between the malicious and deceitful irony of Aristophanes and Theophrastus on the one hand and the rhetoricians' obvious trope through which nothing is hidden on the other, there is no question where Socrates belongs.

That dilemma, however, is not real. The essential connection between irony and superiority shows that even when it is not straightforwardly deceptive as it was in Aristophanes, irony always includes an element of dissimulation, a distancing between speaker and audience. That is the point Lionel Trilling made when he wrote that irony implies "a disconnection between a speaker and his interlocutor, or between the speaker and that which is spoken about, or even between the speaker and himself."[45] I want now to use this sense of disconnection, which is directly relevant to the superiority I have already mentioned,[46] in order to construct a different interpretation of Socratic irony.

Let us begin with Thrasymachus' well-known attack on Socrates during the course of their discussion of justice in the first book of the *Republic*: "Heracles!" he said. "This is Socrates' habitual shamming ($\epsilon i \omega \theta v \tilde{\iota} a$ $\epsilon i \rho \omega v \epsilon i a$). I had predicted to these people that you would refuse to answer and would sham ($\epsilon i \rho \omega v \epsilon \acute{v} \sigma o \iota o$) and would do anything but answer if the question were put to you."[47] Vlastos's translation of *eirôneia* as "shamming" allows him to argue that Socrates' opponents regularly saw him as an Aristophanic deceiver: "Thrasymachus is charging that Socrates lies in saying that he has no answer of his own to the question he is putting to others: he most certainly has, Thrasymachus is protesting, but pretends he hasn't to keep it under wraps so he can have a field-day pouncing on ours and tearing it to pieces while he is shielded from attack" (24).[48] Thrasymachus' only complaint is that Socrates is lying about knowing or, rather, about believing that he knows what justice is.

But, in fact, Thrasymachus' point is more complex. The sophist has been silently fuming at Socrates' discussion of the nature of justice for some time; unable to contain himself any longer, he has just exploded with a vicious attack. Socrates responds calmly by asking Thrasymachus not to be angry at Polemarchus and him: if they have so far failed to determine what justice is, Thrasymachus can be sure that they have done so unwillingly; they would never have intentionally compromised their search, he says, for what is to them even more precious than gold. Thrasymachus must not for a moment suppose that they were anything less than completely serious about finding what justice is: "You surely mustn't think that," Socrates continues, "but rather—as I do—that we're incapable of finding it. Hence it's surely far more appropriate for us to be pitied by you clever people than to be given rough treatment."[49]

It is only this last statement that prompts Thrasymachus' attack against Socrates' "habitual *eirôneia*." Must we think that he accuses Socrates of shamming or deceiving? Thrasymachus is drawing attention to what *he* takes as Socrates' mock humility, through which he claims to be able easily to see and which, in his eyes, Socrates has laid on so thick that it cannot deceive anyone. Thrasymachus does not accuse Socrates of lying; he blames him for not meaning what he says and, in addition, for not hiding his lack of sincerity. Socrates obviously doesn't believe, Thrasymachus is saying, that the sophist is more clever than he. He charges Socrates with pretending to be innocent of his real meaning (which here is, in fact, the contrary of what he says) and with failing, intentionally, to hide his mockery. Thrasymachus claims not just that Socrates is trying to deceive him— his ploy is too transparent for that—but that he is evading the issue: he says things he does not mean, he distances, disconnects himself from the words he is actually using; he appears to flatter Thrasymachus while in reality he shows his contempt for him. Not Socrates' intention to deceive, but his transparent refusal to take responsibility for his real meaning, is what enrages Thrasymachus. He knows that Socrates does not consider him wise or clever. He feels that he has been taunted successfully, not that he has been swindled to no effect. Taunting and mocking are at best peripheral features of Aristophanic *eirôneia*, the point of which, like the point of all lying, is to pass unnoticed. But they are essential to irony as we understand it today.

This passage shows that even the most negative uses of *eirôneia* against Socrates do not centrally involve the notion of deceit, understood simply as lying. But what about those cases when the term is used positively, not as an accusation but as a mere description or diagnosis of Socrates' personality, perhaps even as a compliment? Do these absolutely exclude the notion of deceit, as Vlastos argues? They do not. But "deceit" is too strong a word for my purposes. The simple contrast between truthfulness and lying cannot capture either Socrates' character or his way of doing philosophy.

In his great drunken speech in the *Symposium*, Alcibiades promises to reveal Socrates as he really is to their friends. One of the first things he says is that Socrates "spends his entire life *in eirôneia* (εἰρωνευόμενος) and jesting with people."[50] Vlastos offers us a choice between an irony that is ultimately transparent on the one hand and a case of intentional deceit on the other: "If we follow Quintilian we shall understand Alcibiades to be saying that Socrates is a lifelong ironist. If we follow [a group of contemporary scholars] we shall understand him to be saying that Socrates is a lifelong deceiver" (34).[51]

A little later, Alcibiades uses the adverb *eirônikôs* ("ironically") to describe the manner in which Socrates, some time ago, had appeared to reject the younger man's sexual advances. Alcibiades had offered Socrates his beautiful body in exchange for Socrates' wisdom. Socrates, he now tells his audience, heard him out to the end. He then answered, "most ironically (*eirônikôs*) in his extremely characteristic and habitual manner" (218d6–7), that if indeed he was as wise as Alcibiades thought, the offer would not be to his own advantage: since wisdom is so much more precious than beauty, why should Socrates exchange one for the other? But, Socrates continued, perhaps Alcibiades was wrong: Socrates might not be wise and might have nothing to offer him. "Here, I submit," Vlastos writes, "it is incontestably clear that 'ironically' has to be the sense of *eirônikôs*, for the context gives no foothold for the notion of pretence or deceit. Socrates is turning down flat the proposed exchange, saying that it is a swindle" (36). But is the clarity Vlastos discerns incontestable?

Throughout his discussion of this passage, Vlastos equates the notions of deceit and pretense. He claims that those who take Socrates as a deceiver do so because they understand Alcibiades to be saying that Socrates is pretending either not to know the answers to his questions or something more vague and more general.[52] Of course, some cases of pretending are also cases of deceiving. But others are not. Such cases are not weak enough to turn pretense into a totally transparent game that takes no one in, but they imply precisely the distance, the disconnection from one's own words, even from one's own self, that we have already mentioned. The *Symposium* presents us with one of them.

Irony allows us to pretend we are something other than our words suggest. It enables us to play at being someone, without forcing us to decide what we really are or, indeed, whether we really are anyone. Ironists can maintain a distance that allows them to say, when pressed, "But that is not what I meant, not what I meant at all," and to get away with it. I say "get away with it" not because I presume always to know what an ironist means but precisely because I believe that it is often not clear what iro-nists mean, even though we can strongly suspect it is not what they say. Their words do not bind them.

Irony always and necessarily postulates a double speaker and a double audience. One speaker does and one does not mean what is said; one au-dience does and one does not understand what is meant. Fowler gets part of this right when he writes that irony consists in "the use of words in-tended to convey one meaning to the uninitiated part of the audience and another to the initiated, the delight of it lying in the secret intimacy set up between the latter and the speaker."[53] The sense of superiority that al-ways accompanies irony has its source in this intimacy between the speaker and the initiated part of the audience.[54]

With these general points in mind, let us now look at Alcibiades' speech in the *Symposium* in more detail. Alcibiades is relating past events, an in-cident between Socrates and himself that occurred some time ago. He has now come to realize that Socrates' self-control is unassailable. But though Socrates might never have intended to deceive him when he re-fused his offer, his ironical manner need not at that time have been free of pretense. And in fact it was not. It entailed the pretense involved when you detach yourself from the obvious interpretation of your words, when you hint that what you say may not be what you really mean, when you suggest that you just might possibly be of two minds about what you are saying. And so you allow your audience to act on its interpretation of your meaning, whatever it takes it to be, rather than on its understanding of your words. An ironic refusal of someone's offer to go to bed with you may suggest coyness rather than virtue.

Coy is just what Alcibiades took Socrates to be when they were alone together at dinner. Inexperienced as he was, Alcibiades had just asked Socrates to help him improve his soul, and in return he offered his body to him. Now suppose for a moment that Alcibiades had not used the ad-verb *eirônikôs* in his account of Socrates' reply:

Dear Alcibiades, it looks as though you are not stupid, if what you say about me is true and there really is in me some power which could make you a better man: you must be seeing something inconceivably beautiful in me, enormously superior to your good looks. If that is what you see and you want beauty for beauty, you mean to take a huge advantage of me: you are trying to get true beauty in exchange for seeming beauty—"gold for brass". But look more closely, blessed boy, lest you have missed that I am nothing. The mind's vision grows sharp only when the eyesight has passed its peak, and you are still far from that.[55]

Socrates could well have uttered these words without a trace of irony, speaking as a sober man who is rejecting an impetuous boy's offer. In that case, he would have meant to deny that he was capable of accomplishing what Alcibiades expected of him, and he would have allowed Alcibiades to see that he did. But add the qualification "ironically" that Plato puts in Alcibiades' mouth, and what do we have? We have a young boy faced with a radical uncertainty about whether an older man does or does not mean what he says to him. Is Socrates serious or is he not? Does he want Alcibiades or does he not? Alcibiades soon learns the answer to those questions when he joins Socrates on his couch and finds him absolutely unmoved. We already suspect it from our general knowledge of Socrates' character. But why should Alcibiades know it, at the time when Socrates spoke to him as ironically as he did? And why should we not even suppose that Socrates might have been for a moment uncertain of his own feelings, at least while he was making his ironic and therefore ambiguous response?

Socrates does not offer Alcibiades a "riddle" with a clear answer that he expects him to reach on his own.[56] Through his irony, Socrates dissociates himself from his words; he does produce a riddle, but it has no easy solution. Vlastos believes that when Socrates tells Alcibiades "that it looks as if you are not stupid," he means precisely the opposite: that Alcibiades really is stupid and that he would never even conceive of accepting his offer (36). But is it clear that Alcibiades, even if he were the most gifted interpreter, should have taken that as Socrates' point? Should he have realized that Socrates could be valuable to him only as a fellow searcher for the truth and not as a source of information about it?[57] Why should he? What evidence does he have for that conclusion? Socrates gives him none. He simply does not let Alcibiades see clearly what he means when he responds to his proposition; he at least suggests that what he says may not really be what he means. It is no wonder that, alone in the middle of the night, the boy, on hearing Socrates' words, joins him on his couch. Socrates has not lied to Alcibiades. But he has suggested that he has not quite meant what he said. By being ironic, he has left his meaning and intention concealed.

Vlastos notes that fact. In Alcibiades' image of Socrates as Silenus (ugly outside, full of the most beautiful statues inside) he sees "the picture of a man who lives behind a mask—a mysterious enigmatic figure, a man nobody knows." But, captive by his stark dichotomy between pure deceit and utter truthfulness, he insists that "to be reserved and to be deceitful are not the same thing. All we can get from the simile is concealment, not deceit" (37).

Concealment, however, constitutes a third and distinct ironical effect. Intermediate between lying and truthfulness, it shares features with both: like truthfulness, concealment does not distort the truth; like lying, it does not reveal it. Once we have rejected the view that irony consists simply in saying the contrary of what you mean, concealment cannot, even when the irony is detected, lead us to the ironist's real meaning.

Vlastos agrees that in his exchange with Socrates Alcibiades was indeed deceived: "But by whom? Not by Socrates, but by himself. He believed what he did [that Socrates wanted to sleep with him] because he wanted to believe it" (41). I don't agree. Even though Socrates may never have intended to deceive Alcibiades, his toying with him, his concealing himself and his real desire behind his words, prompted the boy into the wrong reaction. Perhaps Alcibiades did want to believe that Socrates wanted him, but it was Socrates himself, through his irony, who helped him transform his belief into action. Vlastos tries to absolve Socrates of all responsibility for Alcibiades' reaction. I believe he tempted him into it, if only to teach him a further lesson.

Concealment introduces complexity even in the simplest cases of irony. It is also connected to the sense of superiority that is irony's constant companion. For example, when Socrates ironically calls Thrasymachus "a clever person," we cannot immediately say that what he really means is that Thrasymachus is "a fool." That is not false, but it is a poor interpretation because it lacks sufficient texture. Just *how* stupid, for example, does Socrates believe Thrasymachus is? The question has no answer. Socrates does not mean that Thrasymachus is stupid in some well-specified sense; what he lets us know is that, in saying that Thrasymachus is clever, he is implying that it is really he, Socrates, who is the more clever of the two. In hiding his meaning, however simply, Socrates succeeds in concealing himself more deeply than he could have done by saying the contrary of what he meant. And, at the same time, he claims a double superiority for himself. He puts himself above Thrasymachus both by implying that he is more clever than the sophist and by showing that he is keeping something back from him.

If we take irony as saying the contrary of what you mean, the meaning of an ironic statement is perfectly clear. If we take it, more generally, as saying something other than what you mean, the meaning of an ironic statement is much less determinate. It can remain hidden even from those who know full well that you are being ironic. And it always suggests that you are holding something back, something you do not consider your audience worthy of knowing. It constitutes a refusal to put yourself on the same level as your audience. And even though it may intimate that you may be uncertain about your own intention, it still presents you as superior: for that is an uncertainty you do not openly reveal.

Concealment may be very specific, as in the simple cases of saying just the contrary of what you mean. It may be more complex, as in the case of Socrates' exchange with Alcibiades. But it can also be something much broader and longer lasting. And that finally brings us to the irony of Socrates' whole life, of which Alcibiades and, following him, Quintilian speak. With that issue, I will end this chapter and prepare the ground for the next, in which I examine not the reaction of Socrates' interlocutors' to his irony but Plato's own.

The tradition to which some of Quintilian's remarks have given a voice construes Socratic irony as a transparent self-disparaging pretense to know less than he actually does.[58] It is succinctly summarized by D. J. Enright: "Socrates introduced irony into the world. He pretended to be ignorant . . . and, under the guise of seeking to be taught by others, he taught others."[59] Socrates' constant questioning of his companions, therefore, was his ploy to get them to see for themselves what he already knew. That was the Socratic mode of teaching.

Now Socrates did claim that he was ignorant, and he did deny that he was a teacher. Did he or did he not mean what he said? A serious answer to that question was recently given by Gregory Vlastos by means of his notion of "complex irony." In complex irony, instead of simply saying the contrary of what you mean, you play a double game. You use your words in two distinct senses, denying them in one and asserting them in the other. When Socrates, for example, denies that he is a teacher,

> in the conventional sense, where to "teach" is simply to transfer knowledge from a teacher's to a learner's mind, Socrates means what he says. But in the sense in which *he* would give to "teaching"—engaging would-be learners in elenctic argument to make them aware of their own ignorance and enable them to discover for themselves *the truth the teacher had held back*—in that sense of "teaching" Socrates would want to say that he *is* a teacher, the only true teacher: his dialogue with his fellows is meant

to have, and does have, the effect of evoking and assisting their efforts at moral self-improvement. (32)[60]

Socrates thus both does and does not mean what he says: he is a teacher in one sense and not in another. He does not tell his students the answers to the questions he puts to them, though he knows them, but he is willing to lead them to see them for themselves. But this "teacher who holds back the truth" is, in the ancient sense of the term, a dogmatist: he believes that there is a truth to be known about the nature of things, especially the virtues, and that he himself is in possession of it. He is as "Socratic" as any professor of torts in the first year of contemporary law schools—that is, not at all. His ironic insistence that he neither knows what virtue is nor is capable of teaching it, once interpreted in this manner, disappears into a protreptic device, a mechanism for motivating otherwise unenthusiastic students.[61]

Complex irony is actually a sophisticated version of the simplest cases of rhetorical irony we have already discussed. It still depends on the idea that Socrates means precisely the contrary of what he says, though now in a sense of his words his audience is not likely to understand. It also presupposes that, however mysterious and enigmatic Socrates may have appeared to his interlocutors, he did not present a mystery to Plato, who understood the nature of his irony and depicted its workings in his early works. In the same way, Socrates is no longer enigmatic to his modern readers who have deciphered the double code he used to communicate with his contemporaries. According to this view, Plato understood Socrates as well as Socrates understood himself—perhaps even better—and planted in his works the same hints for understanding him that Socrates himself had included in his own conversations.

Should we allow Socratic irony to transform itself so easily into an educational ploy? Is that still irony at all? In *The Magic Mountain*, Settembrini, Hans Castorp's humanistic pedagogue, proclaims that when irony "is not employed as an honest device of classical rhetoric, the purpose of which no healthy mind can doubt for a moment, it becomes a source of depravity, a barrier to civilization, a squalid flirtation with inertia, nihilism, and vice." But, as Hans Castorp remarks just a little later, "if 'no healthy mind can for a moment doubt its purpose,' what sort of irony is that for heaven's sake, if I may ask? . . . That would just be dry pedantry."[62] Hans Castorp is right. In any but its coarsest varieties, where it shades into cheap sarcasm, irony exercises healthy minds and leaves them in doubt about its purpose. Friedrich Schlegel, too, though he praised "a rhetorical species of irony which, sparingly used, has an excellent effect, especially in polemics," claimed that "compared to the sublime urbanity of the Socratic muse, it is like the pomp of the most splendid oration set over against the noble style of an ancient tragedy."[63] Rhetorical irony generally leaves its listeners in no doubt about what is said. And though nothing is wrong with that, it is only a very small part of what irony does. Uncertainty, Settembrini notwithstanding, is not depravity; uncertainty, we shall see, is of the essence. Socratic irony is more complex than "complex irony," and Plato's own understanding of Socrates, as we shall see in the next chapter, may have been less perfect than the latter notion allows.

The idea that Plato understood Socrates as if the character of the dialogues is a real person with whom Plato is thoroughly acquainted leaves me deeply dissatisfied. I will explain my reasons for being unhappy with it, and I will make a few suggestions toward an alternative. But first I want to examine the idea of complex irony, which is supposed to reveal Socrates' hidden depths and is essential to the view that Plato saw no mystery in his creature.[64]

In Plato's texts, Socrates sometimes claims and sometimes disavows knowledge of virtue. How is that possible, Vlastos asks, if Socrates is using "knowledge" in the same sense in both sorts of cases?[65] He appeals to complex irony precisely to eliminate such conflicts. Actually, there is no conflict in connection with teaching, since Socrates not once claims the role of teacher for himself.[66] But he often disavows it, and there are other reasons for refusing to read those disavowals (e.g., La. 186d8–e3) as complex ironies. One of those reasons is that Plato's works do not at all show that Socrates' dialogue with his fellows has the beneficial effects Vlastos so confidently attributes to him and on the basis of which he considers him "the only true teacher" of virtue. Who among Socrates' interlocutors in Plato's dialogues is improved by him? Protagoras remains unmoved. So do Gorgias, Polus, Callicles, Hippias, Euthydemus, and Dionysiodorus. The same is true of Euthyphro,[67] Ion, and Meno. "Moral improvement" grossly misdescribes the trajectory of the lives of Charmides and Critias.[68] The Laches and the Lysis end on a positive note: the participants promise to continue the efforts they have begun, but Plato leaves the question of Socrates' long-term effect completely unresolved. As to his influence on Alcibiades, we have, apart from the testimony of history, the confession Plato himself has him make in the Symposium: "I know perfectly well that I can't prove him wrong when he tells me what I should do; yet, the moment I leave his side, I go back to my old ways: I cave in to my desire to please the crowd."[69] How could Socrates, who constantly criticized the failure of the great Athenians to make not only their fellow citizens but also their very own children better,[70] claim success for himself in light of such a record?

Socrates' attitude toward a teacher's obligations provides a second reason for taking him at face value when he denies being a teacher of anything, especially of virtue. In the *Gorgias* (456a4–461b2), the sophist, who has claimed to be a teacher of rhetoric, disclaims any responsibility for the use to which his students might put the knowledge he gives them: his task is to teach them to speak, not to speak with justice—whether they do so or not is their choice and responsibility. Socrates then argues that since Gorgias has agreed that the nature of justice is part of what his course on rhetoric reveals, his students could never be unjust: how could someone who has learned what justice is not act according to that knowledge?[71] Gorgias, slightly confused, accepts the conclusion, but the issue remains unresolved. The implication is that either rhetoric is not after all concerned with justice or that Gorgias does not teach his students what he professes. By contrast, in the *Apology* (33a5–b8), Socrates assumes just the position he refuses to allow Gorgias to occupy: he argues that he cannot be held in any way responsible for the character and behavior of those who listen to his discussions. And the reason he gives is that these people took it upon *themselves* to follow him around Athens; he never was, nor claimed to be, their teacher. I think that if there ever was a sense—any sense—in which Socrates thought of himself as a teacher of *aretê*,[72] he would never have disavowed the responsibility for his students' character which he considered essential to all teaching.[73]

It is true that both his friends and his enemies took Socrates to profess to teach what *aretê* is, though they disagreed about the quality of his influence. But that is no reason for refusing to take his own disavowal of the role at face value. Strange as that may sound, it is difficult for me to imagine that Socrates' contemporaries and near-contemporaries *must* have understood him better than we do today (which is not to say that I believe that we do understand him well ourselves). The fact that his friends and companions composed so many *logoi* or dialogues depicting him in the most contradictory ways and quarreled seriously among themselves suggests that he was never an easy man to understand.[74] Proximity does not always secure understanding. Kierkegaard was right: "Even if I were to imagine myself his contemporary," he wrote, "he would still always be difficult to comprehend."[75] That difficulty is what we must capture. We do not need to find the key that will unlock his secret. His secret is there for all to see: it is that we cannot comprehend him. That is not a secret that can be explained: it can at best be displayed, and the best way of displaying it is by seeing the vast diversity of interpretations he has provoked over the centuries.

Taking Socrates' attitude toward his teaching as a complex irony robs him of much of his strangeness,[76] since complex irony gives us a window into his soul. Taking it as sincere supplies him, paradoxically, with a deeper ironical mask—a mask so profound that it proves difficult, perhaps impossible, to remove: perhaps not even a mask at all, if a mask is supposed to cover a real face. If Socrates believes sincerely that he does not know what *aretê* is and that he cannot teach it to others, he constitutes a real enigma. He held that knowledge of *aretê* is necessary for the good and happy human life. He disavowed that knowledge and the ability to communicate it. And yet he succeeded in living as good a life as anyone had ever done so far, in Plato's eyes as well as in the eyes of the tradition the two of them initiated. And he never let us know how that was possible.

That—we must be very clear—is a case of very deep irony. Irony is acknowledged concealment, and one can decide to conceal or to pretend to conceal oneself for many reasons. To think that irony can always be deciphered, or that ironists are themselves always in clear possession of a truth they are holding back, is often just to miss the point. It is to fail to notice that irony does not always hide an unambiguous truth and that it can be directed toward oneself as well. There is, as Enright writes, an irony that "doesn't reject or refute or turn upside down, but quietly casts decent doubt and leaves the question open: not evasiveness or lack of courage or conviction, but an admission that there are times when we cannot be sure, not so much because we don't know enough as because uncertainty is intrinsic, of the essence."[77] Irony often insinuates that something is taking place inside you that your audience is not allowed to see, but it does not always entail that you see it yourself. Irony often communicates that only part of a picture is visible to an audience, but it does not always entail that the speaker sees the whole. Sometimes, it does not even imply that a whole picture exists. Uncertainty is intrinsic, of the essence.

Irony seems to create a mask. It does not show what, if anything, is masked. It suggests depth. It does not guarantee it. And, I now want to claim, the Socrates of Plato's early dialogues has no depth, no underlying story distinct from the story these texts contain. Difficult and impossible to understand, he is as he seems. Only in Plato's later works, beginning with the *Gorgias* and the *Meno*,[78] do we find an attempt to account for Socrates, a set of views and theories he never had expressed before designed to explain how he could have lived as virtuously as he had. The first effort explicitly to display Socrates' depths, to expose what he is like inside, is made by Alcibiades in his speech in the *Symposium*. And his speech follows the discourse of Diotima on the Form of Beauty, which describes how one will remain indifferent to apparent beauty once one has seen the true beauty of the Form, and thus explains how Socrates could have remained unmoved by Alcibiades' seductive offer. But when Alcibiades opens Socrates like the statue of Silenus, he is still confronted with a mystery: how, after all, did the beautiful statues find their way inside? How did Socrates become the virtuous man he was?

Alcibiades has no answer to that question, and neither — that is the main point — does Plato, up to that time. The *Gorgias*, the *Meno*, and the *Symposium* mark the beginning of Plato's own attempt to provide Socrates with a depth that explains his paradoxical surface, his absurd appearance, his virtuous life. In these dialogues, Plato begins to make an explicit effort to construct his own interpretation, his own reflection of Socrates by means of views and theories new to his philosophical work.[79] But Plato's new reflection of Socrates is also a reflection on him. And what Plato is reflecting on, as we shall see in the next chapter, is nothing but another reflection as well. There is no more to Socrates than this series of reflections.

Socrates confronted Plato with a paradox. Convinced that Socrates was the best man of his generation (*Phd.* 118a15–18), perhaps the best man who had ever lived so far, Plato had to face the fact that, on his own admission, Socrates did not have what he himself considered necessary in order to be what he was. If knowledge of *aretê* is required for having *aretê* and so for living well, then Socrates, who lacked that knowledge, could not have been virtuous and could not have lived well. Yet he was, and he did.

Xenophon, too, faced the same problem and gave it his own answer. The sophist Hippias at one point charges that Socrates only asks questions about the virtues and never offers answers of his own (*Mem.* 4.4.10–11). Socrates responds, perhaps surprisingly, that he constantly demonstrates (ἀποδεικνύναι) what he thinks justice is. And when Hippias asks him to say what justice is, Socrates replies that his demonstration consists in the fact that he never, on any occasion, acts unjustly. And "deeds," he sententiously adds, "are much more serious evidence than words." Xenophon seems to have been satisfied with such an answer.[80] But Plato, who thought that knowledge of justice was necessary for acting justly in a consistent manner over a long period and that such knowledge could always be expressed in words, found it unacceptable.

We have left those texts of Plato in which *eirôneia* is explicitly attributed to Socrates behind. We are now concerned with Socratic irony not as a rhetorical figure but truly as a way of living. This way of living — a life of *aretê* that did not meet the conditions necessary for being such a life—presented Plato with a deep problem of his own, with a personality he could not understand. Part of his genius consists in his ability to have written a number of works (the Socratic dialogues) in which he portrayed that personality, exhibited its irony, puzzled about it, and displayed his puzzlement without offering an explanation of the character who was their central hero.

Plato's early works produce two important effects. One is that they create a particularly silent Socrates, a character whose irony does not allow us to see what made him a possible human being. That has enabled Plato's Socrates to invite, and to survive, the most disparate attempts to try to understand him, to explain how he came to be what he was—we will discuss three such attempts in the second part of this book. The second effect is that Plato's Socratic works created a character who remained a mystery to his own author. That in turn gives that character the verisimilitude and vivacity that account, as we shall see in the next chapter, for the fact that for almost two hundred years now he has appeared to be not just a character, a reflection, but a direct duplicate of his original.

Plato, however, did not remain content with that character. In the works of his middle and late periods, he offered the first explicit interpretation of Socratic irony, the first attempt to take off the mask his Socrates had been wearing and to bring to light what it concealed. For that purpose, he developed most of the ambitious resources that characterize the systematic thought that continues to dominate philosophy up to our own time, and initiated a major philosophical tradition. But his early works, in which Socrates is an unexplained mystery and simply lives a philosophic life, stand at the beginning of a different philosophical tradition, perhaps not as pervasive as the first but still alive and worth pursuing again.

For the moment, I would like to end with Friedrich Schlegel's observation that Socratic irony "aims at deceiving no one except those who consider it deception, and either take pleasure in the wonderful knavishness of tricking the whole world or become upset when they suspect that they too are intended as its targets."[81] Gregory Vlastos seems to have accepted Schlegel's point of view and to have tried to free Socrates from all possible deception. Kierkegaard appears to have taken delight in what he sees as Socrates' tricking the whole world, including those great tricksters, the sophists. Plato, I think, in the end came to see that he too may have been a target of his own creature's irony and tried to strip his mask away. As for me, I would like to think that my refusal to see Socratic irony as deception does not force me to consider it a path to the innermost depths of his, or any other, soul.

3

Socratic Irony
Character and Author

---

*Socrates' life is like a magnificent pause in the course of history:
we do not hear him at all; a profound stillness prevails — until it
is broken by the noisy attempts of the many and different schools of
followers to trace their origin in this hidden and cryptic source. His
irony was not the instrument he used in the service of the idea; irony
was his position — more he did not have.*

Søren Kierkegaard, *The Concept of Irony*

The idea that the most voluble figure in the history of philosophy is someone "we do not hear at all" seems at first to be just a calculated effort to shock and unsettle. But Kierkegaard is serious. Earlier in *The Concept of Irony* he writes much the same: "What Socrates himself prized so highly, namely, standing still and contemplating — in other words, silence — this is his whole life in terms of world history. He has left nothing by which a later age can judge him."[1] And Kierkegaard is right.

Kierkegaard's contrast between the silent figure of Socrates and "the noisy attempts" of his followers is nicely anticipated by Hegel, who described Socrates as the founder of moral philosophy and wrote that "all succeeding babblers about morality and popular philosophy constituted him their patron and object of adoration, and made him into a cloak which should cover all false philosophy."[2] Despite our common picture of Socrates, passionately devoted to talk and conversation, the torrent of words that surrounds him eventually flows on past him and finally leaves him perfectly silent. It is that silence that prompted most of the ancients and many of the moderns to look back at him again and again, some in order to understand him only, others also in order to follow him. The clamor that has always surrounded Socrates is ultimately the echo of a fundamental stillness. It is that stillness I want to recapture through my own noisy efforts in what follows.

Influenced by Hegel's grand view of the development of Greek philosophy, Kierkegaard believed that Socrates ended that early period of Greek civilization when the Athenians acted as they did simply because they adhered without question to the ethical norms they inherited along with the rest of their culture. Socrates fought against the authority of external codes of behavior and emphasized for the first time the primacy of subjectivity and the individual conscience: "Socrates' principle," Hegel wrote, "is that man has to find from himself both the end of his actions and the end of the world, and must attain to truth through himself."[3] Hegel, who rejected Friedrich Schlegel's conception of irony and tried to distinguish Socratic irony from it, argued that irony was only a part of Socrates' method for showing that moral questions must be answered by individuals through self-examination.[4] But Kierkegaard, who followed Hegel in defining irony as "infinite absolute negativity,"[5] insisted that irony was all that Socrates ever had at his disposal: "more he did not have."[6]

Kierkegaard claims that in its most important sense (*sensus eminentior*) irony "is directed not against this or that particular existing entity but against the entire given actuality at a certain time and under certain conditions."[7] In that sense, irony is "infinite" because it does not put in doubt the validity of this or that particular phenomenon of a culture but the culture as a whole. It is "negative" because it undermines what it opposes but is incapable of offering any serious alternative to it. And it is "absolute" because it negates what is actual by means of an implicit appeal to a future that, in a Hegelian sense, represents a higher stage of development but of which the ironist remains unaware. The higher stage toward which Socratic irony was pointing, according to Kierkegaard, was Christianity; but that was not something Socrates could know. The ironist, Kierkegaard writes, "has stepped out of line with his age, has turned around and faced it. That which is coming is hidden from him, lies behind his back, but the actuality he so antagonistically confronts is what he must destroy; upon this he focuses his burning gaze."[8] Socrates, then, introduced subjectivity and individual conscience into the world, but he remained unaware of their nature and their ultimate significance; these were only realized in Christianity as Kierkegaard understood it.

These are heady ideas. I am not sure I can do them justice, nor, indeed, am I sure that justice can be fully done to them.[9] But I do want to appeal to Kierkegaard in order to develop Quintilian's notion that Socrates' whole life was characterized by irony without also accepting Quintilian's further view that Socrates' irony is nothing but feigned ignorance. This most common understanding of Socratic irony[10] must be rejected. Socrates does not feign the ignorance we find him avowing in Plato's early works. I cannot, for example, accept Norman Gulley's view that Socrates already knows what piety, courage, or temperance is but pretends he does not so that his interlocutors will endeavor to discover it for themselves.[11] His ignorance is genuine, and that is perhaps the most important fact about him.

Plato's early dialogues are not instances of "didactic" dialectic, through which a questioner who knows the answer to a question of which the respondent is ignorant brings that respondent to the necessary knowledge by means of a series of cleverly designed questions. Such a view of Plato's works, as Michael Frede notes, assumes that "in each case Socrates . . . is represented as advancing an argument he already has and espouses, because it is an argument Plato has and endorses and which Plato just puts into Socrates' mouth." But that makes nonsense of the early "elenctic" or "aporetic" dialogues we are trying to understand. These works, in contrast to dialogues like the *Phaedo* and the *Republic*, do not represent Socrates "as leading a respondent by an argument in didactic fashion to come to see the truth on some matter. They rather lead the respondent by an argument to come to see the ignorance out of which he made some claim."[12] But the respondent's unconscious ignorance also reflects the ignorance that prompts Socrates, who is at least conscious of his lack of knowledge, to ask his questions in the first place.[13]

Socrates is often ironic when he claims to believe that his interlocutors know the answer to his questions. He is also ironic when, for example, he calls Thrasymachus "clever" in *Republic* i.[14] But he is honest when he says that he himself does not know what virtue is, and he is earnestly devoted to finding someone who might actually have that knowledge and communicate it to him. But to say that Socrates really does not know what virtue is, as Aristotle did when he rightly wrote that "Socrates used to ask questions and not to answer them—for he used to confess that he did not know,"[15] raises a number of serious questions about his philosophical practice.

Central among those questions is how Socrates' profession of ignorance, if it is sincere, fits with the fact that he often accepts a number of ethical views and principles. One of these principles, in Socrates' own words in his *Apology*, is "that to do injustice and to disobey a superior, whether divine or human: that I know to be bad and shameful."[16] Another, considerably more controversial, idea is that "one should never return an injustice nor harm another human being, no matter what one suffers at their hands" (*Cr.* 49c10–11). How can we understand Socrates' disavowal of knowledge when we are confronted with his claims to know that these things are true? Is he just contradicting himself? Or is the conflict, in some way or another, merely apparent?

Plato's representation of Socrates in his elenctic works has given rise to many different interpretations. One possible way of resolving the conflict we just noted is by means of the common contemporary distinction between knowledge and true belief. Though Socrates can disavow knowledge of virtue and ethical truth, he is under no obligation to disclaim all true belief about them. His beliefs, which are not supported by the strong justification only the understanding of the essential nature of virtue can provide, fail to qualify as knowledge; but they can still be true. That is the interpretation of T. H. Irwin, who writes that "a disclaimer of knowledge does not require a disclaimer of all positive convictions. Socrates . . . allows knowledge about virtue only to someone who can . . . say what it is. . . . If Socrates demands this stringent justification . . . it is not surprising that he claims no knowledge for himself. But he can still claim positive beliefs, which lack this stringent explicit justification but are still reliable."[17]

However, Socrates in the *Apology* claims more than true belief about the principle he articulates: he says that he *knows* that disobeying a superior is bad and shameful. The conflict between the conviction he expresses here and his various disavowals of knowledge is starker than Irwin allows. This problem has led Gregory Vlastos to propose another alternative. He rejects Irwin's appeal to the distinction between knowledge and true belief and argues that the paradox created by Socrates' simultaneous disavowals of and claims to knowledge can be resolved if we distinguish between two different conceptions of knowledge itself.[18]

What are those two conceptions? There is, first, the knowledge that is based on deducing a truth from some fundamental, self-evident principles. This kind of knowledge requires necessity and produces certainty: what we know this way cannot be otherwise and we cannot doubt it. It is what Plato has in mind when he claims that knowledge is infallible (*Rep.* 477e6–7) and what Aristotle is thinking of when he argues that "we all suppose that what we know is not capable of being otherwise."[19] It is the knowledge that the ancient philosophers, according to Vlastos, generally aspired to; for that reason he calls it "philosophical" or "certain" knowledge. In that sense of knowledge, Socrates, who was never concerned with deduction from fundamental axioms, certainly knows nothing, and his disavowals of knowledge are perfectly sincere.

Socrates, however, is no less sincere when he says he knows a number of ethical truths since, in those cases, what he means by "knowledge," according to Vlastos, is something weaker, more common and homespun. That is the knowledge Socrates derives from his own dialectical practice. It applies to whatever statements remain standing at the end of one or, preferably, more engagements in the conversational bouts we call the elenchus. Such "elenctic" knowledge (if knowledge it is) is weaker than "certain" knowledge because it is essentially fallible. No matter how often you have won an argument that depends on a particular view, there is no guarantee that you will not lose the argument next time around. In that case, what had seemed secure, perhaps even unassailable, will collapse in pieces. The view on which you had so often depended in the past, on which you might even have staked your life, will prove to have been indefensible after all. But as long as you have not yet lost an argument that depends on that view, you might feel justified in claiming that you know it. That, according to Vlastos, is just what Socrates feels in connection with the principles he states in the *Apology* and the *Crito*: since he has never lost an argument when he depended on them, he considers that he can claim to know them.

Socrates' disavowal of knowledge turns out to be one more instance of Vlastos's "complex irony."[20] When Socrates says that he lacks ethical knowledge, he means what he says if knowledge involves deductive certainty and infallibility; but he does not mean it if knowledge is understood as the fallible product of his dialectical victories. That is a knowledge he can and does claim for himself.

A central problem with this view is that the notion of a "philosophical" knowledge as Vlastos understands it is systematically articulated only in the middle and later writings of Plato and in the works of Aristotle.[21] Unless the concept of philosophical knowledge was reasonably current at the time of Plato's early dialogues, Socrates could not be made to deny possessing it without any explanation; and the evidence that it was current is very weak indeed. Vlastos cites two passages from Democritus: "In reality we know nothing, for the truth is in the depths" and "In reality we know nothing with certainty."[22] But Democritus' traditional skepticism, which goes at least as far back as Xenophanes,[23] seems a popular commonplace rather than a philosophical theory; it certainly is not developed enough to suggest that a well-defined concept of a knowledge that was certain and infallible had been articulated and was generally available at the time, even among the natural philosophers. Vlastos also appeals to the strong claims Parmenides had made on behalf of his view of the world.[24] But the Eleatic school, which Parmenides initiated, relied on deductive proof (though mostly on proof by reductio ad absurdum, which does not begin from the fundamental principles Plato and Aristotle were later to require of knowledge) almost exclusively in order to refute the commonsense views of most people and not in order to establish positive results of their own. Socrates, who on Vlastos's own account had no interest in natural philosophy or in the theory of knowledge,[25] would have had no access to what was still at best an esoteric epistemological innovation.[26] And even if Plato was familiar with such philosophical debates, he could not have allowed Socrates to rely on them without a single word of explanation.

My own view of the matter combines the sincerity Irwin attributes to Socrates with Vlastos's idea that there are two kinds of knowledge. With Irwin, I take Socrates quite literally when he says that in respect of virtue (*aretê*) he lacks the sort of knowledge he would truly consider worthy of that name. With Vlastos, I take Socrates to believe that he does have a kind of knowledge in regard to some ethical principles, like the idea that it is better to suffer rather than to commit injustice or that the fear of death makes it shameful to disobey the orders of one's superior.

The knowledge Socrates has is the knowledge he has gained through his lifelong practice of the elenchus; the knowledge he contrasts it with is not the knowledge of the philosophers (which, I have just argued, had not been properly articulated at the time) but the knowledge he believes craftsmen and artisans possess. Though he denies that such people know anything about the ethical topics that interest him, Socrates speaks generously of their mastery of their craft in the *Apology*. He was sure, he says, that they knew many fine things (πολλὰ καὶ καλά), and he was not wrong: they knew things he did not, and to that extent they were wiser than he.[27] The problem with the artisans was that they seemed to believe that knowledge of their crafts also gave them knowledge of the good life, though it did not. In that respect, the artisans proved as ignorant as anyone else and to that extent less wise than Socrates, who was aware of his ignorance. But the artisans' knowledge of their crafts is solid and indisputable, even though they know nothing of the ethical subjects that Gorgias, Prodicus, Hippias, and Evenus claim to understand and teach (*Ap.* 19e1–20c3).[28] The latter, too, obviously have no interest in philosophical knowledge, certainty, or infallibility: dialectical and rhetorical success is all that concerns them. They simply lay claim to technical or expert knowledge of *aretê;* as artisans do with their techniques, they can articulate and transmit this knowledge to others with a reasonable chance of success.[29]

Socrates, of course, thinks that the sophists are wrong. They possess nothing like the technical knowledge of *aretê* he is after. Technical knowledge can be more or less articulated; one can transmit it to others, even if it sometimes takes time and trouble to do so. It enables you to give reasons for what you are doing in many particular cases. It generally results in products that people can agree are good, or at least better than others. It is by no means a foolproof method,[30] and not everyone was capable, or allowed, to learn a craft. Socrates, himself a statuary and a statuary's son,[31] knew perfectly well that the crafts were at the time most often transmitted along with their secrets within a single family from generation to generation.[32] The evidence suggests very strongly that fathers trained their sons and that training began earlier than in modern times.[33] The knowledge involved in the crafts is not purely rational, and it certainly cannot be fully expressed in rules. Habituation is as essential to the practice of the crafts as it is to their appreciation. And disputes cannot always be easily settled. The famous case of the constant competition between Zeuxis and Parrhasius is only one of many; the invective heaped by the author of *On Ancient Medicine* on those who don't share his conception of how medicine is to be practiced is another.[34]

All those qualifications notwithstanding, the knowledge of artisans is stable: once you acquire it and practice it, you cannot lose it; your products are generally of high quality; you can also, at least in principle, explain and transmit it to others. Socrates would have considered that such knowledge, if he but had it, would allow him to live a virtuous and therefore a happy life.[35] But he lacked it and knew that he did. Thinking that it was the most precious human possession, he spent much of his life searching in regard to *aretê* for the kind of knowledge that enables sculptors, doctors, and shoemakers to produce results that are by and large good and allows them, at times, to explain to others how they were able to bring them about.

Socrates knows that he lacks knowledge of *aretê.* And it is his knowledge of that ignorance that produced his amazement, as we learn in the *Apology*, when the Delphic oracle said, in response to the question posed by his friend, Chaerephon, that no one in Athens was wiser than he: "What on earth does the god mean? What is he hinting at? For I am aware of being wise in nothing, great or small. What then could he mean by saying that I am wise?" (21b2–5; Cf. 21d2–6).[36] What Socrates would count as wisdom regarding the good life, even when it concerns "small things," is not simply the fact of holding some views about ethical matters; like everyone else, he naturally has certain beliefs about what is right and wrong. What he wants is the ability to articulate and justify those views to himself and thus to be able to transmit them to others—an ability he is painfully aware he lacks.[37]

That too is why in the *Apology* Socrates makes such a point of contrasting himself with the sophists who have a reputation for teaching people how to be successful (19d7–20c3). He disavows precisely what these people claim for themselves. It is also why, once he has learned of the oracle, he follows the procedure he describes (20b9–22e5). For those he approaches in order to locate someone wise in the matters that concern him are statesmen and poets (people with the reputation of being themselves good and of making others better as well) and artisans (people who possess, at least in their own fields, the type of knowledge he considered necessary for being a teacher of *aretê*).[38]

So far, I have translated *aretê* loosely as "virtue." It is of course a commonplace that "virtue" is not an accurate translation of the Greek term. "Virtue" is simply too narrow a concept, while the more recent "excellence" is, I believe, too weak, colorless, and vague. *Aretê* applies to many more human qualities than "virtue"; it can also refer perfectly well to features of nonhuman and even inanimate beings. That is obvious in those passages in the *Republic* where Plato discusses, without any indication that he is being innovative or revisionary, the *aretê* of utensils and instruments and, by implication, of animals (352d8–353c10). Homer attributes *aretê* to horses.[39] Inanimate objects, too, have their own characteristic *aretê*: Herodotus assigns *aretê* to Indian cotton, which he considers a superior form of wool (it grows on trees rather than sheep), and to fertile soil as well,[40] while Thucydides too speaks of the *aretê* of good earth.[41]

In regard to human beings, we would do well to construe *aretê* as "success" or as the quality or qualities that account for it. If nothing else, such an interpretation would explain why the Greeks were so concerned whether *aretê* can or cannot be taught and would show that their debates are immediately relevant to our situation today.[42] A vast industry is now devoted to imparting the secrets of success in innumerable fields of endeavor either through manuals or through "seminars" held around the world by experts who, for an appropriate fee, are just as eager to travel from place to place as the sophists were in their time. All those are versions of the sophists' promise and they prompt Socratic and Platonic responses from everyone who doubts that success in such contemptible endeavors constitutes anything of which one can be truly proud: is it really praiseworthy to succeed in real-estate get-rich-quick schemes? can anyone consider it "real" success? Benjamin Jowett was surely wrong to construe *areté* strictly as moral virtue and so to conclude that "no one would either ask or answer in modern times" the question how *areté* can be acquired with which Plato's *Meno* begins.[43] The nature of success and the means of acquiring it are central issues in contemporary life. As always, Plato once again proves to be very much with us.

But since *areté* applies to inanimate objects as well as to human beings, it is better to try to understand the term in a more general manner. We could do no better, I suggest, than to think of it as that quality or set of qualities that makes something an *outstanding* member of the group to which it belongs. *Areté* is the feature that accounts for something's being *justifiably notable*. Both suggestions, which come to the same thing, involve three elements: the inner structure and quality of things, their reputation, and the audience that is to appreciate them. And this is as it should be. From earliest times, the idea of *areté* was intrinsically social, sometimes almost equivalent to fame ($\kappa\lambda\acute{\epsilon}o\varsigma$). That dimension of the term is clear in the Homeric epics, but it survives in the classical period as well: on an inscription commemorating the Athenians who fell at Potidaea (432 BC) we read that "having placed their lives onto the scale, they received *areté* in return."[44] And in his *Funeral Oration*, which was delivered much later, after Alexander's death in 323 BC, Hyperides wrote that those who die for their city's sake "leave *areté* behind them" (41).

The question, then, whether *areté* can be taught is the question whether one can teach what it takes to have a justifiably high reputation among one's peers. Socrates knows that he cannot do that, since he does not know what *areté* is in the first place, and his elenctic examination of others proves to him that they are no better at it than he is. In fact, their conviction that they know and can teach it, their ignorance of their limitations, makes them, in his awareness, inferior to him. As he puts it in the *Apology*, "I asked myself on behalf of the oracle whether I would prefer to be as I am, being neither wise in respect of their [sc. the artisans'] sort of wisdom nor ignorant of their ignorance, or whether I would prefer to have both. And I answered to myself and to the oracle that I am better off just as I am" (22e1–5).

It is crucial to the ability Socrates disavows that it has nothing to do with deduction and certainty. It is important for teachers of all subjects to be masters of the systematic structure of their fields, but such a structure is far weaker than the rigorous set of relationships that underwrite the deductive validity that mathematical thought manifests. What really makes a difference here is a reasonable degree of reliability, a likely consistency of results, even if disagreements among artisans, as we have seen, may have been more frequent than Socrates suggests.[45] The art of medicine, for example, which Socrates often uses as his paradigm of what a craft is, was much less neat than he claims. One always had to be on one's guard: "Since doctors tended to be itinerant, it was practically impossible to hold them responsible. Hence there were many quacks and incompetent doctors; one had to try to make some informed judgment about whether one should trust the competence of the doctor who offered his help."[46]

However vexed the question of identifying a reliable expert in medicine may have been, it is minor in comparison to the immense complexity of recognizing an expert in *aretê*. The latter involves two problems. First, even though the question whether *aretê* can be taught may have been a commonplace, and even if we understand *aretê* as a justifiably high reputation among one's peers, a prior question is still unanswered. For none of these terms is noncontroversially connected with any particular set of human qualities. We know neither the proper domain within which one is supposed to be outstanding nor the qualities that justify such a person's reputation nor the proper group that is qualified to recognize an outstanding person: in short we don't know what constitutes the very idea of being outstanding. And that, as Socrates is made to insist throughout Plato's early works, is not to know what *aretê* itself is at all.

Second, the problem of recognizing an expert is particularly acute for someone who approaches the problem as Plato's Socrates does. Consider, in this context, the passage in the *Protagoras* where Socrates warns the young Hippocrates, who can't wait to run to the sophist's side, not to rush to Protagoras for instruction in *aretê* (313a1–314c2). The sophist, Socrates says, is "a merchant or peddler of the goods [learning, μαθήματα] that nourish the soul" (313c4–5). Sophists are for the soul what greengrocers are for the body. Merchants praise their products indiscriminately, whether they are good or bad (πονηρὸν ἢ χρηστόν, 313d1–3), even though they know nothing about them. Buyers cannot make the right discriminations themselves; unless they are themselves physicians or teachers of gymnastics (313d3–5), they must ask such experts for advice regarding what to buy and eat. The peddlers of mental nourishment, too, may well be "ignorant whether their wares are harmful or beneficial to the soul" (πονηρὸν ἢ χρηστὸν πρὸς τὴν ψυχήν, 313d8–e1). And the same is true of their

clients, unless one of them happens to be "a physician of the soul" (περὶ
τὴν ψυχὴν ἰατρικός, 313e1–2).

Only if you are yourself an expert (ἐπιστήμων) regarding what benefits and what harms the soul, Socrates tells Hippocrates, is it "safe for
you to buy learning from Protagoras or from anyone else" (313e2–5). If
you are not, you will endanger yourself much more than if you were to
buy unhealthy food. For you can take the food away in a basket and ask
an expert to examine it before you eat it (314a3–b1). Not so for food for
thought: "You cannot carry learning away in a jar. Once you have paid
for it, you must accept it directly in your soul, and having learned it you
must leave with the harm or benefit already inside you" (314b1–4).

Experts on the soul's nourishment, unlike experts on the body's food,
cannot be consulted after the initial transaction: that transaction is all there
is. One must determine in advance whether approaching a professor of
areté will help or harm one's soul—whether it will lead to *areté* or to vice
(κακία). But there is an additional problem. In the case of *areté*, and in
contrast to medicine or gymnastics, there are no acknowledged experts—
people can't even agree on what *areté* is in the first place. And therefore
the same difficulty that originally applied to the sophist will now apply
to those putative experts as well: how will you be able to tell whether their
advice regarding the sophist's wares will be in its own turn harmful or
beneficial? And the predicament gets even worse. One should not approach professors of *areté* unless one already knows whether what they
offer will help or harm the soul. But to benefit the soul is to make it better, to impart *areté* to it; to harm it is to make it worse, to fill it with vice
(κακία, 318a6–9, d7–e5). So one should not approach a professor of *areté*
unless one is sure that the professor really does teach what *areté* is and
thus, to that extent, really will enable one to possess it.

Let's now turn for a moment to Plato's *Laches*. The dialogue begins with
the question whether training in fighting with armor is good for boys of
good families, but Socrates, who is as always concerned with *areté* in general, quickly turns the discussion to the issue how the boys can be made
to be as good as possible. To decide that, however, they must know what
they are talking about. Is there anyone in the group, he now asks, who is
an expert (τεχνικός) in the care of the soul and who therefore knows how
to turn the boys into good men (185a4–6)? To know how to accomplish
that, Socrates continues, one must know what is that which, when present in the soul, makes it better than it was without it. But what makes the
soul better is *areté*, and therefore only someone who knows what *areté* is
will also know how to make the boys good men (189d3–190c6).

In order, therefore, to judge whether a sophist's course on *aretê* will help or harm the student, the expert of the *Protagoras* (ἰατρικός, ἐπαίων) must, like the expert of the *Laches* (τεχνικός), know what *aretê* itself is. But if such an expert exists, why go to the sophist in the first place and not learn directly from the one who has already been determined to know?

The reason we cannot is that no one has been determined to know—no one, as we have said, is an acknowledged expert on *aretê*. So, prospective students of professors of *aretê* cannot appeal to an independent authority. They can be sure that a course in *aretê* will benefit them only if they themselves can tell that it will. But to know that it will do so, as we have just shown, requires knowing what *aretê* is. And if one knows that, one needs no instruction from anyone. Professors of *aretê* should be approached only by those who already know what these people profess to teach. Professors of *aretê* are totally useless!

Experts in *aretê* therefore present a very complex problem. Do such experts exist at all? And, if they do, how they are to be recognized? In the case of shoemakers or doctors, we can tell whether the shoe fits or the fever has gone: we have relatively clear ways of recognizing them. But in the case of ethical experts, it is not clear that we can recognize the experts independently of the fact that we find their views and their reasons for them—their reasons for living as they do—convincing. But to find such reasons convincing is already to follow them.

That is clearly suggested by Socrates' refusal to agree with Euthyphro's definition of piety as doing what the gods love (*Eu.* 9e1–3). Socrates claims that this reverses the right order of things: the gods love the pious because it is pious, they don't *make* it pious by their love (9e4–11b1). The gods—experts in *aretê* if anyone is, despite Euthyphro's traditionalist view that they often disagree with one another—love the pious for a particular reason. And that reason explains why the pious is pious in the first place and why the gods command us to do it. But then that reason itself, not the gods' love, constitutes piety. What matters is only the gods' reason for wanting us to act in one way rather than in another. And that reason can be convincing only if we understand it and find it rationally acceptable.

But what would it be to find such a reason rationally acceptable, to recognize it as the definition of the nature of piety? It is clearly more than being unable to refute it when someone proposes it in a dialectical bout. It is also to be able to make that definition our own, to realize how it fits with definitions of the other virtues, and to make it part of the reasons for which we do what we do. Plato's Socrates believes that knowledge is sufficient for virtue, that if you know the right thing to do, you cannot fail to do it.[47] If therefore we recognize a statement as the definition of piety, we must have to that extent accepted it and become pious ourselves.

More generally, to recognize an expert in *aretê*, someone who truly is good, one must be good oneself. For to be able to recognize the expert, to know that someone is in fact a good person, is to be convinced of that person's views; and to be convinced of those views is to act on them in a rational, articulate manner. That is one of the most crucial and paradoxical consequences of Socratic ethics: only one good human being can recognize another.[48]

But if that is so, we are faced with an additional problem: how does one become, how does one learn to be good? Socrates believes that being good requires knowledge of the definition of *aretê*. His only method of searching for that definition is the elenchus. But, as everyone knows, the elenchus is essentially negative: it shows only that someone's beliefs do not cohere with one another and that at least one of them must be abandoned; the elenchus itself does not logically determine which view must be rejected.[49] The elenchus, it seems, can have a positive result only if, after many efforts, the respondent's account of *aretê* remains intact and the questioner finds it personally acceptable and becomes able to act upon it. And even such a result is tentative at best: the next encounter may uncover a contradiction where none had been suspected before; one's mode of life can collapse in ruins at any moment.

Socrates seems to realize that, since he constantly emphasizes his willingness to continue the elenchus as long as anyone wants:[50] the elenchus can succeed positively, if at all, only if both parties reach the relevant understanding together. The questioner realizes that the proposed definition cannot be refuted, the respondent becomes convinced that the definition is secure, and both can act on the basis of that definition without falling into conflicts with the rest of their beliefs and principles. The recognition of an expert in *aretê* through the elenchus can in the end only be mutual. The two participants must become noncoercively convinced of the views and therefore of the ways of each other.

I said above that "everyone knows" that the elenchus is a negative procedure.[51] Socrates, according to Grote, "assigned to the negative an intrinsic importance by itself. . . . He thought that the natural state of the human mind, among established communities, was not simply ignorance, but ignorance mistaking itself for knowledge—false or uncertified belief—false persuasion of knowledge. The only way of dissipating such false persuasion was, the effective stimulus of the negative test, or cross-examining elenchus."[52] The most important recent discussions of the elenchus make the same point. Richard Robinson, for example, writes that in its strict sense the elenchus is simply "a form of cross-examination or refutation."[53] Gregory Vlastos, in his introduction to the *Protagoras* which has been the most widely known introduction to Socratic method for many years, believes that Socrates himself realizes that the aim of the elenchus "cannot be final demonstrative certainty, and that its practice is quite compatible with suspended judgment as to the material truth of any one of its conclusions."[54] All these views share the assumption that the elenchus cannot reach any positive results, that it cannot ever prove that someone is right. Socrates refutes various definitions of the virtues by showing that they are inconsistent with certain other views that he elicits from his respondents. Those views are not tested for their truth. The fact that they are inconsistent with the definition does not show that the latter must be given up but only that one cannot hold all of them together at the same time. And, as a matter of fact, none of the dialogues in which Socrates searches for the definition of the virtues ever reaches a positive end. No one is ever proved right.[55]

It is now time to deny what everybody knows. For there is a definite, indisputable case in Plato's early dialogues of an elenchus that leads Socrates to the positive conclusion that someone's view is indeed correct. As far as I know, this enormously interesting case has not been noticed before; and we have not appreciated its immense significance either in regard to the notion of truth that is at play within dialectic or in relation to its implications for the structure of the rest of Plato's Socratic dialogues.

When Socrates tells the court that he received Apollo's oracle that no one in Athens was wiser than he, he also tells them how puzzled he was by the god's pronouncement. And though he knew that the god could not lie, he decided to test the oracle by means of a search (ζήτησις): he turned to those with a reputation for wisdom in order to provide an *elenchus* of the oracle by proving that some of them were wiser than he despite the oracle's message (*Ap.* 21b1–c2). Though the word he uses (ἐλέγξων), which is cognate with "elenchus," is perfectly clear, Socrates' general attitude is not. He knows that the god cannot lie and thus that what he needs to do is to *interpret* the oracle. But he also intends to *refute* it by means of an elenctic demonstration that he is not as wise as some other Athenian.[56]

Since Socrates cannot address the oracle directly, he performs his elenchus by examining the Athenians who are thought to be wise. Those examinations are in turn elenchi in their own right. None of them is successful: Socrates' interlocutors know no more about the virtues than he does, and they are all in addition unaware of their ignorance. Socrates therefore concludes that he is wiser than everyone else, at least because he knows he is ignorant. He therefore concludes that the oracle was right after all. His successful elenchi of the Athenians have convinced him that his elenchus of the oracle has failed. He accepts the god's pronouncement; he concedes its truth. He continues to practice the elenchus, he says, in order to "help the god and to show that those who seem to be wise really are not " (*Ap.* 23b6–7).

From a logical point of view, Socrates has no right to infer that the oracle is right on the basis of his examinations. As we have already said, a new encounter can always destroy whatever confidence the elenchus has given us so far. And yet Socrates, and Plato with him, has no hesitation in thinking that his conclusion is impregnably true, pure and simple: the god was right. That implies that we cannot identify the notion of truth Plato's early works presuppose with any stronger philosophical notion. Even though, logically, a new case can undermine our conclusions so far, a broad enough examination of reasonable alternatives can establish, dialectically, the truth of a particular conclusion. In that respect, dialectic is akin to the law: questions of guilt and innocence are still determined by eliminating all reasonable competing alternatives. In dialectic, as in the law, disposing of the alternatives that have been offered as a matter of fact is sufficient to establish the truth of a conclusion. There is no sense in which such truth is second best: it is completely determined within these practices, by the laws that govern them, and not by reference to any other practice or institution.

Plato, then, actually describes an elenchus that proves that someone is right. That elenchus is positive because Socrates failed to find a single Athenian who was wiser than he was. How could he have found such a person? Obviously, through an elenchus that convinced him that at least one of his respondents actually knew some of the "great" things of which Socrates knew he was ignorant. But such an elenchus, a meeting between Socrates and someone who knew what *aretê* is, valuable as it might have been for Socrates, would have made a liar of the god! Anyone who knew the nature of *aretê* would be wiser than Socrates, though the oracle had said that no such person existed. If the god were to be proved right, then, it was imperative for Plato not to show a single case in which Socrates reached the definition of *aretê* through the elenchus. And that now gives us a new, strategic explanation for the negative conclusions of all of Plato's elenctic dialogues. The dialogues of search don't fail to determine the nature of *aretê* because the elenchus is structurally incapable of establishing truths: we have seen that it can. They fail because if they did not Socrates would not have been the wisest man in Athens, and the god of Delphi would have been wrong. Plato has a literary, not simply a philosophical reason, for closing his dialogues of search on a consistently negative note. Not the nature of the elenchus, but the character of Socrates, dictates the way the dialogues end.

I have avoided many complex issues in my interpretation of Socrates' ethics and method so far. This is not because they are unimportant or uninteresting.[57] But, however we ultimately specify the precise sense of Socrates' disavowals of ethical knowledge or his views regarding the nature of *areté* and its role in the good life, we will leave the main question I want to raise here unanswered. We may attribute to Socrates fallible beliefs about *areté*, or the uncertain assurance that consistent dialectic victory affords, or any other cognitive state weaker than knowledge in the strictest sense of the term. We may construe the strict knowledge he desires in any manner we want—as deductive knowledge, as technical or expert knowledge, or even as the knowledge only the gods possess. But the fact remains that in Plato's eyes Socrates, though he lacked that knowledge, always acted in a virtuous manner. No one was ever more consistently virtuous, no one managed to act as well as he did, without exception, over the course of his whole life. Without exception: but also without explanation. For being reliably good is one of the central results of possessing the strict knowledge that Socrates considered necessary for *areté*[58] and that he was convinced he lacked. That is the real paradox of Socrates.

Within the world of the dialogues (it makes no difference at this point whether that world is fictional or historical), how Socrates managed to live as he did remains a mystery. Contrary to the prevailing approach to Plato's early works, my central claim is that we should not assume that Plato understands what enabled Socrates to be the type of person he was. Plato has no deep account of the paradox Socrates constituted for him. His early portrait of Socrates exhibits that paradox and lays it out for our inspection. It does not offer a successful solution to it, nor does it even attempt to solve it in the first place.

What exactly is that paradox, and why does it remain unresolved? Let me illustrate it with a pair of quotations from Gregory Vlastos's essay on Socrates' disavowal of knowledge. Early on, Vlastos writes that Socrates "holds that virtue 'is' knowledge: if he has no knowledge, his life is a disaster, he has missed out on virtue and, therewith, on happiness. How is it then that he is *serenely* confident that he has achieved both?"[59] Toward the end of the essay, he claims that Socrates, when he hears that the Delphic oracle said that no one was wiser than he, can "hardly bring himself to believe that his own understanding of the good life, chancy, patchy, provisional, perpetually self-questioning, endlessly perplexed as it is, should have any value at all in the eyes of the god who enjoys . . . the perfect security, the *serene* completeness of knowledge.."[60]

The paradox is involved in Vlastos's use of the term "serene" both to characterize Socrates' confidence that he possesses *aretê* and happiness and also to describe the completeness of the knowledge only the god can have—the knowledge that is the only guarantee that one will invariably, infallibly, and with absolute reliability do what *aretê* and happiness require. How can Socrates, whose knowledge is so different, be as serene as the god?

With the exception of his clear statement that committing injustice is worse than suffering it, Socrates does not really make any explicit claim to knowledge in Plato's early works.[61] But his explicit claims are not to the point if he honestly disavows the knowledge he considers necessary as a guide to the art of living. For Plato depicts him as the only master of that art. Socrates' paradox is that he is aware that he lacks what he believes the art of living requires but is still its best practitioner.

Socrates is a paradox not only for the dialogues' readers but, more important and also more paradoxical, for his own student, his own author. That paradox animates those works and their hero and makes it necessary to return to them again and again in the search for the "real" Socrates.

Our discussion must now return to irony. We have seen that irony does not always, and never in its more interesting cases, mean the contrary of what it says. More often, ironists distance themselves, in a variety of ways, from the words they use. They are unwilling to accept full responsibility for what they say, but they are equally unwilling to deny it explicitly: as Kierkegaard put it, they remain "negatively free."[62] Irony presents what seems at first sight a mask. Sometimes it presents a real mask. Sometimes it leaves the question open whether we really see a mask or, if we do, what, if anything, it is a mask of. Irony creates an essential uncertainty. It makes it impossible to decide whether ironists are or are not serious either about what they say or about what they mean. Sometimes it makes it impossible to know whether ironists even know who they really are.

That is Socrates' final and most complex irony. He disavows the knowledge he himself considers necessary for a life of *aretê*. But he is also "serenely" confident in thinking that he has actually lived such a life. And we have no reason to believe that he himself had a view about how that, how *he*, was possible. But since he did live a good life, does he or does he not think that he really has that knowledge? Does he or does he not mean his disavowal seriously?

Does Socrates think that he knows what virtue is after all or doesn't he? Plato's early works do not answer that question, and they thus endow Socrates with a further ironical dimension. Not just ironical with his interlocutors, he is ironical toward Plato himself (and so toward Plato's readers) as well, for even Plato cannot answer the question Socrates poses for him. Though Socrates is Plato's creature, his own literary character, he remains opaque to him: he is a character his own creator admits he cannot understand. I can't think of a single other case in world literature or philosophy in which an author presents a character and, totally implicitly, acknowledges that his character is incomprehensible to him.[63] Yet that is exactly what Plato acknowledges in regard to the central figure of his early works.

So far I have been speaking consistently of Plato's early works.[64] The reason is that with the dialogues that inaugurate his middle period Plato embarks on a long and ambitious effort to understand and explain the paradox that Socrates had earlier constituted for him. That effort is part of what allows me to consider that works like the *Gorgias* and the *Meno* introduce a new stage in Plato's thought. In the *Gorgias*, though Socrates still persists in disavowing knowledge in general (509a4; cf. 506a3–4), he also, for the first time, asserts more than once and with considerable self-confidence that a number of his elenctic conclusions are true (486e5–6, 512b1–2). In this dialogue, we also find for the first time in Plato's work the distinction between knowledge and belief: since belief ($\pi\iota\sigma\tau\iota\varsigma$) can be either true or false but knowledge ($\epsilon\pi\iota\sigma\tau\eta\mu\eta$) can never be false, "it is clear that they are not the same" (454d5–8).

The distinction between knowledge and belief, in turn, becomes the pivot on which the *Meno* revolves. This work introduces us to the theory of recollection, according to which our immortal souls possess "within" them true beliefs ($\delta\delta\xi\alpha\iota$) they gathered when they were not incarnate. Prompted by correct and systematic questioning, these beliefs can eventually turn into knowledge (81c5–86c2; cf. 97e5–98b5). This epistemological model allows the Socratic elenchus a much more positive role in establishing ethical views than ever before. Dialectic no longer defines the sense of truth involved in the elenchus. Some of the views the elenchus elicits can now be known to be true independently, by being recognized as truths we learned during another stage of our life. The theory of recollection explains how we learned them at first and how we can recognize them when we meet them again.

The *Meno* also argues that since only knowledge can be taught and since *aretê* appears not to be teachable, *aretê* may after all be mere true belief. That is, if one holds the right views, however one arrived at them, one can act correctly and well: knowledge is not necessary for right conduct. But, as Plato says, beliefs, which are not systematically connected with one another as the elements of knowledge must be, are inherently unstable. The elements of knowledge, especially of knowledge modeled on the axiomatic structure of mathematics, support one another. It is difficult to forget what we know because every single thing we know is related to everything else and cannot, so to speak, be forgotten in isolation. But beliefs are haphazard. As long as they remain in the soul, true beliefs produce all sorts of benefits: while they last, they are as good a guide to *aretê* as knowledge itself. But precisely because they are not systematically connected to one another, beliefs can be easily lost. They are not likely to stay long in the soul: like Daedalus' statues, so lifelike that they would take off on their own unless they were tied down, beliefs, no matter how true, can be easily forgotten.[65] To stay permanently in the soul, beliefs need to be tied down by what Plato mysteriously calls "reasoning about explanation," which he identifies with the recollection he has already said transforms belief into knowledge (97b5–98b5).[66]

With Callicles' radical attack on Socratic ethics in the *Gorgias* and with the fundamental doubts regarding Socratic dialectic expressed in the *Meno*, Plato abandons his project of presenting Socrates simply as he saw him and makes instead an effort to explain the phenomenon Socrates constitutes.[67] His effort is the first in a long series and is perhaps the most remarkable among them because Plato tries to explain a character he himself had created—a character who, though he is a reflection of a lost original, gradually assumes the role of the original for which any subsequent attempt to come to terms with Socrates must account. It is almost as if Plato's later works try to articulate the deep structure of a Socrates whose surface structure is the subject matter of the early dialogues. Plato wants to understand how the beauty Alcibiades discerned in Socrates made its way there in the first place. The theory of recollection provides him with an answer.

That answer is not entirely successful. If belief, as the *Meno* argues, is unstable, then Socrates' remarkable reliability in always acting well is still left unexplained. True belief about *aretê* can explain how one can act well on some, perhaps many, occasions. But Socrates' consistently unerring behavior requires something considerably stronger—something much closer to the knowledge he disavows having. Further, the *Meno* identifies *aretê*, tentatively, with true belief. But the theory of recollection holds that belief cannot be taught: it inheres in the soul and provides the material that, through the questioning the dialogue identifies with teaching, becomes knowledge. But then there is no good reason why some people are better than others, why, that is, some have more true beliefs in their soul than others do. Plato is forced to conclude that people have *aretê* neither by nature nor by teaching but by divine dispensation (θεία μοῖρα, 99e3–100c2). Plato is therefore forced to conclude that Socrates is a divine accident (cf. *Rep.* 492a1–5, θεῶν τύχῃ), and we cannot possibly count on the continued existence of *aretê* in the world: why should another such accident occur? *Aretê* would appear consistently in the world only if its true practitioners, truly good statesmen capable of creating other good statesmen like them, were born with each new generation.

Plato puts this last claim in Socrates' mouth at the end of the *Meno*. And the claim returns us to the *Gorgias*. Here Socrates argues that he may perhaps be the only Athenian who truly practices politics, which he identifies with speaking for the sake of truth, not pleasure (521d6–8),[68] and with making one's fellow citizens better (515a1–b4). Had he been successful, had he made people better, we might have concluded that Socrates somehow possessed the knowledge he craved. But nowhere in Plato's early works, perhaps in contrast to Xenophon's *Memorabilia*, does Socrates succeed in making someone else good. Does Socrates then lack that knowledge after all?

If only matters were simply that complicated! For consider the following point. Plato's early works never allow their readers to doubt that Socrates is a good human being, the best exemplar of *aretê* so far. But, on Plato's own terms, only one good human being can recognize another.[69] Who is it, then, who saw him as what he really was and enabled the rest of us to make a similar evaluation, even if we often make it in the throes of self-deception?[70]

Asked this way, the question answers itself. The one person who recognized Socrates as the good human being he was is the one who never appears in the dialogues — Plato himself. Although, absent as a character, he cannot make that claim explicitly, Plato, as author of the dialogues, issues it with every word he writes, and that is the reason I described him as Socrates' student above. His claim is subtle, complex, and not a little arrogant. It implies that Plato is the only other good person in the world of the dialogues, even though he is not explicitly a character within them. His absence, which at first appears an act of humility, turns out to be a further ironical act of disdain.[71]

Still, until Plato composed the *Republic*, which spells out the content of *aretê* and the method of acquiring it through the theory of Forms and its immense metaphysical, epistemological, political, psychological, and educational system, Socrates remained a mystery to him—an ironic creature through whom he could not see. Socrates invited people to agree that one will do the good if one knows what it is and to confess with him that they did not. He urged them to search with him for the knowledge without which doing the good is impossible but lived as if he actually possessed it. Could he then perhaps have known more than he said?

Socrates might appear as an expert on *aretê* because his behavior was reliably good and he finally proved (in the single case of Plato) capable of transmitting it. But he was not capable of articulating what he knew. And yet that is as necessary for knowledge as anything else: "We can surely say what that which we know is," he is made to say in the *Laches*.[72] Did Socrates then perhaps keep something back even from his author, who presents himself as his greatest student?

Plato never knew. He always regarded Socrates a mystery, a divine accident. He outlined the city of the *Republic* partly to ensure that people like Socrates, those whom he was the first to call "philosophers," would be part of every generation.[73] He articulated and gave formal expression to the knowledge that, he came to believe, Socrates had somehow come to possess in an inarticulate, unsystematic manner—a manner that qualified it at best for the status of belief. Once that knowledge was articulated, people with sufficient talent could be educated to acquire it through a lifetime of practice. That practice was modeled on, but was much more extensive and ambitious than, education in the crafts: in particular, it was made to include the rigorous study of the mathematical sciences, which were beginning to flourish in Athens and, not by accident, in Plato's own Academy.

In the *Republic*, philosophers rule the city so that its educational system can continue to be successful, so that the state can be governed by the best people in it, and so that what happened to Socrates in Athens can never happen again. Socrates' trial and execution convinced Plato that in a corrupt state the internal aspects of *aretê* and its external face can become totally disconnected from each other. But the philosophers, who possess the internal psychic harmony that Socrates regarded as *aretê*, also possess, as the city's rulers, the *aretê* of tradition, the recognition and reputation that were part of the archaic ethos that Socrates himself may have tried to annihilate. In that respect, Plato's political radicalism has a deeply conservative side. His new heroes are famous, just like the old Homeric and Athenian heroes he would like them to displace. But they are famous for a new reason: they are good, their soul has the right structure. The two aspects of *aretê* have now become inseparable. And a population has been created that will be ready to recognize the best among them as worthy of being their leaders. The three elements required by *aretê*—internal structure, public recognition, and the right audience—are now woven inextricably together.

If this idea is at all correct, the grand philosophical system of the *Republic* is in the first instance an effort to make sure that Socrates and others like him (perhaps people like Plato himself) will arise consistently with every new generation. But this does not alter the fact that in Plato's own early works, Socrates remains a divine accident, a surd, an inexplicable phenomenon, a lucky stroke who, ironically concealing himself from his interlocutors, remains opaque to his own author as well.[74]

"In fiction," Amélie Rorty has written, "characters are dear to us because they are predictable, because they entitle us to the superiority of gods who can lovingly foresee and thus more readily forgive what is fixed."[75] Socrates may in a sense be predictable: we know that in the end he will almost always win his argument and that he will do the right thing. But the gods are superior because they also understand why things happen as they do. Socrates never allows us to see that. He is both predictable and incomprehensible. In relation to him, we are both gods and victims.

Incomprehensible and opaque, to his author as well as to us, Plato's early Socrates has acquired a solidity and robustness few literary characters can match.[76] That is why he appears more real than fictional. Plato's implicit admission that he does not understand him, his amazing success in reproducing Socrates' irony not only toward his interlocutors but also toward himself, is the mechanism that explains why generations of readers have inevitably returned to these texts, convinced that they provide a transparent window that opens directly onto the light of reality.

What is the window that leads to such light? It is, ironically, Socrates' opaqueness, the darkness that prevents us from feeling that we can see through him as we can see through other literary characters who, however complex they may be, ultimately hold no secrets. But Plato's Socrates seems to hold a secret, and his own creator does not pretend to understand it. Socrates' opaqueness makes him solid and three-dimensional, and his solidity creates an unparalleled sense of verisimilitude and realism. Plato's Socrates, to the extent that he remains incomprehensible, is an incomplete character. And incompleteness is essential to verisimilitude: "Leonardo," E. H. Gombrich has written, "achieved his greatest triumphs of lifelike expression by blurring precisely the features in which the expression resides, thus compelling us to complete the act of creation. Rembrandt could dare to leave the eyes of his most moving portraits in the shade because we are thus stimulated to supplement them."[77] Plato's leaving Socrates opaque is the literary analogue of these visual strategies. His early works present a character who is subject neither to our will nor to Plato's own. Resistance to the will is one of the most crucial features of the real. Plato's Socrates resists our will to an extent unmatched by any other literary or philosophical figure. That is why he seems more than a fictional character.

Does this make Plato's picture of Socrates accurate, a portrait of the man as he really was? I am not at all sure. The temptation is great to say that Plato has portrayed a real person, an ironist who kept his secrets to himself. But that temptation, I believe, is the product of a literary strategy that was not and could not have been appreciated until German Romanticism, primarily through the writings of Friedrich Schlegel, generalized irony from a rhetorical trope into a basic literary and philosophical device.

We may leave aside the ironic taxonomy of irony Schlegel supplies in his essay "On Incomprehensibility" and ask with him, "Of all things that have to do with communicating ideas, what could be more fascinating than the question of whether such communication is actually possible?"[78] Schlegel's answer, expressed with characteristic hyperbole, is that human beings are constantly oscillating between the desire to understand things fully and the realization that complete understanding is impossible. Acknowledging that predicament and being able to live with it is, very roughly, what he understands by irony. That is the point he makes, in terms that are themselves not fully comprehensible, when he writes of "the indissoluble antagonism between the absolute and the relative."[79] Schlegel believes that ironic authors describe their subject matter with the greatest seriousness, but at the same time, like Goethe in *Wilhelm Meister*,[80] keep themselves at a distance from their work. They suggest to their readers that, despite appearances, they cannot play God: they are not in total control of their materials and characters. Such are, sometimes, the authors of Old Attic Comedy, whose characters seem to leap out of their fictional confines during the course of the *parabasis* to address their audience directly, as the chorus of Aristophanes' *Frogs* rebukes the Athenians for the decline of their great city. And that is why Schlegel once characterized irony as such a permanent *parabasis*.[81]

Socrates' irony toward Plato results in such a permanent parabasis: it makes it hard to remember that the figure who addresses his interlocutors and, by implication, the dialogues' readers is a literary character in the first place.[82] But, like the Aristophanic chorus that regularly berated its Athenian audience, Socrates does not thereby cease to be a literary character. Verisimilitude is not reality. Socrates does not literally step out of the dialogues and into our world any more than the Aristophanic chorus ever does so. On the contrary, he sweeps Plato's readers into his own fictional world and seems to include them in his fictional discussions. He thus appears more real than a character who acts as if the audience does not exist and who is therefore free (or forced) to reveal everything that makes him what he is. Socrates is real because we inhabit his world, not because he inhabits ours.

It is often thought that "the Socratic problem," the task of distinguishing the real person from his literary representations, was first posed in the nineteenth century by Friedrich Schleiermacher. That is not quite true. The problem has a slightly longer history: a number of Enlightenment scholars at the end of the eighteenth century had already attempted to establish the facts of Socrates' life, particularly in connection with his trial and execution in 399 BC.[83] Still, it was Schleiermacher who posed the Socratic problem in the starkest form. He believed that both Xenophon and Plato were reporting on the historical Socrates, though they did not always understand him in the same way. And he proposed a principle by means of which he hoped the discrepancies between them could be eliminated or at least minimized. That principle, sometimes known as "Schleiermacher's Canon," was expressed by the following question: What *could* Socrates have been like to have exhibited without contradiction those traits of character and principles of action the pedestrian Xenophon attributed to him, and what *must* he have been like so as to give the inspired Plato the right and grounds for presenting him as he does in his dialogues?[84]

It may, of course, have all been a coincidence, but Schleiermacher was a particularly close friend of Friedrich Schlegel. Despite his deep religious commitment, which eventually pulled them apart, Schleiermacher had worked closely with Schlegel during the last years of the eighteenth century and the first years of the nineteenth. He had belonged to the group Schlegel gathered together to publish the *Athenaeum* in 1798. The two even lived together for a number of months in 1798 and were planning to translate Plato's works into German together—a project from which Schlegel finally withdrew and that Schleiermacher almost completed on his own before his death in 1834. Schleiermacher, therefore, may have become interested in the historical aspects of Plato's Socrates partly because Schlegel's new emphasis on irony endowed Plato's writings with a verisimilitude they had never been seen to have before. That is a speculation, but neither without historical evidence nor without interpretative force.[85]

In his study of the Socratic problem, Mario Montuori has written that

> Schleiermacher and even more Hegel . . . as well as Grote and Zeller, Labriola, Gomperz, and all those who have followed their traces up to own day, have considered the *Apology* and Alcibiades' speech in the *Symposium* as an historically faithful description of Socrates' personality and one which was capable of containing a mass of dissimilar ideas. Whether he be conceptualist or moralist, metaphysician, dialectician, protreptic or problematic, Socrates the man could not really be different from the picture given by Plato in the two apologetic essays.[86]

None of the figures Montuori mentions predates Romanticism, even though Alcibiades' picture of Socrates as Silenus has a long history in European thought, going back all the way to Erasmus.[87] The real authority of Plato as the true source for the historical Socrates is the product of Romanticism, and I am convinced that the importance of irony both to Plato and to the Romantics played a crucial role in that transformation. For a transformation indeed it was. Hegel, in particular, occupies a fascinating transitional position between our present attitude toward Socrates and the approach that, until his time, had relied on Xenophon as the primary source for Socrates' views and character:

> If we inquire whether [Xenophon] or Plato depicts Socrates to us most faithfully in his personality and doctrine, there is no question that in regard to the personality and method, the externals of his teaching, we may certainly receive from Plato a satisfactory and perhaps a more complete representation of what Socrates was. But in regard to the content of his teaching and the point reached by him in the development of thought, we have in the main to look to Xenophon.[88]

Hegel, though he despised Schlegel's version of romantic irony,[89] was still enough under its sway to believe that the ironic Socrates of Plato's early dialogues must have been the person one might meet in the streets of Athens. But that Socrates had very little to say, while the Socrates of Plato later's works, full of complex philosophical views and theories could have been, as the eighteenth century had by and large assumed,[90] nothing but Plato's own mouthpiece. Accordingly, Hegel divided the issue. He accepted Plato's robust, impenetrable character as what Socrates must have really been like in everyday life. But he continued to rely on Xenophon's picture of an inveterate purveyor of commonplace views, opinions, theories, and pieces of advice for Socrates' philosophical positions.[91]

Xenophon's Socrates, on whom Hegel and many others before him relied, holds explicitly positive doctrines. Xenophon attributes them to a particular source, the *daimonion*, the divine voice that he claims advised Socrates not only negatively, as Plato says, but positively as well.[92] Today, relatively few people turn to Xenophon as a source either for Socrates' personality or for his philosophical views.[93] The Romantics changed our taste away from what (had he not been a classical author) we could call Xenophon's neoclassical style, so congenial to the eighteenth century: clarity, crisp outlines, absence of ambiguity, the obvious fitting together of parts, his constant reminders that he speaks as an eyewitness.[94]

And yet we still read Socrates primarily for the content of his positive philosophical views—his denial of retaliation, his view that no one errs willingly, his conviction that knowledge of the good is sufficient and even necessary for doing it. As long as Xenophon was our main source for information about Socrates, our exclusive interest in Socrates' theories presented no problem.[95] But as Plato began to displace him, the question what it was that Socrates believed, if he believed anything, became considerably more urgent. I do not mean to argue that Plato's Socrates holds no views of his own or that they are not deep and important. But no analysis of those views, valuable as it may be in itself, can answer the question in which I am interested, the main question I am asking here: How did Socrates manage to live as he did, how did he become who he was?

We have seen that the Platonic Socrates presents the following problem. He holds that you need to know the good in order to do it and that, if you know the good, you will in fact do it; he also claims that he does not himself know what the good is: and yet, as Plato presents him, he seems to do the good as consistently as anyone ever had. But is that really possible? It is reasonable to think that if one does not know the good, one may still succeed in doing it from time to time. But Socrates' consistent success suggests that he had the knowledge he denied. Is he then toying with all of us after all?

Nietzsche attacks Socrates because he believes that we act well only when we don't do the good knowingly, when we do not rely on independent reasons for our action, when our actions are simply expressions of our whole personality.[96] Nietzsche's view is that one acts well only when one acts "instinctively," by which he means through habits that no longer need rational articulation and justification. But is that so different from the way the Platonic Socrates acts? If, as we should, we take his disavowal of knowledge seriously, how can we describe his actions except by saying that he became accustomed (no one knows how) to doing the good and acted well without knowing the reasons he himself considered necessary for such behavior? What Socrates considers the good thing to do differs greatly from what was considered good in his time. He originated a new set of customs, a new art of living.[97] How did he devise that art? That is the question the Platonic texts don't answer for us. On his own assumptions, Socrates could not have established such an art of living, such a τέχνη τοῦ βίου. But he did, and we don't know how.

That, to me, is the real Socratic problem. Though Socrates holds a number of extraordinary philosophical views, each one of which repays serious study, his main concern, as Plato eventually was to put it, is how to live (*Rep.* 352d6). And his major accomplishment is that he established a new way of life, a new art of living. Holding philosophical views is of course essential for living a philosophical life: the philosophical art of living combines practical activity with philosophical discourse. But Plato's early dialogues do not make clear the exact connection between the views one holds and the life one leads. Socrates' views are simply not sufficient for explaining his mode of life. And perhaps that is always so. What we can at best expect from a philosophic life is that the views and the actions that make it up be in harmony with one another, not that the views will entail the actions. Both "views" and "actions" are equally parts of life; there is no reason one should be prior to the other.

Socrates seems certain that his way of life—the examined life of the *Apology* (38a5–6)—is the best life for all human beings. But he has no argument to convince those who disagree with him or who simply don't care. He has nothing to say to Euthyphro to make him stay when the latter walks away from their conversation (*Eu.* 15e3–16a3). He cannot press his proposal to start his discussion with Protagoras from the very beginning all over again when the latter says that the time has come to talk about something else (*Pr.* 361d5–362a4). Socrates issues an invitation that no one is obliged to accept. His art of living is intended to apply to all, but he has no argument by which to prove that it does.

To produce such an argument is just what Plato undertakes in the *Republic*. Here he produces a grandiose set of considerations to show that the life of philosophy—inspired by the life of Socrates but not strictly identical with it[98]—is really best for everyone, philosophers and non-philosophers alike. And for that, he needs to describe what human beings are really like, the nature of the human soul and the good life, the kind of political system that gives philosophy the preeminence he believes it deserves, the educational system that will allow people to value the life of philosophy above all others, the kinds of objects that such an education will lead them to know and value (the Forms), as well as the limits and limitations of philosophy's alternatives—sophistry, science, poetry, traditional ethics, and religion. Those are philosophy's "perennial" problems. The *Republic* inaugurates philosophy as most of us understand it today.

Plato's project has two important implications. First, it is intended to apply to everyone without exception: it aims to show that the philosophic life is in everyone's best interest and that therefore everyone has a reason for following it as closely as possible. Plato's art of living produces only one work, which everyone should try to imitate. Second, Plato's universalist approach cannot proceed without answering a vast number of substantive ethical, educational, political, aesthetic, epistemological, and metaphysical questions. The interest and importance of these views give them a life of their own. And it is easy—at least, it has become easy—to believe that the sole purpose of philosophy is to ask and answer those questions with no regard for the further purpose to which they were once subordinate. There is no question in my mind that these questions deserve to be asked and answered. But that should not obscure the fact that another, vital purpose of philosophy is not the production of views for their own sake but the establishment of a mode of life. And the mode of life, the art of living Plato presented through Socrates in his early works, was not obviously one that everyone was obliged, on rational grounds, to follow.

Socrates' invitation to his interlocutors is protreptic and nondogmatic. His attitude is moderate: he wants people to follow his new way of life but has no arguments to convince them they must do so. Plato's position is more ambitious and more extreme: he believes that a particular philosophical way of life is best for everyone and is convinced that he can prove it. But in addition to those two approaches, there is a third, more individualist alternative. Philosophy might also be an effort to develop a mode of life that is unique to a particular individual, neither an imitation of nor a direct model for anyone else. Such an approach centers on the novelty of Socrates' art of living and considers that novelty as his great achievement. It pays less attention to the specific contents of his views, the substance of the particular life he advocated, and concentrates instead on his having constituted himself as a radically new type of person, a new sort of individual. That is what Montaigne, Nietzsche, and Foucault, whose own arts of living will occupy us from now on, took philosophy to be.

In reading these philosophers, I will keep two issues in mind. First, the assumption that those who can truly be considered philosophers must produce positive views—in a sense of "positive" that I will try to make clear as we go on. Though I believe that a large part of philosophy is devoted to producing views of that sort, I will argue that this is not its only legitimate concern. Second, the fact that even philosophers whose goal is to construct a totally original mode of life and who, particularly like Nietzsche and Foucault, have profound disagreements with Socrates' views and way of living keep returning to him as a model for their own work. Why is that? What allows Plato' Socrates to function as a model in an enterprise that seems, through its emphasis on originality, to require that no model exist? And why is it that even those who think of themselves as his enemies find themselves returning to him? The answer involves Kierkegaard's view, with which this chapter began, that a real philosopher can sometimes remain silent. In the remainder of this book, I shall try to articulate and give voice to Socrates' silence; better, I shall try to open a space where his silence can be heard.

Socrates' ironic gaze is turned not only toward his interlocutors but toward his interpreters as well. Many of them, beginning with Plato himself, have tried to see through it, to fill in the outlines of the hero of the Socratic dialogues. But there seems no way to do that securely, no way to understand once and for all who Plato's Socrates really was: however much we learn about him, we shall never know how he did what he did. We can try instead to take advantage of his silence. Though the enterprise is hard and for most of us unlikely to succeed, we can try to establish, as he did, our own way of doing things, our own combination of views and actions, our own philosophic art of living. We can emulate the structure of his project without accepting the particular shape he gave his own life. There are innumerable ways of pursuing that goal. Even looking at thinkers who shared that purpose with him and thinking about how they constructed their individual reflections of Socrates by means of reflecting on him may be a way of practicing the philosophic art of living.

PART TWO

Voices

4

A Face for Socrates' Reason

Montaigne's "Of physiognomy"

[A]What I write here is not my teaching, but my study; it is not a lesson for others, but for me. . . . It is many years now that I have had only myself as object of my thoughts, that I have been examining and studying only myself, and if I study anything else, it is in order promptly to apply it to myself, or rather within myself. . . . What does Socrates treat of more fully than himself? To what does he lead his disciples' conversations more often than to talk about themselves, not about the lesson of their book, but about the essence and movement of their soul?

Michel de Montaigne, "Of practice"

The Socrates of Plato's early works says very little. The Socrates of Plato's middle and late works says too much; his views are too complex and grandiose: his voice has always been considered to be unmistakably Plato's own. But Xenophon's Socrates both speaks—he speaks constantly—and says things that are obvious enough not to seem to require the mediation of Plato's genius. Xenophon's Socrates holds views that even someone of Xenophon's modest philosophical gifts—perhaps especially someone of Xenophon's modest philosophical gifts—would have been able to reproduce.[1] In addition, Xenophon's constant reminders that he was himself present at many of the conversations he reports, as opposed to Plato's magisterial (and calculated) absence from his work, once helped convince generations of readers that Xenophon's image corresponded to Socratic reality.[2]

During most of the two hundred years preceding the nineteenth century, the writings of Xenophon were the main source for the life and views of the historical Socrates. One of the crucial texts was François Charpentier's *Life of Socrates;* based on Xenophon, this "biography" appeared in 1650, was reprinted many times, and was widely disseminated. Fénelon also composed a Xenophontic life of Socrates, which he included in his *Lives of the Philosophers* of 1726.[3] Plato's Socrates began to displace Xenophon's loquacious reflection only when irony acquired the prominence Romanticism attributed to it.[4]

We generally think that philosophers must have positive views of their own. "Positive views" usually include theories about the nature of things in general and human beings in particular, about the essence of knowledge, truth, and goodness and about everything else that is considered necessary for understanding one's place in the world and how to live well within it. That is the tradition initiated by Plato's *Republic*, in which the philosophers are the experts of life, who both live best and determine how everyone else in the city should live. Plato's philosophers are such experts because their theoretical knowledge enables them to live well themselves, and their understanding of human nature enables them to know what is best for their fellow citizens. They are the craftsmen, the artisans, the artists of life. They secure the good life for themselves and help others come as close to it as their abilities allow them.

Today most people, including most philosophers, no longer believe that the life of philosophy is the best human life. That has made it impossible for philosophers to play the role that Plato (and, following him, Aristotle) envisaged for them and that many played, though intermittently and with enormous variations, until recent times. Even in ancient times, the Platonic-Aristotelian view that the practical significance of philosophy derives directly from its theoretical nature was rejected by various schools — moderately by Stoicism, vehemently by Cynicism. But our present-day emphasis on theoretical (including, of course, moral and political) investigation has caused us to lose sight of the different conceptions of philosophy that were prevalent in antiquity. Michael Frede has written that "we do not as a rule assume that somebody who does not have any demonstrably distinctive philosophical views of his own does not for that reason count as a philosopher. If we went by this assumption, there would not be many persons who would count as philosophers."[5] But as Frede's own discussion of Euphrates of Tyrus demonstrates, that assumption is more common than we suppose. Euphrates was an enormously respected philosopher of the end of the first century

AD who, partly because he seems to have produced no original views we are willing to consider philosophical today, has all but disappeared from the philosophical canon. But Euphrates was at least according to Epictetus "a philosopher who had conspicuously succeeded in doing what on Stoic theory a philosopher is required to do: to live up to in practice to what one has learned or seen to be true in theory."[6] Euphrates' life seems to have been a life of ease and public success, opposed both to the asceticism of Cynicism and to the theurgical trappings of the life of Apollonius of Tyana. But it qualifies as a philosophical life, even though Euphrates produced no great theoretical innovations and issued no prescriptions for others, because it resulted from Euphrates' effort to make his views, derived from Stoicism, harmonious with the rest of his life.

Though still concerned with the nature of goodness and the right political organization, philosophy today is faced with the irreparable loss of the authority it once derived from being thought to constitute the best way of life. One could argue, of course, that the idea that philosophy represents the best life was just Plato's dream and that philosophers have never been better than the rest of the world (except, perhaps, at dreaming). Plato's dream was for a long time most people's wakefulness, but it has finally lost its hold on our imagination. The life of philosophy has gradually lost its exemplary status and philosophy has increasingly retreated into its theoretical component: we no longer believe that the life of philosophers constitutes a model that others should follow. But that has not stopped philosophers from thinking that they still have much to say about how life in general should be lived. What is the good of philosophy, after all, if it does not tell people what to do?[7]

Now, suppose we combine Plato's view that philosophers must have positive views with Xenophon's depiction of Socrates as someone who never missed an opportunity to tell others what was right or wrong. In that case, once Plato's Socratic dialogues replaced Xenophon's texts as the source for the "real" Socrates, it appeared natural to appeal to Plato in order to discover Socrates' positive views. If Socrates was a philosopher and Plato's dialogues show us who he really was, and if philosophers must have positive views, then Plato's Socrates must have had such views himself. And then the temptation to read the dialogues only in order to determine Socrates' views becomes virtually impossible to resist — virtually, though not actually: I have been resisting it in the course of this book, reading the dialogues instead for the life and character they present, for Socrates' mysterious art of caring for himself.

Montaigne, too, tried to understand Socrates in similar terms.[8] He did not only try to interpret him but also followed him in his project of self-fashioning: "[A]I am myself the matter of my book."[9] Montaigne's inward turn animates his writing: "[C]I dare not only speak of myself, but to speak only of myself; I go astray when I write about anything else, and get away from my subject."[10] He dedicated much of his life to depicting his life—and only his life—in a book that, having became its most important part, gave his life its shape and substance:

> [C]And if no one reads me, have I wasted my time, entertaining myself for so many idle hours with such useful and agreeable thoughts? In modeling this figure upon myself, I have had to fashion and compose myself so often to bring myself out, that the model itself has to some extent grown firm and taken shape. Painting myself for others, I have painted my inward self with colors clearer than my original ones. I have no more made my book than my book has made me—a book consubstantial with its author, concerned with my own self, an integral part of my life; not concerned with some third-hand, extraneous purpose, like all other books.[11]

The work and the life, the book and the self became inextricable parts of one another.

Montaigne's "only real aim," according to Hugo Friedrich, "is . . . to grant every person the same right to the freedom of being himself that the author claims for himself."[12] Montaigne's is not a project we commonly associate with philosophy today. But apart from philosophy as we most often conceive it—as an effort to offer systematically connected answers to a set of independently given problems—another tradition, equally philosophical, is concerned with what I have called the art of living, the care of the self, or self-fashioning. That is the tradition to which Montaigne, following Socrates, belongs. Its aim is less to construct a theory of the world as it is to establish and articulate a mode of life. It comes, as we have seen, in three varieties. In its first version—Socrates' project in Plato's early works—it constructs a mode of life its author considers appropriate for the world as a whole, but it offers no arguments to show that everyone is rationally obliged to follow it. The second—Plato's aim in the *Republic* as well as the goal of philosophers from Aristotle to Kant—is to construct an art of living that does in fact apply to all.[13] The universalism of this version needs to be justified by a number of positive theories that account for its general application. And the inherent interest of such theories underlies the modern understanding of philosophy as a discipline concerned with such theories solely for their own sake. The third variety of philosophy as an art of living is designed to establish a mode of life that is appropriate for its author and not necessarily for anyone else. Remarkably, this individualist version of the art of living has always returned to find its source in Socrates, even though his own approach occupies a middle ground between individualism and universalism. At first, that appears paradoxical: why should such a tradition of self-fashioning appeal to anything outside the author's own consciousness? Is it possible to appeal to a model and also to construct a mode of life that is unique to its author and not an imitation of the model's achievement? And what is it about Socrates in particular that makes him an appropriate model for this tradition? These are questions that I will try to answer as we go along.

Socrates' name occurs fourteen times in the 1580 edition of Montaigne's *Essays;* twenty new additions were made in the 1588 edition; and no fewer than fifty-nine more appear in the posthumous edition of 1595.[14] How did Montaigne use Socrates? What did he learn from him? What can we learn about depending on someone else in fashioning our own selves from Montaigne's example? And how are *we* to use Montaigne if that is a project we want to make our own?

These questions are pressing because Montaigne's project is so intensely individualist: "[C]It is many years now that I have had only myself as object of my thoughts, that I have been examining and studying only myself; and if I study anything else, it is in order promptly to apply it to myself, or rather within myself."[15] His task is unusual; others "[B]form man; I tell of him, and portray a particular one, very ill-formed."[16] Yet Montaigne often appeals not only to Plato's silent figure but also to the garrulous Socrates of Xenophon, who is full of advice for others and is always ready to show them how to live.[17] Is it possible to take Xenophon's reflection of Socrates seriously and consider one's task to be, as Montaigne did, the description and formation only of one's own self?[18]

Though Xenophon's Socrates was always crucial to Montaigne, Plato is absolutely central to the essay "Of physiognomy," to which I shall soon turn, as well as to the rest of his work. The sixteenth century, however, did not distinguish among Plato's early, middle, and late works. The Platonic Socrates was the dialectical searcher of the *Euthyphro* and the *Laches,* the cosmologist of the *Phaedo,* the epistemologist, political theorist, educational reformer, and metaphysician of the *Republic,* and the metaphysical dialectician of the *Sophist* and the *Philebus.* Montaigne, who had been reading Cicero and Seneca since childhood, wove all his Socratic sources together, and it is not always easy to say who among the ancients was his main source for each particular version of Socrates we meet in the various essays.

Whatever his sources, Montaigne always used them selectively. His Socrates confines himself exclusively to ethics, and that is more a feature of Xenophon's version than of the picture we get from Plato's middle and late dialogues, which Montaigne cites, though more rarely than the works we now classify as early. Montaigne often alludes to Cicero's famous statement that "Socrates was the first to call philosophy down from the heavens and establish it in the towns and introduce it into homes and force it to investigate life, ethics, good and evil."[19] Cicero's picture reflects the Socrates of Plato's *Apology* and his other early dialogues more than the hero of the *Phaedo*, the *Republic*, and the *Philebus* or the *Timaeus*.[20] Later authors probably took Socrates as a purely ethical thinker under the influence of the *Memorabilia*, according to which Socrates turned completely away from the investigation of nature and devoted himself instead "to a dialectical examination of human [that is, ethical] matters" (1.1.11–16).[21] It is this purely ethical Socrates who is essential to Montaigne, though it was less his avuncular garrulousness than his ethical focus that attracted him to Xenophon's figure.

Plato's Socrates, no less than Xenophon's, placed great importance on the Delphic precept, "Know yourself." Plato appeals to the precept implicitly in the *Apology*, when the Delphic oracle spurs Socrates into his search and his eventual realization that his wisdom is his knowledge of his own ignorance.[22] In the *Memorabilia* (4.2.24–29), Xenophon identifies self-knowledge more broadly with the knowledge of the nature and limits of one's powers ($\delta \nu \nu \acute{\alpha} \mu \epsilon \iota \varsigma$). That knowledge allows you to be aware of what your needs are and what your accomplishments can be. It enables you to get what you want for yourself and for your friends. It is a knowledge of how far your abilities extend. Montaigne's own gloss on Apollo's maxim characteristically combines his two sources: "[B]'Except for you, O man,' said that god, 'each thing studies itself first, and, according to its needs, has limits to its labors and desires. There is not a single thing as empty and needy as you, who embrace the universe: you are the investigator without knowledge, the magistrate without jurisdiction, and all in all, the fool of the farce.'"[23]

Montaigne believes that there is an essential connection between self-knowledge and the awareness of the limits of one's powers, the ability to live within the constraints of one's nature. And though Montaigne's idea of "nature" is extraordinarily complex, idiosyncratic, and in need of explication,[24] his view is a development of an idea that is explicit in Xenophon: Socrates, according to Xenophon, "consistently praised the verse 'Render sacrifice to the immortal gods according to your power' and claimed that in our relations both to friends and strangers and in all our activities, 'to render according to one's power (καδδύναμιν)' was a noble principle" (*Mem.* 1.3.3). Montaigne comments: "[B]'According to one's power,' that was the refrain and favorite saying of Socrates, a saying of great substance," and he derives from it the advice to "direct and fix our desires on the easiest and nearest things."[25] Self-knowledge is the awareness of one's limitations. But these are not simply the universal limitations of human wisdom, of which the Platonic Socrates, followed by Montaigne, makes so much in the *Apology*.[26] They are the moral and psychological limitations of each particular individual. That is perhaps a more homely lesson, perfectly in tune with Xenophon's figure but important enough to Montaigne to have had an Italian version of it inscribed in many of his own books.[27]

Xenophon's Socrates is full of advice, a conventional teacher, almost a schoolmaster, always prepared with an appropriate recommendation for those who approach him for counsel and whom he often approaches himself first.[28] He has none of the arrogance and very little of the irony of his Platonic counterpart.[29] He is so innocuous that Kierkegaard wondered why the Athenians would have ever been tempted to put such a man to death.[30] But, of course, the answer is that Xenophon's purpose was precisely to show that it is totally incomprehensible why a man like Socrates should have been executed in the first place: "I have often wondered what arguments Socrates' accusers can possibly have used to convince the people of Athens that he deserved execution"—that is the very first sentence of the *Memorabilia*.[31] Xenophon succeeded admirably in his purpose, even though we are lucky that his work was not the only one that survived. For suppose for a moment Plato's account of Socrates had been lost. It would then be a complete mystery to us why the Athenians had put Socrates to death; but that mystery would have deprived us of the greater and deeper mystery of the figure around whom the Platonic dialogues revolved. Xenophon's victory would have been, to that extent, our loss.

Montaigne, then, combines elements from a number of ancient sources to form his own portrait of Socrates. The character who cares only about ethical issues derives more from Xenophon and from Plato's early works than from the *Phaedo* or the *Republic*. Both Plato and Xenophon (though more the latter) provide elements of the background of Montaigne's claim that

[A] the wise man should withdraw his soul within, out of the crowd, and keep it in freedom and power to judge things freely; but as for externals, he should wholly follow the accepted fashions and forms. Society in general can do without our thoughts; but the rest—our actions, our work, our fortunes, and our very life—we must lend and abandon to its service and to the common opinions, just as the great and the good Socrates refused to save his life by disobedience to the magistrate, even a very unjust and very iniquitous magistrate.[32]

And though Xenophon's Socrates, like Plato's, takes the Delphic oracle seriously,[33] it is only the latter who interprets it, like Montaigne, as a warning about the limitations of human reason:

> [C]When Socrates was advised that the God of wisdom had given him the title of Sage, he was astonished; and, examining and searching himself through and through, he found no basis for the divine judgment. He knew of men as just, as temperate, as valiant, as learned as himself, and more eloquent, handsomer, and more useful to their country. Finally he concluded that he was distinguished from the others, and wise, only in that he did not think himself so and that his God considered the opinion that we possess learning and wisdom a singular piece of stupidity in man; and that his best knowledge was the knowledge of his ignorance, and simplicity his best wisdom.[34]

What use did Montaigne make of this complex compilation of his sources? What role did this many-sided portrait of Socrates play in his thought? What was the function of this intricate character in his own self-fashioning? To answer these questions we must turn to Montaigne's next-to-last essay, "Of physiognomy." The essay is immensely complex, apparently disorganized, often contradictory, difficult to place in a broader context, and impossible to discuss with anything approaching the care it deserves in this context.[35] It addresses, among other things, the shortcomings of learning, the fortitude of the common people, the evils of the civil war and the troubles it caused Montaigne, the fear of death, the stature of Socrates, and the nature of Montaigne's own writing. Physiognomy itself appears so fleetingly in it that a number of scholars actually doubt that it really constitutes its main theme.[36] We shall see if they are right.

The essay begins abruptly: "[B]Almost all the opinions we have are taken on authority and on credit. There is no harm in this: we could not make a worse choice than our own in so feeble an age. The version of the sayings of Socrates that his friends have left us we approve only out of respect for the universal approval these sayings enjoy, not by our own knowledge. They are beyond our experience. If anything of the kind were brought forth at this time, there are few men who would prize it."[37] Montaigne will use this temporal contrast between a golden past and a fallen present to criticize his age because it can no longer perceive anything that is natural and not artificially inflated. The contrast between the natural and the artificial, the inner and the outer, will allow him in turn to introduce the main image that, though it appears only in a few places, governs the structure of his text: the contrast implied by the image of Socrates as Silenus, ugly on the outside, a paragon of "natural beauty" inside — in appearance as well as in his views, which were as superficially commonplace as they were deeply original.

The image of Socrates as Silenus was a commonplace of Renaissance humanism. It was made famous by Erasmus in adage 2201, *Sileni Alcibiadis*, which transforms the ugly Socrates into a forerunner of Christ, "the most extraordinary Silenus of all."[38] Erasmus even ended his *Convivium religiosum*, in which he compares Socrates to St. Paul, by imagining that one could address him in these words: "Sancte Socrates, ora pro nobis."[39] Rabelais circulated the image even more widely when he included it in his preface to Gargantua. His books, he writes, are just like Socrates ("without any argument the prince of philosophers"), for whom, if you were to try "to weigh him from the outside, you wouldn't give a bite of onion." But even though his own books, he continues, are superficially silly and coarse, "you'll find all sorts of flavors here . . . and secret learning, which will open in front of you the highest sacraments and the most hair-raising mysteries, not only concerning religion, but also politics, even economics."[40]

Many discussions of "Of physiognomy" assume that Montaigne is working solely with Alcibiades' speech in Plato's *Symposium*, where the image of Socrates as Silenus is so marvelously developed.[41] That the *Symposium* was Montaigne's main inspiration is beyond doubt. But in his reference to the episode, Montaigne introduces a Xenophontic element that, so far as I know, has not been noticed before: "[B]Socrates makes his soul move with a natural and common motion. So says a woman, so says a child. [C]His mouth is full of nothing but carters, joiners, cobblers, and masons. [B]His are inductions and similes drawn from the commonest and best-known actions of men; everyone understands him. Under so mean a form ["si vyle forme"[42]] we should never have picked out the nobility and splendor of his admirable ideas." Everything here comes from Alcibiades' speech,[43] except for one element that is in stark contrast with Alcibiades' actual words in the *Symposium*: "If you are foolish," Plato makes him say there, "or simply unfamiliar with him, you'd find it impossible not to laugh at his arguments. But if you see them when they open up like the statues [of Silenus], if you go behind their surface, you'll realize that no other arguments make any sense." Alcibiades maintains that only very few people are capable of opening Socrates up and seeing him for what he is—he claims that he may even be the only one among his intimates who does really know him: "You can be sure of it, *none of you* really understands him" (216c–d).⁴⁴

Where, then, does Montaigne's *"everyone* understands him" come from? It comes directly from Xenophon, whose Socrates always argued from the most widely agreed premises and who, unlike Plato's figure (who found it difficult to make himself understood, let alone believed), "whenever he argued, made his listeners willing to agree with him better than any man I have ever known."⁴⁵

Montaigne is pursuing a double strategy. First, he is stitching together various accounts of Socrates to suit his particular purposes. Second, he is constructing a nonesoteric Socrates, a Socrates who is as common, straightforward, and "natural" as can be. For one of the essay's central ideas is that we should admire and try to emulate Socrates because he is the best example of a natural human being, free of artifice and contrivance. Montaigne keeps returning to Socrates' artlessness: "[B]I can easily imagine Socrates in Alexander's place; Alexander in that of Socrates, I cannot. If you ask the former what he knows how to do, he will answer, 'Subdue the world'; if you ask the latter, he will say, 'Lead the life of a man in conformity with its natural condition'; a knowledge much more general, more weighty, and more legitimate."⁴⁶

Xenophon considered Socrates' self-control (ἐγκράτεια) as his most important virtue, and he described it as the foundation (κρηπίς) of *aretê* (*Mem*. 1.4.4–5). Montaigne, too, emphasizes Socrates' self-control, which he considers to be the virtue that enabled Socrates to follow nature and act according to his power: "[B]He was also always one and the same, and raised himself, not by sallies but by disposition, to the utmost point of vigor. Or, to speak more exactly, he raised nothing, but rather brought vigor, hardships, and difficulties down and back to his natural and original level, and subjected them to it" (1037; 793F). Above all else, however, Xenophon was determined to demonstrate that Socrates was supremely useful and beneficial to his friends. Unlike Plato's character, who mostly kept his own counsel and asked questions designed primarily to show him what *aretê* was, Xenophon's character "was so helpful in every activity and in every way that anyone who considers the matter and estimates it fairly must see that nothing was more profitable than associating with Socrates and spending one's time with him in any place or circumstances."[47] That infuriated Kierkegaard: "Xenophon portrays in Socrates not that beautiful, harmonious unity of natural determinant and freedom indicated in the term σωφροσύνη [temperance, self-control] but a graceless composite of cynicism and bourgeois philistinism. . . . Instead of the good, we have the useful, instead of the beautiful the utilitarian."[48] Nevertheless, in that respect, it is Xenophon's and not Plato's image that is reflected in Montaigne's own portrait: "[B]At a gentle and ordinary pace [Socrates] treats the most useful subjects [*utiles discours*]" (1038; 793F).[49]

Montaigne's Socrates has compound sources and a compound character. He is both Silenic and natural, both self-controlled and useful to others, both unusual and easy to understand. That, I believe, is the result of a conscious strategy on Montaigne's part, and it plays a serious role in his writing. Montaigne himself evaluates his sources: "[B]It happened fortunately that the man most worthy to be known and to be presented to the world as an example should be the one of whom we have the most certain knowledge. We have light on him from the most clear-sighted men who ever lived; the witnesses we have of him are wonderful in fidelity and competence" (1037; 793F).[50] This statement, however, conflicts with the opening of the essay, which, as we saw, claims that we approve of Socrates' views "not by our own knowledge," since they are "beyond our experience," but because they have already come to be universally respected. It also conflicts with the fact that Montaigne appears not to trust any one of his sources completely. That is surely part of the reason that, in the course of the essay, he gradually constructs a new composite image of Socrates that combines the views of Plato and Xenophon as well as the testimony of Cicero and Plutarch.

The essay "Of physiognomy" is striking because it is full of conflicts of that sort—and others we shall soon face. What do these conflicts signify? Montaigne, I believe, uses them to warn us against accepting the testimony of Socrates' "witnesses" without question. Even Alcibiades' description of Socrates as Silenus must be read as a "Silenic" description: it cannot be taken for granted; it must be deciphered if it is to be understood. Nothing in the essay, neither Socrates' nor Montaigne's various stories, nor even Montaigne's own writing, can be taken at face value. How, after all, can we trust appearance, since we live in a world that allows us to "[B]perceive no charms [*graces*] that are not sharpened, puffed out, and inflated by artifice. Those which glide along naturally and simply easily escape a sight as gross as ours. They have a delicate and hidden beauty; we need a clear and well-purged sight to discover their secret light.

Is not naturalness, according to us, akin to stupidity and a matter for reproach?" (1037; 793F).

Montaigne introduces Socrates as a model of someone who lives according to nature and not by artifice in order to set our world apart from an earlier time when life was simpler and more forthright: "[B]Socrates makes his soul move with a natural and common motion. . . . Our world is formed only for ostentation. . . . This man did not propose to himself any idle fancies. . . . We are each richer than we think, but we are trained to borrow and beg; we are taught to use the resources of others more than our own" (1037–38; 793–94F).

In connection both with Montaigne's essay in particular and with the philosophical issue of self-fashioning in general, we might naturally ask whether relying on Socrates is not itself a case of using the resources of others more than our own. Can a philosopher try to articulate a new, individual mode of life and still depend on someone else as a model? When does dependence become imitation? But Montaigne does not allow us to raise these questions. Before we can even formulate them, he has already moved on to an attack on learning, of which, he argues, Socrates had no need: "[B]See him plead before his judges. . . . There is nothing borrowed from art and the sciences; even the simplest can recognize in him their means and their strength. . . . He did a great favor to human nature by showing how much it can do by itself" (1038; 793–94F). Learning was merely useless to Socrates; to the rest of us it can be positively harmful. To prove his point, Montaigne repeats almost verbatim the passage of the *Protagoras* that denounces buying knowledge from the sophists; and he concludes that food for the soul, most of the learning "[C]which we swallow . . . as we buy . . . under color of curing us, poisons us" (1039; 794F).[51]

Montaigne illustrates the uselessness of learning through an attack on Cicero: "[C]Should I have died less cheerfully before having read the *Tusculans*? I think not" (1039; 794F). But just a page earlier he had relied on the authority of that very work for his description of Socrates as the figure who brought human wisdom from heaven, "[C]where she was wasting her time, down to earth" (1038; 793F).[52] Another conflict of the sort we were just discussing confronts us. Are we to trust learning, and Cicero in particular, or are we not? Once again Montaigne seems to be warning us that his obvious practice may be less than we need to understand this essay.

The attack on learning continues. Montaigne now denounces the practice, common even among "[C]the most compact and the wisest" authors of his time, of piling up many worthless arguments around a few good ones: "[C]These are nothing but verbal quibbles, to deceive us." Here, too, learning is more an obstacle than a means to wisdom. At this point, we may well begin to think that we are faced with another expression of the skepticism that is the central theme of the "Apology for Raymond Sebond."[53] But that is not an impression that lasts long: Montaigne's attitude toward the practice and the authors he has just condemned suddenly changes: "[C]But inasmuch as this may be done usefully, I do not want to expose them any further." He may himself occasionally engage in it: "[C]There are enough of that sort in this book in various places, either from borrowing or from imitation" (1039–40; 795F).[54] There may (who knows?) even be some "worthless arguments" in the very essay we are in the process of reading. It is up to us to guard ourselves against them, not to read complacently, not to take things, not even Montaigne's prose, or the self his prose constructs, at face value.

The attack on learning—to which he is himself, in light of his constant quotations, allusions, and elaborate discussions, extremely vulnerable—turns into a praise of ordinary people. Common and uneducated, they "[B]know neither Aristotle nor Cato, neither example nor precept. From them Nature every day draws deeds of constancy and endurance purer and harder than those that we study with such care at school" (1040; 795F). Perhaps these people are the only real followers of Socrates in Montaigne's age. But Montaigne does not pursue that seemingly obvious point. Instead, he interrupts himself almost immediately in order to give an account of his life during the civil war and the plague that accompanied it; only after an elaborate discussion of that new topic does he return to the issue of learning (1048; 802F).

Many of Montaigne's readers have found it difficult to integrate the passage on the civil war into the essay as a whole.[55] But in fact the discussion of the war serves a variety of important reasons. First, the misery the civil war has brought to France functions as a metaphor for the breakdown of the natural order of things in Montaigne's world with which the essay begins. Second, the idea of a war in which a single country is divided against itself is an image writ large of the psychological breakdown of the self, with two or more of its parts fighting against each other. Socrates and the common people Montaigne had just begun praising have escaped such a psychological civil war: relying on "nature" and shunning "artifice," avoiding the conflict between them, keeps one whole. Third, the civil war gives Montaigne the opportunity to describe his own self-controlled behavior under extreme circumstances and thus also to introduce into the essay what we know he considers his "only subject," his own self. During all the troubles the war brought, Montaigne himself, on his own account, remained consistently moderate; for that reason, he writes, "[B]I incurred the disadvantages moderation brings in such maladies. . . . [T]o the Ghibellines I was a Guelph, to the Guelph a Ghibelline" (1044; 798F). And though, Silenuslike, he presented different aspects to different people,[56] he was never formally accused of treason: "[B]I never transgress the laws, and if anyone had proceeded against me, he would have been found guiltier than I," he writes (1044; 799F) in what may well be one more allusion to Xenophon's *Memorabilia* and an identification of himself with Socrates that becomes clearer as the essay continues.[57]

Whatever people say about him, Montaigne continues, he never justifies himself: "[C]And as if everyone saw into me as clearly as I do myself, instead of retreating from the accusation, I advance to meet it and rather enhance it by an ironic and mocking confession, if I do not flatly keep silent about it as something unworthy of an answer" (1044; 799F). The reference to irony and mockery, I believe, is Montaigne's first clear hint that his purpose in this work, as it is throughout the *Essays*, is to liken himself to Socrates. It is a strong hint, especially since the conclusion he draws from the troubles the civil war brought him resonates with Socratic self-sufficiency: "[B]I recognized that the surest thing was to entrust myself and my need to myself; and that if it happened that I was lodged only coolly in fortune's favors I should recommend myself all the more strongly to my own favor, and attach myself, and look all the more closely to myself. . . . [C]Everyone rushes elsewhere and into the future, because no one has arrived at himself" (1045; 799F). Montaigne, too, despite his differences from the artless and uneducated common people, has something of Socrates about him.

In the end, Montaigne realizes that the civil war furnished him with "[B]useful troubles" ("utiles inconveniens"), which drove two lessons home to him. First, since his own rational powers had proved inadequate, they taught him "[B]by the rod" to keep to himself: "[B]I have long been preaching to myself to stick to myself and break away from outside things; nevertheless I still keep turning my eyes to one side. Inclination, a favorable word from a great man, a pleasant countenance tempt me" (1045; 800F). The dangers of the war showed him the advantages of keeping one's own counsel. Second, the troubles he had were a preparation for facing worse ones in the future; where one difficulty exists, others, probably worse, are possible. His troubles taught "[B]me in good time to restrict my way of life and arrange it for a new state of things. True freedom is to have power over oneself for everything" (1046; 800F).

In both cases, Montaigne succeeded in replacing some natural inclinations of which he was ashamed with learned behavior of which he could be proud. But apart from their contribution to the improvement of his character, the troubles the war had brought also contained a crucial lesson: they showed that chance events can help to eliminate natural weaknesses and to arrive at a balance within oneself, to construct a better self than one had before. The materials for the art of living can come from anywhere. In addition, Montaigne's use of his troubles for constructing a different self shows that he needed to work upon his own nature in order to improve it. But that distinguishes him from "[B]the people round about," to whom he now finally returns. They needed no such lessons. They acted well and nobly without ever having learned how. Learning once more turns out to be nature's opponent: "[B]We have abandoned Nature and we want to teach her a lesson, she who used to guide us so happily and so surely" (1048; 803F).

Even so, however, and despite the fact that learning has been declared to be nature's opponent, "[B]the traces of her teaching and the little that remains of her image—imprinted, by the benefit of ignorance, on the life of that rustic, unpolished mob—learning is constrained every day to go and borrow, to give its disciples models of constancy, innocence, and tranquillity" (1048; 803F). In other words, even though natural dispositions seem in general to be superior to learned ones, it is necessary for the people who lack the simplicity of the uneducated to use their learning to recapture the natural tendencies they have lost in their corrupt age and state.

Montaigne's hesitations seem to have created a muddle. If nature is so elusive, if we have left it so far behind, how can he think that we can still recapture it and, inspired by the example of Socrates, follow it and be truly ourselves, truly who we are? And if, as Montaigne has just suggested, learning can help in that search, why has he been attacking it so relentlessly?

Once again, however, Montaigne refuses to face these obvious problems. Instead, he lets his reference to the common people remind him of their resoluteness in the face of death—a seemingly new subject altogether. Philosophy had traditionally been taken as "a preparation for death"—a tradition Montaigne himself had accepted in his early essay, "That to philosophize is to learn to die." But now he has a different view: "[C]Death is indeed the end, but not therefore the goal, of life" he writes in what seems to be a direct attack on the Socrates of Plato's *Phaedo*, on Cicero, and on Stoicism in general. "[C]Life should be an aim unto itself, a purpose unto itself; its rightful study is to regulate, conduct, and suffer itself" (1051; 805F). He claims, quite unconvincingly, that the common people do not spend their time contemplating and preparing for death and concludes that the learned should follow their example.

With that idea, Montaigne finally returns to Socrates, whom he seemed to have forgotten during his long digression. "[B]We shall have no lack of good teachers, interpreters of the simplicity of nature. Socrates will be one. For as far as I can remember, he speaks in about this sense to the judges who are deliberating over his life" (1052; 805). Socrates shows how to approach our own death properly; more important, he shows how to recapture our nature and be ourselves again.[58]

There now follows a remarkable passage, a condensation, rearrangement, and eclectic paraphrase of Plato's *Apology*, from which Montaigne has excised Socrates' references to his divine voice and his tentative view that the soul may survive the body's death. Montaigne warns his readers that he is quoting from memory and that his words are not a strict repetition of Socrates' apology. Still, he asks, "[B]Is this not a [C]sober, [B]sane plea, [C]but at the same time natural and lowly, [B]inconceivably lofty, [C]truthful, frank, and just beyond all example?"[59] He contrasts the speech he has just cited with the address, "[C]excellently fashioned in the forensic style, but unworthy of so noble a criminal," which, we are told, the orator Lysias had prepared for Socrates.[60] "[C]Should his rich and powerful nature," he continues, "have committed his defense to art, and, in its loftiest test, renounced truth and sincerity, the ornaments of his speech, to bedeck itself with the make-up of the figures and fictions of a memorized oration?" (1054; 807F).

But the oration Montaigne has put in Socrates' mouth is itself a version of a speech originally written for him by a third party — Plato himself. Further, that version is in fact one that Montaigne has just admitted he has himself composed for Socrates! If this procedure is not artful and fictional, what is? And as if to underscore once again his refusal to trust any single source for his view of Socrates, Montaigne immediately appeals to Xenophon's view (which we never find in Plato) that Socrates' manner in court was due to his unwillingness "[C]to prolong his decrepitude by a year and betray the immortal memory of that glorious end."[61] He also describes Socrates' way of dying as "[B]nonchallante," which strikes me as a direct echo of Xenophon's use of the word $\phi\alpha\iota\delta\rho\acute{o}\varsigma$ (which means, precisely, "blithe," "cheerful," "nonchalant") to describe Socrates' demeanor as he left the court[62] — an attitude in stark contrast to his solemn tone at the end of Plato's *Apology*. This description of the blithe Socrates in turn echoes another, which Nietzsche, we shall see in the next chapter, should have kept better in mind. It is Montaigne's own description of Socrates in "On Some Verses of Virgil," where, having said that he loves "[B]a gay and sociable wisdom,"[63] he continues, "[C]Socrates had a settled expression, but serene and smiling, not settled like that of old Crassus, who was never seen to laugh. [B]Virtue is a pleasant and gay quality."[64]

Despite his various sources and his own manipulation of them, Montaigne insists that Socrates' speech, as he has rendered it, is perfectly natural: "[C]In an unstudied and artless boldness and a childlike assurance [B]it represents the pure and primary impression [C]and ignorance [B]of Nature" (1054–55; 807F). How is that possible? What can "nature" mean here if it describes such artful composition? But our questions remain unanswered yet again.

Montaigne's reflections on the naturalness of Socrates' apology open still another twisting path within the maze of this essay. They send him off on a meditation on writing. Montaigne has just praised Socrates for having given a simple and "natural" speech (which, we have just seen, it is not). He now claims that such a way of speaking involves "[B]the extreme degree of perfection and difficulty: art cannot teach it"; it could only have been accomplished in a simpler past. Today we no longer follow our natural "[B]faculties." Instead, "[B]we invest ourselves with those of others, and our own lie idle" (1055; 808F).

Doesn't that complaint, however, which was probably made the first time human beings ever realized they had a past, also apply directly to Montaigne's own writing? Isn't the charge true that "[B]I have here only made a bunch of other people's flowers, having furnished nothing of my own but the thread to tie them"?[65] Montaigne admits that it is. He pleads guilty to his extensive use of quotation, allusion, and paraphrase throughout his book. But he justifies his dependence on such "[B]borrowed ornaments" by claiming that he defers to the fashion of his times — the very fashion for artifice he denounced on the essay's opening page. Yet he defends himself on the grounds that his own borrowings are not intended to "[B]cover and hide" him. That, he claims, "[B]is the opposite of my design, I who wish to make a show only of what is my own, and of what is naturally my own" (1055; 808F).

Can we accept Montaigne's defense? I believe that we can. As we have seen in Socrates' own case, the path to the self must cross the paths of others, sometimes, cruel as that seems, almost purely as means. There is no such thing as a direct confrontation with oneself: that way only emptiness lies. To the extent that Montaigne uses earlier texts for his own purposes (as in the case of Socrates' speech), using them to fashion something truly his own by their means, his defense is legitimate. Whether it is successful in general depends on the importance of the particular purposes to which he puts his "borrowed ornaments." The question is whether his borrowings are really ornaments and not part of his very substance.

Not all of Montaigne's allusions and quotations are clear and explicit. His game is more complex:

> [C]I, among so many borrowings of mine, am very glad to be able to hide one now and then, disguising it and altering it for a new service. At the risk of letting it be said that I do so through failure to understand its original use, I give it some particular application with my own hand, so that it may be less purely someone else's. These others put their thefts on parade and into account; and so they have better credit with the laws than I. We naturalists judge that the honor of invention is greatly and incomparably preferable to the honor of quotation. (1056; 809F)[66]

Through his discussion of Socrates' speech and his own borrowings, Montaigne has raised, as explicitly as any author of his degree of indirectness ever could, the question whether the surface of his texts indicates their real meaning, whether their appearance expresses their nature. That is the central question of physiognomy, and it is only at this point, near the end of the work, that Montaigne finally comes to the topic that gives his essay its title.[67] What is the relationship between the outer and the inner? What does the appearance of something show us about its nature?

Montaigne has just been preening himself on his use of quotation. But as we should expect by now, he suddenly changes tacks and puts himself down. He forgets his nimble use of the ideas of others in fashioning his own. His mind, he writes, has grown "[B]constipated and sluggish" with age, and "[C]there is nothing I treat specifically except nothing, and no knowledge except that of the lack of knowledge." All that life now holds for him is the prospect of his death. And at this point, in a manner apparently both strained and abrupt, he turns once again to Socrates: "[B]About Socrates, who was a perfect model in all great qualities, it vexes me that he hit on a body and face so ugly as they say he had, and so incongruous with the beauty of his soul, [C]he who was so madly in love with beauty. Nature did him an injustice. [B]There is nothing more likely than the conformity and relation of the body to the spirit" (1057; 809F).

What does that have to do with anything that preceded it? To answer the question, we must read further. And what we find next is Montaigne's repetition of Cicero's story that "[B]Socrates said of his ugliness that it had betrayed what would have been just as much ugliness in his soul, if he had not corrected it by training" (1058; 810F).[68] By contrast, he goes on, "[B]I have very simply and crudely adopted for my own sake this ancient precept; that we cannot go wrong by following Nature, that the sovereign precept is to conform to her. I have not, like Socrates, corrected my natural disposition by force of reason, and have not troubled my inclination at all by art. I let myself go as I have come. I combat nothing" (1059; 811F). That is very puzzling, since Socrates, who has up to now been held up as a paradigm of naturalness, is now said to have fought against his original nature, while Montaigne, who lives in an age that glorifies artifice, describes himself as nature's true follower.

But matters get worse. In a manner so maddeningly typical of him, Montaigne immediately undercuts his own contrast: "[C]What I like is the virtue that laws and religions do not make but perfect and authorize, that feels in itself enough to sustain itself without help, born in us from its own roots, from the seed of universal reason that is implanted in every man who is not denatured. This reason, which straightens Socrates from his inclination to vice, makes him obedient to the men and gods who command in his city,[69] courageous in death not because his soul is immortal but because he is mortal" (1059; 811F). So far, Montaigne has claimed both that he is different from and similar to Socrates, both that Socrates' virtue is natural and that it is the result of his correcting his natural disposition. He now accentuates their differences. He proceeds to relate two episodes when his life and property were saved because of his "[B]favorable bearing both in itself and in others' interpretation . . . one very unlike that of Socrates" (1059–60; 811F). Perhaps then, in the end, the differences between them are greater than the similarities?

Socrates, Montaigne writes, changed himself so that his ugly face, which he could do nothing about, no longer corresponded to the beautiful interior he constructed for himself as a result of eliminating, through training, the ugliness inside. In Socrates' case, the physiognomic principle, according to which the outside should reflect the inside, seems not to hold. But Montaigne's own face does reveal his soul: the principle does hold for him. Twice in his life, once within his castle, another time in a forest, Montaigne was captured but eventually freed. His first enemy was disarmed by Montaigne's "[B]face and . . . frankness" (1061; 813F); the second was captivated by "[B]my face and the freedom and firmness of my speech" (1062; 814F). And once those incidents have been related, the essay closes with some seemingly inconsequential but actually crucial remarks, to which I will come at the very end of this chapter.

From the skein of these disordered thoughts, let me now try to produce some whole cloth. My general question is how Socrates, whose main concern was to care for himself, a man who neither presented himself as, nor was, a teacher of anyone, could function as an model for another. The question is more pressing when that other, like Montaigne, is also concerned only with the care of his own self: "[C]My trade and my art is living."[70] Montaigne's reasons for undertaking to portray and simultaneously form himself are complex. We shall never know exactly why he undertook that task. His own explanation is that "[A] a melancholy humor . . . first put into my head this daydream of meddling with writing. And then, finding myself entirely destitute and void of any other matter, I presented myself to myself for argument and subject."[71] Another reason, which motivates all the philosophers of the art of living with whom I am concerned, is a fear of death or — as Socrates says in the *Apology* (40c3–41c7) — an ignorance of its nature. For if death is "dreamless sleep" (*Ap.* 40d1), the only immortality one can hope for lies in the memory of others and in the effect on the world one can have once one has died. The fear of death is not a fear of what it will be like for me when I am dead — that is a silly, incoherent feeling: it will be *nothing* for me when I am dead. The real fear is that the world will go on without me. The prospect of my death confronts me with the incontestable fact that I am not irreplaceable, that I am and will be nothing unless I do something that will make a significant difference, particularly if that is a difference the world knows that *I* and not someone else has made. Writing, especially about oneself, often makes such a difference. Nietzsche was obsessed with that idea, but Montaigne too was moved by it. Having lost his faith in the immortality the church promised, Montaigne responded to death, as Jean Starobinski has written, "not by an act of faith in the divine promise, but by recourse to literature, to art, in order to fashion an image of his life to be bequeathed to posterity. To exist in the pages of a book is better than to vanish into nothingness and oblivion. The *Essays* are to have the value of a *monument*."[72] Socrates, who left his own portrait to history without writing anything on his own, is Montaigne's model as he draws himself with his own pen.[73]

Montaigne's Socrates is the result of stitching together the testimonies of Plato and Xenophon, Cicero and Plutarch. That, I have argued, suggests that Montaigne is qualifying his stated view that these witnesses are absolutely trustworthy (1038; 793F). What is the main idea Montaigne derives from these various authors? It is that Socrates is the great model of naturalness, of turning away from idle speculation to a life according to one's power. But that is an empty thought. It provides him with no substantial advice, no concrete counsel. From Cicero, Montaigne gets the idea that Socrates turned philosophy to the study of the soul. From Plato, he takes Socrates' courage in the face of death and the naturalness with which he faced and discussed it. Xenophon provides him with the principle that one should live according to one's power. We shall see what he takes from Plutarch in a moment. Turning to oneself, following nature, living according to one's power: these are vague ideas; they give no explicit guidance. The Socrates Montaigne puts together from his various sources is in the end closer to Plato's figure than to anyone else's. His model of naturalness is the silent Socrates to whom we ourselves have been listening so far.

Toward the end of his essay, Montaigne seems to insist that Socrates' naturalness is itself a product of some sort of art—not an art of shallow artifice but an art he characterizes, in Stoic terms, as the pursuit of "universal reason." To display Socrates' plain and unadorned reaction to his impending death, Montaigne found it necessary to *create* a speech for him. That speech is itself a highly artful work: it derives from the elaborate speech Plato wrote on Socrates' behalf, but it is also deeply different from it; and though it is supposed to be much less rhetorical than the speech Lysias had composed, Montaigne does not hesitate to embroider it with anecdotes from Xenophon and Plutarch.[74]

Socrates' ability to live according to nature, as Montaigne understands it, is therefore the product of two highly artful processes. One is his own correction of the natural disposition, which, according to Montaigne, is still evident on his face. The second is Montaigne's combination of his various sources for his portrait of his model and his composition of Socrates' "natural" apology for him. Art and nature interpenetrate, but their mixture creates three problems. How is it possible for nature to be the product of art if the essay, from its very beginning, asserts that there is a deep contrast between them? Does Montaigne think that Socrates did really change his nature so that his ugly face was no longer an accurate indication of his beautiful soul? How did Montaigne himself succeed in following nature, and what is the character of his success, given that nature appears to be the product of art?

To answer these questions we must consider the possibility that Montaigne does not think that nature constitutes only an origin from which we have all fallen but also an end that some can still reach. Despite the rhetoric of the essay's opening sentences, there may still be a sense in which art and nature are not opposed to one another.[75] Montaigne's "need to borrow a speech from Socrates," Terence Cave has written, "seems to prove the point: in order to articulate nature, a borrowed image of nature is necessary; so that the self may say about death what is proper to it, a borrowed first person singular is used."[76] Montaigne wants to speak of his own death (1057; 809F): he uses Socrates' fabricated speech. He wants to show that unlike the rest of his world he has not interfered with nature: he appeals to the naturalness of Socrates he has so equivocally constructed. Cave writes that Montaigne uses a "borrowed" Socratic speech, a "borrowed" image of nature, a "borrowed" first-person singular. But is that term appropriate?[77] Montaigne insists that he uses quotation and allusion for his own purposes, often deforming their original meaning ("[C]originel usage"). Since he does use both the speech he writes for Socrates and his combination of his sometimes contradictory sources for his own particular purposes, those are not just "borrowed" material but original works. They bestow upon him not "[C]the honor of quotation" but "[C]the honor of invention " (1056; 809F). Similarly, Joshua Scodel has written that "Montaigne . . . avoids undue reliance on others by appropriating the Socratic message and making it his own [another instance of 'borrowing'], by not simply *reading about* Socrates but instead *writing as* Socrates. Montaigne finds himself by recreating Socrates."[78] But it is not clear to me that Montaigne is writing "as" Socrates, if "Socrates" is the creature of tradition;[79] the Socrates Montaigne is writing "as" is a creature of his own art and imagination: perhaps recognizable in the traditional figure, he is still a new character with his own face.

Montaigne has therefore fashioned a Socrates of his own, a creature that exemplifies what it is to be natural, how one can oneself be the object of one's primary care, how one can fashion oneself. He writes that Socrates followed nature by changing his soul through training ("[B]institution") and universal reason ("[C]la raison universelle"). There seems to be a conflict here, since Montaigne claims that for his own part he has not corrected his own disposition either by force of reason ("[B]par force de la raison") or by art ("[B]par l'art"). But "force of reason" need not signify the same as "universal reason," nor need all art suggest the "ornamentation" the essay denounces throughout. As Jean Starobinski has written, "Montaigne is in no doubt as to the correct moral choice: insistence on *veracity* remains his undying standard of judgment, his permanent criterion for criticizing morals and for governing his own behavior." At the same time, however, though "the note to the reader lets it be known that Montaigne has set himself a rule of avoiding show and artifice . . . to paint oneself is an art, and no art can do without artifice in one form or another."[80]

In Montaigne's world, perhaps everywhere, it is impossible to show oneself as what one really is; artifice permeates nature. To be heard truly, one must follow the fashion of the age and use ornaments, though not in order to "[B]puff" and "[B]inflate" (1037; 793F), not "[B]to cover and hide," but "[B]to make a show only of what is [one's] own, and of what is naturally [one's] own" (1055; 808F). Simple purity may be the product of intricate complexity. That is what Socrates accomplished, that is how Montaigne has depicted him, and that is, finally, how he presents himself as well. Let me try to explain.

Montaigne's insistence that Socrates defeated his original inclination to vice through reason allows him to think of nature not as a lost original state but as a state achieved through rational self-restraint. Despite the apparently central thesis of the essay "Of physiognomy," one does not start as a natural being; that is something one becomes.[81] Especially in the world into which Montaigne is born, where (he believes) one grows inevitably through and into artifice, nature is reached through the gradual acculturation of one's tendencies, one's "powers," into mutual respect and compatibility. That is not a return; it is forward progress. Nature is, as Montaigne's Socrates taught, self-control and the ability to live according to one's power: "[B]The solitude that I love and preach is primarily nothing but leading my feelings and thoughts back to myself, restraining and shortening not my steps, but my desires and cares."[82] Respect and compatibility are achieved through effort, training, and even through truthful art. But the powers of each person are different from the powers of everyone else. Those who take that difference seriously and try to organize their powers in new and unprecedented ways produce lives and selves that differ from all others. Montaigne was one of them.

Respect among our various tendencies, among the various parties that make each one of us up, is exactly what was lacking, on a large scale, in the civil war. This is another reason the war is so important to this essay on physiognomy:

> [B]Monstrous war! Other wars act outward; this one acts also against itself, eats and destroys itself by its own venom. It is by nature so malignant and ruinous that it ruins itself together with all the rest, and tears and dismembers itself with rage. . . . All discipline flies from it. It comes to cure sedition and is full of it, would chastise disobedience and sets the example of it; and employed in defense of the laws, plays the part of a rebel against its own laws. What have we come to? Our medicine carries infection. (1041; 796F)

Montaigne learned from the civil war to withdraw into himself and to be ready for worse troubles. We now see that the war, as a metaphor for nature fighting against nature, also taught Montaigne how to establish a new order within himself. As a result of his experience, Montaigne established a new discipline in himself. Being the accommodation of elements like inclination and reason, which are themselves natural, that discipline has every right to being itself considered a new nature. Nature, therefore, is not simply the origin where individuals or society begin. More important, it is the final state in which our various inclinations work for a common purpose, refusing to trespass on one another's ground, and enable each individual to accomplish the best—the different best—of which each is capable. Once again, play and seriousness, art and nature, blend together: "[B]There is nothing so beautiful and legitimate as to *play* the man well and properly, no knowledge so hard to *acquire* as the knowledge of how to live this life well [C]*and naturally*."[83]

Unlike Montaigne, Socrates (so far as we know) did not learn his lesson from an actual civil war. Instead, he fought his own inner war from which he emerged victorious, self-controlled, and self-sufficient, aware of what he could and could not accomplish, reconciled to his various powers—in a word, natural. Just as nature is not an origin but an end, so the self, too, is the product of fashioning. And since, as we have said, everyone's features and circumstances are different, there is no general method for composing nature, for constructing the self. For the same reason, no exemplar can ever be followed directly, since that results in imitation—not in creation.

Montaigne uses Socrates, "[B]the man most worthy to be known," as his model. At the same time, he distances himself from him because Socrates' face, unlike Montaigne's own, does not reflect his inner character. The way to rely on Socrates, to follow him in making oneself the object of one's primary care, is after all not to be like him—at least not like any of the versions that have come down to us. Rather, like the quotations Montaigne puts "[C]to a new service," it is to use him, perhaps even to deform him, for one's own purposes. Socrates has no specific lesson to teach, and neither does Montaigne: "[B]I do not teach, I tell."[84] Though, of course, he discusses and accepts many general ideas in his work, what he keeps returning to is himself: "[C]We arrange our thoughts in generalities, and the causes and conduct of the universe, which conduct themselves very well without us, and we leave behind our own affairs and Michel, who concerns us more closely than man in general."[85] Perhaps we can use what we learn from Michel for our ourselves; but what we learn from Michel is that we must know ourselves.

What of the contrast Montaigne draws between Socrates and himself? Socrates' Silenic aspect masks the beauty and reason that reign within; if anything, it suggests a vicious nature. But Montaigne's internal harmony, as he rather archly tells us, reveals itself even to his enemies as they are plotting to destroy him: "[B]I let myself go as I have come. I combat nothing" (1059; 811F). Has Montaigne then made no effort to discover or fashion his own nature?

He has. Part of what he has become is a product of the discipline he followed as a result of the civil war. But recall also the essay's first paragraph: nothing like Socrates' sayings, which we accept because of their age-old authority, is available today; "[B]if anything of the kind were brought forth at this time, there are few men who would prize it." Of course, something of just that kind—a new set of Socratic sayings—is being brought forth in the essay those words introduce and in the whole book of which this essay is a part. But Montaigne is right: that is still a difficult thing to prize.

His time would find it difficult to prize Montaigne's Socratic sayings because, he complains, its preference for artifice blinds it to simple charms ("[B]graces") which have "[B]a delicate and hidden beauty . . . [a] secret light" (1037; 793F). Montaigne finds it necessary to write in a way that will please a large audience. Such writing depends on artificial rhetorical means and extensive quotations. It may even, for good measure, require an account of the civil war, since people enjoy war stories and, as we read in "Of physiognomy" itself, "[C]good historians avoid peaceful narratives as if they were stagnant water and dead sea, in order to get back to the seditions and wars to which they know that we summon them" (1046; 800F).

"Of physiognomy" is written in the fashion of the age, but Montaigne gives enough hints that more is going on within his text than a casual reading would suggest. Few of his readers may prize what he offers, because what he offers has its own delicate and hidden beauty, its own secret light that is obscured by the dazzling artifice that surrounds it. Socrates is not the only Silenus. Montaigne's essay and Montaigne himself are also instances of Alcibiades' image. Montaigne's protestation, "[B]I let myself go as I have come. I combat nothing," rings hollow when we recall what the war has taught him. In fact, the essay suggests that Montaigne is Socrates' mirror image. Socrates had an ugly, sensual face; he changed his interior so that his face was no longer in line with it. Montaigne changed his interior so that it would be in harmony with his frank and innocent face.

Montaigne, then, is anything but the easygoing character he describes in the closing pages of his essay on physiognomy. More of a Silenus than he explicitly admits, he even suggests that the harmony between his exterior and his inside may not be as perfect as his explicit claims boast. Having praised himself as lavishly on his accomplishments as on his honest face, which saved him from so many troubles, he calls himself in his very last paragraph "only a jack of clubs" ("[B]qu'escuyer de trefles"). He even intimates that his character may not be as simple as he professes, since he says that both versions of what Plutarch said of Charilaos of Sparta are true of him as well. According to one version, Charilaos "[B]could not possibly be good, since he is not bad to the wicked"; according to the other, "[B]he must certainly be good, since he is good even to the wicked." Montaigne's "[B]favorable bearing" is after all not really "[B]very unlike that of Socrates" (1060; 811F). Like Socrates' ugly exterior, it is not a clear indication of what is found inside. Both Socrates and Montaigne need to be interpreted in order to be understood: Montaigne's two enemies, who let him go on the basis of his honest face, may have been fools. Physiognomy cannot be trusted, especially when one, like Montaigne, is still in the process of fashioning himself.

The essay closes with these words: "[B]As I do not like to take a hand in legitimate actions against people who resent them, so, to tell the truth, I am not scrupulous enough to refrain from taking a hand in illegitimate actions against people who consent to them" (1063; 814F). Who are these people who consent to illegitimate actions against themselves? Perhaps Montaigne had some real people in mind and a particular action he did or might undertake against them. But that is unlikely. Montaigne is writing on a very abstract level here. These people are a metaphor for those readers who take him at face value, who ignore his hints that his book ("[C]consubstantial with its author, concerned with my own self, an integral part of my life"[86]) and therefore Montaigne himself are other than they seem. They are both still in process of being made even as they are being read: "[B]I cannot keep my subject still. . . . I do not portray being: I portray passing. Not the passing from one age to another, or, as the people say, from seven years to seven years, but from day to day, from minute to minute."[87]

Socrates taught Montaigne a few general precepts, like "Live according to your power" or "Follow nature," which do not describe their end and offer no instructions for reaching it. To apply them, one must determine one's particular powers, which, as we shall see in more detail in our discussion of Nietzsche, are different in each individual case. Socrates also taught Montaigne that there is little to learn *from* him, even though one can learn a lot *through* him. And he taught him that to learn through Socrates is not to follow and re-create him but, as Montaigne himself does in this Silenic text, to become his own model of nature.

Montaigne uses the ironic Socrates ironically and puts himself in his place. He assumes Socrates' Silenic aspect and shows his readers, in a manner as empty as Socrates' own, how he became himself and how, if that is what we want, we can do the same ourselves. Montaigne produced a self, a work of the art of living, but neither he nor we can articulate how he accomplished his task. His example is as paradoxical as Socrates' own: "[B]Example is a hazy mirror, reflecting all things in all ways."[88] As models of how one can engage in self-fashioning—the issue that consumes Montaigne throughout the book in which he creates himself—examples play an equivocal role: "Manifesting their own uniqueness," Starobinski has written, "exempla point to a world composed of unique, dissimilar entities. . . . They testify only to their singular existence. . . . Thus the only thing exemplified is that a possibility was in fact realized."[89] But that a possibility was in fact realized shows that other possibilities, too, can be realized as well, that the realm of possibility is not exhausted. To follow such an example, therefore, is to try to be different from it; it is to try to realize a new and different possibility. Anything short of that is mere imitation. That is how examples function within the individualist strain of the art of living; that is the role they play for those who want to make something unprecedented of themselves, if any such people exist.

Do they? Montaigne was one of them. Can they succeed? As in all matters, Montaigne was cautiously optimistic about that question as well: "[B]There may be some people of my temperament, I who learn better by contrast than by example, and by flight than by pursuit."[90] And behind all such artists of living, Montaigne included, there stands the figure of Socrates, supremely successful and irresolubly dark, rejected when pursued and followed when denied.

A Reason for Socrates' Face

Nietzsche on "The Problem of Socrates"

I know of only one writer whom, in point of honesty, I can rank with Schopenhauer, and even above him, and that is Montaigne. The fact that such a man has written truly adds to the joy of living on this earth. At any rate, since my first encounter with this freest and most vigorous of spirits, I feel moved to say of him what he said of Plutarch: "No sooner do I look at him than I sprout a leg or a wing." If my task were to make myself at home on this earth, it is to him that I would cleave.

Friedrich Nietzsche, *Schopenhauer as Educator*

Nietzsche, whose task never was to make himself "at home on this earth," wrote this passage in *Schopenhauer as Educator*, the third of his *Untimely Meditations*, one of his earlier and most absorbing works.[1] It is, not accidentally, the work in which we find his first adaptation of Pindar's verse "Having learned, become who you are":[2] "Those who do not wish to belong to the mass need only to cease taking themselves easily; let them follow their conscience, which calls to them: 'Be yourself! All that you are now doing, thinking, desiring is not you yourself'" (*UM* III:1; 1:338). Nietzsche eventually simplified that idea to his most central slogan, "How one becomes what one is" (the subtitle of his intellectual autobiography, *Ecce Homo*), which expresses the task he actually took on, his gradual fashioning of himself into the singular character we know by that name today.

Officially, Nietzsche wrote the essay to praise Schopenhauer for having shown him, more through his own personal example than through his philosophical theories, how to start on the process of becoming who he really was. But the work is also Nietzsche's declaration of independence from his teacher and model. Eventually, he took the *Untimely Meditations* to have been not about their various ostensible topics but about a very different subject altogether. All four of the essays, he wrote in *Ecce Homo*, "at bottom speak only of me. The essay *Wagner in Bayreuth* is a vision of my future, while in *Schopenhauer as Educator* my innermost history, my *becoming*, is inscribed. . . . [A]t bottom it is . . . not 'Schopenhauer as Educator' that speaks here, but his opposite, 'Nietzsche as Educator'" (III: "The Untimely Ones": 3; 6:320).[3] The fourth essay, *Richard Wagner in Bayreuth*, is even more explicitly a criticism and attack, although Wagner, rather uncharacteristically, seems to have missed the point.[4] Still, neither essay even begins to suggest the vehemence with which Nietzsche eventually was to turn against his two early "educators."[5]

Nietzsche's vehemence, in this as in almost everything else about him, was never unqualified, never without ambivalence. On the one hand, he can claim in one of his unpublished notes "that the history of all phenomena of morality could be simplified in the way Schopenhauer believed— namely, so that pity is to be discovered as the root of all moral impulse hitherto—only a thinker denuded of all historical instinct, and one who had eluded in the strangest way even that strong schooling in history undergone by the Germans from Herder to Hegel, could have attained to this degree of absurdity and naiveté."[6] On the other, he can write that Schopenhauer and Hegel, whom he also did not like much, are "two hostile brother geniuses in philosophy who strove apart toward opposite poles of the German spirit and in the process wronged each other as only brothers can wrong each other" (*BGE* 253; 5:195). And even though Schopenhauer is "a genuine *philosopher*," Nietzsche can still describe his views on the primacy of the will as "superstition," an adoption and exaggeration of "popular prejudice,"[7] and denounce them in the most bitter and biting terms.

Among Wagner's innumerable faults Nietzsche will also count "a great corruption of music. He has guessed what it means to excite weary nerves—and with that he has made music sick" (*CW* 5; 6:23). Still, he is delighted to have been his friend: "I must say a word to express my gratitude for what has been by far the most profound and cordial recreation of my life. Beyond a doubt, that was my intimate relationship with Richard Wagner. I'd let go cheap the whole rest of my human relationships" (*EH* II.5; 6:288). Such a combination of enmity and generosity on Nietzsche's part is important and not at all uncharacteristic. It is worth emphasizing, for we shall soon enough find a contrary case.

Nietzsche does not mention Montaigne often,[8] but only under his influence could he have written a number of passages in his middle works. In one of these, Nietzsche argues that "almost all the physical and psychical frailties of the individual derive from . . . being unknowledgeable in the smallest and most everyday things." The world teaches us to turn away from "the closest things," our own habits and needs, away from ourselves:

> Priests and teachers, and the sublime lust for power of idealists of every description, the cruder and the more refined, hammer even into children that what matters is something quite different: the salvation of the soul, the service of the state, the advancement of science, or the accumulation of reputation and possessions, all as the means of doing service to mankind as a whole; while the requirements of the individual, its great and small needs within the twenty-four hours of the day, are to be regarded as something contemptible or a matter of indifference.[9]

What could that be but an echo of the *Essays*, on the final page of which Montaigne writes, as he has written countless times already, that "we seek other conditions because we do not understand the use of our own, and go outside because we do not know what it is like inside"?[10] Nietzsche was aware of the connection: Montaigne signifies for him, he writes, "a coming to rest in oneself, a peaceful being for oneself and relaxation" (*UM* IV.3; 1:444). Nietzsche now puts Montaigne together with Socrates, and with that we come to our own topic: "Already in ancient Greece Socrates was defending himself with all his might against this arrogant neglect of the human for the benefit of the human race, and loved to indicate the true compass and content of all reflection and concern with an expression of Homer's: it comprises, he said, nothing other than 'that which I encounter of good and ill in my own house.'"[11]

Nietzsche derives the story about Socrates' quotation of Homer from Diogenes Laertius.[12] But such a positive image of a Socrates who has turned away from "the service of the state, the advancement of science, of the accumulation of reputation and possessions" brings to mind elements that are common to Montaigne's and Xenophon's portraits. Interestingly, however, Nietzsche is in the end no more faithful to his sources than Montaigne was to his. His Socrates, for example, does not attend to "the benefit of the human race," as Xenophon's did. His concern is only with the care of himself—in that respect, he is much closer to the image we find both in Plato's early dialogues and in Montaigne himself. Despite his fondness for world-historical generalization, Nietzsche makes a lot of the idea of the importance of such an inward turn, which he himself makes in all his later works. In *The Twilight of the Idols*, for example, he claims with characteristic hyperbole that "one misunderstands great human beings if one views them from the miserable perspective of some public use. That one cannot put them to any use, that in itself may belong to greatness."[13]

It is strange and difficult to explain why, while he was composing the *Untimely Meditations* and *Human, All-Too-Human* and while he was gradually emancipating himself from Schopenhauer and Wagner, Nietzsche became fond of Socrates, whom he had attacked so bitterly in *The Birth of Tragedy* just a few years earlier.[14] In *The Birth of Tragedy*, for example, he describes Socrates as the murderer of tragedy (*BT* 12; 1:87) and his dark metaphor for Socrates' influence is that of "a shadow that keeps growing in the evening sun" (*BT* 15; 1:97). Two years later, however, in *Schopenhauer as Educator* he writes that "conditions for the production of genius have *not improved* in modern times, and . . . aversion to originality has so increased that Socrates could not have lived among us and clearly would never have reached the age of seventy."[15]

Nietzsche's change of mind, though temporary, was serious. In a note from 1875, he wrote that "Plato's Socrates in a very real sense is a caricature, an excessive Socrates."[16] By 1878, he felt that it is possible to agree with Socrates and Plato that "whatever one does one always does the good, that is to say, that which seems to one good (useful) according to the relative degree of one's intellect, the measure of one's rationality" (*HH* 102; 2:99). His agreement with this moral position, however, did not last long. Nietzsche eventually abandoned the thesis that all action is aimed at the good in the most uncompromising terms. As his attitude toward Socrates changed once again into a condemnation — even more radical than his rejection in *The Birth of Tragedy* — Nietzsche came to believe that Plato held that view despite himself, because of Socrates' pernicious influence: "This type of inference smells of the *rabble* that sees nothing in bad actions but the unpleasant consequences and really judges, 'it is *stupid* to be bad,' while 'good' is taken without further ado to be identical with 'useful and agreeable'" (*BGE* 190; 5:111).

Mention of "the rabble" brings us to "The Problem of Socrates," the last extended discussion of Socrates in Nietzsche's published works and our main topic in this chapter:[17] "In origin, Socrates belonged to the lowest class: Socrates was plebs. We know, we can still see for ourselves, how ugly he was."[18] The personal (one might say, nonphilosophical) tone of this particular passage is not at all exceptional: the whole essay reeks with disdain and animosity. Almost every criticism Nietzsche makes of Socrates in his late works is a personal one. Why?

Apart from Schopenhauer and Wagner, no figure was more important to Nietzsche's individual and intellectual development than Socrates. Actually, he was more deeply involved with Socrates than with either of the other two, and he knew it: "Socrates, to confess it simply, stands so close to me, that I am almost always fighting a battle with him."[19] But why, apart from the truce he struck with him during his middle works (and with one exception we shall discuss as we go along), did Nietzsche never show Socrates the generosity of spirit, the respect, the gratitude, and even the love he retained for his other educators? Why, in the single case of Socrates, does Nietzsche's uncanny ability to see everything from many points of view, to be in *his* sense objective, "to employ a variety of perspectives and affective interpretations in the service of knowledge," abandon him (*GM* III:12; 5:364–65)? Is Nietzsche as one-sided as his writing on Socrates generally indicates? Or are things not as they appear? His extraordinary bitterness suggests they are not. Nietzsche generally refuses to take absolute positions for granted. For example, he refuses to believe that the denial of earthly pleasures which Christian asceticism preaches so shrilly really is, as it appears to be, a denial of life. Perhaps we should apply his diagnosis of asceticism to his own treatment of Socrates. Perhaps we should say that his unequivocal condemnation of Socrates, like the ascetic's hatred of life, "must be a kind of provisional formulation, an interpretation and psychological misunderstanding of something whose real nature could not for a long time be understood and described *as it really was*" (*GM* III:13; 5:365).

Before we interpret that most suspicious of interpreters with such suspiciousness ourselves, it is reasonable to ask whether Socrates was in fact one of Nietzsche's "educators." Did Socrates play anything like the role Schopenhauer and Wagner played in Nietzsche's thought, or was he simply his enemy? If he did not play such a role, then Nietzsche's unequivocal rejection may mean very little indeed. But though the question is good, Nietzsche's image of doing battle with Socrates must not mislead us into denying that the Greek philosopher had a place that was very similar to the place of Schopenhauer and Wagner in Nietzsche's life and thought. Nietzsche never believed that resistance excludes learning. A beautiful passage from *The Gay Science* makes this absolutely clear: "*Undesirable disciples.*—What shall I do with these two young men! cried a disgruntled philosopher who 'corrupted' youth as Socrates had once done; they are unwelcome students. This one cannot say 'No,' and that one says to everything 'Half and half.' Supposing that they adopted my doctrine, the former would *suffer* too much, for my way of thinking requires a war-like soul, a desire to hurt, a delight in saying No, a hard skin; he would slowly die of open and internal wounds."[20] This "disgruntled" philosopher, who may not be so different from Nietzsche himself,[21] wants disciples who are able to say "No." If they can say "No" in general, they must also be able to say "No" to their teacher as well: "One repays a teacher badly if one always remains nothing but a pupil."[22] Yet clearly it was not enough for Nietzsche to have done battle with Socrates to have been his disciple. To see whether he was, whether Socrates was after all one of Nietzsche's educators, we must look further.

Throughout his writings, from *The Birth of Tragedy* to *Ecce Homo*, Nietzsche associated Socrates with a complex of views and attitudes that we can characterize — very roughly — in the following way. First, Socrates denied the importance of instinct and stressed instead the value of reason and dialectic, which he considered as the most central human activity. Second, he introduced morality into the world. That, for Nietzsche, means that Socrates introduced a way of thinking that justifies human action by appealing to the reasons for which people engage in it.[23] So understood, Socrates' emphasis on morality is a special case of his view that reason is our essential feature. And since Nietzsche thinks that reasons are by their nature universal — if something is in fact a reason, then it is a reason for all rational creatures — he also believes that morality is supposed to apply to everyone in the same way.[24] Morality, as Nietzsche sees it, implies that if any people are in the same circumstances, then, since in every morally relevant respect these people are the same — which is to say that they are rational — they will in fact perform the same action. Morality is therefore for Nietzsche essentially universalist, or, as he puts it, dogmatist. It envisages one set of motives and one code of conduct to which everyone must conform.[25] Third, by means of reason and morality, Socrates destroyed the tragic Greek world and its art and introduced the seeds of what we now are: he is in a serious sense the first modern individual.

In *The Birth of Tragedy*, as we have seen, Nietzsche had denounced Socrates as the murderer of tragedy.[26] According to Nietzsche's rather naive image of archaic and classical Greece, the culture that expressed itself through the tragedies of Aeschylus and Sophocles did not believe that the world, or life within it, require explicit justification.[27] The early Greeks accepted both the world and life as they found them and celebrated even their most horrible aspects. In particular, tragedy, their greatest art, glorified the inevitably doomed efforts of all great individuals to tame and use for human purposes those aspects of the world that are totally indifferent to our fate and to which we are of no account. According to Nietzsche, tragedy exalts, in the person of the hero, the individual who stands in vain against a world impervious to human action while, in the guise of the chorus, it rejoices in that very world of which that individual is in the end a part. Individuals belong to nature and their efforts to subdue it are themselves natural and products of the nature they are intended to vanquish. The conflict between individual and collectivity, between culture and nature, is only apparent. Individuals who pit themselves against the world, like whole cultures that try to change the course of history, are for Nietzsche nothing more than "artistic" creations of the world itself. In a famous passage, Nietzsche writes that neither is art

> performed for our betterment or education nor are we the true authors of this art world. On the contrary, we may assume that we are merely images and artistic projections for the true author[28] and that we have our highest dignity in our significance as works of art—for it is only as an *aesthetic phenomenon* that existence and the world are eternally *justified*—while of course our consciousness of our own significance hardly differs from that which the soldiers painted on canvas have of the battle represented on it. (*BT* 5; 1:47)

Tragedy, Nietzsche believed, reveals that individuals and their actions, like cultures and their products, are ultimately of no significance. They cannot affect the world, which remains "eternally the same, despite the changes of generations and of the history of nations." But tragedy also shows that we are creatures, part and parcel of a life that "is at the bottom of things, despite all the changes of appearances, indestructibly powerful and pleasurable" and allows us to enjoy the power that, as such, we share with the whole to which we belong (*BT* 7; 1:56). Respect for tradition and authority, Nietzsche nostalgically believed, were bred into the aristocratic inhabitants of a world that produced such art: they were "at home on this earth," aware perhaps of its cruelty and of their lack of final importance, but willing to accept both their world and themselves just as they were. They were willing to continue to live and to act, although they were aware that their actions would not alter the world in any fundamental way because they knew the limitations of reason. They knew that there is no final systematic understanding of the world and no ultimate rational justification of action. The weight of tradition was the only source of the authority of their actions: they lived as they did because people like them (those with the aristocratic background) had always lived in that manner.

Socrates, according to Nietzsche's interpretation, was amazed by the power of tradition: neither the artists nor the great individuals of the tragic age of the Greeks possessed a rational understanding of their way of life or of the world in which they lived. Most important, they could not give an answer when Socrates, as we constantly see him doing in Plato's dialogues, asked them "Why?" Their way of life, in general, contained no rational "Because." They acted "only by instinct." "'Only by instinct': with this phrase we touch upon the heart and core of the Socratic tendency. With it Socratism condemns existing art as well as existing ethics. Wherever Socratism turns its searching eyes it sees lack of insight and the power of illusion; and from this lack it infers the essential perversity and reprehensibility of what exists" (*BT* 13; 1:89). Moral Socratism identifies virtue with knowledge. Its companion is "aesthetic Socratism," which collapses beauty into intelligibility (*BT* 12; 1:85). Tragedy finds beauty and goodness where no reason can be given. Socratism, the idea that nothing is beautiful or good unless it is understandable, destroyed tragedy as it destroyed a whole world, Nietzsche writes, "to touch whose very hem would give us the greatest happiness" (*BT* 13; 1:89–90).

How did Socrates manage to destroy a whole world? His "one great Cyclops eye" saw in it and in its art only "something rather unreasonable, full of causes apparently without effects, and effects apparently without causes" (*BT* 14; 1:92). He rejected the idea that the world cannot finally be understood, that it was not made for us, that nothing we can do, as tragedy showed, can change that world effectively and for the better. Socrates was horrified by the tragic vision of heroes destroyed even though they have made no errors and have done nothing wrong. He repudiated the pessimistic view that, far from guaranteeing success and happiness, knowledge and virtue can bring about the hero's destruction.[29] He refused to follow the path of irrational tradition. Instead, Socrates constituted himself as "the prototype of the theoretical optimist who, with his faith that the nature of things can be fathomed, ascribes to knowledge and insight the power of a panacea, while understanding error as the evil *par excellence*" (*BT* 15; 1:100). He established dialectic, which aims to offer a reason for everything that is done, and defended it against attack—something neither the society nor the art he questioned could do. His attack proved fatal because the culture Socrates assaulted lacked the reasons he demanded for being as it was, and he convinced his contemporaries to think of such a lack as an inexcusable infirmity.

It is time to put *The Birth of Tragedy* aside: this rough discussion was intended only to introduce the themes that would occupy Nietzsche in regard to Socrates throughout his life. But though the themes remained stable, Nietzsche's attitude did not. We have seen that during his middle period, while he was turning away from Schopenhauer and Wagner—the heroes of *The Birth of Tragedy*—Nietzsche seems to have made peace with Socrates. Dialectic, so viciously attacked in *Birth of Tragedy*, now acquires a positive color; Plato's dialogues vibrate with the joy of its invention. Those moderns who dislike it are soundly denounced:

> In those days there still lingered on the palate of the Greeks that other, more ancient and formerly all-powerful taste: and the new taste presented so magical a contrast to this that they sang and stammered of dialectics, the 'divine art', as though in a delirium of love. That ancient way, how- ever, was thinking under the spell of custom, for which there was noth- ing but established judgements, established causes, and no other reasons than those of authority. . . . It was Socrates who discovered the antithet- ical magic, that of cause and effect, ground and consequence: and we mod- ern men are so accustomed to and brought up in the necessity of logic that it lies in our palate as the normal taste and, as such, cannot help being re- pugnant to the lustful and conceited. (*D* 544; 3:314–15)

The truce was uneasy, and Nietzsche remained suspicious of Socrates; he was never unwilling to ridicule him: "The daemon of Socrates was perhaps an ear infection which, in accordance with the moralizing man- ner of thinking that dominated him, he only *interpreted* differently from what it would be interpreted now."[30] And even this uneasy respite did not last long. By the time of "The Problem of Socrates," to which I now return, Nietzsche had decided that Socrates' theoretical optimism, for which he had attacked him in *The Birth of Tragedy*, was a sign of the deep- est degeneration. Socrates, he now argued, was a sick man; he perceived— experienced and lived—life as a disease.[31] Socrates' last words in Plato's *Phaedo*, "I owe Asclepius the Savior a rooster," seem to refer to the cus- tom of sacrificing a rooster to the god of medicine when one was cured of a disease; Nietzsche claims that the disease Socrates is grateful of be- ing cured of is life itself.[32] Nietzsche had already begun to formulate that view a little earlier, when he wrote that he wished that Socrates, who had never said too much, "had remained taciturn also at the last moment of his life." "Is it possible," he asked, "that a man like him, who had lived cheerfully and like a soldier in the sight of everyone, should have been a pessimist?" (*GS* 340; 3:569). But he did not really try to come to terms with the problem of Socrates until he wrote *Twilight of the Idols*.

The essay begins with the view of Socrates and "the wisest men of all ages" that life "*is no good*." But Nietzsche refuses to accept their judgment. He claims that not life but these sages themselves are no good: "Were they perhaps shaky on their legs? late? tottery? decadents? . . . Indeed? All these great wise men— they were not only decadents but not wise at all?" (1; 67).

Like Montaigne, Nietzsche is fascinated by Cicero's story regarding Socrates' face: "The criminal is a decadent. Was Socrates a typical criminal? At least that would not be contradicted by the famous judgment of the physiognomist which sounded so offensive to the friends of Socrates. A foreigner who knew about faces passed through Athens and told Socrates to his face that he *was a monstrum*— that he harbored in himself all the bad vices and appetites. And Socrates merely answered: 'You know me, sir!'" (3; 69). Though he had consistently emphasized Socrates' trust in reason and self-control throughout his writing, never before had Nietzsche tried to offer an explanation for it. Here, for the first and last time, he does. Socrates' rationality is both a symptom and a result of his effort to escape the "disease" from which, according to Nietzsche, he suffered.

That disease, which is evident in Socrates' face, is "decadence." It "is suggested not only by the admitted wantonness and anarchy of his instincts, but also by the hypertrophy of the logical faculty and that *sarcasm of the rachitic* which distinguishes him" (4; 69).[33] Socrates' reverence for reason, Nietzsche continues, must have been at first repellent to his noble Athenian companions: "Wherever authority still forms part of good bearing, where one does not give reasons but commands, the dialectician is a kind of buffoon: one laughs at him, one does not take him seriously. Socrates was the buffoon who *got himself taken seriously*: what really happened here?" (5; 70). How did this repugnant figure win one of the greatest intellectual victories of all time? How did Socrates manage to "fascinate" his world (8; 71)?

Nietzsche believes that Socrates was successful for two reasons. The first is that Socratic dialectic represented a new form of the contest (ἀγών) to which the Athenians were devoted: Socrates "fascinated by appealing to the agonistic impulse of the Greeks— he introduced a variation into the wrestling match between older men and youths. Socrates was also a great *erotic*" (8; 71).[34] In other words, Socrates took the general structure of an existing institution and gave it a new content and meaning: he adapted the nature of competition, and of Athenian pederasty, to his own purposes. That, for Nietzsche, is a perfect manifestation of "the will to power," which is the ability to use the materials that already exist in the

world in a new and different way; that is for him the mechanism that accounts for all major changes in history: "Whatever exists, having somehow come into being, is again and again reinterpreted to new ends, taken
over, transformed, and redirected by some power superior to it; all events
in the organic world are a subduing, a *becoming master*, and all subduing
and becoming master involves a fresh interpretation, an adaptation
through which any previous 'meaning' and 'purpose' are necessarily obscured or even obliterated. . . . The form is fluid, but the 'meaning' is even
more so."[35]

The first reason for Socrates' victory was his will to power. The second
was that his case was not at all unusual: "He saw *through* his noble Athenians; he comprehended that his own case, his idiosyncrasy, was no longer
exceptional." His society was already falling apart, though it did not know
it: "Everywhere the instincts were in anarchy; everywhere one was within
five paces of excess: *monstrum in animo* was the general danger. 'The impulses want to play the tyrant; one must invent a *counter-tyrant* who is
stronger'" (9; 71).

Socrates put up a mirror to his contemporaries. He was fascinating because he was the most extreme case "of what was then beginning to be a
universal disease"—the anarchy of instinct.[36] "His awe-inspiring ugliness
proclaimed him as such to all who could see." Most important, "he fascinated, of course, even more as an answer, a solution, an apparent cure
of this case" (9; 71–72). In Socrates' mirror, the Athenian nobles thought
they saw a way out of the decadence to which they were themselves becoming subject.

Socrates, then, attracted an audience that should have been repelled
by him because he showed them their own central problem in himself
and offered them a solution: "When the physiognomist had revealed to
Socrates who he was—a cave of bad appetites—the great master of irony
let slip another word which is the key to his character. 'This is true,' he
said, 'but I mastered them all.' *How* did Socrates become master over *himself?*" (9; 71).[37] Nietzsche answers that Socrates became master over himself by turning "*reason* into a tyrant" (10; 72). The "apparent" cure he
offered his contemporaries claimed to be the path to self-mastery.

But why is self-mastery only an apparent cure for the "anarchy of instinct"? Because, Nietzsche believes in very classical style, a way of life
that needs to *fight* instinct is as "sick" and "decadent" as a life in which
instinct is out of control. Socrates did indeed show his degenerate contemporaries a way of becoming masters of themselves. But true self-mastery requires moderating the impulses, acculturating them into mutual

accommodation and respect, giving everything of which one consists some voice in self-government. Instead, Socrates chose one impulse, strengthened it into a domineering master, and willingly submitted the rest to its tyranny. Reason, after all, is for Nietzsche no less an "instinct" — a natural feature and development — than the rest of our impulses and faculties. By giving it absolute preeminence, Socrates convinced us not to think we comprise many things, all of them equally part of what we are. Instead, he persuaded us to identify ourselves with this one impulse, to consider it the seat of the self, the mark of the human, and to distrust everything else about us as lower, degenerate, as features simply of the body or our fallen nature. Instead of integrating our various capacities, he convinced us to try to subjugate, perhaps even to destroy them. But *"destroying* the passions and cravings, merely as a preventive measure against their stupidity and the unpleasant consequences of this stupidity — today this itself strikes us as merely another acute form of stupidity. We no longer admire dentists who 'pluck out' teeth so that they will not hurt any more" (*TI* V:1; 6:82). Curing is not excision but, as almost every ancient doctor would have agreed, a harmony of opposites.

Nietzsche believes that in general the features that characterize each one of us cannot be eliminated: "Castration, extirpation . . . is instinctively chosen by those who are too weak-willed, too degenerate, to impose moderation upon themselves."[38] Moderation can be imposed, for example, by spiritualizing, beautifying, even by "deifying" a craving (*TI* V:1; 6:83), by using it to accomplish what has never been accomplished before. It depends crucially on what Freud was later to call sublimation. It requires the long, hard effort to give what Nietzsche calls "style to one's character."[39] Perhaps surprisingly for many of his recent admirers, Nietzsche's ethical ideal is in the end an expression of the aesthetics of classicism, the ability to "possess *all* the strong, seemingly contradictory gifts and desires — but in such a way that they go together beneath one yoke." Morality, the subjugation of desire, is "in itself a contradiction of the classical. . . . Precisely such a preponderance of one virtue over the others (as in the case of a moral monster) is hostile to the classical power of equilibrium" (*WP* 848; 12:434). Nietzsche's Socrates, by contrast, was classicism's great enemy.

Socrates' ugly face is an outward reflection of the total chaos within. Reason is just his means of keeping that chaos at bay. His face reflects an anarchy of instincts, a civil war (to return to Montaigne's metaphor) that resulted in tyranny, not peace. In contrast to Montaigne's figure, he provides a perfect application of the physiognomic principle. That is why his solution was merely apparent.

Socrates is therefore for Nietzsche the figure who first identified the nature of what it is to be human with rationality. He thus introduced the elements that eventually led to the idea that each human being is, in origin and essence, an indissoluble unity; but such a unity is achieved only by disregarding the rest of our features, the rest of ourselves. Socrates was also, for the same reason, the first to establish the notion that the soul (which he identified with rationality) is fundamentally different from the rest of us—from everything that according to Nietzsche in reality constitutes the human individual. He was not only the first modern but also the first Christian.[40]

It was therefore Socrates' unconditional faith in reason that secured his apparent success: "The most blinding daylight; rationality at any price; life, bright, cold, cautious, conscious, without instinct, in opposition to the instincts—all this was a mere disease, another disease, and by no means a return to 'virtue,' to 'health,' to happiness. To *have* to fight the instincts— that is the formula of decadence: as long as life is *ascending*, happiness equals instinct" (11; 73).

We have been talking rather freely about instinct and reason, and we must be more careful. We must never, when we read Nietzsche on this topic, understand him as if he were a vulgar Freudian. Nietzsche does not consider the instincts simply as the basic tendencies or impulses that constitute the bedrock of the self and to which he urges us to return. He is neither an irrationalist nor an atavist.[41] By "instinct" and "instinctive," Nietzsche generally understands any mode of behavior that is performed more or less unselfconsciously, without explicit awareness of the steps it involves. Instinctive behavior in that sense, though some of it may in fact be basic and unlearned, can also be the result of acculturation, effort, and practice. In particular, it can include the unquestioned codes (if such they were) of behavior of the early Greek aristocracy—codes that by Socrates' time may have broken down enough to drive Socrates' audience into disordered and inconsistent modes of life.

Nietzsche's way of thinking about instinct allows him to believe that even knowledge can become instinctive: "To this day the task of *incorporating* knowledge and making it instinctive is only beginning to dawn on the human eye and is not yet clearly discernible" (*GS* 11; 3:383). That instinct represents something learned is one of his most central ideas: "The great rationality of all education in morality has always been that one tried to attain to the certainty of an instinct: so that neither good intentions nor good means had to enter consciousness as such. As the soldier exercises, so should one learn to act. In fact, this unconsciousness belongs to any kind of perfection."[42] "We must in fact seek perfect life where it has *become* least conscious (i.e., least aware of its logic, its reasons, its means and intentions, its utility)" (*WP* 439; 13:313). In most cases, instinct is for Nietzsche, as the self and nature are for Montaigne, not an origin but an end, not given but achieved.

Nietzsche's complaint against Socrates, therefore, is that he was unable to act as he would have wanted "instinctively," as a result of a harmony between his various impulses. Accordingly, he forced himself to act well by appealing to reasons. And reasons, for Nietzsche, mark precisely the absence of real self-mastery, when "necessity [is] freedom itself" (*Z* III: "On Old and New Tablets," 2; 4:248). Self-mastery is a state where all our desires, beliefs, and values dictate a single course of action, performing which is all we want to do. The very issue of choosing between alternatives seems to disappear. Reasons, as we commonly think of them, become irrelevant. Nietzsche believes that he has himself attained a state of harmony. His charge against Socrates, who must still act by means of reasons, is that the two of them stand at opposite poles of a single scale. I now want to examine that opposition between them. Here, unfortunately, I shall have to be both rough and dogmatic.[43]

In his early works, Nietzsche believed that philosophers should intervene directly in their world. *The Birth of Tragedy* and the *Untimely Meditations* were conceived as blueprints for regenerating German culture. But once Nietzsche abandoned his early conception of philosophy, he took a radically individualist turn. He saw his task to be that of fashioning himself, or, as he put it, of becoming an individual, of becoming who he was. The task of philosophy is not to improve the culture at large but to cultivate the individual. These two conceptions of philosophy are not necessarily incompatible: new individuals establish new modes of life, and those, as Socrates' case indicates, can in turn have the greatest effect on the world at large.[44]

To achieve his end, to become who he was, Nietzsche first had to accomplish at least two subsidiary tasks. The first was to put absolutely everything he was faced with—events peculiar to him alone: accidents of birth and growth, health and sickness, choices made consciously and unconsciously, friendships made and lost, works composed or left unfinished, features liked and despised—into a single, unified whole that he could affirm altogether. Some of these elements, taken in isolation, might be objectionable. But one of his central ideas is precisely that no human feature (or any other thing in the world) can be judged in itself: "There is much filth in the world; that much is true. But that doesn't make the world itself a filthy monster" (*Z* III: "On Old and New Tablets," 14; 4:256). The value of everything depends on its contribution to a whole of which it can be seen as a part:

> *One thing is needful.* — To "give style" to one's character — a great and rare art! It is practiced by those who survey all the strengths and weaknesses of their nature and then fit them into an artistic plan until every one of them appears as art and reason and even weaknesses delight the eye. . . . In the end, when the work is finished, it becomes evident how the constraint of a single taste governed and formed everything large and small. Whether this taste was good or bad is less important than one might suppose, if only it was a single taste! (*GS* 290; 3:530)

But what is it to affirm the whole of which all these features and events have been made parts? The answer is provided by the thought of the eternal recurrence. This is not the senseless view that everything in the world has occurred and will occur again exactly in the same way infinitely many times. Rather, it is the thought that if one were to live over again, one would want the very life one has already had, exactly the same down to its tiniest detail, and nothing else:[45] "My formula for greatness for a human being is *amor fati*: that one wants nothing to be different, not forward, not backward, not in all eternity. Not merely bear what is necessary, still less conceal it . . . but *love* it" (*EH* II:10; 6:297). In Zarathustra's words, "Have you said Yes to a single joy? O my friends, then you have said Yes too to *all* woe. All things are entangled, ensnared, enamored; if ever you wanted one thing twice, if ever you said, 'You please me, happiness! Abide, moment!' then you wanted *all* back. All anew, all eternally, all entangled, ensnared, enamored — oh, then you *loved* the world" (*Z* IV: "The Drunken Song," 10; 4:402). To want the eternal repetition of one's life is to be perfectly happy with the life one has lived.

The second task presupposed by the effort to become who one is requires that the whole one constructs, the self one fashions, be significantly different from all others. If it isn't, then one is not distinguishable from the rest of the world: one has not become an individual. But to be different in a significant way, one will have to produce, one will have to *become* something significantly new. To become something significantly new, one must develop an unprecedented way of doing things, of thinking, feeling, and living. And to accomplish that, in turn, it will be necessary to break some long-accepted rules, some principles and practices that have been taken for granted so far. That is the first aspect of Nietzsche's "immoralism": "If a temple is to be erected *a temple must first be destroyed*: that is the law" (*GM* II 24; 5:335).

Nietzsche's self-fashioning, like Montaigne's, is an essentially individual project. It does not allow you to follow, in any straightforward sense, the example set by someone else; for instead of creating yourself you would then be imitating that other person. Individuality, however, is threatened not only if you imitate someone else but also, in a darker, more dangerous manner, if others imitate you. Nietzsche is remarkable among the philosophers of the art of living because he was so conscious of that danger and so disturbed by its possibility. Success in creating yourself may cause its own failure. For if others in fact imitate you, if your way of life appeals enough to the rest of the world and can become a paradigm of how life can be lived, then what distinguished you from your world becomes part of that world. It is no longer you; it becomes, as Nietzsche would have put it, a fact: "*Imitators.*—A: 'What? You want no imitators?' B: 'I do not want to have people imitate my example; I wish that everybody would fashion his own example, as *I* do.' A: 'So?'"[46] Individuality, like style, requires multiplicity and opposition. If everyone adopts a particular style, the style disappears: it becomes just the normal way to act, living degree zero. The individuality of one's own story is threatened both because it may be an imitation of a model supplied by someone else and because it may itself become a model that others will in turn imitate. The combination of these two dangers is one of the reasons Nietzsche's attitude toward Socrates turns out to be so complex, as we shall see.

Nietzsche is well aware that the life he fashioned for himself need not, cannot, and probably should not be held as a direct example of imitation. That is one aspect of his "perspectivism." He believes, as Montaigne did, that each individual's life consists of a unique combination of events. There is no general method for putting one's own story together—if, that is, it will be one's own story and not the story dictated by the standards accepted generally by one's world. Individuals must be at least partially independent of the standards that govern their world. But Nietzsche believes that these standards generally determine which actions count as moral and good. He insists that human beings are "herd animals" because he believes that to be good is to fit in with one's world, not to stand out, not to threaten or upset the lives that most people are capable of living. The standards of good action enjoin everyone to act alike. They have even been used to convince many of those who could have acted differently to deny their difference, to become members of the herd.[47]

That is the second part of Nietzsche's immoralism. Morality, as he sees it, is an effort to prevent the creation of new possibilities, to prevent the temple's destruction: "'Whom do [the good] hate the most?' The *creator* they hate the most: the creator breaks tablets and old values and is a breaker,

whom they call lawbreaker. For the good are *unable* to create; they are always the beginning of the end: they crucify him who writes new values
on new tablets" (*Z* III: "On Old and New Tablets," 26; 4:266).[48] In very
general terms, morality begins by focusing on the principles dictated by
the needs of a particular group. These principles depend, they are "conditional," on the group's desire to survive as it is: no one who rejects that
desire need follow them. But morality hides the interested and partial origins of such conditional principles. It requires that they be accepted not
because they are useful to a particular and common type of person and to
that type of person only. It claims that they are unconditional, that they
must be accepted simply because they are the right principles of action in
general and therefore binding on all people, whatever their particular views,
needs, and desires, and not only on some particular group for its own purposes. For example, the moral imperative not to cause harm, "listened to
calmly and without previous bias, really amounts to no more than: 'we
weak ones are, after all, weak; it would be good if we did nothing *for which
we are not strong enough*'; but this dry matter of fact, this prudence of the
lowest order which even insects possess . . . has . . . clad itself in the os-
tentatious garb of the virtue of quiet, calm resignation, just as if the weakness of the weak—that is to say, their *essence*—were a voluntary achievement, willed, chosen, a *deed*, a *meritorious* act" (GM I:13; 5:280). Morality
turns prudence into virtue and necessity into choice.

It was Socrates who, Nietzsche has claimed, first made value judgments
moral. In their original context within early Greek culture, value judgments were made as a matter of course, on the unspoken assumption that
the culture and its survival demanded them. They were therefore conditional on the welfare of that particular culture—in Kantian terms, they
were "hypothetical" and prudential. But Socrates claimed that value
judgments should be unconditional. He argued that if they were to be
binding on anyone, they had to be supported by reasons that apply to
everyone alike, whatever their different needs and purposes. Socrates
therefore originated the view that the fact that a mode of life advances
the interests and purposes of particular people or groups is never a moral
reason for accepting it. We should adopt a course of action only if it is
right, if it embodies values that are real and views that are true. Following a way of life for prudential reasons is a matter of choice, a question
of wanting to be like those whose way of life it is, whether that life is or
is not a good one. Following a way of life for moral reasons is a matter
of obligation, a question of recognizing its rightness. Goodness and truth,
like virtue and knowledge, go together.

Nietzsche rejects the "dogmatism" that recognizes only a single mode of life as good. His perspectivism denies that truth and value are inherently connected and insists that different people need to live in different ways.[49] Perspectivism has two components. The first is epistemological. It is a denial of "the correspondence theory of truth," the idea that all our true views are true because they bear a particular relation—the relation of correspondence—to the world. Nietzsche, who wrote that "facts are precisely what there is not, only interpretations" (*WP* 481; 12:315), cannot possibly accept that idea. But are "interpretations" or perspectives simply a matter of taste? Or are some of them true? And if they are, what accounts for their truth?

Arthur Danto has answered that Nietzsche believed that perspectives are true if and only if they "enhance and facilitate life." Nietzsche, according to Danto's influential interpretation, "advanced a pragmatic criterion of truth: *p* is true and *q* is false if *p* works and *q* does not."[50] A few passages in Nietzsche might seem to suggest that he was sometimes tempted to accept such a theory.[51] But others show that he rejects Pragmatism in the most uncompromising terms: "*Life no argument.*—We have arranged for ourselves a world in which we can live—by positing bodies, lines, planes, causes and effects, motion and rest, form and content; without these articles of faith nobody could now endure life. But that does not prove them. Life is no argument. The conditions of life might include error"[52] The most basic ideas and judgments that secure survival may, for all we know, still be false. Nietzsche refuses to accept the Pragmatists' identification of truth with utility.

Textual reasons aside, to attribute this identification to Nietzsche is to open his thought to one of his own central objections against dogmatism. Why do we believe that the value of truth is unconditional, that "*nothing is needed more* than truth, and in relation to it everything else has only second-rate value"? No calculation of utility can lead to that conviction: "What do you know in advance of the character of existence to be able to decide whether the greatest advantage is on the side of the unconditionally mistrustful or the unconditionally trusting? But if both should be required . . . from where would science then be permitted to take its unconditional faith or conviction on which it rests, that truth is more important than any other thing? Precisely this conviction could never have come into being *if both truth and untruth constantly proved to be useful, which is the case.*"[53] Pragmatism denies just this divergence between truth and value. In that, it is at one with classical Rationalism; but though Rationalism generally explains value by grounding it on truth, Pragmatism collapses truth into value. Nietzsche is not a Pragmatist, nor does he accept any other theory of the nature of truth. He holds instead the controversial and important view that there is no point in trying to explain what truth is. He does not believe that a definition of truth, a single informative explanation why all our true views are true, exists. Many people believe that unless there is such a definition, none of our views can ever be true; or that, if they are, they are true for no reason at all. But that is wrong. We can give specific reasons, sometimes very complex ones, for everything that we know: such reasons are different in each particular case; some are as simple as the fact that the cat is on the mat, others as complex as the arguments that support contemporary physics. Perspectivism denies that all those reasons can be generalized into a formula that is both informative and correct. If our definition of truth is correct, it will turn out to be trivial; if it is informative, it will fail to apply to all truths.

Nietzsche often tries to explain why people believe that some views are true: sometimes he claims that their reason is their faith in their utility;[54] sometimes he writes that such views enhance their own feeling of power.[55] But these reasons explain only why we are *willing* to consider that some of our beliefs, whether that is or is not in fact the case, are true. They have nothing to do with the truth of the beliefs themselves.

It might seem that if we lack a general theory of truth we cannot judge whether any particular view is or is not true. If you don't know what truth is, how can you recognize it when you come upon it? Some people, in fact, might be tempted to believe that if you don't have such a theory you are not entitled to claim that anything is true: a theory of truth can be conceived, in part, as a standard that allows us to decide which of our beliefs are and which are not true; without such a standard, it would be impossible to make that decision. I do not accept that position, which is, ironically, a version of what has been called "the Socratic fallacy."[56] This latter view, which is in fact a fallacy but which, even more ironically, Socrates did not hold, is that if you don't know what, for example, justice or courage is you cannot recognize any of its instances. But of course you can, and the Socratic elenchus requires it: Socrates, for example, could not refute Laches, who said that courage is standing one's ground against the enemy, by arguing that the Scythians fight courageously while they retreat unless he was able to recognize that their behavior was courageous. But he clearly admits that he does not know what courage is. The fact is that without a theory of courage we cannot *always* decide whether an action is courageous; without a theory of truth we cannot *always* decide whether a belief is true. But it does not follow from the fact that we lack such a theory that we can *never* recognize when we are being confronted with an instance of courage or truth.[57]

Perspectivism entails that some cases are not decidable, not that none is. There probably are perspectives that share so little ground that though they compete with one another—though no one can live with both of them at the same time—it is still impossible for their adherents to resolve their differences even under the best possible conditions of communication. That all such differences can be resolved, at least in principle, is the dream of dogmatism. If there are general ahistorical standards of correctness that establish what does and what does not count as true once and for all, and if these standards are at least in principle acceptable to everyone, then with enough time and good will no case would be left unresolved. But that is just a dream; I am not even sure it is pleasant.

Perspectivism holds that there are only "interpretations" because no single overarching view of the world is binding on everyone. But that may seem to undermine itself: "Does perspectivism entail that perspectivism itself is but a perspective, so that the truth of this doctrine entails that it is false?"[58] It does not. Perspectivism entails only that it is itself a perspective—nothing follows from that regarding its truth. To decide whether perspectivism is or is not true, we need to argue the case in detail and, as we do in all cases of disagreement, offer specific arguments against it. To be a perspective and "*but* a perspective" are not at all the same. For one view is "but" a perspective only relative to another, acknowledged to be superior. It is only in relation to such a superior perspective (which has yet to be produced) that perspectivism can appear *merely* as a perspective and to that extent false. Perspectivism may be false—that is to be decided by argument—but it does not, as many people believe and in contrast to relativism, undermine itself on purely logical grounds.

In slightly more detail, the situation is this. You try to refute my view that all views are interpretations by arguing that my view is itself only an interpretation. But to show that my view is *only* an interpretation, you must produce your own alternative view. If that view is itself an interpretation, then perspectivism is not refuted. If it is not, however, then we need to discuss it. We may decide that you are wrong and that your view was after all an interpretation (in that case, it would be appropriate to say that it was only an interpretation!) or that you are right—that you produced a view that is not an interpretation. In that case, perspectivism turns out to be false, but *not because it undermined itself*. It is false because it has been proved to be so by a better view. But that is the way in which every

view, perspectivist or dogmatist, is refuted. There is therefore nothing logically vicious or even suspicious about perspectivism.

Perspectivism may therefore be true after all, and perspectivists have
no difficulty in holding that many of their views are themselves true. But
does the fact that a perspective, or a view, is true give us enough of a reason to accept it? We generally think that it does: what other good reason
could we have for accepting a position? But Nietzsche answers that question in clearly negative terms. That is the second, evaluative, and more
controversial component of perspectivism: people need not believe something just because it is true, just as they need not reject it just because it
is false. This apparently paradoxical view is very important to him; anything else would commit him to the idea that the value of truth is unconditional, that no other value can compete with it and that nothing is
really valuable unless it is also true—a Platonist position that, we shall
now see, he rejects in the strongest terms.

We must be careful here; we need to distinguish between someone who
is already within a perspective and someone who is looking at that perspective from the outside. From a first-person point of view, if I already
accept a certain view, I cannot also believe that I have a choice whether
to believe it or not. Belief is just the attitude we take toward (what we
consider) the truth. From within a perspective, the value of truth cannot
be overridden: I only accept the views I consider true and reject the views
I consider false. It makes no sense for me to say that I believe something
because it is in my interest to do so even though I know it is not true.[59]

From a third-person point of view, however, perspectivism becomes
more disturbing. From a third-person point of view, truth and value diverge. I may agree with Nietzsche to "reject the Christian interpretation
and condemn its 'meaning' as counterfeit" (GS 357; 3:600), but I may also
think that there is no reason to convince Christians to give up their faith:
"Christianity, it seems to me, is still needed by most people in old Europe even today; therefore it still finds believers" (GS 347; 3:581). It is not
at all obvious that it would be better for all Christians to lose their faith.
Perhaps they might then live in the truth, but it is not clear that they could
survive that life.

Truth and falsity are not relative concepts for perspectivism, as they are
for relativism: a view either is true or is not, whatever anyone thinks.[60] What
is relative—to particular people, to their abilities, needs, and desires—is
value. Section 344 of The Gay Science makes it absolutely clear that both
truth and falsehood are essential to survival. So truth does not have an unconditional value: it is not always and in all circumstances good. Whether

it is or not depends on the kind of person you are and on the circumstances in which you find yourself. There is therefore no obligation on the part of those who know (or think they know) the truth to try to convince all others of it. For the truth may be harmful to those others: so, for example, Nietzsche thinks that the idea of "the death of God" is harmful to most people, who need to believe that their values are given to them independently of their own idiosyncrasies and preferences.[61] Perspectivism holds that I can believe both that your views are false and that it is good for you to hold them. It also holds that you can believe the same about me.[62]

Such an attitude is haughty, disdainful, and contemptuous—just as it should be if it is to be true to Nietzsche. But it does not make him what most people generally accuse him of being: an authoritarian, perhaps totalitarian thinker who believes that his point of view (or the point of view of some "select" group) must be imposed on everyone else. On the contrary, Nietzsche's perspectivism implies that it is impossible for most people to accept the perspective that he himself articulates in his work. The effort to convince others of it—the effort that Zarathustra makes, in vain, in the early stages of his return to the world and in the early parts of Nietzsche's book about him—is bound either to fail or to cause them harm.

Perspectives are therefore to be judged, as Danto claimed, by their contribution to life. But "life" here cannot mean, as he meant, life as a whole, the life of all people. In evaluating a perspective, we must always ask, "To whose life does it contribute?" There is absolutely no reason to think that a perspective that is good for one type of person will also be good for another—not to speak of "all others." We share no common ground that makes what is good for one good for all or good in itself. Moralities must "finally reach agreement that it is *immoral* to say: 'what is right for one is right for the other'" (*BGE* 221; 5:156).

It is just for that reason that Nietzsche does not simply reject Christianity (or any of the many other perspectives he abhors).[63] Maudemarie Clark, who claims that Nietzsche "opposes" Christianity, says that Christianity is "harmful."[64] But, once we see that the question we must ask is "Harmful to whom?" the issue no longer is whether Nietzsche "opposes" Christianity—though of course he does not "accept" it either. False as it is, Christianity is, according to Nietzsche, good for most people: they would be totally asea without it. Capable of separating truth from value and of seeing Christianity from both points of view, Nietzsche here manifests perfectly what he means by "objectivity"—not "'contemplation without interest' (which is a nonsensical absurdity)" but, as we have seen, "the ability to control one's Pro and Con and to dispose of them, so that one knows how to employ a variety of perspectives and affective interpretations in the service of knowledge" (*GM* III:12; 5:364–65). Contrary to the view that Nietzsche can only condemn Christianity if he commends "the opposed ideal to universal attention,"[65] I think that he never participates in what is simply another version of the apostolic mission.

Instead, Nietzsche advocates his own personal view of the world and life but does not insist that many, or any, others should, or could, accept it. Only dogmatists insist on that: "What is regressive in the philosopher? That he teaches that *his* qualities are the necessary and sole qualities for the attainment of the 'highest good' (e.g. dialectic, as with Plato). That he orders human beings of all kinds *gradatim* up to *his* type as the highest. . . . The typical philosopher is here an absolute dogmatist" (*WP* 446; 12:377). Dogmatists, Nietzsche claims, believe that the mode of life that is best for them in their particular circumstances is also best for all human beings, whatever their varying needs, desires, and abilities. The following passage ties together a number of themes we have already discussed and finally brings us back to the issue with which we began: "The struggle against Socrates, Plato, all the Socratic schools, proceeds from the profound instinct that one does not make human beings better when one represents to them that virtue is demonstrable and asks for reasons. Ultimately, it is the measly fact that the agonal instinct in all these born dialecticians compelled them to glorify their personal ability as the highest quality and to represent all other goods as conditioned by it" (*WP* 441; 13:330–31).

On Nietzsche's own account, he fashioned—created—himself by using everything he was faced with, good and evil, and producing a coherent self that he but no one else needed to, or indeed could, affirm. He finally reached "maturity and mastery in the midst of doing, creating, working, and willing—calm breathing, *attained* 'freedom of the will'" (*TI* V:3; 6:85). He constructed a harmonious self, capable of acting in the instinctive manner he praises as the mark of perfection.

According to the same account, Socrates, by contrast, looked into himself and found within a mass of unruly, battling impulses. But instead of simply acknowledging that he was, in Nietzsche's terms, a sick man, Socrates attacked his illness. He denounced all his impulses save one as evil and used that one—reason—to master the rest: in the end he thought that reason was the only part of himself that was truly good and that made him who he really was. He forced himself to act only when he found reasons for doing so and convinced the world that everyone should try to be like him. And, at the hour of his death, Socrates realized that his whole effort—that *he*—had been a huge mistake: "Did he himself comprehend this, this most brilliant of self-outwitters? Was this what he said to himself in the end, in the *wisdom* of his courage to die: not Athens, but he himself chose the hemlock; he forced Athens to sentence him. 'Socrates is no physician,' he said softly to himself; 'here death alone is the physician. Socrates himself has merely been sick a long time'" (12; 73). Socrates was not a "physician"; only death could cure him of the misery his life had constituted. While Nietzsche could write, "I do not want in the least that anything should become different than it is; I myself do not want to become different" (*EH* II 9; 6:295), Socrates died denouncing himself and life, wishing he had been someone else altogether. It is difficult to think that the opposition between them could have been more stark.

If only, as I remarked earlier, matters were only that complicated! By and large, Nietzsche's image of Socrates depends on Plato. Socrates' dying words, which are essential to that image, come from the *Phaedo*, in which Plato has left the silent figure of his early works behind and has begun to give expression to his own otherworldliness. The dogmatism that Nietzsche attributes to both[66] may then be Plato's and not Socrates' invention. Nietzsche actually admits as much in this very complex passage:

> The worst, most durable, and most dangerous of all errors so far was a dogmatist's error—namely, Plato's invention of pure spirit and the good as such. . . . It meant standing truth on her head and denying *perspective*, the basic condition of all life. . . . Indeed, as a physician one might ask: "How could the most beautiful growth of antiquity, Plato, contract such a disease? Did the wicked Socrates corrupt him after all? Could Socrates have been the corrupter of youth after all? And did he deserve the hemlock?" (*BGE* Pref.; 5:12)

Nietzsche's questions suggest that he saw that philosophical dogmatism, the effort to articulate an ideal mode of life that all ought to approximate so far as they are able, is Plato's creation. But he insists on blaming Socrates, the creature, for his creator's fault. And the question I return to is, Why? Why such obvious twists and turns? Why such unforgiving vehemence? Why this smallness of spirit that is so uncharacteristic of Nietzsche in all his other serious personal and intellectual relationships?

Another passage from *Beyond Good and Evil* (212; 5:145–47) may provide us with the beginnings of an answer: "Genuine philosophers, being *of necessity* people of tomorrow and the day after tomorrow, have always found themselves, and *had* to find themselves, in contradiction to their today: their enemy was ever the ideal of today." But who are those "genuine philosophers"?[67] Nietzsche offers only one example. Amazingly, it is Socrates. In the situation in which he found himself, surrounded by the degenerate aristocrats of his time who pursued pleasure but still repeated "the ancient pompous words to which their lives no longer gave them any right, *irony* may have been required for greatness of soul, that Socratic assurance of the old physician and plebeian who cut ruthlessly into his own flesh, as he did into the flesh and heart of the 'noble,' with a look that said clearly enough: 'Don't dissemble in front of me! Here— we are equal.'"[68] Nietzsche goes on to credit Socrates with introducing the radically new principle of equality in opposition to the bankrupt hierarchical ideals of his time. Socrates rejected the anti-intellectual values and fashions of his age that allowed some people to act differently from others, relied instead on the universal reason that dictates that all should act alike, and convinced the rest of the world to follow him. But such a radical revaluation of values makes Socrates as surely an "immoralist" in relation to his world as Nietzsche wished to appear in relation to his own. And now the neat and extreme contrast Nietzsche has drawn between Socrates and himself begins to lose its clear outlines. What exactly are the opposite poles of the scale each is supposed to occupy if both, unlike mere "philosophical laborers," refuse to accept the values of their world and instead create new ones?

Well, one could reply, Socrates was a "decadent,"[69] a sick man who could not control his inner chaos and tyrannized it by means of reason and dialectic. But, by his own admission, Nietzsche was a "decadent" too. He opens *Ecce Homo* by writing that he has inherited his dead father's delicacy. He explicitly connects his sickliness to his own dialectical abilities: "In the midst of the torments that go with an uninterrupted three-day migraine, accompanied by laborious vomiting of phlegm, I possessed a dialectician's clarity *par excellence* and thought through with very cold blood matters for which under healthier circumstances I am not mountainclimber, not subtle, not *cold* enough." But his readers know, he confesses, "in what way I consider dialectic as a symptom of decadence; for example in the most famous case, the case of Socrates." "Need I say after all this," he concludes, "that in questions of decadence I am *experienced?*" (*EH* I:1; 6:264–65).

But Nietzsche, he goes on to tell us in this strange book, was more complex than Socrates: "Apart from the fact that I am a decadent, I am also the opposite." Decadents, he claims, consistently choose disadvantageous methods o relieve themselves of their pains; by contrast, he has always "instinctively chosen the *right* means." That is, decadents always harm themselves in the end, while healthy people do not. Who are those healthy people? What allows us to recognize "who has turned out well"? Nietzsche answers:

> A well-turned out person . . . has a taste only for what is good for him; his pleasure, his delight cease where the measure of what is good for him is transgressed. . . . He exploits bad accidents to his advantage; what does not kill him makes him stronger. . . . He is always in his own company, whether he associates with books, human beings, or landscapes. . . . He believes neither in "misfortune" nor in "guilt": he comes to terms with himself, with others; he knows how to *forget* — he is strong enough; hence everything *must* turn out for his best.

That allows him to conclude: "Well then, I am the *opposite* of a decadent, for I have just described myself" (*EH* I:2; 6:266–67). Perhaps he is right. But I cannot help thinking that his description of the person "who has turned out well" applies perfectly to the Socrates of Plato's early works, who also always knew what was good for him, whose pleasure, too, ended where he saw harm to himself begin, who was consistently in his own company, who believed neither in misfortune nor in guilt. What is remarkable to me is that as astute an observer and as sensitive a reader as he was, Nietzsche did not see the parallel between Socrates and himself. Or did he?

Compare Nietzsche, sick most of his life (and making his sickness part of the subject of his writing), with Socrates, who was the embodiment of health; Nietzsche, constantly bundled up against the cold, with Socrates, who wore the same tunic winter and summer and always went barefoot; Nietzsche, confessing that "a single glass of wine or beer a day is quite sufficient to turn my life into a vale of misery" (*EH* II:1; 6:280), with Socrates, whose prodigious drinking always left him perfectly sober; Nietzsche, squinting his way through the world, with Socrates, who prides himself that his bulging eyes allow him to see not only ahead but sideways as well;[70] Nietzsche, spending his life writing frantically, away from everyone, with Socrates, who was always in public, always in conversation, and never wrote a word — compare them in these and in many other respects, and the question who is decadent and who is healthy begins to appear perfectly senseless.

Perhaps all these are merely superficial features. Real health and decadence as Nietzsche understood them may depend on the goal one sets for oneself — stability or growth, conformity or distinction — and on the life one constructs. That is true. But even here, the difference between

Socrates and himself turns out to be slighter than Nietzsche would want to believe. To see that, we must return to the question why Nietzsche attacked Socrates with such unrelenting passion.

The reason is that Socrates was the only one among Nietzsche's "educators" from whom he could never be sure he had emancipated himself. In Nietzsche's own eyes and on his own terms, Socrates, whatever else he thought of him, was one of the world's truly great individuals. It is true that Nietzsche also believed that, though he was an individual, Socrates created a universalist conception of human life that became the signpost of a culture Nietzsche detested. Socrates and dogmatism are never far apart. But perhaps that is what happens to all great individuals. However much one anticipates and defends oneself against the dogmatic appropriation of one's life, of one's self, one can never be sure of preventing it. Nietzsche fought more passionately than any of the philosophers of the art of living to make it unforgettable that his views, his values, his life were *his own*, not models for the world as a whole. He tried to convince his readers that when the question is (as Socrates had put it) how we are to live, being admirable is more important than being convincing.[71] But he knew that he had no control over the future, that in that respect great individuals are at the mercy of their followers. In most cases, those are their readers, who may take their views and try to apply them dogmatically, as if they were intended for everyone. But, in addition, Socrates was also at the mercy of his own author, who created one of the greatest universalist philosophical systems in history. What, then, if Socrates' own project had not after all been so different from Nietzsche's? What would that say about Nietzsche's own philosophical work?

One could argue that Socrates and Nietzsche differ most deeply because Nietzsche articulated a mode of life in which one's actions follow essentially and effortlessly from one's nature while, as he saw it, Socrates always had to appeal to reasons—to force—to choose and justify his life. Is that true of Socrates? We have seen that Plato's early works show that Socrates spent his life searching for the technical or expert knowledge of the nature of *aretê* that would have provided him with reasons for action. But since that was a knowledge he never acquired, his actions, which Plato depicts as invariably moral and right, were not produced by such reasons; they constituted a mystery: *they had no source*. Being able always to do the right thing without effort or hesitation and without reason, however, is exactly what Nietzsche praises as "instinctive" action. And if that is so, it may also be true that, whatever his theoretical views, Socrates had succeeded in living as "instinctively" as Nietzsche claimed he had lived himself.

And since Nietzsche, I believe, sometimes suspected that just that was the case, Socrates constituted an immense problem for him. Nietzsche took his project to be to attack traditional, dogmatic philosophy and to make a conscious effort to fashion himself as an inimitable individual. But he could never be sure that his own project was not also the project of the character who animated the tradition against which he defined himself. He could therefore never be sure that his project was not the same as the project of the tradition he denounced. Was he perhaps, Nietzsche must have asked himself, part and parcel of the philosophy from which he wanted to dissociate himself? Was Socrates perhaps not part of the opposing tradition but Nietzsche's ally? And if he was an ally, what did that say about the originality of Nietzsche's project? Can one be liberated from philosophy or from Socrates as long as one is still writing about them, even if only to condemn them?

The problem of Socrates was for Nietzsche the problem raised by all these questions, and he could never resolve it to his satisfaction. *Ecce Homo* begins with an acknowledgment of Nietzsche's gratitude to his whole life because of what he had accomplished in its last three months and also, of course, because of everything that had led him there. But Nietzsche's gratitude to his whole life seems to stop short of Socrates, despite the fact that he was one of its most important parts. That, I believe, is because he felt so close and in such competition with him that to acknowledge him would have seemed to him an acknowledgment that he himself was not, after all, who he said he was.

Nietzsche's attitude toward Socrates was therefore fundamentally ambivalent. Socrates was neither his "model" nor his "villain."[72] His constant problem, forever gnawing at him, was that he could never be sure that Socrates' ugly face was not after all a reflection of his own.[73] Could the great ironist, in whom Nietzsche discerned "three souls,"[74] have yet another, which was not so different from that of his great opponent? Could Socrates, too, have been a self-fashioner in Nietzsche's manner?

But that would make Nietzsche a self-fashioner in Socrates' manner. What, then, would there be for Nietzsche to fight against? I believe there was still much—especially Plato and the image of Socrates of his middle works that Nietzsche, for his own purposes, identified with the original behind the reflection. In addition, Nietzsche might have realized that in following Socrates, he was still establishing a life of his own and very different from that of Socrates himself; that in following, in "imitating" Socrates, he was still fashioning his *own* example (as Socrates also had). But I also like to think that there might have been moments in his life when Nietzsche could have simply enjoyed the Socrates of Plato's early dialogues and might have appreciated a passage he had written years before he denounced Socrates as life's great enemy. Let me end by quoting it, especially because it returns us precisely where we began:

> *Socrates.*— If all goes well, the time will come when one will take up the memorabilia of Socrates rather than the Bible as a guide to morals and reason, and when Montaigne and Horace will be employed as forerunners and signposts to an understanding of this simplest and most imperishable of intercessors. The pathways of the most various philosophical modes of life lead back to him; at bottom they are the modes of life of the various temperaments confirmed and established by reason and habit and all of them directed towards joy in living and in one's own self; from which one might conclude that Socrates' most personal characteristic was a participation in every temperament.[75]

But to participate in every temperament is to participate in none, to be blank, almost not to have a face at all, however pronounced one's features happen to be. And that, once again, leads us back to the Socrates whose silence I am trying to hear among its many echoes.

6

A Fate for Socrates' Reason

Foucault on the Care of the Self

What runs through the whole cycle concerning Socrates' death is the establishment, the foundation, in its specifically non-political nature, of a form of discourse which is primarily occupied with, which cares for, care—whose care is the care of the self.

Michel Foucault, Lecture at the Collège de France,
15 February 1984

Nietzsche left us two pictures of Socrates: his earlier portrait of the Montaignesque, cheerful, silent Socrates of the *Untimely Meditations* and of *Human, All-Too-Human* and the decadent, pessimistic, gruesome figure of his later works whose last words revealed that he had suffered life as a disease. Though the former is far preferable, Nietzsche needed to construct the later, negative figure because his own feelings toward Socrates were so deeply ambivalent. He never could be sure that he and Socrates were not involved in the same project of self-creation. And if they were, if they were after all allies and not enemies, the originality and importance of Nietzsche's own project might appear disputable. More dangerous, his individualist task ran the risk of collapsing into the dogmatist view that one and only one type of life is good for all human beings, for which Nietzsche came to hold Socrates responsible and which he took upon himself to unmask and fight.

Nietzsche's interpretation of Socrates' last words—"O Crito, we owe Asclepius a rooster. Do sacrifice it to him; do not forget" (*Phd.* 118a7–8)—

has by now become almost canonical.[1] Michel Foucault came to these words near the end of his own life.[2] He found them difficult to understand. In particular, he was puzzled by the fact that Socrates' very last word was the Greek term for "to forget," "to neglect" (ἀμελεῖν). That word, in various forms, is etymologically connected throughout the *Phaedo*, as well as in the *Apology* and the *Crito*, with the theme of the care of the self (ἑαυτοῦ ἐπιμελεῖσθαι), which is central to all three works. Why, Foucault asked, is that important term now applied "not to the soul, to truth and wisdom, but only to a rooster?"[3] He admits that he was disturbed by that question but was not able to answer it until he read Georges Dumézil's interpretation of Plato's line.[4] And, following Dumézil, he offered a radically new interpretation of Socrates' saying and his attitude toward philosophy and life.

Foucault begins his new interpretation by repeating Nietzsche's question in *The Gay Science*: "Is it possible that a man like [Socrates], who had lived his life cheerfully and like a soldier in the sight of everyone, should have been a pessimist?" (*GS* 340; 3:569). But while Nietzsche answered that with his last words Socrates finally revealed the dark secret he carried within him throughout his life, Foucault refuses to accept such a negative interpretation of Socrates. He claims that Nietzsche's pessimistic Socrates does not fit with the figure we find either in the *Phaedo* itself or in the *Apology*, from which he does not (as I would) distinguish the *Phaedo* chronologically or philosophically. He therefore concludes that Plato could not have meant Socrates' last words as an indication that life is a disease, that health can be found only in another world.

Let us start on our own interpretation of Foucault's Socrates by looking at his version of Socrates' last words. Foucault agrees that Socrates must be referring to a disease: that is the only possible interpretation of the reference to the sacrifice to Asclepius.[5] But if the disease Socrates has in mind is not life itself, what can it be? Foucault approaches that question through Dumézil, who had pointed out that Socrates says to Crito not that "*I*" (as Nietzsche, among many others, had always assumed) but that "*we*" owe Asclepius a rooster.[6] The debt is collective: Socrates and Crito, perhaps others as well, owe it to Asclepius together. What is that collective debt (57)?

Since Socrates addresses his last words to Crito, Foucault assumes that part of the answer to that question is contained in the dialogue of which Crito is the protagonist. In that work, Crito visits Socrates in his prison cell and tries to convince him to escape from jail and avoid execution by appealing to what people will think of him for abandoning his children and of his friends for abandoning him (*Cr.* 45a–46a). Socrates replies that we should pay attention only to the right views, whether or not they are the views most people hold (46b–47a). When we take care of our body, he continues, we do not listen to what everyone says; we pay attention only to the advice of doctors or teachers of gymnastics. Inexpert advice harms and ultimately destroys (διόλλυσι) the body (47a–c). So also when we are concerned with the more important issues of justice, nobility, and goodness, as we are now: we must listen not to the many but to the expert (if one exists, 47d1–2). If not, we shall corrupt and harm (διαφθε-ροῦμεν . . . καὶ λωβησόμεθα) the part of us that is improved by justice and destroyed by injustice, our soul (47c8–d5). And if, as everyone agrees, it is not worth living with a corrupted (διεφθαρμένον) body, it is even less worth living with a corrupted (διεφθαρμένη) soul.[7] We must there-fore pay no attention to what people say; we must discuss the question of escape on our own, with our eye not on opinion but on truth (48a5–11). Socrates and Crito have their discussion, Crito loses the argument, and Socrates remains in prison to die.

Foucault claims that Plato's comparison between the illness of the body and the soul's disease suggests that the soul is sick when it has ideas that are unexamined and untested in regard to truth: "Certainly, this is not a disease that can be treated by medical procedures. But if it is true that it is produced by false opinion, by the opinion of everyone and anyone, then it is opinion reinforced by truth, it is the right *logos*, precisely the *logos* that characterizes *phronêsis* [wisdom], which will be able to prevent this cor-ruption or to enable the soul to return to health from a corrupt state" (61).

Foucault consistently describes the *Apology*, the *Crito*, and the *Phaedo* as a single "cycle" concerned with Socrates' death (e.g., 3, 5, 40). The close connection he envisages to hold between the *Phaedo* and the *Crito* allows him to claim that Socrates' last words refer to the disease of which Crito was cured in the course of his dialogue with Socrates, namely, his false belief, engendered by his faith in popular opinion, that it was proper for Socrates to escape from prison. Socrates and Crito are therefore grateful to Asclepius because Crito has seen that it was right for Socrates to sub-mit to the laws of Athens.

There is nothing obvious about the idea that false belief is a disease, and a disease of the soul at that. To support his claim, Foucault points out that when the company that gathered round Socrates on the day of his execution was dispirited by the strength of Simmias' and Cebes' ar-guments against the soul's immortality, Socrates "cured" them (ἰάσατο) and convinced them to go on with their discussion (*Phd.* 89c). He also draws attention to Socrates' view that an argument that is pursued correctly leads to the kind of health (ὑγιῶς ἔχειν) that all of them should desire—his friends on account of the rest of their lives, he on account of his imminent death (90e–91a). "These two texts," Foucault concludes, "confirm . . . perfectly the *Crito*'s theme, that a badly formed opinion is like an illness that affects the soul, corrupts it, deprives it of health, and from which we must be cured" (67).

But if the false belief that Socrates should escape, and therefore the disease it involves, is only Crito's, why does Socrates use the plural when he refers to the debt to Asclepius? Why is the debt to the god for Crito's cure Socrates' own debt as well? Foucault answers, first, that Socrates is so close to his friends that if any one of them is ill, he himself suffers. This is a weak response: it is arbitrary and speculative; no evidence supports it. Second, he claims that since Socrates runs the risk of being infected with a false belief as long as he is still alive, Crito's disease is potentially his own as well. But this implies that Socrates doesn't see death as a cure that purges him of all false opinion; since he can, and probably will, die with many false beliefs still in his soul, death can only serve to protect him from further infection. In that case, he should not be thanking the god for a cure that he is incapable of effecting. Third, Foucault argues that Socrates believes that the victory of error is everyone's defeat, not just the person's whose error it is (69–71). But this implies that a false belief that harms the person who holds it also harms someone who does not accept either that or, potentially, any other false opinion. And that does not fit well with Socrates' view, expressed in the *Apology* (30c–d), that "no harm can come to a good human being" and his statement that if his judges accept his accusers' lies and condemn him they will harm themselves much more than him. I therefore cannot accept Foucault's idea that the illness Socrates has in mind is Crito's false opinion; I also cannot agree that, if it is, Socrates uses the plural "we" because he believes that Crito's disease is his own as well.

Foucault's case against the otherworldly interpretation of Socrates' last words would be stronger if the *Phaedo* never represented life as a sickness. He gives two reasons to show that it does not. The first is the passage where Socrates claims that suicide is wrong because "the gods care (ἐπιμελοῦνται) for us and we human beings are their possessions"; and possessions, he continues, have no right to kill themselves without their masters' permission (62b–c). Foucault argues that the vocabulary of "caring" is always positive; it suggests not the surveillance of prison guards but the solicitude of parents: "It is therefore impossible to fit together the idea that life is a disease from which we can be freed through death and the idea that down here we are the charge and the concern of the gods" (51). Actually, however, care (ἐπιμέλεια) and disease do not at all exclude one another. On the contrary, the term applies regularly to doctors treating their patients; Plato himself uses it in such a context.[8] Nothing, then, prevents Plato from using the vocabulary of caring to describe a life that he can be convinced is an illness.

Foucault's second reason for thinking Plato cannot believe life is a disease is that Socrates believes that in the other world he will find, "no less than here," good masters and friends (*Cr.* 69e). And even though those will be doubtless better than our present company, "this does not imply that we are here like sick patients who are trying to free themselves, to liberate themselves, to cure themselves of their illness" (51). That is true. But though Socrates' view does not imply that life is a disease, it is perfectly compatible with it: a sick person can always have excellent masters and companions, even though they may not always be able to effect a perfect cure and sometimes accomplish no cure at all.[9]

In my view, the *Phaedo's* animosity toward the body is so intense, so passionate, that it is difficult to believe that Plato is thinking of life—the time when the soul is trapped in a body—as anything other than a disease. But despite my disagreements with him, I believe that Foucault's view of Socrates is both suggestive and important and that his own conception of philosophy, which places him solidly within the tradition of the art of living, should be central to our own understanding of philosophy's prospects. Much that he says is true. His picture of Socrates is worth contemplating. His view of philosophy is worth retaining.

"Those who do philosophy correctly are preparing themselves for death," Socrates says while he is explaining how the body deprives the soul of true knowledge and virtue (*Phd.* 64a4–6; cf. 81a1–2). To think philosophically—that is to say, to live philosophically—one must distance oneself from the body as much as possible and rely on the soul's abilities alone. Since death is the ultimate separation of the soul from the body, to live philosophically is to prepare oneself for death, to live as close to death as being alive allows (64c4–5, 64d4–5).[10] Vulgar virtue, the virtue of the lovers of the body (φιλοσώματοι), as opposed to the virtue of soul philosophers possess, "has nothing healthy [ὑγιές] about it" (69b8). Even by itself, that statement shows that Plato believes that an explicit connection exists between embodied life and disease.

More strongly, in the *Gorgias* Plato had already appealed to the Orphic slogan "the body is a tomb" (σῶμα σῆμα, 493a1; cf. *Crat.* 400c1–4).

Plato there adopted not simply the view that life is a disease but the much more pessimistic position that it is actually a form of death. The body, he now writes in the *Phaedo*, is the main obstacle to wisdom; not even sight and hearing, its most accurate instruments, can show us the truth. Only when the soul thinks rationally, "itself by itself," free of the body's bonds, can we hope to bring truth within our uneasy grasp (65a–d). Rational thought, independent of the body, Plato says, is the essence of philosophy and the substance of the philosophic life.

Plato had always believed that most people live their whole lives in the grip of error and unexamined opinion: that is the underpinning of the elenchus throughout the Socratic dialogues. The *Phaedo*, however, introduces a radically new idea. Plato does not simply exhibit, as he had done before, our susceptibility to error. For the first time, he tries to explain it; and his explanation is that it is caused by the corrupt nature of the body. But if he thinks that the body is the source of error, Plato may well believe that death, when the soul finally leaves the body behind, will liberate Socrates from the false beliefs that, like all embodied beings, he inevitably has. And though life and falsehood are inextricably connected, false belief is not itself the illness of which Socrates suffers. The illness is life itself: the soul's imprisonment in the body. False belief is, so to speak, that disease's central symptom. How is that symptom corrected?

It is corrected, so far as it can be, through philosophy, which is, to repeat, a preparation for death. To practice philosophy is to leave more false ideas behind than other people do and to come closer to the truth than the rest of the world: it is to allow one's life to be ruled by the soul and so to be as far removed from ordinary life as possible. Socrates' final words therefore also allude to the fact that philosophy has helped him and his associates come as close to a cure as it is possible for any embodied being. But the very idea that Socrates has philosophical associates with whom he shares views about the body, the soul, and the intelligible world is a new one in Plato. The Socratic dialogues contain many characters who are sympathetic to Socrates, but none of them, not even Nicias, is in any way his disciple. The group gathered round Socrates in the *Phaedo* reflects Plato's own development and his expansion of Socratic thought into a system that can be communicated from one person to another in more or less explicit terms. The idea that Socrates now has philosophical disciples also allows us to retain the plural subject of his last words and still accept Nietzsche's otherworldly interpretation. Friends, relatives, a philosophical group (ἑταιρία) should all be grateful to the god for curing one of their own. That is why the debt is collective.

Foucault identified Socrates' disease with false belief and asked how he and his associates were (already) cured from it (71). I identified it with life itself, but since I consider that error, false belief, and unexamined opinion are symptoms of that disease, I asked how Socrates' friends came as close as they did to the cure that Socrates (and only Socrates) is about to accomplish completely. Our answer is the same: the cure is reached through the process of taking care of oneself (ἐπιμέλεια ἑαυτοῦ) that constitutes the main task of philosophy. That is the central theme of all of Plato's early works, and it is given a radical expansion in the *Phaedo*.

The care of the self in the *Apology* and the *Laches* is the central theme of Foucault's final lectures. Foucault begins his discussion of the *Apology*, which will be my own main concern in what follows, with the passage in which Socrates tells the Athenians that his task has been to try to convince each one of them, like a father or an older brother, to care for virtue (ἐπιμελεῖσθαι ἀρετῆς). Socrates admits that it may seem strange that he has admonished them only in private: if his task was as important as he claims it is, why did he not try to communicate it to the citizens together, as a whole? Why did he avoid all involvement in public affairs and politics (31c4–d2)? He replies that his divine voice (*daimonion*), which occasionally spoke to him and urged him to avoid certain courses of action, prevented him from doing so. The voice, he continues, was right: had he tried to play a political role, the city would have already put him to death long ago and he would have been of benefit neither to Athens nor to himself (31d7–e1).

Socrates justifies his decision by appealing to two episodes when his life was endangered because of his involvement in politics. But Foucault points out that these are quite ambiguous: they undermine his claim that the risk of death kept him away from politics as much as they support it. In both episodes, Socrates took a public position against the prevailing political system (democracy in one case, the Thirty Tyrants in the other) because he thought "it better to be in danger along with law and justice rather then take your side while you were contemplating injustice, out of fear of prison or death" (32c1–3). The examples show that getting involved in politics was really dangerous but also that the fear of death did not deter Socrates from doing what he thought was right.

Was then the fear of death Socrates' real reason for avoiding politics? Yes and no. No, because it wasn't precisely the fear of death that kept him out of public life: his examples show that he was not afraid to risk his life for the sake of right conduct. Yes, because if he had died, he would have been useful neither to Athens, Foucault claims (16), nor—I add with

Socrates—to himself.[11] Socrates' voice kept him true to his "divine mission"; that mission was personal: politics was irrelevant to it.[12]

Socrates' mission is a radical new enterprise within the ethical and intellectual world of Athens. It has two central features. First, it requires that one assume the task of always telling the truth, even when that is unpleasant and distasteful to one's audience. That is a version of the complex Greek notion of *parrhêsia*, which Foucault addressed in some detail in the last two years of his life.[13] *Parrhêsia*, which means literally "saying everything," was traditionally used to describe the activity of certain individuals who addressed the city or the monarch and confronted them with difficult truths. It was, generally, a political category. It was Socrates, according to Foucault, who for the first time extended the concept and the practice of *parrhêsia* to the communication between individuals, one of whom—the truth-teller—is usually (as was often the case in the political context as well) of a lower rank than the other. This confrontation of individuals constitutes a new, different mode of truth-telling: it is the truth-telling associated not with politics but with what we have come to know as philosophy. In the person of Socrates, philosophy emerged as the activity through which one individual confronts another with an important but not often welcome truth.

Philosophy, according to Foucault's interpretation, began not so much as an effort to present some general doctrines about the world or our knowledge of it: its purpose was, rather, to change people's lives on an individual level. The view that philosophy was in ancient times primarily a way of life and not a purely theoretical activity has been forcefully expressed by Pierre Hadot, who had a considerable influence on Foucault's own thought. Needless to say, theory was never far away and very often closer than Hadot believed. The Greek philosophers, from Socrates to the Neoplatonists (with the possible exception of the Skeptics), were generally committed to many doctrinal views, but those were often instruments in their effort to live the good life and not purely objects of pursuit in their own right.[14] Eventually the philosophical life was pursued not so much by individuals on their own but by members of distinct schools.[15] But Socrates, at least in the *Apology* (23c2–7, 33a5–b8), insists that he never established a school and that he undertook his divine mission completely by himself. He addressed individuals individually and only as individuals.

The first feature of Socrates' mission, then, is his individual attempt to confront other individuals with some potentially unpleasant truths about themselves. In the *Apology*, Socrates describes his practice in general terms, though he also exemplifies it by telling the court a number of things that please them not at all. In the *Laches*, the actual practice of *parrhêsia* becomes a central theme.[16]

Socrates' philosophical truth-telling exhibits three crucial features. First, its origin is very traditional: it springs from a divine source, the Delphic oracle, which said that no one was wiser than he (*Ap.* 20e6–21a8). What is not traditional, however, is Socrates' reaction to the oracle. He does not either wait for its fulfillment or try to make an effort to interpret it and then avoid it—that is what happens, for example, in the *Oedipus Rex* and the *Ion*.[17] Socrates' reaction to the oracle consists in a search ($\zeta\acute{\eta}\tau\eta\sigma\iota\varsigma$) and a test; in fact, the word he applies to his treatment of the oracle is the very same word ($\dot{\epsilon}\lambda\acute{\epsilon}\gamma\chi\epsilon\iota\nu$) that refers to his usual dialectical practice of refutation, the elenchus. Socrates, Foucault claims, does not interpret the oracle; he discusses it in order to determine whether or not it is true (20–22).[18]

Second, the test to which Socrates puts the oracle consists in his examining ($\dot{\epsilon}\xi\epsilon\tau\acute{a}\zeta\epsilon\iota\nu$) his fellow citizens to determine whether in fact they surpass him in wisdom. If anyone does, then the oracle will have been refuted (20b9–c2). Testing the oracle is therefore testing the souls of the Athenians. It is an effort to see what they do and do not know, especially about themselves, a confrontation of their souls with Socrates's own, which therefore becomes, in Foucault's word, the touchstone ($\beta\acute{a}\sigma\alpha\nu o\varsigma$) by which their own metal is tested.[19]

Third, Socrates' test of the oracle, which consists in the elenchus, produces great hostility, including the charges that are about to bring him to his death.[20] But the dangers of his mission do not in any way prevent Socrates from persevering in it. A crucial feature, then, of Socratic *parrhêsia* is that the risk of death, the risk that (he had said) prevented him from playing a political role is also at the very heart of his own enterprise: one should remain at one's appointed task "and risk danger, taking nothing into account, neither death nor anything else, aside from what is shameful" (*Ap.* 28d8–10). Foucault, who defines *parrhêsia* as "the courage of truth . . . the courage of speaking truly," describes Socrates as a soldier who remains always at his post, defending himself and his fellow citizens (26–27).

The importance of *parrhêsia*, then, is the first central feature of Socrates' mission. But *parrhêsia* has a specific purpose, and that purpose constitutes the mission's second feature. That purpose, Foucault claims, is to attend to his fellow citizens like a father or an older brother in order to show them that what is important is not money or reputation but the care of themselves (ἐπιμελεῖσθαι ἑαυτοῦ, 31b4–5; cf. 36c5–7)—not a concern for the world but for wisdom, truth, and for their own soul (φρόνησις, ἀλήθεια, ψυχή, 29e1). Socrates' purpose is to make people care for themselves. And Foucault defines such care as the use of one's reason in order to find out who one is and how one can be best (28).

The divine voice that prevented Socrates from practicing politics, therefore, marks an immensely important distinction. It sets on one side traditional, political *parrhêsia*, the public practice of telling one's rulers or fellow citizens a truth they might not want to hear and for which they might punish the truth-teller. It sets on the other a different, more private practice of telling the truth, which, as Socrates' fate itself testifies, is equally risky and dangerous (31). As Foucault sees it, Socrates' divine voice inaugurates the practice of philosophy.

Socratic truth-telling is different from other modes of establishing the truth: from prophecy, from the wisdom of the sage, and from the teaching of the expert. Unlike the prophet, the diviner, or the ordinary person who receives an oracle, Socrates, as we have seen, does not take divine communications for granted. Unlike the sage, who intervenes only when necessary, Socrates, so to speak, never leaves his post.[21] Most important, unlike the expert, Socrates does not transmit what he knows, or thinks, or pretends to know to others. He has no knowledge to communicate. As Foucault puts it, he shows courageously to others that they do *not* know and that they must attend to themselves: "If I attend to you," Foucault writes, uncannily identifying his own voice with that of Socrates as he does throughout these lectures, "it is not in order to transmit to you the knowledge you lack, but so that, having realized that you know nothing, you will learn thereby to care for yourselves" (35–36).[22]

We have seen that Foucault reads the *Apology*, the *Crito*, and the *Phaedo* together, as a single "cycle" concerning Socrates' death. He establishes a brilliant thematic link between these texts by connecting the theme of care (ἐπιμέλεια) with the idea of the family. We have seen that in the *Apology* Socrates refers to himself as a father or older brother of his fellow citizens (31b4–5). But the family motif appears again at the very end of the dialogue, when, after having been condemned to die, Socrates bids his judges farewell. He asks them for a favor. He wants his fellow citizens to treat his sons just as he himself has treated his fellow citizens: they are to scold them if they care for anything more than *aretê* (ἐπιμελεῖσθαι ἀρετῆς) and to reproach them if they do not care for the proper things (οὐκ ἐπιμελοῦνται ὧν δεῖ) or if they believe they are praiseworthy when they are not (41e1–7). Socrates wants his fellow citizens to act, in their turn, as fathers or older brothers to his own children, to take on, individually, for his family the role he has taken on for them.

In the *Crito*, the family motif first appears in Crito's argument in favor of Socrates' escape on the grounds that if he were to die he would be betraying his own children. He would be relinquishing his responsibility toward them because he would no longer be able to make sure that they were being brought up properly: "A good and brave man must continue to do what he originally chose, especially one who claims that he cared (ἐπιμελεῖσθαι) for *aretê* throughout his whole life" (45d6–8). In the course of his long reply to Crito, Socrates eventually shows that his just death is better for his children than his disgraceful survival. Moreover, one of his main reasons for refusing to escape is that, in his famous personification of the laws of the city, he argues that he owes them even more respect than he owes his own parents. The laws have cared for him even more than his own parents ever could and they therefore do not deserve the violence his escape would do them. The city is his true family (49c–52d).

The theme of the family also appears in the *Phaedo*, when, close to its end, Crito asks Socrates for his last wishes concerning his children or any other matter: what can they do to please him (115b1–4)? Socrates replies that they should do what he has always been telling them to do: "If you care for yourselves [ὑμῶν αὐτῶν ἐπιμελούμενοι] you will please me and mine and yourselves the most, even if you don't see the point right now" (115b5–8).

Socrates' last wish, prompted by his concern for his family, is that his friends care for themselves; only in that way will they be able to care for his children or, for that matter, for anyone else. The care of the self, as I have argued, precedes, or perhaps constitutes, the care of the other. And Foucault finds that the theme of the care of the self also appears, in a more subtle form, both at the very beginning of the *Apology* and at the very end of the *Phaedo*. For in the first full sentence of the *Apology*, Socrates says that his accusers have spoken so artfully that he almost forgot who he actually was (ὀλίγον ἐμαυτοῦ ἐπελαθόμην, 17a3). If oratory can provoke self-forgetting, then Socratic *parrhêsia*, his plain and direct truth-telling, is a way of finding out who one is; and that, Foucault argues, is the goal of the care of the self. The opening of the *Apology* is therefore, he claims, a "negative overture" to the theme of the care of the self, while the closing of the *Phaedo* is a negative coda. For Socrates' very last words to Crito, after his statement about the sacrifice, are "Do not forget" (μὴ ἀμελήσετε) — a word that is derived from the very same root from which "care"

($ἐπιμέλεια$) and its cognates are derived. The term therefore harks back, in a negative way, to Socrates' overarching concern with care, particularly with the care of the self.

In addition to the central place of the care of the self within it, Foucault's image of Socrates consists of two other essential elements. The first is his emphasis on the courage required to tell others an unpleasant truth about themselves (in Socrates' case, the truth that they are ignorant about the most important things) to motivate them to determine that truth for themselves and to act accordingly. *Parrhêsia*, as we have said, is an issue not only in the *Apology* but also in the *Laches*. The latter dialogue, which addresses the education of, or care for ($ἐπιμέλεια$), the sons of two well-to-do Athenians often appeals to the idea of speaking frankly, of saying exactly what is on one's mind, both by the word *parrhêsia* itself (178a4, 179c1–2, 189a1) and in more general terms (187e7–188c3). The *Laches* also concerns courage both because the definition of that virtue is its subject and because, according to Foucault, courage keeps getting displayed in a number of contexts within it.[23] Courage is central to Foucault's image of Socrates.

The second element in that image is Foucault's insistence on Socrates' usefulness to his city, on his importance to his fellows, on his benefits to his friends. Socratic *parrhêsia*, Foucault claims, is good for the city as a whole. And, mixing once again his voice with the voice of Socrates almost as if he were assuming Socrates' role himself, Foucault says: "In urging you to care for yourselves, I am being useful to the whole city. And if I try to protect my life, it is precisely in the city's interest that I am doing it; it is in the city's interest to protect true discourse, the courageous truth-telling which urges the citizens to care for themselves" (37).

I believe that Foucault emphasized Socrates' usefulness, which Nietzsche had derided in the most biting terms,[24] and which Foucault may well have derived from his extensive reading of Xenophon,[25] for two reasons. The first is that Foucault, who gradually came to see his writing as part of philosophy understood as the art of living, also believed that philosophers of his sort, self-fashioners who create new possibilities for life, are directly useful to the public. They are particularly useful to excluded, oppressed groups that have not been able to speak in their own voice so far—he, in particular, was primarily (though by no means exclusively) concerned with homosexuals. And he took his project, his care for his own self, to be to develop a voice that others like him might be able to appropriate in their own terms, use it for their own purposes, and through it care for themselves in the way their own selves and particular circumstances required. He wrote, after all, that he was trying to develop "a way to work on ourselves" that would allow us "to invent—I don't mean discover—a way of being that is still improbable."[26] To understand how Foucault reached such a position, we must take a look at his work as a whole.

It is worth following this longer path, even though it will postpone my examination of Foucault's second reason for thinking that Socrates was very beneficial to his contemporaries. My view that Foucault belongs to the individualist strain of the tradition of philosophy as the art of living is not uncontroversial. It took Foucault a long time—most of his life—to come to think of himself as a philosopher who had always been concerned with the care of the self and whose project, despite its general applications, was essentially individual. Many will disagree with my interpretation, especially since it depends centrally on the notion that change is in general both possible and desirable—a notion Foucault was charged with denying during most of his career.

For many years, it is true, Foucault regarded the very idea of change, of making something radically new either of society as a whole or of a single individual, with the deepest suspicion. In many of his early works, he argued that every effort to reform an institution—the clinic, the madhouse, the prison—is doomed to perpetuate it. In *Madness and Civilization*, for example, he argued that Samuel Tuke's replacement of the prisonlike confinement of the insane in the asylums of the early nineteenth century with a more humane mode of treatment simply produced a new prison, a new form of punishment. Part of Tuke's reforms depended on holding the insane responsible for their actions; but that, Foucault argued, was to treat them no better, perhaps worse, than before. Leg irons and the bonds of conscience are one: "Liberation of the insane, abolition of punishment, constitution of a human milieu—these are only justifications. The real operations were different. In fact, Tuke created an asylum where he substituted for the free terror of madness the stifling anguish of responsibility; fear no longer reigned on the other side of the prison gates, it now raged under the seals of conscience."[27] "The soul," he once wrote, reversing the Platonic formula that, during the last months of his life, he denied Socrates could ever have accepted, "is the prison of the body."[28]

Two central premises govern Foucault's thought. The first, which he derived from Nietzsche and never abandoned, is that most of the situations in which we find ourselves are products of history, though we are convinced they are natural facts. This prevents us from seeing that our particular views, habits, and institutions are contingent: just as there was a time when they did not exist, so there could be a time when they will no longer be part of our world. And though many of his specific historical claims have been disputed,[29] Foucault still had an uncanny ability to discern history and contingency where others had seen only nature and necessity. He was a master of exhibiting the emergence of radically new objects—insanity, illness, even the human individual—where others detected only a change in the appearance of unchanging realities.

Foucault's second premise, which he modified in his later years, was a relentless suspiciousness of "progress." He was always able—indeed, eager—to see the dark side of every step toward the light, to grasp the price at which every advance had to be bought. And he believed that the price was never a bargain. Whether it was Tuke's and Pinel's treatment of the insane or the penal reforms of the early nineteenth century, which exchanged physical torture for constant surveillance, Foucault always displayed one horror replaced by another.

The central idea those two premises generated was that both individuals and groups were parts of a vast network over which they had little or no control. Foucault tried to describe that network; he exhibited its historical basis and he hinted darkly that it was self-perpetuating. Reversing Clausewitz's formula, he sometimes claimed that politics is war continued by other means and that power, the nature of which was one of his most central concerns throughout his writing, is "a sort of generalized war which assumes at particular moments the forms of peace and the State. . . . Peace would then be a form of war, and the State a means of waging it."[30]

Foucault's early views were to a great extent consciously opposed to the Existentialist humanism of Jean-Paul Sartre,[31] for whom Foucault never had any kind words: "When I was young," he once said, "he was the one—along with everything he represented, the terrorism of *Les Temps modernes*—from whom I wanted to free myself."[32] Sartre had argued that human beings are the ultimate subjects of their actions, free sovereign agents, even if freedom itself is not the product of choice: "Man," he had written in a famous formulation, "is condemned to be free."[33] Foucault detested that view and argued that, far from being free, human individuals are not even the agents and guides but merely the creatures of their own history. The "subject" is itself the product of historical forces beyond conscious control, and different conditions produce different sorts of subjects. In his early works, Foucault claimed that what we are today is a creation of the last two hundred years, brought about by the specific oppressive arrangements he discussed in books like *Madness and Civilization*,

The Birth of the Clinic, and *Discipline and Punish* and by the changes in the human sciences he outlined in *The Order of Things*. His own formulation, which is becoming as famous as Sartre's, was this:

Man is an invention of recent date. And one perhaps nearing its end. If those arrangements were to disappear as they appeared, if some event of which we can at the moment do no more than sense the possibility—without knowing either what its forms will be or what it promises—were to cause them to crumble, as the ground of Classical thought [beginning in the 16th century] did, at the end of the eighteenth century, then one can certainly wager that man would be erased, like a face drawn in sand at the edge of the sea.[34]

Foucault's position was extremely radical. His suspiciousness of individualism led him to think that even "the author," a special case of the "subject" and the individual, is a recent, oppressive invention, better left alone and undiscussed. Far from being the origin of the meaning and value of a literary or philosophical work, the author is for Foucault a creation that aims at preventing literature from being read, as he thought it ought, in radically novel ways, unconstrained by considerations of genre, intention, or historical plausibility: "The author is the principle of thrift in the proliferation of meaning."[35]

This idea is easily misunderstood. "The death of the author" does not imply that writers do not exist, that books get written by themselves, any more than "the death of Man" implies that people are not real. Foucault's argument is that certain apparently natural ways of treating both books and human beings are specific to particular historical periods. In particular, literary and philosophical works, which are open to radically divergent readings, have been treated as the products of a special kind of writer—the author—who (unlike, say, the writer of a modern scientific treatise) is accorded ultimate power over their meaning. By and large, we now read works of literature and philosophy to find out what their authors meant in composing them. But what, Foucault asks, is the real justification of this comparatively recent practice? The real aim of this conception of authorship, he answers, is not so much to glorify an individual (though it does do that) as to create a mechanism "by which one impedes the free circulation, the free manipulation, the free composition, decomposition, and recomposition of fiction."[36]

Foucault's view of the historical, contingent, and ultimately oppressive nature of both "the subject" in general and the author in particular, his conviction that history is governed by the blind operations of impersonal powers, makes it difficult to see how he could ever come to the position he seems to have adopted in his final lectures on Socrates. How could individuals who inhabit the kind of world he had described throughout most of his life "care for themselves" and produce something with which they could be justifiably satisfied? Still, in rough terms at least, we can trace a clear trajectory from his early to his late views and connect them with one another.

Like Nietzsche and Georges Bataille, Foucault was always fascinated by what an individual or a social group has to exclude and suppress to form a positive conception of itself. He argued that our conception of what we are like as individuals or "subjects" depends essentially on excluding and controlling whole classes of people who do not fit the categories the Enlightenment developed precisely in order to establish what it would count as "normal." Foucault believed that the mechanisms used to understand and control marginalized and ostracized groups were also essential to the understanding, control, and even the constitution of "normal" individuals. For example, the constant surveillance of prisoners that replaced physical torture as a result of penal reform was eventually applied to schoolchildren, factory workers, and population groups as a whole. In fact, it is today becoming the norm for the treatment of average citizens, whose police records, medical reports, and credit ratings are constantly becoming increasingly more detailed and more easily available. What counts as an individual, who one is, is whatever our many varieties of information regarding people describe.

Such information is always produced through the exercise of power—the power of the state, the medical profession, the institution of banking. Who we are, therefore, on Foucault's account is itself the result of the exercise of power. In that sense, power is "productive" and the other side of knowledge: "It is not possible for power to be exercised without knowledge, it is impossible for knowledge not to engender power."[37] That is what Foucault meant by his compound term "power/knowledge": "Power produces knowledge . . . power and knowledge directly imply one another. . . . [T]here is no power relation without the correlative constitution of a field of knowledge, nor any knowledge that does not presuppose and constitute at the same time power relations."[38] To know something is to have power over it; to have power over something, we must know what it is. Knowledge is, indeed, power; but power is, no less, itself knowledge.

Foucault's was a vision in which everything is paid for. "Ah, reason, seriousness, mastery over the affects, the whole somber thing called reflection, all these prerogatives and showpieces of man," Nietzsche had written; "how dearly they have been bought! how much blood and cruelty lie at the bottom of all 'good things'!"[39] But Nietzsche did not believe that nothing can ever change for the better. Eventually, Foucault came to agree with him. But for many years, partly owing to the influence of Heidegger's uncompromising disdain of modernity and partly owing to his own political commitments, Foucault found it impossible to believe that any change in what he regarded as an essentially corrupt era and political system could produce any improvement. Power might be exercised in different forms, but its amount and, more important, its quality remained constant. Indeed, as the expressions of power came to be increasingly cloaked in the vocabulary of humanism and humanitarianism, the conditions of oppression actually became worse. For the benevolent appearance of modern power makes it that much more difficult to resist.

In his early works, Foucault studied the "archaeology" of the human sciences—psychiatry, medicine, linguistics, economics, and biology.[40] He investigated the rules underlying and determining their practice. He showed that these rules often underwent radical shifts ("ruptures") that could be explained neither by the usual appeals to universal scientific progress nor by the innovations of great individuals. Foucault's aim seemed to be to subvert the objective status of the human sciences, their claim to arrive at an independent truth, and to expose them instead as a tool of power, a means for creating and controlling the modern "subject."[41]

The work Foucault undertook from the late 1960s to the late 1970s, which coincided with his activist political period, was even more disturbing. During those years he shifted his attention from the human sciences to the disciplinary practices of the nineteenth century and to the direct analysis of the power relations that he believed traverse everything we do and provide no possibility for escape. The "genealogical" researches of this second period of his writing were his most pessimistic. They were intended to show that everything we take as orderly and rational (the prison, the court system, the school, the statistical information government collects about its citizens) is a product of domination and subjugation, in short, of power; and that no system can be created from which domination and subjugation can ever be even partially absent.

It was one of Foucault's most central ideas that power is not only something exercised by a central authority and thus primarily an agent of prohibition. This "juridical" conception of power is at best part of what power is and does. More important, power is a productive agent. It is not exercised by subjects; it creates them. Though power flows through individuals, it is most often not under their control. On the contrary, established relationships of power, despite the intentions of those who try to control or modify them, reassert themselves in constantly changing forms. Efforts to humanize, to rationalize, even to renounce power result only in the exercise of new forms of it—in the creation of new ways of knowing what individuals or "subjects" are, indeed, in the creation of new individuals or "subjects." People who are subject to the sovereign's absolute and total vengeance, though only when they act in deeply unusual ways, are radically different from people whose every movement is constantly observed and catalogued by minor functionaries, themselves observed by someone else.[42] New forms of knowledge and new forms of control, of power, thus go together. That is why Foucault refused, throughout that period, to offer alternatives to the "intolerable" situations he exposed in his writings and in his political activities. Any alternative would simply perpetuate power relations.

For more than twenty years, Foucault seemed dedicated to exposing the seamy underside of the Enlightenment, conceding to it no positive accomplishment and refusing any vision of a better future. He explicitly denied that reason can transcend time and accident and lead us out of the impasse he thought was confronting us, since reason itself is an instrument and part of the program of the Enlightenment. Reliance on rationality, too, constituted a form of the exercise of power that determined what sort of people the individuals envisaged by the Enlightenment would be.

Distant and ironic, an anatomist but not a physician, Foucault seemed to withdraw more and more into a sort of solitary philosophical despair. As Maurice Blanchot wrote, in *The Archaeology of Knowledge* (and in all the works of Foucault's middle period) "you will be surprised to rediscover . . . many a formula from negative theology. Foucault invests all his talent in describing with sublime phrases what it is he rejects: 'It's not . . . , nor is it . . . , nor is it for that matter . . . ,' so that there remained almost nothing for him to say" in his own person.[43] Amazingly prolific as he was, Foucault seemed condemned to a peculiar kind of philosophical silence. His critics did not miss that point, and his "nihilism" was widely criticized.

And yet matters were not quite so simple. As early as 1961 Michel Serres had noticed something very important in *Folie et déraison*, which he wrote was not simply a scientific treatise on madness but "also a cry." Serres realized that Foucault's detachment, forbidding language, and abstract formulations could not hide his own deep feelings for those who have been treated as insane: "At the heart of the meticulous erudition of historical inquiry, a deep love circulates . . . for this obscure population in which the infinitely close, the other oneself, is recognized. . . . Consequently, this transparent geometry is the pathetic language of men who undergo the greatest of tortures, that of being cornered, of disgrace, of exile, of quarantine, ostracism, and excommunication."[44]

Serres's description is true of everything Foucault wrote on the disenfranchised—the poor, the delinquent, the prison population, the sexually deviant, factory workers, even children attending the rigorous schools of the nineteenth century. But Foucault's "deep love" seemed to exhaust itself in letting the voices of these groups be heard. He exposed their plight, invited his readers to react to it with horror, but had nothing to say about eliminating or reducing it.[45]

In the early 1970s, Foucault began a work on the history of sexuality. The first volume in the series argued that, contrary to common views, the period between the sixteenth and the nineteenth centuries did not so much repress sexuality as it produced, literally, an explosion of writing about it. Foucault asked "not, Why are we repressed? but rather, Why do we say, with so much passion and so much resentment against our most recent past, against our present, and against ourselves, that we are repressed?"[46] His thesis was that the proliferation of talk about sexuality, especially concerning children and perversion, brought new aspects of sexuality into existence. Instead of being repressed, sexuality was to a great extent *created* in the nineteenth century, and with it new capacities for understanding and controlling human beings—that is, new types of human beings—came into existence. The connections with the approach of *Discipline and Punish* were clear.[47]

After writing the introductory volume, however, Foucault put the project aside. Or rather, he began to think about it in drastically new terms. The next two volumes were totally different from what had been earlier announced in subject, style, and approach. They appeared only eight years later, a few days before his death, at the time when he was addressing Socrates' dedicated service to his city and his effort to change himself and his contemporaries. Foucault's own change, obviously enough, was enormously radical. His unqualified vilification of the Enlightenment was replaced by a serious if qualified respect. In a late piece entitled, like Kant's, "What Is Enlightenment?" he argued that the project of the Enlightenment is still not over. Following Kant, he urged that we engage in a constant critique of ourselves and the world; departing from him, however, he claimed that our approach must be thoroughly historicist. Instead of trying to establish those unchanging and universal human features that give rational thought dominion over tradition and prejudice, we must ask the question, "In what is given to us as universal, necessary, obligatory, what place is occupied by whatever is singular, contingent, and the product of arbitrary constraints?"[48] That, of course, was one of his old ideas, but Foucault's discussion strikes a startling new note. Our critique, he wrote, "will be genealogical in the sense that it will not deduce from the form of what we are what it is impossible for us to do and to know; but it will separate out, from the contingency that has made us what we are, the possibility of no longer being, doing, or thinking, what we are, do, or think. . . . It is seeking to give new impetus, as far and wide and possible, to the undefined work of freedom".[49]

"The undefined work of freedom": these words represent a stunning reversal for the philosopher who had earlier argued that the Enlightenment's reforms did not in reality liberate the spirit but subjugated the body in darker and more efficient ways. Foucault had clearly come to a new view of human possibilities.

Why the change? My own view is that Foucault's earlier pessimism was partly due to his inability to imagine who would profit from new social and individual formations. At times he wrote as if there were no such "who," taking perhaps his own "dissolution" of the subject too literally: if individuals are simply the playthings of power, nothing they do can produce a real, lasting change in a continual war of forces beyond their conscious control. But Foucault began to see that the situation was more complicated, partly, I believe, as a result of his increasingly frequent trips to America. In the United States, the full complexity of Nietzsche's slogan "Beyond good and evil" became clear to him. He grasped its double implication: not only—as he had thought so far—that everything good has its bad side; but also that everything bad can turn out to be good in the right circumstances. Every original virtue, as Nietzsche had said, had once been a vice. And out of the sometimes silly, often valuable, and to him always fascinating self-absorption of his California friends, colleagues, and students, Foucault formulated his deepest and most important idea, the idea of the care of the self. Among the barrage of numberless obsessions with improving this or that aspect of one's personality, Foucault discerned the possibility for the serious work on the self to which he devoted his last years.

But hadn't Foucault simply eliminated the very concept of the self during his earlier antihumanist phase? Was he now rejecting all that he stood for? Not quite. Blanchot had once again read him correctly: "Were not his principles more complex than his official discourse with its striking formulations led one to think? For example, it is accepted as a certainty that Foucault got rid of, purely and simply, the notion of the subject: no more oeuvre, no more author, no more creative writing. But things are not that simple. The subject does not disappear; rather its excessively determined unity is put in question."[50] Foucault sometimes wrote as if the self is a fiction, but in fact he had never denied that the subject exists. What he had tried to show is how different periods constitute subjects differently and how the subject is not the final ground of thought and history but their complex product.

The self may not be not the final reality underlying history, but it is not exactly a fiction, either; and though it is not ultimately (or "metaphysically") free, it is not exactly a puppet. Moreover, every form of power, in Foucault's new view, contains the potential of its own undoing, since every prohibition, he came to realize, creates the possibility of a new transgression. Since power is productive, the subjects it produces, being themselves forms of power, can be productive in their own right.

That the subject is a construct of history implies that there is no such thing as a true self, remaining always the same underneath the changes of appearance. Foucault never abandoned his belief that such a "true self" is a chimera. Instead, that belief became the unexpected foundation for his most important idea. He returned yet again to Nietzsche, who had written that "we want to be the poets of our lives" (GS 299; 3:538) and began to think of life and art together: "From the idea that the self is not given to us, I think that there is only one practical consequence: we have to create ourselves as a work of art. . . . Couldn't everyone's life become a work of art? Why should the lamp or the house be an art object, but not our life?"[51]

Foucault's "rediscovery" of the self and the art of living was accompanied by two other important developments. One was his increasing public acknowledgment of his homosexuality. He came to see that if movements like gay liberation were to be successful—as Foucault truly hoped they would be—he had to find a way out of his earlier pessimism about the finality of power.[52] The second was his interest in Greek attitudes toward pederasty in particular and friendship and pleasure in general, and in their place in the ethical enterprise of the classical and later pagan world, in the ancient understanding of the good person.[53]

In ancient ethical practice, Foucault found a wide range of different techniques, ranging from practical exercises to self-examination to the extensive writing of daily diaries, all aiming to make oneself into a kind of person of which one could be proud. These techniques constituted what he called, following his ancient authorities, "the care of the self." He connected these instruments of morality explicitly to medical thought and practice and used something approaching the language of therapy regarding them. He became, like Freud, supremely interested in the correct management of pleasure. But unlike Freud, he did not believe in repression; he denied the existence of natural or historically constant needs denied by social constraints or individual pathology. More important, he believed that the care of the self was not a process of discovering who one truly is but of inventing and improvising who one can be. Foucault's model for the care of the self was the creation of art.[54]

Art would seem to provide an unlikely model for Foucault's thought. Talk of artistic creation always provokes thoughts of genius, unlimited freedom, absolute spontaneity—the very ideas of which Foucault remained resolutely suspicious throughout his life. But in the end there is no contradiction. For creativity, too, is always historically situated. Not everything is possible at every time. Like everyone else, artists have to work within the limitations of their traditions. Creation demands rearranging the given; innovation requires manipulating the dated. Lives, seen aesthetically, are no different: the artistic creation of the self, as both Montaigne and Nietzsche testify, must necessarily use the materials with which one is always and already faced.

In Foucault's case, the most important materials he had to work with during the last ten years of his life were his erudition and his homosexuality. In particular, he became progressively more fascinated with the sadomasochistic subcultures of New York and San Francisco. Was this an adventitious event, better left out of an examination of his work, or was it integrally connected with his philosophical writing, as James Miller argued in *The Passion of Michel Foucault*? And did Foucault succeed in integrating it into the life he constructed for himself?

The answer is that he did. Reversing yet another received view, Foucault argued that the traditional picture, according to which the tolerant Greek attitude toward pederasty was replaced by centuries of Christian repression, was crude if not totally inaccurate. Austerity was a constant concern, and self-control a regular goal, from the fourth century BC to the third century AD. But the forms of discipline, the reasons for which it was undertaken, and the objects in relation to which it was practiced changed radically over time. They could therefore be adapted to still other situations, perhaps even to Foucault's own.

Foucault came to believe that he might combine ancient ethics (which "was not a question of giving a pattern of behavior for everybody [but] a personal choice for a small elite"[55]) with the stuff of his own life and thereby fashion a self of his own. In volumes 2 and 3 of *The History of Sexuality*, he showed that the ancient world was centrally interested in the control of pleasure by means of the serious and concerted effort, which he rightly called *askêsis* or "asceticism." The purpose of the complex exercises[56] of which *askêsis* consisted was not to deny the pleasures—of sex, of food, of worldly ambition—but to avoid excess. The point was not to be mastered by pleasure but to become its master and therefore to become the master of oneself as well. Asceticism is not the repression but the regulation of pleasure. Its objective is not denial but satisfaction. The conventional ascetic ideal of denying pleasure altogether is not a fact of nature but the product of centuries of Christian theorizing.[57]

In the third and final period of his writing, Foucault turned from the power exercised on, and forming, individuals to the power individuals exercised upon, and through which they formed, themselves. That was part of what he meant by "ethics"—the subject that preoccupied him during the last years of his life. Morality, Foucault argued, is not exhausted by our relations to others, by codes of moral behavior that govern the interaction of various individuals and groups with one another. It also concerns the ways in which individuals relate to and regulate themselves—the ways in which we practice self-government and at the same time constitute ourselves as the moral subjects of our own desires and actions.[58] Ethics is the care of the self.

At the same time that Foucault turned to thinking about ethics, he became more outspoken about his own personal attitudes toward the theoretical issues he was addressing. He also turned explicitly to the Nietzschean project of fashioning himself as a subject, of creating himself as the author he in fact became. This is less banal than it sounds. Not all who write books are thereby authors, and not all that writers write resonates within their own lives.[59] To become an author in this sense is to be unified and original; to produce nothing less than a new model of how life can be lived, a new art of living. Foucault applied his historicism to himself, unifying his life with his thought, and enlarged our understanding of what a "subject" can be, much in the way that great artists enlarge our sense of what art can accomplish.

Foucault had always tried to allow the voices of excluded groups to sound out on their own. Toward the end of his life, he included his own voice explicitly among them. He tried, as James Miller has argued, to put together his literary and philosophical gifts and ideas, his homosexuality and sense of exclusion, his strong political commitments, his dangerously close lifelong relationship with madness, and even his fascination with death into a coherent and beautiful whole.[60] In particular, Foucault's sado-masochism, about which he became increasingly outspoken in his last years, proved in the end to be a kind of blessing in his life, a perfect il-lustration of Nietzsche's idea that the value of everything depends on the contribution it makes to the whole to which it belongs. It provided the occasion to experience relations of power as a source of delight. It was the theater of power, in which discipline could bring happiness and dom-ination itself be dominated, partly by submitting to pain voluntarily, partly by controlling its intensity, partly by exchanging roles.[61]

Such freedom was unprecedented in Foucault's earlier experience and not completely warranted by his earlier thought. Having written about the ways the self had been created in history, mostly by the power exer-cised on us by others, Foucault undertook to exert power upon himself and, in Nietzsche's words, to "become who he was" on his own. He wrote about control and exercised it on himself in what became a single project. The point is philosophical, not biographical.[62] Foucault extended the lim-its of what could count as an admirable human life, even if his was a life of which few might approve. But, as with all works of art, approval and admiration often do not go together.

To some, Foucault's personal, aestheticist turn may seem like an ab-dication of responsibility, an indulgence for the sake of one man's hap-piness, an abandonment of politics. But it is not. In the cases of great in-dividuals like Socrates, Montaigne, Nietzsche, and Foucault, the private and the public, the aesthetic and the political, are as entangled with one another as the "life" and the "work." It is by transforming themselves that such philosophers effect the greatest changes in the lives of others, for good or ill. By turning to the self in his later works and by living in a way consonant with his ideas, Foucault finally managed to express his "deep love" for the excluded and the marginalized in practical terms. He made himself into a model of autonomy, of a voice of one's own. Politics, as he might have put it, begins with the care of the self. His private project was of public significance. That was just what he claimed Socrates—the only philosopher Foucault ever discussed as an individual in his own right and not simply as a source of ideas—had been telling his own uncom-prehending contemporaries. That (to remind ourselves why we under-took this long discussion) is the first reason Foucault insisted on Socrates' usefulness to his contemporaries.

But Foucault had a second reason for thinking Socrates was useful to Athens, and that was that he read the *Apology*, the *Crito*, and the *Phaedo* as if they formed a single unit. For though Socrates does make a point of his importance to Athens in the *Apology*, it is primarily in the *Phaedo* that Plato gives that importance an explicit and detailed content.

In the *Phaedo*, Plato attributes to Socrates an articulate view of the nature of philosophy and its relationship to the immortal soul and to the corrupt body. Plato makes Socrates speak of the proper objects (the Forms) to which philosophy is directed and supplies him with an epistemological theory (Recollection) that accounts for our knowledge of them. He supplies him with a method for investigating change, a "resort to argument" ($\kappa\alpha\tau\alpha\phi\upsilon\gamma\grave{\eta}$ $\epsilon\grave{\iota}\varsigma$ $\lambda\acute{o}\gamma\upsilon\varsigma$, 99e5) that competes directly with the methods of the natural philosophers, whose interests Socrates had completely disavowed in the *Apology*. Socrates' last wish in the *Phaedo*, that his friends care for themselves, makes the content of that care clear: it is the complex practice of philosophy as the dialogue itself has defined and exemplified it; it is the "preparation for death" and all it implies.

But what is the content of the care of the self in the *Apology*? What is the only activity in which Socrates urges his fellow citizens to engage? It is the elenchus, the constant questioning of one's views as one questions the views of others. The elenchus—Foucault is absolutely right—requires a tremendous amount of courage. But its usefulness to the city as a whole is more disputable, especially since part of Socrates' mission has been to urge the Athenians not to attend to the affairs of the city before they attend to themselves.[63] One can argue that such care of the self will ultimately make both the citizens and the city as a whole better.[64] But when we recall the permanently unfinished state of Socrates' elenctic project, we may wonder whether a life devoted to the elenchus is at all compatible with life in a political community.[65]

In the *Apology*, Plato makes Socrates interpret the elenchus as his effort to improve his fellow citizens. But the fact remains that through the elenchus Socrates primarily and in good conscience tries to find someone who knows what *aretê* is. And he does this primarily for his own sake: if he can convince himself that he has found such a person, he can also be sure that from then on he will act rightly in all circumstances. For, as we have seen, to recognize that someone is good one must know what goodness is, which in turn guarantees that one actually is good, given Socrates' view that virtue is knowledge. Socrates welcomes others as companions in his search, he urges them to join him, but (unlike the Plato of the middle and late works) he makes no effort to demonstrate that his mode of life is best for everyone. Socrates' primary object of care is his own self, his own soul, not the souls of others. That is not to say, of course, that

Socrates disregards others, that he does not care for them. But to care for others is not the same as to devote oneself to them.

It is true that other people became what we may call Socrates' disciples — but the elenctic dialogues contain no such evidence. In the *Apology*, Socrates strongly denies that he has any disciples like those that surround him in the *Phaedo*. He admits that young men follow him around Athens, but he insists that all they learn from him seems to be how to use the elenchus to annoy their parents (23c2–7, 33a1–b8). The elenctic dialogues attribute to Socrates a negligible effect on his interlocutors. What is certainly true is that in a sense Socrates used his contemporaries for his own purpose — to understand the nature of *aretê* and to live the good life. We must not assume that "using" can have only negative connotations. It was naturally in Socrates' interest to find a person who possessed an understanding of *aretê* and to convince others to join him in his search. But his enterprise was in the most literal terms a care of the self — his own. In method, his project was essentially social: the elenchus cannot exist without those on whom it is practiced. In purpose, however, it was an essentially individual undertaking. Others might benefit from it, especially if, through Socrates' questioning, they came to realize they actually knew what *aretê* was and started living as that knowledge dictated. But in no case does anyone come to such knowledge. Socrates only managed to demonstrate to his interlocutors that they were ignorant of their ignorance. But, not being convinced, they did not follow his example and did not live in order to acquire that knowledge.

The elenchus required courage not so much because of the unpleasant truths Socrates revealed to his contemporaries. Most of the time he revealed nothing to them — not even their own ignorance — as he has revealed nothing to the generations that followed him. He needed courage because he asked his interlocutors to offer him their most valuable possessions — their views and their values, their own selves — and then consistently rejected them. He asked them to open their souls to him and let them know he did not like what he saw. He did not so much reveal to them their dark, shameful underside as refuse to accept their surface as his own, as a mode of life he could follow. He needed courage not only because he made his contemporaries face some difficult truths but mostly because he displayed his own disdain toward them.

But Michel Foucault made it his own life-work to reveal just that dark, shameful underside of the individuals and especially of the institutions that surrounded him. Where official ideology saw directed progress, he saw mindless change; where it found improvement, he discerned the exchange of one evil for another; where it proclaimed humanitarian reform, he detected the invention of new and unnoticed forms of cruelty. The courage the self he fashioned for himself required was different from the courage of Socrates. Like Nietzsche, Foucault became what he was by openly and explicitly denouncing the greatest accomplishments of his age. He felt he had to dislodge what was in place as the good and the true in order to find a place for himself, for his own truth and goodness. Nietzsche and Foucault were both essentially adversarial thinkers. And though both were great ironists, neither hid himself or his criticisms of his times with anything like Socrates' single-mindedness. Though Socrates was also clearly a critic of his times, he was far more reticent about what he rejected in his world. His irony covered him like the mantle he never wore. His main concern was to chart a path he could follow. That path led through, literally through, other people: he often discarded them once they were no longer useful to him.

Foucault emphasized the courage of Socratic *parrhêsia* because he was looking in Socrates for a model of his own manner of caring for himself. Like Nietzsche, he read Socrates as an adversarial thinker of his own sort. Unlike Nietzsche he did not feel he had to denounce him as the wrong kind of adversarial thinker. In fact, one of the most attractive features of Foucault's late lectures is his accommodation with Socrates. This emerges through the content and style of the lectures, which celebrate him with affection and kindness, but also through a feature to which I cannot stop returning: Foucault's speaking in Socrates' place, obliterating the lines that separate quotation, paraphrase, accepting another's views, putting words in another's mouth, and finally taking another's self as one's own.

But Montaigne's example shows that the project of fashioning the self does not necessarily require the opposition that Nietzsche and Foucault may have considered essential to it. To fashion a self, to become an individual, one has to do something that is both significant and very different from whatever has been done before. But that need not be accomplished only by objecting to the tenor of one's time. Montaigne fashioned himself by writing a new sort of book, breaking old conventions and establishing new ones: henceforth how one wrote and what one could write about would never be the same. And though Montaigne certainly did not approve of everything in his world, he was very much at home in it— which does not imply, of course, that one must be "at home on this earth" in order to fashion oneself. Becoming who one is has only one essential element: the rules for accomplishing it can be formulated only after each singular project has been completed, and they can be formulated and applied only once. Which is to say that the art of living has no rules, that there is no such thing as *the* art of living. There are only arts of living—many arts, recognizable only after they have already been practiced and after their products have been brought into being.

By reading the *Apology*, the *Crito*, and the *Phaedo* together, Foucault gave a fascinating twist to Nietzsche's interpretation of Socrates. Nietzsche, too, read Plato's early works along with the *Phaedo*. The otherworldliness of the latter made him think that Plato's early works were also otherworldly, and he concluded that Socrates had always been a "pessimist": "He had merely kept a cheerful mien while concealing all his life long his ultimate judgment, his inmost feeling. Socrates, Socrates *suffered life!*" (*GS* 340; 3:569–70). By contrast, the cheerfulness of Plato's early works prompted Foucault to find the same joy in the *Phaedo* and to refuse to believe that in that work Plato makes Socrates turn his back to life.

Perhaps more prosaic is my preference to separate the *Phaedo* from Plato's early works, to see it as the first in a series of efforts, continued, among others, by the Cynics, the Stoics, the Skeptics, the Neoplatonists, Montaigne, Kierkegaard, Nietzsche, and Foucault, to understand Socrates and to explain what made him what he was. Among the philosophers of the art of living we have discussed, Plato is the only one who is explicitly universalist: he uses various means already at his disposal and many he invents for the purpose—logic, metaphysics, epistemology, and ethical, aesthetic, and political theory—to articulate a single mode of life that is best for everyone. But one might also think that Plato's goal was to establish philosophy as a purely theoretical investigation of independently given problems, including the problem of knowledge, of the nature of things and persons, as well as the problem of the good life. That is the goal of most of the philosophy we recognize as such today.

Socrates gave rise to all these traditions. The first derives from those works of Plato that reflect Socrates but do not reflect on him, that present his mode of life as Plato saw it without an effort to interpret or systematize it. The second originates in those dialogues that not only reflect Socrates but also reflect on him. They suggest that Socrates' indistinct recollection of the eternal Forms allowed him to lead a good life, and they contain a set of guidelines for making sure that versions of Socrates, with knowledge and not mere belief regarding the Forms, paradigms of the good life, and experts on it will always be among us. And that second tradition, in turn, gave rise to the theoretical conception of philosophy that dominates our own thought.

It is remarkable enough that Socrates stands at the head of almost every ancient philosophical school.[66] But it is even more remarkable that he marks the point where these most different traditions within Western philosophy are created and, ever since their very first moment, begin to diverge from one another. These traditions, these different fates of Socrates' reason, have their common origin in the writings of a single author and of his two different reflections of his master. Through Socrates, Plato created the most lasting conceptions of philosophy available to us: philosophy as a purely intellectual discipline and philosophy as a way of life, an art of living, combining, in its various versions, life with discourse, doing with writing.[67]

I have tried to isolate a certain image of Socrates in Plato's early works. That image did not satisfy Plato for very long, and he made a vast effort to reveal its underpinnings, to construct, so to speak, the solid object of which he felt his early works offered a two-dimensional projection. That original image — original only as an image, not identical with its model — has in turn given rise to many different reflections that keep returning to it as if it somehow captured the real historical figure who, in my opinion, is by now lost forever.

The philosophers who have produced their own reflections of Socrates have made selective and eclectic use of various sources. But they have always come back to Plato's early works, especially to the *Apology*. Nietzsche, for one, went so far as to write that "some ancient writings one reads in order to understand antiquity; others, however, are such that one studies antiquity in order to be able to read *them*. To these belongs the *Apology*."[68] I have tried to explain that preoccupation by arguing that the Socrates of Plato's early works is a fundamentally empty figure. Though he spent much of his life obsessively engaged in conversation, his legacy — to his interlocutors, to his own author, to his author's readers — was a profound silence. And though his facial features were pronounced enough to provoke so many different interpretations, his face ultimately proved to be blank, a face from which his soul could not, in the end, be read. Though he seems to spring off the page, vivid and alive, Plato's early Socrates is not a concrete figure but a half-empty page that later philosophers have tried to complete with their own words.[69]

Plato's early Socrates is the first and strangest example of the art of living, an art of which there can only, in the nature of the case, be many sorts. Philosophy as such an art, as a way of life, of self-fashioning, of becoming what one is, of caring for the self, cannot ever follow examples straightforwardly. To choose a model and try to replicate its features results in the many imitations and caricatures to which Nietzsche, in particular, has given rise. To follow such examples we must focus not on their particular characteristics but on their more abstract, higher-level features. We need to turn to their successful integration of their various particular characteristics, whatever those are (and they are always different), into coherent wholes: that integration gives them a self. And we must note that the wholes they construct are different from the wholes to which we have become accustomed: that difference makes them individuals. Socrates is such an abstract model, the best and most abstract model of all.

Perhaps, however, it is not even possible to follow the higher-level features of a model if these include, for example, the opposition to their world that enabled Nietzsche and Foucault to become what they were or Montaigne's magnificent equanimity. For even such aspects, the manner in which specific features like character traits, accidents of life and birth, setbacks, and strokes of good luck are put together may well depend on the nature of the features they are intended to harmonize. The manner of organization often depends on the features to be organized. And since those are different in each case, the manner of organizing them will also itself be different. We are then left with some very abstract principles, like "Be relevantly different," "Accept everything about yourself," "Organize your features in an artistic manner," which are as empty as they are banal and useless. Once again, the art of living, like any art, does not obey rules that are both general and informative.

It was part of the fate of Socrates' emphasis on reason that he inaugurated that art, in all its varieties and with all its different products, because he let us see so little about how he accomplished his own task. We know less about him, his motives and needs, than about most of his followers. What we do know is that he cared for himself, searched for answers to questions he considered necessary for the good and happy life, failed to find them, and still was as good and perfect a character as any in world history. And who—to ask the question in Socrates' own terms—would not want to know how to be as perfect as possible?

Montaigne was right: "[B]In Cato we see very clearly that his is a pace strained far above the ordinary; in the brave exploits of his life and in his death we feel he is always mounted on his high horse. The other [Socrates] walks close to the ground, and at a gentle and ordinary pace treats the most useful subjects and behaves, both in the face of death and in the thorniest trials that can confront us, in the ordinary way of human life."[70] Or, better, Montaigne was almost right. For the "ordinariness" of Socrates, not unlike the ordinariness of Hans Castorp, the little hero with whom we began, is one of his most extraordinary features. Partly in the world and partly outside it, Socrates never allows us to see either exactly who he was or how he came to be that way.

Here then is another reason Socrates is crucial for those who want to practice the art of living. Self-fashioning always begins in the middle. It is only after one has become someone or other, once one realizes that one has already had a life consisting of all sorts of events that appear haphazard, disconnected, imitative, and insignificant, that one can begin to try to put them together and to become not just someone or other but oneself. Montaigne did not begin his project until, at the age of thirty-eight, he decided to abandon his public career. Nietzsche did not resign his position at the University of Basel until he was thirty-five. Foucault did not turn to the care of the self until the last ten years of his life, when he had already established himself as the leading thinker of his generation in France.

We know what all these authors had been doing until they turned to the project of self-fashioning, and we can use our knowledge in telling their philosophical tales. But about Socrates' early life we know nothing. We have a number of ancient reports: perhaps he studied with Archelaus,[71] perhaps he helped Euripides write his plays, perhaps he was also a student of Anaxagoras and Damon. He may have been a stonemason, removed from that life by Crito, who, "charmed by the beauty of his soul," educated him and enabled him to turn to the study of ethics.[72] But what was it that won for him the reputation that prompted Chaerephon to ask Delphi whether anyone else was wiser? We have no idea. We don't even know if the oracle (assuming the story is true in the first place) preceded or followed Aristophanes' *Clouds* (423 BC), in which Socrates appears as a character with whom the audience is quite familiar. Socrates' mystery includes the manner in which he cared for himself, the reasons for his success, as well as the reasons for which he undertook to care for himself in the first place. It makes his role as the prototypical artist of life less determinate and therefore more broadly applicable. We can write more of ourselves onto him.

When I started to think about the lectures that have resulted in this book, I thought they would belong to the history of ideas: on the one hand, various treatments of Socrates, on the other, my account of their features—a work of clarification, standing slightly to the side of its subject, perhaps capable, in the ideal case, of reaching some lasting conclusions. I did not then realize that Socrates himself would turn out to be like the books Montaigne had in mind when he asked, "[B]Who would not say that glosses increase doubts and ignorance, since there is no book to be found, whether human or divine, with which the world busies itself, whose difficulties are cleared up by interpretation? The hundredth commentator hands it on to his successor thornier and rougher than the first one had found it. When do we agree and say, 'There has been enough about this book; henceforth there is nothing more to say about it'?"[73] I did not realize that, in my mind at least, I would leave my Socrates thornier and rougher than I had found him.

I have been looking at various ways in which Socrates has been treated, in antiquity and modernity; in presenting these treatments I often criticized or modified them. While I have been trying to extract from Plato's texts a figure of utter simplicity and to show how that figure has been treated by others, Socrates has steadily become more complex. Gradually, it has become apparent to me that I too have been following in part Montaigne, Nietzsche, and Foucault. My own choice of sources for understanding Socrates has been at least eclectic, if not actually manipulative. I, too, have tried to construct a particular character — more ironical than Vlastos's or Montaigne's, more individualist than Foucault's, less absolutist than the hero of the *Republic*, relatively more "at home on this earth" than Nietzsche's. Like them, I too have used the voices of most of the authors I address. I too have written from their points of view and looked at the world, at myself, and at my own construct of Socrates through their eyes. I have even used the voice of that Socrates. And in producing that Socrates, I have composed a tragelaphic sort of work, partly a work of classics, partly of philosophy, partly of literary criticism, full of quotations acknowledged and deformed, indebted to various and perhaps not always compatible approaches. These are all combined here in a manner I cannot justify explicitly, apart from presenting this book to its readers. My hope is that my own reflection on Socrates, depending as it does on everything I understand, however imperfectly, and on everything I know how to do, however defectively, may have resulted in a slightly different manner of doing things. The art of living comes in many guises. The pursuit of Socrates' reflections is one of its variations.

Notes

Introduction

1. I am not unaware of the scholarly debate surrounding the issue whether Aristotle does ultimately prefer the theoretical over the "mixed" life that combines "theory" with participation in public affairs. The controversy does not affect my claim, since Aristotle is in either case envisaging philosophy as a particular mode of life.

2. Another figure who played a role not unlike that of Socrates is Diogenes of Sinope, the main representative of Cynicism. Diogenes is reputed to have written a number of dialogues, including a *Republic*, as well as seven tragedies, though there seems to have been some disagreement about the authenticity of those works (see Diogenes Laertius, *Lives of the Philosophers*, 6.2.80). But Diogenes' importance was mostly due to the stories circulating about his life and activities.

Let me say a few words about my method of citing ancient authors. For most of those authors, there is a standard system of citation. With Diogenes Laertius, as also with Xenophon's *Memorabilia* and with Plutarch, Cicero, and Quintilian, their works are generally cited by book, chapter, and section (6.2.80 in the present citation). Plato's and Aristotle's works are cited by an abbreviation of each work's title (many of the abbreviations can be found on pp. xxix–liv of Simon Hornblower and Antony Spawford, eds., *The Oxford Classical Dictionary* [Oxford: Oxford University Press, 1996]), and by a reference to page, column, and line number, which are common to all editions.

3. On the thematic and chronological order of Plato's dialogues, see n. 33 in chapter 1 below.

4. Johann Wolfgang von Goethe, "Plato als Mitgenosse einer christlichen Offenbarung," in *Werke* (Stuttgart and Tübingen, 1827–34), quoted by Paul Friedländer, *Plato*, trans. Hans Meyerhoff, 2d ed., vol. 1 (Princeton: Princeton University Press, 1969), 137.

5. In his later works, beginning with the *Parmenides* and the *Phaedrus*, which I do not discuss at all in this book, Plato offers a different conception of philosophy and of the philosophical life. But his universalist intent and his inspiration by Socrates remain the same.

Chapter 1

1. Hermann J. Weigand, *"The Magic Mountain": A Study of Thomas Mann's Novel* (1933; reprint, Chapel Hill: University of North Carolina Press, 1965), 63.

2. In what follows, when I cite an English version of Thomas Mann's *The Magic Mountain* I will mostly use the older translation by H. T. Lowe-Porter (New York: Alfred A. Knopf, 1927) instead of the newer version by John E. Woods (New York: Alfred A. Knopf, 1995). Lowe-Porter tends to take greater liberties with the texture of Mann's prose; compare, for example, the last sentence above with Woods's "He did not feel all that well rested, but fresh enough to meet the morning," which, though not perfect as a rendering of "Sehr ausgeruht fühlte er sich eben nicht, aber frisch mit dem jungen Tage," keeps closer to the German syntax. Still, in my opinion, Lowe-Porter conveys more of the atmosphere of Mann's German and in particular the ambiguity of the narrator's view of the events related. In this context, note the occurrence of the word *frisch*, which recurs throughout this section and will occupy us again. In all citations to Mann's text, the first page number is that of the English translation, the second that of the German original.

3. See 112/154–55 (where beer, music, and a sense of decay and death are all present), 178/246 (where Hans watches his cousin's physical examination and ponders over the fact that Joachim's disease is eating up the inside of his healthy-looking body), and 219/302–3 (Hans is now looking at the x-ray of his own hand and thus feels that he is looking "at his own grave . . . and for the first time he understood that he was going to die. . . . At the thought there came over his face the expression it usually wore when he listened to music: a little dull, sleepy, and pious, his mouth half open, his head inclined toward his shoulder"); see further n. 9 below and 292/401, 389/533, 476/649, 557/761, 622/853.

4. Self-deception, as Mark Johnston has argued, involves purposive but not thereby intentional action; it is thus mental but not conscious, less a deliberate activity than a sort of "mental tropism, a characteristic pattern whose existence within the mind is no more surprising, given what it does for us, than a plant's turning toward the sun" ("Self-Deception and the Nature of Mind," in Brian McLaughlin and Amélie Oksenberg Rorty, eds., *Perspectives on Self-Deception* [Berkeley: University of California Press, 1988], 86).

5. In fact, the woman's story has a strong connection with Hans and Joachim. Just as Castorp is diagnosed with tuberculosis during his visit to his cousin, so the woman's second son comes to visit his sick brother and, like so many other visitors to the magic mountain, becomes ill and eventually dies.

6. As I mentioned in n. 2 above, the word *frisch* and its derivatives pick up the earlier reference to the "fresh" morning and appear again a number of times within this section. The whole passage is setting up in subtle terms a contrast between the freshness of the mountain landscape where the Berghof is located and the dissolution within the sanatorium.

his weakness to anemia (103/142). Similarly, when on his very first day he discovered that he had coughed up some blood into his handkerchief, he "had not enough energy to think about the fact, though he was rather given to worrying over himself and by nature inclined to hypochondria" (78/109). The effect of this incident is quite complex. Castorp's not thinking about the blood makes it appear less important than it is, especially since we are told he worries about himself a lot. By the same token, however, the reference to Hans's hypochondria predisposes us not to take his symptoms and complaints as seriously as we might otherwise have.

18. Hans and James have a late supper at the sanatorium's restaurant upon the latter's arrival, just as Hans had eaten with Joachim when he first arrived. "James ate and drank heartily, as was his custom" (431/588), like Hans, who regularly "ate heartily . . . he always ate a good deal, out of pure self-respect, even when he was not hungry" (13/23). We are told that during the meal James's temples were swollen, reminding us of the fact that Hans's "face was like fire" in the restaurant on his own first night at the sanatorium (14/24). James bursts out in surprising and uncharacteristic laughter: "He fairly snorted, but recovered himself immediately, horrified; coughed, and tried his best to disguise the senseless outbreak" (432/589). Hans, too, had laughed a lot his first evening at the Berghof, first when he heard about the bodies being moved by bobsled and then throughout supper: "Hans being taken by another fit of laughing, his cousin laughed too" (14/25). James's "tongue was a little thick" and "his weariness became at length so overpowering that the meeting broke up at about half past ten, and he was scarcely capable of attending when he was introduced to . . . Dr. Krokowski" (432-33/590). So it was with Hans. During their dinner together, Joachim suddenly realized that "his cousin was overcome with sleep, that in fact he was actually nodding" (15/26). And when, on leaving the restaurant, the cousins met the same Dr. Krokowski, "it was touching to see Hans Castorp labour to master his drowsiness and be polite" (16/27). The parallels can be multiplied. On first meeting them, the head nurse tells both Hans (167/230) and James (436/594–95) that they are ill. James becomes almost immediately attracted to a Frau Redisch (437–38/597), just as Hans began to fall in love with Clawdia Chauchat long before he realized it. James asks Behrens about the human body (438/598) in the same exalted, poetic tones Hans had earlier used for his own questions on the same subject (265/365), revealing his incipient preoccupation both with disease and with Clawdia, and Behrens answers them both in exactly the same reductive, deflationary, materialist mode (265/365; 438–39/598–99). "'Certainly, of course,' said the Consul," to the Hofrat's bizarre physiological disquisition. "The next morning he had vanished" (439/599), but not before having already had a physical examination under the pretext of discussing Hans's case with the chief of staff (437/596). What are we to make of this? Are we to say that James, too, was after all ill? Or do the extensive parallels with Hans's case and behavior suggest that the young engineer was not? Is their illness, if illness it is, physiological or psychological in origin? These are vexed questions, which we shall discuss, though only briefly, in what follows.

19. It is also relevant to mention here the episode of the woman who was reported to have been seen leaving the room of a male patient—the lawyer Einhuf—at a very late hour. The event "was a scandal; not only to the general, but even

more to Hans Castorp's private sense, and derogatory to his spiritual endeavours" (297/408). Eventually Hans becomes incapable of reactions of this sort.

20. The present incident is explicitly connected to Hans's original experience not only through the allusion to music but also because Mann accentuates the Russians' activities and Hans's indifference to them: "Man hörte das Ehepaar vom schlechten Russentisch. . . . Und Hans Castorp nahm Seitenlage ein, in Erwartung des Schlafes" (279).

21. I have tried to show how deeply equivocal the etiology of the disease of all the main characters in the novel is in "Getting Used to Not Getting Used to It: Nietzsche in *The Magic Mountain*," *Philosophy and Literature* 5 (1981): 73–89. In that article, however, I drew too sharp a distinction between Hans's case and those of the rest of the characters, and I would like to qualify my view in what follows.

22. Stock, *"Magic Mountain,"* 501.

23. This view runs contrary to that of C. J. Reed, *Thomas Mann: The Uses of Tradition* (Oxford: Clarendon Press, 1974), who argues that Mann originally conceived of Hans's illness as caused, in a Freudian manner, by his erotic fixations but then, as a result of working on the novel for more than a decade, decided to attribute it instead to the "hollowness" of the age in which Hans lived. Reed finds both views present in the novel and explains their presence developmentally. He considers the later conception quite implausible (235). But what is even more implausible is that Mann was taking any sort of unambiguous attitude toward the origins and nature of Hans's illness. The medical history of Hans's family, as we have seen, suggests that the illness is solidly grounded in physiological factors as well. Similarly, Reed considers "the expectation of Clawdia's return [as] the true reason why Hans Castorp declines to leave the sanatorium when Behrens pronounces him cured" (248–49), and he thus commits himself to a psychosomatic account of Hans's illness. But though such an account is doubtless true so far as it goes, it does not go far enough. To say that Behrens "pronounces" Hans "cured" is to simplify matters beyond justification. During the episode where this scene occurs, Behrens is shown to be already furious when the cousins go to visit him. He has been smoking, which always makes him "melancholy," and he is seething about an affair between two of his patients, which had caused him to dismiss them along with the third patient who, out of jealousy, had revealed their relationship (416/568). At that point, Joachim walks into his examining room and announces that, whatever Behrens thinks, he is terminating his cure and returning to his regiment. Behrens is driven to distraction. He lashes out at Castorp, and when the latter says that *he* will not leave without the doctor's permission, he conducts the most cursory examination and, just like that, tells him that he is "cured." In the process, he contradicts his own earlier diagnosis of the source of Hans's fever (419/572) to which, once he relents, he returns without explanation or apology (474/646). His examination, as we said, is not serious: "He . . . began to tap and listen. He did not dictate [as he always does]. It went rather fast." It is, instead, the result of an acute fit of pique, and it does not result in any straightforward pronouncement that Hans is cured. Why Hans chooses to stay, despite this formal pronouncement, however, is another question.

24. Weigand, *"Magic Mountain"*, 63.

25. C. E. Williams, for example, in "Not an Inn, but a Hospital" (in Harold Bloom, ed., *Thomas Mann's "The Magic Mountain": Modern Critical Interpreta-*

tions [New Haven: Chelsea, 1986], 39), writes that "under the influence of external forces an originally base matter is purged and transformed into something of
a higher order." This, however, strikes me as both too unequivocal a reading of
the progress of Castorp on the mountain and too simple an account of the young
man's nature. His matter is not "base" in the sense Williams has in mind—that
is precisely part of Mann's point: Hans saw "no positive reason for exertion,"
he had been in love with Pribislav Hippe and on that account (or as a result of
it) developed his first "moist spot" which is a sign of not belonging to the flatland, he was exposed to death early on in his life, and so on. He is, in other words,
despite his ordinariness, an unusual person; but Mann's irony, which we shall discuss in what follows, does not allow the judgment that he is therefore *only* unusual. A classic presentation of the view that Hans does accomplish a transcendence of opposites that none of the other patients is able to do can be found in
Jens Rieckman, *"Der Zauberberg": Eine geistige Autobiographie Thomas Manns*
(Stuttgart: Heinz, 1977). See also, among others, Walther Weiss, *Thomas Manns
Kunst der sprachlichen und thematischen Integration*, Hefte zur Zeitschrift *Wirkendes Wort* 13 (Düsseldorf: Schwann, 1964), and Theodore Ziolkowski, *Dimensions of the Modern Novel* (Princeton: Princeton University Press, 1969).

26. On the episode as a whole, see Ludwig Völker, "'Experiment,' 'Abenteuer,'
'Traum' in Thomas Manns Roman *Der Zauberberg*: Struktur-Idee-Tradition," in
Heinz Saueressig, ed., *Besichtigung des Zauberbergs* (Biberach: Wege und Gestalten, 1974), 157–82. Reed, *Thomas Mann*, agrees with Mann's description of the
italicized sentence "For the sake of goodness and love, man shall let death have
no sovereignty over his thoughts," which Hans utters during his dream while lost
in the snowstorm (496–97/677), as the *Ergebnissatz* of the novel (Thomas Mann,
Fragment über das Religiöse, in *Gesammelte Werke*, vol. 11 [Frankfurt: Fischer, 1960],
423f.). Reed believes that Mann "himself was quite clear that Hans Castorp undergoes a positive development whose essence is in the chapter 'Schnee' and that
the meaning of that chapter is the novel's message, the already extralinguistic thing
that the reader takes away with him from his reading" (254).

27. See Jürgen Scharfschwerdt, *Thomas Mann und der deutsche Bildungsroman*
(Stuttgart: Kohlhammer, 1967), 142ff.

28. Jill Anne Kowalik, "Sympathy with Death: Hans Castorp's Nietzschean
Resentment," *German Quarterly* 58 (1985): 27–48. Kowalik offers a purely negative reading of Castorp, as a man who cannot overcome resentment. "The *Zauberberg*," she writes, "does not relate how a representative young man comes to
synthesize two opposing forces; rather, it documents the consequences for those
who cannot or will not recognize their points of identity. . . . Castorp leaves the
magic mountain with his own sense of resentment more solidly in place than when
he arrived . . . but he does not go forth as a man who has undergone spiritual or
emotional growth" (28, 40). In addition, Hans returns to the facile humanism of
Settembrini once his vision in the snow is over, despite his statement that he has
been liberated from both his "pedagogues," Settembrini no less than Naptha, the
hedonistic Jesuit who battles Settembrini for the possession of Hans's intellectual soul and who also is, naturally, himself stricken by the disease. In short, nothing much happens to him on the mountain. Given my view that the novel resists
all unequivocal approaches of this sort, I find Kowalik's article, though quite engaging, ultimately unsatisfactory.

29. On narratorial ambivalence, see Francis Bulhof, *Transpersonalismus und Synchronizität: Wiederholung als Strukturelement in Thomas Manns "Zauberberg"* (Groningen: Drukkerij van Denderen, 1966).

30. Paul Friedländer, *Plato*, 2d ed., vol. 1 (Princeton: Princeton University Press, 1969), 137, has observed that Mann's irony bears a strong resemblance to the irony of Plato. Friedländer's whole chapter on Platonic irony is very suggestive, but Friedländer does not pursue the connections he alludes to systematically enough and finally satisfies himself with a few generalities. That is doubtless what has led R. B. Rutherford, in *The Art of Plato: Ten Essays in Platonic Interpretation* (Cambridge, Mass.: Harvard University Press, 1995), 77 n. 20, to describe Friedländer's writing on Plato's irony as "helpful if a little mystical."

31. The expression comes from Richard Rorty's essay, "Philosophy as a Kind of Writing," in *Consequences of Pragmatism: Essays, 1972–1980* (Minneapolis: University of Minnesota Press, 1982).

32. Arthur C. Danto, "Philosophy as/and/of Literature," in *The Philosophical Disenfranchisement of Art* (New York: Columbia University Press, 1986), 154.

33. I count as Plato's early dialogues the following works, listed in alphabetical order: *Apology, Charmides, Crito, Euthyphro, Hippias Minor, Ion, Laches, Protagoras*. A little later than these dialogues, connected with them, working with problems raised within them but offering first stabs at new solutions, are the following: *Gorgias, Hippias Major, Lysis, Menexenus, Meno*. Among Plato's middle works I count the following, in probable chronological sequence: *Symposium, Phaedo, Republic, Euthydemus, Cratylus, Parmenides, Phaedrus, Theaetetus*. Plato's late works include, again in probable chronological sequence, *Timaeus, Critias, Sophist, Politicus, Philebus, Laws*.

My list follows pretty closely that of Leonard Brandwood, *A Word Index to Plato* (Leeds: W. S. Maney and Son, 1976), xvii. It also is not so different from the list offered by Gregory Vlastos, *Socrates: Ironist and Moral Philosopher* (Cambridge: Cambridge University Press, 1991), 46–47. But in contrast to Vlastos, who counts the *Gorgias* as a central early dialogue, I place the *Gorgias*, with Brandwood, among the dialogues of the second (sometimes called "transitional") group. It is important for Vlastos to count the *Gorgias* as an early dialogue so that he can interpret the work's doctrines as expressing the views of the "historical" Socrates, whose reconstruction is part of the aim of his book. But his main argument for this classification is that the *Gorgias* deploys Socrates' elenctic method "with great panache," unlike any other work in the second group (47 n. 8). That is not true. The elenchus, Socrates' traditional question-and-answer method, is used centrally in the *Meno* as well as in the first book of the *Republic* (on the strength of which Vlastos, implausibly, believes that it was composed separately from the rest of the work and along with the other early dialogues).

A radically different chronology of Plato's "Socratic" dialogues is offered by Charles H. Kahn, *Plato and the Socratic Dialogue: The Philosophical Use of a Literary Form* (Cambridge: Cambridge University Press, 1996). The main outlines of his view are contained in a series of articles dating from 1981. See particularly "Plato's *Charmides* and the Proleptic Reading of Socratic Dialogues," *Journal of the History of Philosophy* 85 (1988): 541–49. See also Holger Thesleff, *Studies in Platonic Chronology*, Commentationes humanarum litterarum 70 (Helsinki: Societas Scientiarium Fennica, 1982), now supplemented by his "Platonic Chronology," *Phronesis* 34 (1989): 1–26.

34. The King Archon (βασιλεύς) was in charge of religious functions for the Athenian state and thus also for religious prosecutions (cf. *Pol.* 290e6). Since the accusation against Socrates involved his not believing in the gods of the city and his introducing new deities (Cf. *Ap.* 24b8–c1 and Xenophon, *Ap. Soc.* 10), it was a writ of impiety (ἀσέβεια) and thus subject to the King Archon's jurisdiction. So too was Euthyphro's suit, since murder was believed to bring on a religious pollution (μίασμα) that affected whole families and communities. See also Richard J. Klonoski, "The Portico of the Archon Basileus: On the Significance of the Setting of Plato's *Euthyphro*," *Classical Journal* 81 (1986): 130–37.

35. Plato, *Eu.* 4a–b. See John Burnet, ed., *Plato's "Euthyphro," "Apology of Socrates," and "Crito"* (Oxford: Clarendon Press, 1924), 21.

36. James A. Arieti, *Interpreting Plato: The Dialogues as Drama* (Savage, Md.: Rowman and Littlefield, 1991), 143, 144, 148. Though Arieti is right in emphasizing the importance of Euthyphro's "self-delusion" to the dialogue as a whole, he vastly underestimates the intrinsic importance of the dialectical discussion.

37. R. E. Allen, *Plato's "Euthyphro" and the Earlier Theory of Forms* (London: Routledge and Kegan Paul, 1970), 5.

38. The "introductions" to dialogues like the *Laches*, the *Charmides*, the *Protagoras*, the *Lysis*, and the *Hippias Major* occupy between one fifth and fully one half of these works. Even to call them "introductions" is to make a controversial choice as to the main purpose of each dialogue (cf. George Grote's description of "the Platonic purpose" of the *Euthyphro*: "the enquiry into the general idea of holiness" [*Plato and the Other Companions of Sokrates*, vol. 1 (London: Russell, 1865), 317]) and thus to adopt a disputable approach to the interpretation of the works even before one has begun reading them.

39. A short listing of such works would include the following. Arieti, *Interpreting Plato;* Charles L. Griswold Jr., ed., *Platonic Writings/Platonic Readings* (New York: Routledge, 1988), an interesting volume that confronts those who consider the dialogue form paramount with those who prefer to disregard it, though the book ultimately fails to engage its authors into a dialogue with each other; James C. Klagge and Nicholas D. Smith, eds., *Methods of Interpreting Plato and His Dialogues* (*Oxford Studies in Ancient Philosophy* 10 [1992]: Supplement), meticulously reviewed by Stephen G. Salkever in *Bryn Mawr Classical Review* (electronic edition, 1992); Gerald A. Press, ed., *Plato's Dialogues: New Studies and Interpretations* (Lanham, Md.: Rowman and Littlefield, 1993), which mostly takes issue with exclusive attention to Plato's arguments; David Roochnik, *The Tragedy of Reason: Toward a Platonic Conception of the Logos* (New York: Routledge, 1990), which is not primarily devoted to the dialogue form but occasionally makes some extravagant claims on its behalf; Kenneth Seeskin, *Dialogue and Discovery: A Study in Socratic Method* (Albany: State University of New York Press, 1987), a balanced discussion of a number of issues of method and substance; and C. Jan Swearingen, "Dialogue and Dialectic: The Logic of Conversation and the Interpretation of Logic," in Tullio Maranhâo, ed., *The Interpretation of Dialogue* (Chicago: University of Chicago Press, 1990).

40. The extant fragments of the early Socratics, with the exception of those of Aeschines, can be found in Carlo Giannantoni, *Socratis et Socraticorum reliquiae* (Rome: Bibliopolis, 1990). For Aeschines, see Heinrich Dittmar, *Aischines von Sphettos: Studien zur Literaturgeschichte der Sokratiker* (Berlin: Weidmann, 1912).

See also A. E. Taylor, "Aeschines of Sphettos," in *Philosophical Studies* (London: Macmillan, 1934).

41. Diogenes Laertius, *Lives of the Philosophers*, 2.14.3, writes that Simon, a shoe-maker whose shop Socrates used to frequent, "is said to be the first to compose Socratic dialogues."

42. Frederick Rosen, "Piety and Justice: Plato's *Euthyphro*," *Philosophy* 43 (1968): 109.

43. Leo Strauss, *The City and Man* (Chicago: University of Chicago Press, 1964), chap. 2. See also Allan Bloom's "Interpretive Essay" in his translation of the *Republic* (New York: Basic Books, 1968) for a fuller exposition of Strauss's reading of the work.

44. Among the many books that follow such an approach one could mention Jacob Klein's *Plato's Trilogy: "Theaetetus," the "Sophist," and the "Statesman"* (Chicago: University of Chicago Press, 1977) and Ronna L. Burger's *Plato's "Phaedrus": A Defense of a Philosophic Art of Writing* (Birmingham: University of Alabama Press, 1980): Burger's very title, in view of the apparent Platonic attack on writing in the *Phaedrus*, is indicative of the approach in question here.

Strauss's approach to Plato depends on another principle: since Plato wrote dialogues in which he did not appear as a character, he "concealed his opinions" (*City and Man*, 59), and therefore the distance he creates between himself and the views expressed in his works produces an irony that is absolutely all-pervasive. This approach has recently been defended, among others, by Stanley Rosen, *Plato's "Symposium"* (New Haven: Yale University Press, 1968), xxv: "Platonic irony means that every statement in a dialogue must be understood in terms of its dramatic context." To this, of course, it must be objected that the question when the context is not itself the product of an ironical author is not any easier to answer than that of the meaning of the statement in question. Similarly, Charles C. Griswold Jr. believes that "Plato's distance from his characters supplies the basis for Platonic irony" (*Self-Knowledge in Plato's "Phaedrus"* [New Haven: Yale University Press, 1986], 12). I find that position too extreme, both as an account of irony and as a principle for the interpretation of Plato, partly for reasons given by Christopher Rowe, "Platonic Irony," *Nova Tellus* 5 (1987): 83–101. Rowe's article, which makes a number of good points, takes Platonic irony as a kind "that in fact serves to deflate the pretensions of the author himself" (89) — a kind of irony reminiscent of the description of Mann's irony given by Hermann Weigand (see p. 20 above). But Rowe, despite his view that such irony applies to the Platonic dialogues as wholes (95), mostly confines his attention to those passages in the *Phaedrus* in which Plato, as he interprets him, combines serious and playful elements. So, for example, he takes it that the reference to Socrates' *daimonion* (242b8–d2) and to his bare feet (229a3–4), as well as the funny poem about Eros (252b8–9) and the praise of poets (245a1–8) in Socrates' Great Speech, are all such combinations: "By the introduction of actual elements of *paidia*, Plato cuts himself down to size: despite appearances, we are not meant to follow him all the way in his flights of imagination as he later makes Socrates tell us directly" (98). The difficulty here, however, is that such a combination of seriousness and play in no way helps Plato accomplish what he apparently wants to do in the *Phaedrus*, namely, to distinguish written from spoken discourse: such combinations occur perfectly naturally in both media.

45. Commentators on the dialogue don't even agree on whether a definition of piety is or is not reached during its course. Grote explicitly denied that piety is defined either in the *Euthyphro* or in any other Platonic text (*Plato and the Other Companions of Sokrates*, 1:322). J. Adam, ed., *Platonis "Euthyphro"* (Cambridge: Cambridge University Press, 1890), xii, argued by contrast that the dialogue does succeed in defining piety as the proper service of the gods. More recently, W. G. Rabinowitz has given a complex esoteric reading of the dialogue, aiming to show that piety is finally defined as assisting the gods in contemplating the Platonic Forms ("Platonic Piety: An Essay towards the Solution of an Enigma," *Phronesis* 3 [1958]: 108–20). Allen, however, asserts confidently that "the *Euthyphro* ends in failure: no definition of holiness is stated, and none is implied. There is no 'mask' which can be stripped off the dialogue to reveal its true meaning; it bears its meaning on its face" (*Plato's "Euthyphro" and the Earlier Theory of Forms*, 6).

46. See *Crat.* 396d4–8, where Socrates claims that Euthyphro's enthusiastic disquisition on etymology has inspired him in his own efforts. At 399a1, the same effect is attributed to him, and other references to his passion for etymology can be found at 400a1, 407d6–8, 409d1–2 and 428c7. This information is of little use for the interpretation of the *Euthyphro*, though, unconnected as it is with Euthyphro's concerns in that dialogue, it vaguely suggests that Euthyphro may in fact have been a genuine historical character.

47. This is the procedure followed, for example, in the *Crito*, the *Laches*, the *Protagoras*, the *Meno*, and the *Hippias Minor*. Even in dialogues like the *Gorgias*, in which Socrates seems to take the lead, Plato usually supplies him with a very good reason for doing so: the *Gorgias* begins with Callicles telling Socrates that, though he missed a public session during which Gorgias answered every question, on whatever subject, that was put to him, Socrates can have the opportunity of meeting with Gorgias and asking him whatever he likes, in private. The image of Socrates wandering through the Agora and addressing people almost at random, though it has some (debatable) basis in the *Apology* (29d–30c, 31b), is much less prevalent in the Platonic dialogues than we commonly believe. For some of the debate, see my "What Did Socrates Teach and to Whom Did He Teach It?" *Review of Metaphysics* 46 (1992): 279–306.

48. Tὰς ἐν τῷ Λυκείῳ διατριβάς, 2a1–2; cf. *Eud.* 271a1, *Symp.* 223d8, *Lys.* 203a1, *Phdr.*, and Aesch. fr. 2: ἐκαθήμεθα μὲν ἐπὶ τῶν θάκων ἐν Λυκείῳ, οὗ οἱ ἀθλοθέται τὸν ἀγῶνα διατιθέασιν. Socrates actually seems to have spent more time in the Lyceum than in the Agora, despite the testimony of *Ap.* 17c8.

49. On Socrates' δαιμόνιον, see *Ap.* 31c7–d6, 40a2–b6; *Eud.* 272e3–4; 496c3–5; *Tht.* 151a2–5; *Phdr.* 242b9–c3, as well as *Alc. I* 103a4–b1 and *Theag.* 129e1–9. See also Xenophon, *Memorabilia* 1.1.2, 4; 4.8.1, 5, where the δαιμόνιον is occasionally given a positive as well as a negative voice; *Ap. Soc.* 4, 13. Later discussions of the δαιμόνιον, which go much further than the sparse evidence supplied by Plato and Xenophon, include Plutarch, *De genio Socratis*, and Apuleius, *De deo Socratis*.

50. So Burnet, ed., *Plato's "Euthyphro," "Apology of Socrates," and "Crito,"* 5, followed by Klonoski, "The Portico of the Archon Basileus," 133–34.

51. So Maurice Croiset, ed., *Platon: Oeuvres complètes*, vol. 1 (Paris: Les Belles Lettres, 1920), 179, followed by William D. Furley, "The Figure of Euthyphro in Plato's Dialogue," *Phronesis* 30 (1985): 201–8.

52. What of Euthyphro's prediction that Socrates will win his case? Arieti, *Interpreting Plato*, 144, writes that Euthyphro "presents himself as a man infinitely confident of his abilities. A moment later Euthyphro predicts that Socrates' case will come out well (3e) — and we realize from the dramatic irony how good a prophet he is." From Euthyphro's point of view, where success means acquittal, Arieti's point is well taken. But is it so clear that Socrates' case, from Socrates' own point of view, does not turn out well? During his trial, Socrates refuses to engage in any unjust action, and, in view of his position that no unjust person can harm a just one, he emerges from his trial convicted but unscathed. In a further irony, then, Euthyphro may have been right in his prediction after all!

53. Euthyphro's statement, "ἐάνπερ ἀκούωσί γέ μου λέγοντος," suggests that he is accustomed to not being taken very seriously.

54. Μαθητής: 5a4, a8, b5; μάθω: 15c12; μαθών: 15e6; μεμαθηκότας: 12e4. Διδάσκειν: 6d2, d10, e3, 7a4, 9a1, c3, d8, 11e3, 12e1, 14c1; διδάσκαλος: 5b2. Σοφία, σοφός, σοφώτερος: 5b1, 9a2, b3, 12a5 (twice), 14d4, 16a1. Cf. εἰδέναι: 15d4, e1.

55. The original definition is at 6e10–7a1, improved slightly at 9e1–3.

56. Friedländer, *Plato*, 1:142.

57. Gregory Vlastos, "The Paradox of Socrates," in *The Philosophy of Socrates: A Collection of Critical Essays* (Garden City, N.Y.: Doubleday, 1971), 6.

58. Laszlo Versenyi, *Socratic Humanism* (New Haven: Yale University Press, 1963), 38.

59. Seeskin, *Dialogue and Discovery*, 78.

60. Roslyn Weiss, "Euthyphro's Failure," *Journal of the History of Philosophy* 24 (1986): 437.

61. It is only at 14e8, close to the end of the dialogue, that Euthyphro shows his first signs of impatience.

62. This is the view of Versenyi, *Socratic Humanism*, 38.

63. On common attitudes toward Hesiod, see Isocrates, *Bousiris*, 38, 40; Euripides, *Hercules Furens*, 1346.

64. Versenyi, *Socratic Humanism*, 38.

65. Arieti, *Interpreting Plato*, 143.

66. In actual fact, there are dissenters from this view. Diogenes Laertius (2.5.29) claims that Euthyphro actually dropped his suit against his father as a result of his conversation with Socrates! He has found a modern follower in R. E. Allen: "If Euthyphro persisted in his suit, he did so on another day; he will not now wait to see the King. His action, though not his words, indicates that he has begun to learn the lesson which Socrates' questioning was designed to teach: that he is ignorant of the thing in which he thought himself wise" (*Plato's "Euthyphro" and the Earlier Theory of Forms*, 64). This view is dramatically untenable: it fits with nothing we are told about the character of Euthyphro in the dialogue. Allen, in a tour de force of literalism, claims that Euthyphro (despite Burnet's claim to the contrary [*Plato's "Euthyphro," "Apology of Socrates," and "Crito,"* 2]) cannot have seen the Archon Basileus before his conversation with Socrates began ("if that were true, the introduction to the dialogue would surely have suggested it, and it does not" [Allen, *Plato's "Euthyphro" and the Earlier Theory of Forms*, 64 n. 1]) and that therefore his sudden departure from the scene shows that he has begun to have second thoughts about his action. Needless to say, it is clear that the dialogue simply does not give us enough information to decide the issue of Eu-

thyphro's interview with the King Archon one way or the other. The issue is not, in fact, part of the dialogue's concerns.

67. Lionel Trilling, *Sincerity and Authenticity* (Cambridge, Mass.: Harvard University Press, 1971), 16.

68. Michael Frede, "Plato's Arguments and the Dialogue Form," in James C. Klagge and Nicholas D. Smith, eds., *Methods of Interpreting Plato and His Dialogues, Oxford Studies in Ancient Philosophy* 10 (1992): Supplement, 215.

69. Ibid., 216.

70. That is, if I understand him right, Griswold's view in *Self-Knowledge in Plato's "Phaedrus."* Griswold presents a sophisticated version of the Straussian approach to the reading of the dialogues, and he explicitly denies that irony, along with other literary and dramatic devices, is "a stratagem for creating an inaccessible 'esoteric doctrine' or 'secret teaching.'" But his notion of Platonic irony is much broader than mine. Platonic irony, for Griswold, "depends on the difference between the fact that the dialogue is written and the fact that what is written is supposed to be a nonwritten spoken dialogue" and requires a distinction "between the apparent significance of a particular passage and the significance it possesses as part of a larger whole" (13). Platonic irony, that is, consists generally in the fact that Plato does not himself appear within his works—not, as I have argued, in his putting his audience in the same position he puts the characters he incites them to disdain. The "dialogical" approach Griswold advocates "insist[s] that the various levels of words and deeds be integrated into the interpretation" (13–14). My own view is that even though the dialogues depend on action as well as on argument, there is no a priori reason to assume that every action is essential to the interpretation of the dialogue (just as there is no reason to believe that absolutely everything everyone says in a dialogue is essential to its understanding). Whether it is or not depends on whether it can be interpreted as relevant to the work, and that can only be decided on a case-by-case basis.

71. See, for example, *Pr.* 351b–359a, *M.* 77b–78b. A huge literature has developed around this theme. A good selective bibliography can be found in Richard Kraut, ed., *The Cambridge Companion to Plato* (New York: Cambridge University Press, 1992).

72. Such a view is attributed to Nietzsche by Randall Havas, *Nietzsche's Genealogy: Nihilism and the Will to Knowledge* (Ithaca: Cornell University Press, 1995), chap. 1.

Chapter 2

1. Michel de Montaigne, "Of the art of discussion," in *The Complete Works of Montaigne*, trans. Donald M. Frame (Stanford: Stanford University Press, 1942), 709.

2. Friedrich Nietzsche, "The Problem of Socrates," in *Twilight of the Idols*, in *The Viking Portable Nietzsche*, ed. and trans. Walter Kaufmann (New York: Viking Press, 1954), 475–76.

3. D. C. Muecke, *The Compass of Irony* (London: Methuen), 31.

4. Since the proper understanding, even the exact translation, of the Greek term is in question, I will not use "irony" and its cognates in discussing Greek

texts until we have settled on their proper construal. Instead, I will simply transliterate the Greek word εἰρωνεία.

5. John Burnet, ed., *Plato's "Euthyphro," "Apology of Socrates," and "Crito"* (Oxford: Clarendon Press, 1924). 159. I leave aside the question whether εἰρωνεία in its original sense, which we shall examine below, can apply to the Socratic professions of ignorance. Burnet is followed by R. E. Allen, *Socrates and Legal Obligation* (Minneapolis: University of Minnesota Press, 1980), 58 ("You will think that I am sly and dishonest"). Allen comments: "That is, an εἴρων. 'Irony' was regarded as a defect of character, not a virtue, as Theophrastus' portrait in the *Characters* of the ironical man makes clear" (135 n. 30). We shall discuss Theophrastus below. See also Henry George Liddell and Robert Scott, eds., *A Greek–English Lexicon*, rev. Sir Henry Stuart Jones (Oxford: Oxford University Press, 1968), s.v. εἰρωνεία, iii.2. (This work by Liddell, Scott, and Jones is the standard Greek dictionary and is usually referred to by the abbreviation LSJ.) Others prefer to translate more straightforwardly, with different forms of "irony," e.g., Thomas G. West and Grace Starry West, *Four Texts on Socrates* (Ithaca: Cornell University Press, 1984), 92 (but see n. 6, on their interpretation); G. M. A. Grube, trans., *Plato: Five Dialogues* (Indianapolis: Hackett, 1981), 41; Lane Cooper, *Plato on the Trial and Death of Socrates* (Ithaca: Cornell University Press, 1941), 73. There is a similar translation in Maurice Croiset, *Platon: Oeuvres complètes*, vol. 1 (Paris: Les Belles Lettres, 1920), 167. Gregory Vlastos also disagrees with Burnet's approach, though, unfortunately, he does not offer his own explicit interpretation of the passage; see Vlastos, *Socrates: Ironist and Moral Philosopher* (Cambridge: Cambridge University Press, 1991), 25 with n. 15; further references to this work will be given parenthetically in the main text.

6. That is why the Wests' comment on the text cannot be right: "'To be ironic' (εἰρωνεύεσθαι)," they write (*Four Texts on Socrates*, 92 n. 71), "is to dissemble, to say less than one thinks, to present oneself as less than one is. The opposite of irony is boastfulness, claiming to be more than one is." That is in general true, but what Socrates says here is that his judges would consider that his irony would consist in claiming to be *more*, not less, than he was. The fact is that though the translation "irony" is perfectly adequate for Socrates' words, the traditional understanding of irony as pretending to be less than one is or as saying the opposite of what one means, which we shall discuss in detail as we proceed, does not apply at all well to the present case. Exactly the same point must be made in connection with Léon Robin, *Platon: Oeuvres complètes*, vol. 1 (Paris: Gallimard, 1950), 177, who translates the Greek as "feinte naiveté" and who in his n. 1 claims that the passage presents a case strictly parallel to those in which Socrates feigns ignorance in order to seduce others into conversation. But what Socrates says here is that, *from the point of view of his judges*, he would appear to be boasting if he claimed he had orders from God to engage in philosophy.

7. It is not my purpose here to go over the ground originally covered in Otto Ribbeck's classic article on the concept of the εἴρων in classical Greek thought and literature, "Über den Begriff des *Eiron*," *Rheinisches Museum* 31 (1876): 381–400. Despite a number of attempts to refute and refine it, Ribbeck's study still defines the general outlines of our understanding of ancient εἰρωνεία. See also W. Büchner, "Über den Begriff der Eironeia," *Hermes* 76 (1941): 339–58; Frederic Amory, "*Eirôn* and *Eirôneia*," *Classica et mediaevalia* 33 (1981–82): 49–80; Dietrich Roloff, *Platonische Ironie* (Heidelberg: C. Winter, 1975).

8. Aristophanes, *Clouds* 448–50 (where, interestingly, no clear distinction is drawn between the εἴρων and the ἀλαζών, the boastful person, from whom Aristotle, as we shall see, distinguishes the former); see K. J. Dover, ed., *Aristophanes: "Clouds"* (Oxford: Clarendon Press, 1968): "'Deceitful' in pretending to be innocent when one is up to mischief. . . . Εἰρωνεία approximates to 'making excuses', 'pleading inability'." In Aristophanes' *Wasps* (174–75), the adjective, applied to Philokleon's lying about his intention to sell his donkey so that he can get out of the house and participate in the law courts as a judge, is translated "insinuatingly" by Amory, "*Eirôn and Eirôneia*," 51, and "mockingly" in LSJ; Douglas M. MacDowell, ed., *Aristophanes: "Wasps"* (Oxford: Clarendon Press, 1971), 155 n., suggests "'disingenuously', 'hypocritically'," while Hilaire van Daele, trans., *Aristophane*, 5 vols., ed. Victor Coulon (Paris: Les Belles Lettres, 1928–40), 2:24, translates as "Quel pretexte il met en avant avec quelle dissimulation." At *Peace* 623, the Aristophanic coinage διειρωνόξενος describes the Spartans' lack of hospitality despite their superficial friendliness: Maurice Platnauer, ed., *Aristophanes: "Peace"* (Oxford: Clarendon Press, 1964), 122 n., comments, "'Very (διά) tricky (εἴρωνες) with' or 'thoroughly unreliable about strangers'; possibly a reference to the Spartan practice of ξενηλασία = 'expulsion of foreigners'"; van Daele translates as "faux frères envers les étrangers." At *Birds* 1210–1211, the term is applied to Iris simply on the grounds that she has lied so that she can enter the new city of the birds; van Daele, *Aristophane*, 3:82, translates this as "Tu entends comme elle fait l'ignorante?" In all these cases, deception seems to be the term's primary sense, even though, in the case where it is applied to some character, the deception has failed to be at least fully successful.

9. *Lg.* 908e2, applied to hypocritical religious offenders; *Soph.* 268a7, b3, applied to the sophist as the dialogue finally succeeds in defining the species.

10. 1 *Philippic* 7. See the commentary of Robert Whiston, *Demosthenes, with an English Commentary*, vol. 1 (London: Whittaker, 1959), 82 n.: "It appears . . . that εἰρωνεία generally signified 'to say one thing and mean another'; . . . in fact, to 'confess and avoid' with dissimulation and evasion. The use of the word then in Demosthenes is peculiarly appropriate, and the Athenians would at once understand by its marked contrast with πράττειν, that he meant to rebuke them for making loud professions and ready acknowledgments of their duty, which nevertheless were nothing but substitutes for, and evasions of, the discharge of it" (Whiston's division of the speech includes the relevant passage in section 9). See also section 37: "οἱ δὲ τῶν πραγμάτων οὐ μένουσι καιροὶ τὴν ἡμετέραν βραδύτητα καὶ εἰρωνείαν"(which Whiston translates as "Our delays and evasions" [97 n.]).

11. This is the traditional view, clear already in Ribbeck and recently defended by Vlastos, *Socrates: Ironist and Moral Philosopher*, chap. 1. For the view that the positive understanding of εἰρωνεία does not emerge until Aristotle's discussion in the *Nicomachean Ethics*, see P. W. Gooch, "Socratic Irony and Aristotle's *Eirôn*: Some Puzzles," *Phoenix* 41 (1987): 95–104.

12. See *Rh.* 2.2, 1379b30–35, 2.5, 1382b18–21; slightly more neutral descriptions can be found at 3.18, 1419b8–10, 3.19, 1319b34–1320a2.

13. See *NE* 4.7, 1127a13–b32. The specific passage, cited here in the translation of Jonathan Barnes, ed., *The Revised Oxford Translation of the Complete Works of Aristotle* (Princeton: Princeton University Press, 1984), occurs at 1127b23–25.

Other references to εἰρωνεία in Aristotle include *Eudemian Ethics* 2.3, 1221a24–26, 3.7, 1234a1–4, and *Magna moralia* 32, 1193a28–35.

14. Theophrastus' actual views in his discussion of the εἴρων in chapter 1 of the *Characters* may in fact be difficult to determine. The text is uncertain, and R. Glenn Ussher (*The Characters of Theophrastus* [London: Macmillan, 1960], n. *ad loc.*) suggests that what we have in our hands today is the result of considerable interpolation.

15. See, for example, Joseph A. Dane, *The Critical Mythology of Irony* (Athens: University of Georgia Press, 1991), 21: "The association of irony with Socrates may originate with Plato, but its persistence is largely a product of the rhetorical tradition"; G. G. Sedgewick, *Of Irony, Especially in Drama* (Toronto: University of Toronto Press, 1948), 9–10: "The raw material which was shaped in this notion [Socratic irony] is of course found in Plato. But the first shaping was done by the . . . *Nicomachean Ethics*."

16. Εἰρωνεία "is to say something and pretend that you are not saying it, or else to call things by the names of their contraries. . . . : 'These noble citizens have clearly done great harm to their allies, while we worthless mortals have obviously been the cause of many benefits to them'" (1433b18–30, quoted from Barnes, ed., *Revised Oxford Translation*). It is worth noting that paralipsis, the trope through which one proposes not to discuss a matter but proceeds to present it anyway, is also classified as irony here (it is the first of the two cases mentioned in the quoted passage). The connection between irony and paralipsis remained alive throughout classical rhetoric: see P. J. Corbett, *Classical Rhetoric for the Modern Student*, 3d ed. (New York: Oxford University Press, 1990), 455.

17. Cicero, *De oratore* 2.67.269–70.

18. Quintilian, *Institutio oratoria* 9.2.44: "Contrarium ei quod dicitur intelligendum est." See also 6.2.15, where the relevant contrast, however, is between "something different" ("diversum," not "contrarium") and "what is said" ("quod dicit").

19. This famous formulation forms the point of beginning for many contemporary discussions of irony. See, for example, Vlastos, *Socrates: Ironist and Moral Philosopher*, 21; Dane, *Critical Mythology of Irony*, 1; Muecke, *Compass of Irony*, 5.

20. *EN* 4.7, 1127a20–24, 31–31: ἀληθευτικός, ἀληθής. See the comments of T. H. Irwin, trans., *Aristotle: "Nicomachean Ethics"* (Indianapolis: Hackett, 1985), 329–30. As Irwin correctly notes, "Aristotle refers to Socrates' frequent disavowals of knowledge about the virtues, which was often regarded as self-deprecation [Irwin's translation of εἰρωνεία]. . . . He does not say that Socrates had the vice of self-deprecation; if Socrates' disavowals of knowledge were sincere and truthful, no self-deprecation was expressed." Though I agree with Irwin that Socrates' disavowals of knowledge were in fact sincere, I understand the sense of those disavowals, as we shall see later, in a very different way.

21. Καὶ γὰρ ἡ ὑπερβολὴ καὶ ἡ λίαν ἔλλειψις ἀλαζονικόν, 1127b28–29. Cited from Barnes, ed., *Revised Oxford Translation*.

22. Michel de Montaigne, "Of experience," in *Complete Works of Montaigne*, trans. Frame, 818.

23. *De vitiis* 10, col. 21.37 (included in Ussher's edition of Theophrastus), p. 38J. A full edition of the work is that by Christian Jensen.

24. In fact, this connection is not absent even from the Aristophanic uses of the term, insofar as lying and trying to deceive others are often connected with the sense that, since something is put over on them, they are inferior to the deceiver, whose victims they are intended to be.

25. The literature that surrounds Vlastos's *Socrates* and the essays that preceded the publication of the book (now collected in *Socratic Studies*, ed. Myles Burnyeat [Cambridge: Cambridge University Press, 1994]) is already enormous. It is beyond the scope of my study to give an account of the relevant bibliography. Partial bibliographies can be found in Hugh H. Benson, ed., *Essays on the Philosophy of Socrates* (New York: Oxford University Press, 1992); Thomas C. Brickhouse and Nicholas D. Smith, *Plato's Socrates* (New York: Oxford University Press, 1994); T. H. Irwin, *Plato's Ethics* (New York: Oxford University Press, 1995); and Richard Kraut, ed., *The Cambridge Companion to Plato* (New York: Cambridge University Press, 1992).

26. Søren Kierkegaard, *The Point of View for My Work as an Author*, trans. Walter Lowrie (New York: Harper and Row, 1962), 39–40. In a similar vein, in *The Concept of Irony with Continual Reference to Socrates*, ed. and trans. Howard V. Hong and Edna H. Hong (Princeton: Princeton University Press, 1989), 59, Kierkegaard also claimed that "the ironic consists in this, that Socrates tricks Protagoras out of every concrete virtue, and when he is to lead it back to unity he completely volatilizes it. The sophistical is that by which he is able to do this."

27. This is what Kierkegaard has in mind when he speaks of "simple irony": "The ironic figure of speech cancels itself . . . inasmuch as the one who is speaking assumes that his hearers understand him, and thus, through a negation of the immediate phenomenon, the sense becomes identical with the phenomenon" (*Concept of Irony*, 248).

28. Wayne Booth, *A Rhetoric of Irony* (Chicago: University of Chicago Press, 1974), 12–13. For a similar position, from a logical point of view, see Paul Grice, *Studies in the Way of Words* (Cambridge, Mass.: Harvard University Press, 1989), 34: an ironic speaker "must be trying to get across some other proposition than the one he purports to put forward. This must be some obviously related proposition; the most obviously related proposition is the contradictory of the one he purports to be putting forward"; on 53–54, Grice points out some difficulties with his account, but those don't concern the point above. He is particularly interesting on the connection between irony and the expression of feeling. A criticism of Booth's views has been offered by Stanley Fish, "Short People Got No Reason to Live: Reading Irony," in *Doing What Comes Naturally* (Durham, N.C.: Duke University Press, 1989), 180–96. In particular, Fish criticizes, correctly in my mind, Booth's distinction between "stable" and "unstable" (more radical, less comprehensible) irony on the grounds that interpretation of the ironist's words is equally necessary in both cases.

29. See Muecke, *Compass of Irony*, whose complex and erudite discussion of the many kinds of irony belies his opening statement, "The art of irony is the art of saying something without really saying it" (5). Even that statement, however, addresses a phenomenon more complex than Vlastos's "primary" case. See also Dane, *Critical Mythology of Irony;* Sedgewick, *Of Irony;* J. A. K. Thomson, *Irony* (London: Allen and Unwin, 1926); and the extensive taxonomy of Uwe Japp, *Theorie der Ironie* (Frankfurt: Klostermann, 1983).

30. We have seen that even in the *Rhetoric to Alexander*, irony is introduced as a means of saying something while pretending not to say it, that is, by means of a case of paralipsis. From its very beginnings in the rhetorical tradition, therefore, irony represented a phenomenon more complex than its current common understanding supposes it does.

31. Cicero, *De oficiis* 1.30.108: "De Graecis autem dulcem et facetum festivisque sermonis, atque in omne oratione simulatorem, quem εἴρωνα Graeci nominarunt, Socratem accepimus." The translation is from M. T. Griffin and E. M. Atkins, ed., *Cicero: "On Duties"* (Cambridge: Cambridge University Press, 1991). In his discussion of that passage, Dane claims that Cicero goes on to liken Socrates to Hannibal and Quintus Maximus, who were notorious for being crafty and dissembling: "Callidum Hannibalem ex Poenorum, ex nostris ducibus Q. Maximum accepimus, facile celare, tacere, dissimulare, insidiari, praeripere hostium consilia." But that cannot be right. The contrast that is relevant to Socrates is with Pythagoras and Pericles, who acquired great authority without any levity: "Contra Pythagoram et Periclem summam auctoritatem consecutos sine ulla hilaritate." Cicero then introduces Hannibal and Quintus Maximus as deceptive characters—representing a new trait—and goes on to compare them to Themistocles, Jason of Pherae, and Solon among the Greeks. Solon did, of course, pretend that he was mad ("furere se simulavit") in order to save his life and his city, and his pretense was an outright lie. But Solon is used to illustrate a different character trait, in line with this chapter's overall aim, which is to show that the "differences in men's spirits" are even greater than the differences in their bodies (in animis exsistunt maiores etiam varietates, 1.30.107 *ad fin.*).

32. Cicero, *De or.* 2.67.269–271: "Urbana etiam dissimulatio est, cum alia dicuntur ac sentias. . . . Socratem opinor in hac ironia dissimulantiaque longe lepore et humanitate omnibus praestitisse. Genus est perelegans et cum gravitate salsum."

33. "Non illo genere de quo ante dixi, cum contraria dicas, ut Lamiae Crassus, sed cum toto genere orationis severe ludas, cum aliter sentias ac loquare" (ibid., 2.67.269). The translation of the last sentence is from Vlastos, *Socrates: Ironist and Moral Philosopher*, 28 n. 24. The earlier passage to which Cicero refers here is 2.65, where he is discussing the ironic use of individual words. The case he has in mind is Crassus's reference to the deformed Lucius Aelius Lamia first as "a beautiful youth" ("pulchellus puer") and then, after Lamia replied that he was not responsible for his looks but only for his talents, as "an able orator" ("disertus"), which (in view of Lamia's rhetorical shortcomings) caused even greater laughter among his audience. This case, which Vlastos eliminates from his citation, represents what he has called "the primary use of irony"; the case he actually discusses leaves the issue whether the ironist's mind is open for the audience's inspection quite undecided.

34. See also Cicero, *Lucullus* 5.15: "Socrates autem de se ipse detrahens in disputatione plus tribuebat is quos volebat refellere; ita cum aliud diceret atque sentiret, libenter uti solitus est ea dissimulatione quam Graeci εἰρωνείαν vocant." ("But Socrates, who disparaged himself in his arguments, attributed greater knowledge to those whom he wanted to refute; so, since he would say something *different* from what he thought, he enjoyed using that kind of dissimulation which the Greeks call εἰρωνεία.") Here too we see that the genus to which irony belongs

involves saying something *other* than (not contrary to) what one thinks. Saying the exact contrary of what one has in mind is only a simple variation on the trope.

35. The fullest discussion of the various forms of irony in Quintilian can be found in M. O. Navarre, ed., *Charactères de Théophraste* (Paris: Les Belles Lettres, 1924), 5–14. See also Jean Cousin, *Études sur Quintilien*, vol. 2 (Paris: Boivin, 1936), 70–71.

36. Quintilian, *Inst. orat.* 6.2.15: "eirôneia, quae diversum ei quo dicit intellectum petit."

37. Ibid., 9.2.44: "in utroque enim contrarium ei quod dicitur intelligendum est."

38. Ibid., 9.2.45; Cf. Cicero, *In Catilinam* 1.8.19.

39. Quintilian, *Inst. orat.* 9.2.46: "At in figura totius voluntatis fictio est, apparens magis quam confessa."

40. Ibid., 9.2.46: "Cum etiam vita universa ironiam habere videatur, qualis est visa Socratis." The passage clearly harks back to Plato, *Symp.* 216e4–5, "εἰρωνευόμενος δὲ καὶ παίζων πάντα τὸν βίον πρὸς τοὺς ἀνθρώπους διατελεῖ," which I shall discuss below.

41. Such an explanation does not apply even to some of the simplest cases of irony. Consider, for instance, Vlastos's example (*Socrates: Ironist and Moral Philosopher*, 21) of Mae West's refusal of an invitation to dinner at Gerald Ford's White House: "It's an awful long way to go for just one meal." We do know that the distance from New York to Washington is not that great, but that is not the whole point made by her quip. There is no function that takes us from what West said to its contrary: all we know is that she is not going to dinner—not on account of the distance but for reasons that we, and perhaps she herself as well, can only guess.

42. See Kierkegaard, *Point of View for My Work as an Author*, 41: "In a formal sense I can very well call Socrates my teacher—whereas I have only believed, and only believe, in One, the Lord Jesus Christ."

43. The term comes from George Kerferd's *The Sophistic Movement* (Cambridge: Cambridge University Press, 1981), which offers some considerations linking Socrates to those whom Plato portrays as his great opponents. See also my "Eristic, Antilogic, Sophistic, Dialectic," *History of Philosophy Quarterly* 5 (1990): 3–16.

44. Such deceptiveness was not always attributed to the sophists themselves, even by opponents like Plato. Euthydemus and Dionysiodorus are the only two characters whom Plato portrays as having no concern for truth. He depicts Protagoras, Hippias, and Gorgias in much more respectful terms, despite Gorgias' commitment to rhetoric, which aims at persuasion rather than truth.

45. Lionel Trilling, *Sincerity and Authenticity* (Cambridge, Mass.: Harvard University Press, 1971), 120.

46. This is what, in a different context, Froma Zeitlin characterizes as "discrepant awareness": "Playing the Other: Theater, Theatricality, and the Feminine in Greek Drama," in *Playing the Other: Gender and Society in Classical Greek Literature* (Chicago: University of Chicago Press, 1995).

47. *Rep.* 337a4–7. Since much of the discussion that follows expresses disagreements with Vlastos's interpretation of this and other passages, and with his approach to Socratic irony, I will use his translations of the Greek texts unless I note otherwise. For a similar view of Socratic irony as the refusal to answer ques-

tions to which one knows the answers, cf. Xenophon, *Mem.* 1.2.36, 4.4.9–10 (and, for some discussion, W. K. C. Guthrie, *A History of Greek Philosophy*, vol. 3 [Cambridge: Cambridge University Press, 1969], 446). Vlastos finds no instances of genuine Socratic irony, as he understands it, in the *Memorabilia*, with the exception of 3.11.13, where Socrates tells Theodote that he has "his own girlfriends (φίλαι)" to attend to, meaning quite clearly the young men to whose education in virtue he is, according to Xenophon, devoted. But I think that 4.2.3–5 and 4.2.9, where Socrates interacts with Euthydemus, present us with similar cases. They are both rather artless, even if the former is used to make a serious point about the wrong manner in which Euthydemus is preparing himself for a public career.

48. Cf. *Cr.* 383b8–384a4, where Hermogenes accuses Cratylus of εἰρωνεύεσθαι, on the ground that he is pretending (προσποιούμενος) that he holds certain views that he could make clear if only he wanted to, though in fact he does not. The εἴρων here seems to be pretending to know more, not less, than he says. And Socrates may well have appeared to know more than he said to his contemporaries, although the explicit charge Thrasymachus makes against him differs from Hermogenes' charge against Cratylus. Still, it is clear that Thrasymachus believes that Socrates *thinks* he knows more than he says about justice. Thus the boastful implication of irony, which I have been trying to bring into the foreground, is present in both cases. Kierkegaard, too, saw this point: "It can be just as ironic to pretend to know when one knows that one does not know as to pretend not to know when one knows that one knows" (*Concept of Irony*, 250–51). Cf. also *Soph.* 268a1–b5, where the "ironic" sophist is portrayed as someone who claims to know all sorts of things that only the philosopher can.

49. *Rep.* 336b9–337a2. Translation from G. M. A. Grube, trans., *Plato: "Republic,"* rev. C. D. C. Reeve (Indianapolis: Hackett, 1992).

50. *Symp.* 216e4. The word Vlastos translates as "jesting" is παίζων, which might be better rendered as "toying." That is a term often associated with Socrates, sometimes as a description of what he does, sometimes in order to deny precisely that description; see, for example, *Ap.* 20d4–5, *Pr.* 336d2–4 G. 481b4–5.

51. Vlastos refers to Guthrie, *History of Greek Philosophy*, 3:446; K. J. Dover, ed., *Plato: "Symposium"* (Cambridge: Cambridge University Press, 1980), 168 n.; Suzy Q Groden, trans., *The "Symposium" of Plato*, ed. J. A. Brentlinger (Amherst: University of Massachusetts Press, 1970); and William Hamilton, trans., *Plato: "Symposium,"* (Baltimore: Penguin, 1951).

52. This is in contrast to his earlier view, which we have already discussed, and according to which there can be a pretense that is totally innocent of deceit. Guthrie is the only author among the four Vlastos mentions here who writes that Socrates "deceives" people as to his real character. The others refer to his "pretended ignorance" or to his pretending *tout court*. That is why Vlastos claims they all assume Socrates is a deceiver.

53. H. W. Fowler, *A Dictionary of Modern English Usage*, 2d ed., rev. and ed. Sir Ernest Gowers (New York: Oxford University Press, 1965), 306.

54. This audience may or may not be actual. But even when irony involves only a single speaker and a single victim, the idea that someone can in principle share the joke with the speaker is always present: a notional audience is always involved.

55. Vlastos, whose translation I use again not to beg any questions, separates

this text into two for his own purposes (*Socrates: Ironist and Moral Philosopher*, 36). I have joined his two citations, which form a continuous passage in the Greek, into one.

56. Vlastos, *Socrates: Ironist and Moral Philosopher*, 41–43.

57. That is Vlastos's interpretation, ibid., 36–37.

58. This tradition ultimately goes back to Thrasymachus' reaction to Socrates in *Rep.* 1.

59. D. J. Enright, *The Alluring Problem: An Essay on Irony* (New York: Oxford University Press, 1986), 9.

60. I have italicized the phrase beginning with "the truth." Other statements Vlastos interprets as complex ironies are Socrates' disavowals of knowledge and his disavowal of political engagement. See *Socrates: Ironist and Moral Philosopher*, 31–32, 36–37, 236–42.

61. See Donald Morrison, "On Professor Vlastos' Xenophon," *Ancient Philosophy* 7 (1987): 9–22, who, in the course of an argument to the effect that Xenophon's Socrates is more ironic than Vlastos believes, claims that Vlastos's understanding of complex irony implies that "Socrates would be guilty of trading on an ambiguity: of creating the appearance of paradox and of philosophical depth through failing to distinguish two senses of a word and to state his position clearly in terms of each" (12). Though I suspect that this charge is a little too extreme, I believe Morrison raises an important question: why should Socrates pursue such a roundabout strategy if his goal were, as Vlastos believes, to make his interlocutors better people? Why should he expect them to understand on their own his personal, radically idiosyncratic views of teaching or knowledge?

62. Thomas Mann, *Der Zauberberg* (Frankfurt: Fischer Verlag, 1952), 304, 305; *The Magic Mountain*, translated by John E. Woods (New York: Alfred A. Knopf, 1995), 217, 218.

63. Friedrich Schlegel, *Lyceum Fragments*, no. 42, in *Kritische Schriften* (Munich: Carl Hanser, 1938), 10.

64. The notion of complex irony can actually be found in the discussion of Paul Friedländer, *Plato*, 2d ed., vol. 1 (Princeton: Princeton University Press, 1969), 139–40, though Friedländer did not draw the far-reaching conclusions Vlastos does from the application of that idea.

65. For full references, see Vlastos, *Socrates: Ironist and Moral Philosopher*, 237–38, and idem, "Socrates' Disavowal of Knowledge," in *Socratic Studies*, 39–66.

66. Vlastos cites no text where Socrates avows being a teacher in *Socrates: Ironist and Moral Philosopher*, 237, in contrast to the cases of knowledge and politics, which are well documented. The only evidence he offers for such a conflict in his discussion of teaching from which I quoted above comes from the *Gorgias* (521d6–8), where Socrates' politics, and not his teaching, is the subject.

67. Despite the claims of Diogenes Laertius and R. E. Allen. See chap.1, n. 66.

68. Socrates seems to have been actually accused of being responsible for the brutality of Critias when he joined the Thirty Tyrants who briefly ruled Athens after the end of the Peloponnesian War, as well as for the shameful career of Alcibiades. We can infer that from Xenophon's long and explicit defense of Socrates against those charges (*Mem.* 1.2.12–39).

69. Plato, *Symp.* 216b3–5. Quoted from Alexander Nehamas and Paul Woodruff, trans., *Plato: "Symposium"* (Indianapolis: Hackett, 1989).

70. See, for example, *M.* 93b7–94e1. We should also note that there is no reason to believe that Socrates' own children exhibited the virtue he accused Pericles of not being able to transmit to his own sons.

71. For a contrasting view of the teacher's responsibility, cf. Xenophon, *Mem.* 1.2.19, 23, 27.

72. The common translation of *aretê* is "virtue." In the next chapter, we shall discuss that translation and the proper way of understanding the Greek term.

73. This contrast may, incidentally, provide an additional interpretative reason to think of the *Gorgias* as a later work. For the criticism that Socrates makes of Gorgias here is not unrelated to the criticism of Socratic dialectic Plato puts into Socrates' own mouth in the *Republic* (539b1–d7), which is acknowledged as part of Plato's middle period. The argument here is that Socratic dialectic was practiced with men who were too young to profit from it and who, instead, used the formal methods it taught them in order to disagree with their elders, undermine accepted values, and put nothing in their place. So Plato claims that Socrates did implicitly bear some responsibility for his companions' behavior (even though he was not their teacher in any strict sense) because he exposed them to a method of argument for which they were not ready: the responsibility was therefore not only theirs.

74. That the various Socratics disliked one another on personal as well as on philosophical grounds is stated in a number of places by Diogenes Laertius. See, for example, 2.7.60 (on Aeschines), 2.8.65 (on Aristippus), 3.1.24 (on Plato), and 6.1.4 (on Antisthenes).

75. Kierkegaard, *Concept of Irony*, 12.

76. "Ἀτοπία," literally, "being out of place." See Vlastos, *Socrates: Ironist and Moral Philosopher*, 1, and also Plato, *G.* 494d1, *Symp.* 215a2, 221d2, *Phdr.* 230c6, *Tht.* 149a9. For a different, more complex account of what constitutes Socrates' ἀτοπία, see Pierre Hadot, "Spiritual Exercises," in *Philosophy as a Way of Life* (Oxford: Blackwell, 1995), 57, and *Qu'est-ce que la philosophie antique?* (Paris: Gallimard, 1995), 56–57. Hadot, who connects Socrates' "being out of place" with the philosopher's inability to belong fully either to the sensible or to the intelligible world, also identifies Socrates' ἀτοπία with his unique individuality. If Hadot is right in this latter claim, that would explain why no general account of what Socrates "really" was like ever was, or will be, possible.

77. Enright, *Alluring Problem*, 6. This seems to me a much better account even of Socratic irony than the passage quoted above (63).

78. On my chronology of the dialogues, see chap. 1, n. 33.

79. A central instance is provided by the theory of recollection and the distinction between true belief and knowledge associated with it (*M.* 81a5–86c3, 96e7–100c2). The ideas that the soul may recall views that constitute true beliefs from the time when it was not incarnate, that true beliefs can be as good guides to action as knowledge as long as they remain in the soul, and that who does have such beliefs and who does not is a matter of chance or "divine dispensation" (99e6) seem designed to explain how Socrates, in Plato's eyes, succeeded in acting rightly in a consistent manner despite the fact that he lacked the knowledge that he himself may have considered necessary for such an accomplishment.

80. An analysis of this complex passage is given by Donald Morrison, "Xenophon's Socrates on the Just and the Lawful," *Ancient Philosophy* 15 (1995): 329–48.

81. Schlegel, *Lyceum Fragments*, no. 108, in *Kritische Schriften*, 19.

Chapter 3

1. Søren Kierkegaard, *The Concept of Irony with Continual Reference to Socrates*, ed. and trans. Howard V. Hong and Edna H. Hong (Princeton: Princeton University Press, 1989), 11–12.

2. G. W. F. Hegel, *Lectures on the History of Philosophy*, trans. E. S. Haldane, vol. 1 (1892; reprint, London: Routledge and Kegan Paul, 1962), 388. The original is from Hegel, *Vorlesungen über die Geschichte der Philosophie*, 3 vols. (Leiden: A. H. Adriani, 1908), 1:295.

3. Hegel, *Lectures on the History of Philosophy*, trans. Haldane, 1:386; *Vorlesungen über die Geschichte der Philosophie*, 1:293, 293–95. While Hegel considers this Socrates' greatest achievement, Nietzsche, as we shall see in chap. 5 below, regards what he considers as Socrates' destruction of archaic or "tragic" Greek culture as his gravest fault.

4. Hegel's criticisms of Schlegel and romantic irony can be found, among many other places, in *Lectures on the History of Philosophy*, trans. Haldane, 1:400–402, and in G. W. F. Hegel, *Sämtliche Werke: Jubiläumausgabe*, ed. Hermann Glockner, 26 vols. (Stuttgart: Fromann, 1927–40), 19:640–41.

5. Hegel, *Sämtliche Werke: Jubiläumausgabe*, ed. Glockner, 12:105–6, 221; idem, *Philosophy of Fine Art*, trans. F. P. B. Gemaston, vol. 1 (1920; repr. New York: Hacker Art Books, 1975), 93–94, 217.

6. "When Socrates declared that he was ignorant, he nevertheless did know something, for he knew about his ignorance; on the other hand, however, this knowledge was not a knowledge of something, that is, did not have any positive content, and to that extent his ignorance was ironic, and since Hegel has tried in vain, in my opinion, to reclaim a positive content for him, I believe that the reader must agree with me" (Kierkegaard, *Concept of Irony*, 269). In general, Kierkegaard criticizes Hegel for thinking that because Socratic irony differs from Schlegel's conception, which Hegel identified with irony itself, it is not really irony at all. Kierkegaard believes that both Socrates' and Schlegel's versions are genuine species of irony.

7. Ibid., 254.

8. Ibid., 261.

9. Nor do I want at this point to take issue with Kierkegaard's inclusion of the *Phaedo* among the Platonic texts from which he derives his totally ironic image of Socrates (*Concept of Irony*, 62–79). Kierkegaard's broad conception of irony allows him to find in the *Phaedo* the same sort of character as we find, say, in the *Euthyphro* or the *Protagoras*. But, for me, the *Phaedo* represents a very different Socrates and is part of a very different stage in Plato's philosophical development. The *Phaedo*, in line with the argument of the concluding pages of the previous chapter, is an element in Plato's conscious effort to understand Socrates, to explain what allowed him to live as he did despite the fact that he lacked the knowledge he considered necessary for the good life. It constitutes, for Plato as well as for Socrates (who uses that expression about his own philosophical journey), a δεύτερος πλοῦς, a second or second-best or alternative sailing, a new attempt to accomplish something that Plato's earlier dialogues had not succeeded in accomplishing (and perhaps never intended to accomplish in the first place).

10. See Joseph A. Dane, *The Critical Mythology of Irony* (Athens: University of Georgia Press, 1991), parts 1 and 2.

11. Norman Gulley, *The Philosophy of Socrates* (London: Macmillan, 1968), 39, writes that Socrates claims to be ignorant "as an expedient to encourage his interlocutor to seek out the truth, to make him think that he is joining with Socrates in a voyage of discovery." This is not dissimilar to the view that underlies Vlastos's conception of "complex irony," which we discussed in the preceding chapter.

12. Michael Frede, "Plato's Arguments and the Dialogue Form," in James C. Klagge and Nicholas D. Smith, eds., *Methods of Interpreting Plato and His Dialogues, Oxford Studies in Ancient Philosophy* 10 (1992): Supplement, 208, 209.

13. Though I agree with Frede's description of Socrates' practice, I also believe that when he asks about the nature of the virtues Socrates sometimes hopes, perhaps against hope, that someone may know the answer to one of his questions. The two goals are not incompatible.

14. We saw, however, that Socrates' point is not just to say that Thrasymachus is stupid (see chap. 2, p. 62).

15. Aristotle, *De Sophisticis Elenchis* 34, 183b6–8. Translation from Jonathan Barnes, ed., *The Revised Oxford Translation of the Complete Works of Aristotle* (Princeton: Princeton University Press, 1984). Aristotle's ὡμολόγει, translated as "used to confess" here, carries no suggestion that Socrates dissimulated in his disavowals of knowledge.

16. Plato, *Ap.* 29b6–7. This translation, like all others for which I give no explicit acknowledgment, is mine.

17. T. H. Irwin, *Plato's Moral Theory* (New York: Oxford University Press, 1977), 39, with full references. See also idem, *Plato's Ethics* (New York: Oxford University Press, 1995), chap. 2, esp. pp. 27–29, for a new variant of that view.

18. See Gregory Vlastos, "Socrates' Disavowal of Knowledge," in *Socratic Studies*, ed. Myles Burnyeat (Cambridge: Cambridge University Press, 1994), 42–48. Vlastos, who tries to resolve this conflict by distinguishing, as we shall see, between two different types of knowledge to which Socrates lays claim (43–44), depends crucially on a number of statements Socrates makes in the *Gorgias* concerning his knowledge of moral matters and the truth of his elenctic conclusions (e.g., 472c6–d1, 486e5–6, 505e4–5). However, I am unwilling to use the *Gorgias* as evidence for Plato's early view of Socrates, since I consider it a later work.

I have accepted a later date for the *Gorgias* partly because of stylistic considerations: like the *Meno*, which is acknowledged to belong among the latest of the early dialogues or even among the works of Plato's middle period, the *Gorgias* starts as a dialogue of definition (its subject is rhetoric, that of the *Meno* is virtue) but soon leaves definition aside and faces Callicles' challenge to Socratic ethics — a challenge as radical as that which Meno's paradox (*M.* 80d5–e5) presents to Socratic methodology. I also believe that the issues of ethics, metaphysics, and epistemology presented in those works are new and receive explicit treatment only in the *Phaedo* and the *Republic*.

In addition, I want to draw attention to how differently the thesis that suffering injustice is worse than committing it is treated in the *Crito* (which is acknowledged to be an early work of Plato) and in the *Gorgias*. In the former dialogue, Socrates presents the view as deeply controversial and announces his willingness to discuss it anew (49b3–e2); he admits that people who disagree about it can hold no "common counsel" (κοινὴ βουλή, 49d3). In the latter work, Socrates insists much more dogmatically that everyone, whether they know it or not, accepts the view that being treated unjustly is not as bad as being unjust oneself. The difference is significant.

And that, in turn, makes a significant difference to Vlastos's view that the Socrates of Plato's early dialogues—of *all* the early dialogues—believes that everyone possesses a stock of true beliefs "within" them that entail the negation of any other false ethical views they may also hold. This last thesis is the epistemological heart of the positive moral interpretation of the elenchus that Vlastos proposed in "The Socratic Elenchus," in *Socratic Studies*, ed. Burnyeat, 1–28 (see also idem, *Socrates: Ironist and Moral Philosopher* [Cambridge: Cambridge University Press, 1991], 113–15). If we all have such views within us, then the elenchus, despite the fact that it seems capable only of showing that various beliefs a person holds are inconsistent, allows us eventually to eliminate the false ones and to keep only those that are true (assuming, of course, that we are able to identify our true beliefs in the first place). Vlastos's evidence for his interpretation comes overwhelmingly from the *Gorgias* (see Richard Kraut, "Comments on Gregory Vlastos, 'The Socratic Elenchus,' " *Oxford Studies in Ancient Philosophy* 1 [1983]: 59–70, and Vlastos's reply in the same issue, reprinted with minor changes in *Socratic Studies*, 33–37). But the *Gorgias'* position in Plato's development, if my argument above is correct, forbids us to project views derived from it onto all the dialogues that precede it. In particular, the specific difference between the *Crito* and the *Gorgias* on the "retaliation thesis" suggests that it was only between the time when he wrote the *Crito* and the date when he composed the *Gorgias*, and not throughout his early period, that Plato came (if he did) to the view that all of us possess "within" us the true views that the elenchus, perhaps, reveals. This view is, in my opinion, a later Platonic innovation and not a Socratic thesis—at least not a thesis Plato had ever thought of attributing to the Socrates of his early dialogues. It is expressed for the first time in the *Gorgias* and it receives its first explanation through the theory of recollection in the *Meno*, which is in my view the *Gorgias'* companion piece and belongs, as Vlastos himself believes, to the beginnings of Plato's middle period (*Socrates: Ironist and Moral Philosopher*, 47 with n. 8, and pp. 117–26).

19. *EN* 6.2, 1139b19–20; quoted from Barnes, ed., *Revised Oxford Translation*.

20. See chap. 2, pp. 63–67.

21. For Plato, see, among others, *Rep.* 476e4–478d4; *Tht.* 152c5–6, *Ti.* 51e4. For Aristotle, *APo.* 71b15–16, 72b3–4. These texts (with the exception of the passage from the *Theaetetus*) are cited and discussed by Vlastos, "Socrates' Disavowal of Knowledge," 52–54.

22. Democritus DK B117 and B9, cited in Vlastos, "Socrates' Disavowal of Knowledge," 55.

23. Xenophanes, DK B18, B24, B35, B38.

24. Parmenides, DK B1, B7, also discussed in Vlastos, "Socrates' Disavowal of Knowledge," 55.

25. Vlastos, *Socrates: Ironist and Moral Philosopher*, chap. 2 *passim*, esp. 47–48 (Theses IA and IB). See also idem, "Socrates' Disavowal of Knowledge," 62–63.

26. I have offered a more detailed argument for that conclusion, based partly on the interpretation of *Ap.* 19a8–23c1, in "What Did Socrates Teach and to Whom Did He Teach It?"

27. *Ap.* 22c8–d4, translated by G. M. A. Grube in *Plato: Five Dialogues* (Indi-

anapolis: Hackett, 1981). By contrast, neither the politicians (21c3–e2) nor the poets (22a8–c8) can even understand the principles of their own activities. The problem with the artisans is not that they have no knowledge: they do, but they believe that that qualifies them to speak knowledgeably about the virtues and yet prove incapable of doing so. Socrates also attributes knowledge to physicians and sculptors (toward whom his attitude is much more generous than toward poets — one more indication that Plato was not an enemy of "the arts" as we understand them) at *Pr.* 311b5–c8, by implying that they can teach their craft to others, and in a number of other places.

28. For the argument that Socrates is contrasting himself to the sophists and not to the natural philosophers, as Vlastos has argued ("Socrates' Disavowal of Knowledge," 61–62 with n. 53), see "What Did Socrates Teach and to Whom Did He Teach It?" 291–93. See also C. D. C. Reeve, *Socrates in the Apology* (Indianapolis: Hackett, 1989), 10–11.

29. On such "expert" knowledge, see Reeve, *Socrates in the Apology*, 37–53, and Paul Woodruff, trans., *Plato: "Hippias Major"* (Indianapolis: Hackett, 1982), 79–112. It is possible, however, that not all sophists made such a strong claim. Gorgias, according to *M.* 95c, denied that he was a teacher of *aretê* and claimed only to make people better speakers (though see W. K. C. Guthrie, *A History of Greek Philosophy*, 6 vols. [Cambridge: Cambridge University Press, 1962–81], 3:271–72 with n. 1, for evidence that what Gorgias claimed was not always believed and might have been, perhaps, not believable). Protagoras, according to Paul Woodruff ("Plato's Debt to Protagoras," typescript [Department of Philosophy, University of Texas, 1993]), is aware of the disanalogies between the "craft" of teaching *aretê* and the other crafts, while Socrates pushes the analogy more forcefully than it deserves in order to discredit the sophist's claim to be teaching *aretê* in any way. See also Paul Woodruff, "Plato's Early Theory of Knowledge," in Stephen Everson, ed., *Epistemology* (Cambridge: Cambridge University Press, 1990), 60–84.

30. As suggested by Irwin, *Plato's Moral Theory*, 23, 24, 34, 73.

31. If we can believe Diogenes Laertius, *Lives of the Philosophers*, 2.5.18.

32. Alison Burford, *Craftsmen in Greek and Roman Society* (Ithaca: Cornell University Press, 1972), 82.

33. Ibid., 89. She also writes that "craftsmen . . . had to undergo long and thorough training. Constant application was required of a man if he was to become fully acquainted with his craft. Once he had learnt it, he must continue to exercise his skill, otherwise it would decay and die on him" (p. 69). Pliny (*Natural History*, 35, 84) reports that Apelles used to draw every day in order to maintain his talent in top form. Such statements invite both contrast and comparison with Aristotle's view that *aretê* is almost impossible to lose once acquired since it is by nature such as to be constantly manifested in action (*EN.* 3.5, 1114b30–1115a4; 4.10, 1152a28–33) and perhaps also with Socrates' interpretation of Simonides' poem in the *Protagoras* (341d6–347a5), in which he refuses to attribute to Simonides the view that it is hard to be (that is, to remain) good once one has become good — the really hard thing — in the first place. See also Maurice Pope, *The Ancient Greeks: How They Lived and Worked* (London: David and Charles, 1976), 73.

34. Hippocrates, *On Ancient Medicine* 1.13–19, and see the commentary of A.-J. Festugière in *Hippocrate: L'Ancienne médecine*, ed. A.-J. Festugière (1948;

repr., New York: Arno Press, 1979). On the dispute between Zeuxis and Parrhasius see Pliny, *Natural History*, 35, 61, and on the competition between Apelles
and Protogenes, 35,79; a related story occurs at 36, 79.

35. The literature on the precise connection Plato's Socrates envisaged to hold
between virtue and happiness is immense, and immensely complex. I don't want
to take a position on the many issues it involves here. Irwin's recent discussion
in *Plato's Ethics, passim*, though it advances his own idiosyncratic view, contains
a good discussion of alternative approaches and an extensive bibliography.

36. "Ἐγὼ γὰρ δὴ οὔτε μέγα οὔτε σμικρὸν σύνοιδα ἐμαυτῷ σοφὸς ὤν."
Plato has Socrates use the same verb in connection with self-knowledge at *Phdr.*
235c6–7, "συνειδὼς ἐμαυτῷ ἁμαρτίαν."

37. Contrast Vlastos, "Socrates' Disavowal of Knowledge," 43 with n. 12.

38. More information on the notion of technical knowledge can be found in
Reeve, *Socrates in the Apology;* Woodruff, trans., *Plato: "Hippias Major";* Michael
Frede, "Philosophy and Medicine in Antiquity," in *Essays on Ancient Philosophy*
(Minneapolis: University of Minnesota Press, 1987), 225–42; David Roochnik,
"Plato's Use of the Techne-Analogy," *Journal of the History of Philosophy* 24 (1986):
295–310; J. E. Tiles, "*Techné* and Moral Expertise," *Philosophy* 59 (1984): 49–66;
and Irwin, *Plato's Moral Theory*, 71–86, and *Plato's Ethics*, 47–48.

39. Homer, *Iliad*, 23.276: "ἴστε γὰρ ὅσσον μοι ἀρετῇ περιβάλλετον ἵπποι,"
which Robert Fagles (in Homer, *The Iliad*, trans. Robert Fagles [New York: Viking
Penguin, 1990]) renders as "You know how my team outstrips all others' speed,"
and 374–75, "τότε δὴ ἀρετὴ ἑκάστου [ἵππου] φαίνετο," though Fagles attributes the ἀρετή in question not to the horses but to the charioteers.

40. Herodotus, *Histories*, 3.106.2; 4.198.7. He also speaks of the ἀρετή of
horses, 3.88.

41. Thucydides, *History of the Peloponnesian War*, 1.2.4.

42. The manner in which Meno introduces that question in the dialogue
named after him suggests very strongly that the question was a *topos*, a commonplace of dialectical practice as well as a real issue. The author of the *Dissoi logoi*
(composed probably around 403–395 BC) refers to the "neither true nor new argument that σοφία [wisdom] and ἀρετά [areté] can neither be taught nor learned"
(on the date of this text, see T. M. Robinson, *Contrasting Arguments: An Edition
of the "Dissoi logoi"* [New York: Arno Press, 1979], 34–41). In *Olympian* 2.86–88,
Pindar famously had claimed that the wise (who in this case refers to the poet) is
so by nature, while the others, those who have to learn their craft, are in comparison to him like squawking crows (and cf. *Nemean* 3.41). Isocrates was to argue that ἀρετή (areté) and δικαιοσύνη (justice) are not purely teachable—not,
that is, without a proper nature that is disposed to receive them (*Contra Sophistas* 14–18, 21; cf. *Antidosis* 186–92, 274–75). That position, in fact, is seriously similar to Plato's overall approach in the *Republic*. Even Xenophon attributes a similar thesis to Socrates in *Memorabilia* 3.9.

43. Plato, *The Dialogues of Plato*, trans. Benjamin Jowett (Oxford: Oxford University Press, 1953), 252.

44. Werner Peek, *Griechische Versinschriften*, vol. 1 (Berlin: Akademie, 1955), 20.11.

45. Contrast, for example, the rather idealized version of the agreement
Socrates envisages among sculptors and doctors at *Pr.* 311b5–c8 with the cases cited
in n. 27 above.

46. Frede, "Philosophy and Medicine in Antiquity," 225; cf. 231–34.

47. See Irwin, *Plato's Moral Theory*, 77–86, for discussion.

48. I am grateful to Christopher Bobonich for discussing (not, I am afraid, to his satisfaction) this issue with me.

49. The elenchus proceeds roughly as follows. Socrates usually elicits a proposal for defining a virtue from his interlocutor. He then obtains the interlocutor's agreement with certain other views, for none of which he argues: the interlocutor just accepts them. He then shows that the set that consists of the original proposal along with the other views the interlocutor accepts is inconsistent: the interlocutor cannot hold all those views together. But the elenchus does not, from a purely logical point of view, show which view has to be rejected in order to make the set consistent. Still, Socrates often claims to have shown that the interlocutor's proposed definition is false. How can Socrates do that, Gregory Vlastos asks, "when all he has established is its inconsistency with premises whose truth he has not tried to establish in that argument: they have entered the argument simply as propositions on which he and the interlocutor have agreed"? "This," Vlastos concludes, "is *the* problem of the Socratic elenchus" ("The Socratic Elenchus: Method Is All," in *Socratic Studies*, 4–5). My own position is that Socrates is in general very careful to get his interlocutors to agree to additional views each one of which is more plausible than the proposed definition. That allows him, though not in strictly logical terms, to discard the definition and not any of his interlocutors' subsidiary views. He occasionally gets in trouble when his interlocutor is willing to abandon one of these views, as Thrasymachus prefers to argue that justice is not a virtue than to concede that his definition of justice as the interest of the stronger should be abandoned at *Rep.* 338a8ff.

50. See *Eu.* 15c11–e2; *Ch.* 176a6–d5; *La.* 210b6–c5; *Pr.* 36135–6; *Ly.* 223a1–b3; *M.* 79e5–6, 80e3–4.

51. An exception to this statement is provided by Vlastos, who changed his mind and came to believe that the elenchus could reach positive results because our store of true beliefs within was sufficient to ensure that our false beliefs would be expunged. I discussed that view briefly, and gave some reasons for not accepting it, in n. 18 above.

52. George Grote, *Plato and the Other Companions of Sokrates*, vol. 1 (London: Russell, 1865), 244. In his review of Grote, John Stuart Mill wrote that Plato understood dialectic to consist of two parts: "One is, the testing of every opinion by a negative scrutiny, eliciting every objection or difficulty that could be raised against it, and demanding, before it was adopted, that they should be successfully met. This could only be done effectively through oral discussion; pressing the respondent by questions, to which he could reply either by contradicting views admitted generally or his own original hypothesis. This cross-examination is the Sokratic Elenchus" ("Grote's Plato," *Edinburgh Review*, in Barry Gross, ed., *Great Thinkers on Plato* [New York: Capricorn Books, 1969], 155).

53. Richard Robinson, *Plato's Earlier Dialectic*, 2d ed. (Oxford: Clarendon Press, 1953), 7.

54. Gregory Vlastos, "Introduction," in Benjamin Jowett, trans., *Plato: "Protagoras,"* rev. Martin Ostwald (Indianapolis: Bobbs-Merrill, 1956), xxxi. See also Guthrie, *History of Greek Philosophy*, 4:69: "The method of procedure, governing the structure of the [early] dialogues, is this. A series of definitions is elicited from

the respondents, each a modification of the last necessitated by Socrates' objections, until they arrive at a clear formula. This is then criticized in turn and finally rejected. No definition is finally adopted, and the apparent end is deadlock and bafflement."

55. This is not to say that Plato's readers have not found positive messages hidden within the dialogues themselves. But none of these is implied by the logical structure of the elenchus itself. W. G. Rabinowitz's "Platonic Piety: An Essay towards the Solution of an Enigma," *Phronesis* 3 (1958): 108–20, provides an instance of how the search for such positive views can proceed. In general, the proponents of the Straussian approach to the dialogues try to discern positive conclusions by combining the logical structure of Socrates' method (which, they agree, can only lead to negative results) with the dramatic features of the works. See, for example, David Bolotin, *Plato's Dialogue on Friendship: An Interpretation of the "Lysis" with a New Translation* (Ithaca: Cornell University Press, 1979), 12.

56. Thomas C. Brickhouse and Nicholas D. Smith, *Socrates on Trial* (Princeton: Princeton University Press, 1989), 96–97, object to an earlier interpretation of mine according to which Socrates examines the oracle to see whether it is true ("Socratic Intellectualism," in John J. Cleary, ed., *Proceedings of the Boston Area Colloquium in Ancient Philosophy*, vol. 2 [Lanham, Md.: University Press of America, 1987], 305–6). They are right that I had overstated my case. But they shy away from the implications of Socrates' use of the verb ἐλέγχειν and from his statement that, if he were to find a wiser man, the oracle would be refuted.

57. These issues have been discussed at great length in the extensive secondary literature that has grown around Socrates since the 1970s. Good places to begin looking at that literature are Hugh H. Benson, ed., *Essays on the Philosophy of Socrates* (New York: Oxford University Press, 1992); Thomas C. Brickhouse and Nicholas D. Smith, *Plato's Socrates* (New York: Oxford University Press, 1994); Barry S. Gower and Michael C. Stokes, *Socratic Questions: The Philosophy of Socrates and Its Significance* (London, Routledge, 1992); and, from a different point of view, Paul Vander Waerdt, ed., *The Socratic Movement* (Ithaca: Cornell University Press, 1994). Most of them spring from the work of Gregory Vlastos.

58. On the necessity of the knowledge of ἀρετή for acting with ἀρετή, see *Ap.* 29d2–30a2; *La.* 193d11–e6; and *Ly.* 212a1–7, 223b4–8. A good discussion is in Irwin, *Plato's Moral Theory*, 90–92.

59. Vlastos, "Socrates' Disavowal of Knowledge," 43 with n. 13. The italics are mine.

60. Ibid., 64. "Knowledge" is Vlastos's term for the certain, deductive knowledge for which Socrates had been searching in vain. The italics are again mine.

61. It is important to note that the claim to know that it is bad and shameful to disobey one's superior and refuse to perform one's appointed task whether out of fear of death or anything else (*Ap.* 29d6–10), though not trivial, is not in fact terribly controversial. Polus, for example, readily admits it in the *Gorgias* (474b7–c3). It takes a character of such extreme views as Callicles to deny it (482d7–8). Moreover, though the thesis that it is wrong to consider death worse than disgrace, which is part of Socrates' view in the *Apology*, can be debated at length, it is still not an idea that is easily to be rejected. Socrates, then, relies on substantive though not particularly controversial ideas in making his claim to

knowledge. Note, now, the triviality of *Pr.* 357d7–e1, cited as a case of a Socratic claim to knowledge by Vlastos ("Socrates Disavowal of Knowledge," 46, in his translation): "You yourselves, surely, know that wrong action done *without knowledge* is done because of *ignorance*" (my italics). Another claim is made at *Rep.* 1, 351a5–6: "For injustice is ignorance—no one could still not know this" (referred to by Vlastos, 47, cited here in his translation). But apart from the fact that the dating of this text is a matter of great controversy, I believe that Socrates' verb ἀγνοεῖν ("to be ignorant of") need not be taken too strictly here. He has already driven Thrasymachus into a dialectical corner (350c10–11) and is issuing a further challenge to him here. His use of the term is dialectical, not epistemological. The "rejection of retaliation" thesis in the *Crito* is not presented as a thesis about which Socrates claims certainty: on the contrary, he repeats his willingness to examine it again for as long as necessary. His morally robust attitude is counterbalanced by his dialectical tentativeness.

62. Kierkegaard, *Concept of Irony*, 271–72. Here he describes the elements of Socrates' position as he sees it: "The whole substantial life of Greek culture had lost its validity for him, which means that to him the established actuality was unactual, not in this or that particular aspect but in its totality as such; . . . with regard to this invalid actuality he let the established order of things appear to remain established and thereby brought about its downfall; . . . in the process Socrates became lighter and lighter, more and more negatively free." We do not need to accept all the elements of Kierkegaard's picture to see that the notion of negative freedom implies a distance from what one denies and an unwillingness to attack it directly.

63. Such an *implicit* admission, made by an author who does not appear even as a narrator in his own work, is a very rare phenomenon. Much more common is the explicit admission of a narrator that a character is beyond comprehension. A clear instance of the latter occurs in Thomas Mann's *Doctor Faustus*, whose narrator, Serenus Zeitblom, insists repeatedly that the composer Adrian Leverkühn, whose friend he has been since childhood and whom he considers a true genius, surpasses his own limited understanding. However, I believe that subtle hints in the novel point to a much deeper cunning on Zeitblom's part than the narrator admits. Zeitblom, I am convinced, actually manipulates the data about Leverkühn that he presents with such apparent objectivity. That, however, is a matter for another occasion. In any case, even if Zeitblom fails to understand Leverkühn, the same does not hold either for Mann or for his readers, to whom Zeitblom, perhaps unwittingly, gives all the necessary information. Nabokov's *The Real Life of Sebastian Knight* is a similar case, and his *Transparent Things* depends on an author/ narrator who does not, like Zeitblom, fully belong to the novel's world and who possesses only "limited" knowledge of his central character. The same goes for Robert Musil's Arnheim in *The Man without Qualities*, Gilbert Sorrentino's *Imaginary Qualities of Actual Things*, and Clarence Major's *Reflex and Bone Structure*. Religious figures, also, are often incomprehensible to those who write about them; but divine grace always provides an (unenlightening) explanation. What is remarkable and disturbing about Plato's case is that it involves no assertion, no acknowledgment that an author is creating a character he does not understand. Plato just presents Socrates as a mystery, without the literary self-consciousness that deprives the modernist and postmodernist authors I mention here of the (per-

haps unwanted by them) claim to verisimilitude the dialogues so forcefully make and to which I shall soon turn. I am grateful to Thomas Pavel and Brian McHale, both of whom discussed the issue with me.

64. A serious case for not making chronological assumptions in reading the Platonic dialogues has recently been made by John M. Cooper in his introduction to John M. Cooper, ed., *Plato: Complete Works* (Indianapolis: Hackett, 1997). Cooper argues correctly that the classification of Plato's works into different periods—such as the classification I have been working with in this book, or the different chronology offered by Charles H. Kahn in *Plato and the Socratic Dialogue: The Philosophical Use of a Literary Form* (Cambridge: Cambridge University Press, 1996)—rests on interpretative assumptions. "Such classifications," Cooper writes, "resting as they do on an attempt to interpret the progress of Plato's work, philosophically and literarily, are an unsuitable basis for bringing anyone to the reading of these works. To use them that way is to put the cart before the horse. . . . It is better to relegate thoughts about chronology to the secondary position they deserve, and to concentrate on the literary and philosophical content of the works, taken on their own and in relation to one another" (xiv). This is reasonable as a caution to those who are about to read Plato for the first time (and to those who will teach Plato to such students). But in fact it is impossible to read the dialogues "on their own and in relation to one another" without *at the same time* making serious assumptions about their chronological sequence. For, to take an obvious case, it is often impossible to decide what a particular passage means without knowing whether it is a response to a previous position Plato has already expressed or an anticipation of a thesis he has not yet formulated or stated explicitly. Kahn's chronological rearrangement of the dialogues, for example, rests precisely on reversing such relationships: where others see echoes, he sees anticipations; see his "The Methodology of Plato in the *Laches*," *Revue internationale de philosophie* 40 (1986): 7–21, and "On the Relative Date of the *Gorgias* and the *Protagoras*," *Oxford Studies in Ancient Philosophy* 6 (1988): 69–102. In the end, it is impossible to separate the reading of the dialogues from at least a tentative hypothesis regarding their order. Since the only reliable stylometric evidence we have concerns the very last six works Plato composed (see the recent survey of that evidence by Charles M. Young, "Plato and Computer Dating," *Oxford Studies in Ancient Philosophy* 12 [1994]: 227–50), any hypothesis concerning the chronology of the rest of his writings will have to be interpretative. And the persuasiveness of such a hypothesis will depend on the readings of particular passages along with the attractiveness of the overall narrative of Plato's development it allows us to construct.

65. Though Plato, working out the implications of his simile with Daedalus' statues, writes that true beliefs may "escape" the soul (ἀποδιδράσκειν, δραπετεύειν), the literal content of his view must be that such beliefs are forgotten until they are recalled through the questioning he has already described in his discussion of the theory of recollection. True beliefs, according to the theory, are already within the soul. But, until they become knowledge, they can still come to be forgotten even after questioning elicits them from a respondent.

66. The discussion of these issues is complex. I have tried to offer my own view, and have discussed some alternatives, in "Meno's Paradox and Socrates as a Teacher," *Oxford Studies in Ancient Philosophy* 3 (1985): 1–30.

67. To say that in his early dialogues Plato tried to present Socrates as he saw him does not imply that his representation of Socrates in those works is an accurate reflection of their original. It simply means that he does not try to account for the features of the character he presents.

68. In his effort to locate complex ironies, Vlastos (*Socrates: Ironist and Moral Philosopher*, 240) finds a contradiction between this statement and Socrates' earlier claim (473e6, in his translation: "Polus, I am not a political man"). But apart from the fact that at 521d Socrates says that he is *trying* to practice politics (Vlastos, 240 n. 21, argues, not convincingly, that ἐπιχειρεῖν need not be translated as "trying"), he also says that he is trying "to engage in the *true* political art" (ἡ ὡς ἀληθῶς πολιτικὴ τέχνη). He contrasts the latter with the politics that he does not practice and that he identifies with holding public office. There is no complex irony here. Socrates denies explicitly that what counts as politics in Athens is what he would consider real politics to consist in.

69. One might argue that Crito, who seems convinced by Socrates' argument that he should not escape from prison, or Nicias, who appeals to Socrates for help in deciding whether training in armor is or is not good for boys and who knows that a conversation with Socrates always turns into a defense of one's mode of life (*La.* 180b7–d3, 187e6–188c3), are people who have been made better by Socrates. At least, it could be claimed, they recognized him as a good man. But Crito's response, "Socrates, I have nothing [more] to say," to Socrates's claim that whatever Crito adds to his argument will be in vain (μάτην) but that he should try nonetheless, is a grudging concession, not a whole-hearted endorsement of Socrates' argument (*Cr.* 54d4–8). As to Nicias, he clearly trusts Socrates to find good teachers for children: he has already found a music teacher for his own son (180c9–d1). But that has little to do with Socrates being a good man. And his claim that Socrates turns all conversations into discussions of one's life seems like an expression of appreciation of what he thinks of as a characteristic (οὐκ ἀήθης) and not unpleasant (οὐκ ἀηδής) game of Socrates. Nicias does not resent that game: he even likes it. But there is no evidence that he takes it seriously or that it has had any long-term beneficial effect on him.

70. It should be noted that once the educational and political scheme of the *Republic* is in place, recognizing the good and being good are clearly distinguished. The people in the city are taught to believe that the philosophers are the best people among them even though they themselves fall far below them in respect of ἀρετή (*aretê*).

71. We could also argue, of course, that since Socrates is Plato's literary creation, the irony he exhibits toward Plato and therefore toward Plato's readers is ultimately Plato's own irony as well. What would that irony be? I don't think that Plato is making the implicit claim that he *did* after all know how Socrates did what he did. Rather, he presents himself as an author who implicitly denies that he has full control of his material and creates a character who is "stronger" than he is. That is a point of connection between Platonic and romantic irony, which denies the omnipotence authors had traditionally been accorded over their material.

72. *La.* 190c6; cf. Xenophon, *Mem.* 4.6.1.

73. By the time he wrote the *Republic*, Plato had also developed a number of reservations about Socrates' methods. For example, he criticizes allowing young people—people of the age Socrates surrounded himself with—to practice the

elenchus and dialectic in general. He prefers to wait until they get older and can deal more constructively with the undermining of existing values at which the elenchus excels (539b1–540c4). In the *Sophist* (231b3–8), he describes the elenchus as a kind of sophistry—though a good kind, a sophistry "of noble lineage" as Cornford renders the expression ἡ γένει γενναία σοφιστική (*Plato's Theory of Knowledge* [Indianapolis: Bobbs-Merrill, 1957], 181). William Cobb, ed., *Plato's "Sophist"* (Savage, Md.: Rowman and Littlefield, 1990), translates this as "the nobly born art of sophistry," while Nicholas P. White, trans., *Plato: "Sophist"* (Indianapolis: Hackett, 1993), who, inexplicably, thinks the text here is corrupt, prefers "our noble sophistry" (though neither Burnet, in his *Platonis opera* [Oxford: Clarendon Press, 1900], nor Lewis Campbell, *The "Sophistes" and "Politicus" of Plato* [1867; repr., New York: Arno Press, 1973], nor the new version of the Oxford *Platonis opera*, ed. E. A. Duke, W. F. Hicken, W. S. M. Nicoll, et al. [Oxford: Clarendon Press, 1995], indicate that there is any textual problem here). Some discussion of the topic can be found in Richard S. Bluck, *Plato's "Sophist": A Commentary* (Manchester: Manchester University Press, 1975), 40–52; Bluck prefers his own "sophistry of noble family" to Cornford's "noble lineage" on the ground that it indicates "that this procedure, unlike other aspects or kinds of sophistry, is related (as an imitation) to the noble art of true philosophy" (46). I find this suggestion unconvincing, and I have my doubts about all the translations of the phrase given above. Why should Socrates' method of dialectic be of noble *ancestry*, which is what all these versions imply? Demetres Glenos, in his translation and commentary on the dialogue (*Platona Sophistis*, ed. Giannes Kordatos [1940; repr., Greek-European Youth Movement, 1971], 224 n. 35), accepts the same kind of translation and tries to justify it by claiming that it is intended to remind us that "sophistry" did not originally have a negative sense, and that Plato is trying to reclaim that original sense for Socrates here. But that too is not persuasive. The solution, I think, lies in taking γένος (see LSJ, s.v. γένος, II) to mean not *ancestry* but *progeny*. That is, the elenchus is *a sophistry of noble offspring*, in the sense that by clearing the student's mind of preconceived notions as well as from the ignorance of one's ignorance it prepares the ground for dialectic as Plato now conceives it: it produces good results.

74. Plato, scholars are generally agreed, came to see that the metaphysics and epistemology that support the political structure of the *Republic* presented serious problems, some of which he set out in the *Parmenides*. In his later dialogues, he seems to have made a new start to revise those aspects of his middle views that presented difficulties. In parallel with that change, A. A. Long has argued that the *Theaetetus*, one of Plato's later works, constitutes a new apology for Socrates and for his way of doing philosophy; see his "Plato's Apologies and Socrates," in Jyl Gentzler, ed., *Method in Ancient Philosophy* (Oxford: Oxford University Press, 1997).

75. Amélie Oksenberg Rorty, "A Literary Postscript: Characters, Persons, Selves, Individuals," in *The Identities of Persons* (Berkeley: University of California Press, 1976), 306.

76. A masterful discussion of the various ancient representations to which Socrates gave rise, in various philosophical and literary authors, is given by Olof Gigon, *Sokrates: Sein Bild in Dichtung und Geschichte*, 2d ed. (Bern: A. Francke, 1970). Gigon's study is indispensable for a complete study of the Socratic prob-

lem as it has traditionally been conceived. His conclusion is that the historical Socrates has been irretrievably lost.

77. E. H. Gombrich, *Meditations on a Hobby-Horse* (London: Phaidon, 1963), 10.

78. Friedrich Schlegel, "On Incomprehensibility," in *Friedrich Schlegel's "Lucinde" and the Fragments*, trans. Peter Firchow (Minneapolis: University of Minnesota Press, 1971), 259. The original is in Schlegel, "Über die Unverständlichkeit," in *Kritische Schriften* (Munich: Carl Hanser, 1938), 340–52.

79. Friedrich Schlegel, *Lyceum Fragments*, no. 108, in *Friedrich Schlegel's "Lucinde" and the Fragments*, trans. Firchow, 156; *Kritische Schriften*, 19.

80. Friedrich Schlegel, "Über Wilhelm Meister," in *Kritische Schriften*, 262–82.

81. Friedrich Schlegel, in *Kritische Friedrich-Schlegel-Ausgabe*, ed. Ernst Behler et al., vol. 18 (Munich and Padenborn: Schöningh, 1987), 85.

82. Of course, I do not mean to deny that a historical Socrates existed. But I do believe that we know much less about him than we often believe. See Alexander Nehamas, "Voices of Silence: On Gregory Vlastos's Socrates," *Arion*, 3d ser., 2 (1992): 156–86.

83. A very interesting selection of such writings, along with a surprisingly extensive bibliography, can be found in Mario Montuori, *De Socrate iuste damnato: The Rise of the Socratic Problem in the Eighteenth Century* (Amsterdam: J. C. Gieben, 1981). The Socratic problem has an immensely long and complex history, and it is one more issue I will not attempt to deal with here. I have expressed some of my own views about it in "Voices of Silence." A good discussion is in V. de Magalhâes-Vilhena, *Le Problème de Socrate: Le Socrate historique et le Socrate de Platon* (Paris: Presses Universitaires de France, 1952), and a short overview has been made by P. J. FitzPatrick, "The Legacy of Socrates," in Gower and Stokes, *Socratic Questions*, 153–208. An annotated bibliography has been compiled by Luis E. Navia and Ellen L. Katz, *Socrates: An Annotated Bibliography* (New York: Garland Publishing, 1988). An excellent compilation of sources has been made by John Ferguson, *Socrates: A Source Book* (London: Macmillan, 1970). The latest contribution to the debate is Vlastos, *Socrates: Ironist and Moral Philosopher*. His view that the historical Socrates can be reconstructed through the various points on which Plato, Xenophon, and Aristotle agree (Vlastos disregards Aristophanes' *Clouds*) is nicely anticipated by J. Brucker, who in his *Historia critica philosophiae* (Leipzig, 1767) had already argued that only the issues on which Plato and Xenophon agree with one another constitute good evidence for the views of the historical Socrates. See FitzPatrick, "Legacy of Socrates," 175–76. On Socrates' trial, see the discussion by W. R. Connor, "The Other 399: Religion and the Trial of Socrates," *Bulletin of the Institute of Classical Studies* 58 (1991): Supplement, 49–56. Connor argues, not unconvincingly, that the view, most recently expressed by I. F. Stone in *The Trial of Socrates* (Boston: Beacon Press, 1988), that Socrates was tried and put to death on purely political reasons, as an enemy of democracy, needs to be complicated by the importance of religious reasons in a number of trials of the very same period. Connor's evidence that Socrates' attitude toward sacrifice was at least unusual is strong and adds a new dimension to this very vexed subject.

84. See Friedrich Schleiermacher, "Über den Werth des Sokrates als Philosophen," in *Sämtliche Werke*, vol. 2 (Berlin, 1838), 287–300, esp. 297. The original essay was published in 1818.

85. In this context, we must also not underestimate the increasing significance of the higher criticism of the New Testament, which was aimed at separating the facts surrounding the historical Jesus from his disciples' versions of his life.

86. Mario Montuori, *Socrates, Physiology of a Myth*, London Studies of Classical Philology 6 (Amsterdam: J. C. Gieben, 1981), 32.

87. See chap. 4, p. 109 below.

88. Hegel, *Lectures on the History of Philosophy*, trans. Haldane, 1:414; *Vorlesungen über die Geschichte der Philosophie*, 1:312 (see also 3:1049–54).

89. See Hegel's criticism of Schlegel in the *Lectures on the History of Philosophy*, trans. Haldane, 1:400–402. The original is in his *Vorlesungen über die Geschichte der Philosophie*, 1:302–4. But see also Dane, *Critical Mythology of Irony*, 83: "Hegel, one of the most vehement critics of Friedrich Schlegel's notions of irony, became, somewhat paradoxically, one of the most influential figures in the development of various theories of romantic irony." On his more positive view of Solger's version of irony, see Dane, chap. 6.

90. For an overview of Socrates in the eighteenth century, and for a correction of many of the simplifications offered here, see Benno Böhm, *Sokrates im achtzehnten Jahrhundert* (Leipzig: Quelle und Meyer, 1929). It does remain a fact, however, that the most influential biography of Socrates in the eighteenth century was that by François Charpentier, *La Vie de Socrate*, originally published in Paris in 1650 (reprinted in 1657, 1666, 1668, 1669) and eventually appended to Charpentier's translation of the *Memorabilia: Les Choses mémorables de Xenophon* (Amsterdam, 1699). Though Charpentier makes use of Plato and Diogenes Laertius as well as of Cicero, Seneca, Plutarch, and Apuleius, his reliance on Xenophon is much more extensive. Needless to say, Charpentier's biography was written in the seventeenth century, but it had a very long life, particularly after its translation into German by Christian Thomasius as *Das ebenbild eines wahren und ohnpedantischen philosophi; oder, Das leben Socratis; aus dem frantzösishendes des herrn Charpentier ins teutsche übersetzt von Christian Thomas* (Halle, 1693).

91. This negative assessment of Xenophon's Socrates has been recently challenged by a number of the essays in Vander Waerdt, ed., *Socratic Movement*. See also Donald Morrison, "Xenophon's Socrates on the Just and the Lawful," *Ancient Philosophy* 15 (1993): 329–48. Despite the interest that Xenophon's various writings hold, however, his picture of Socrates still strikes me as considerably less engaging than Plato's.

92. Xenophon, *Mem.* 1.1.4, 4.8.1; *Ap. Soc.* 13.

93. See Eduard Zeller, *Die Philosophie der Griechen*, 4th ed., vol. 2, pt. 1 (Leipzig: Fues, 1889), 91–100. English translation of the relevant part can be found in Eduard Zeller, *Socrates and the Socratic Schools*, trans. Oswald J. Reichel (New York: Russell and Russell, 1962), 82–86. Though adhering to Schleiermacher's canon, Zeller minimized Xenophon's importance. By 1901, Karl Joël, in his *Der echte und der xenophontische Sokrates*, 2 vols. (Berlin: R. Gaentner, 1893–1901), could discount all of Xenophon's testimony, and his view, though attacked by H. Weissenborn in his 1910 Jena dissertation, *De Xenophontis in commentariis scribendis fide historica* (Jena: G. Nevenhahni, 1910), has carried the day (though see the references in n. 90 above). Today, we are in fact faced with a rather ironic reversal. A number of recent authors who want to articulate a version of Socrates influenced by Xenophon's treatment, particularly on the function of the *daimonion*,

are using Plato's texts as the standard against which their interpretation is to be judged: such has been the success of the Platonic Socrates as a reflection that substitutes for its original. That is, for example, Gregory Vlastos's criticism of Thomas C. Brickhouse and Nicholas D. Smith, *Socrates on Trial*, in his review of that book, *Times Literary Supplement*, 15–21 December 1989, 1393 (but see also Brickhouse and Smith's response, *Times Literary Supplement*, 5–11 January 1990, 112, and a number of further exchanges on the issue). The same, I believe, is true of Mark McPherran, "Socrates and the Duty to Philosophize," *Southern Journal of Philosophy* 24 (1986): 541–60.

94. On Xenophon's insistence that he was present for Socrates' conversations, see *Mem.* 1.3.1, 1.3.8, 1.6.14, 2.4.1, 2.5.1, 2.7.1, 4.3.2. Most of these claims are in fact deeply implausible, as is Xenophon's statement that he was present at the party he describes in his *Symposium* (1.1), since the event must have occurred around 422 or 421 BC (cf. Athenaeus, *Deipnosophistai* 5.57.216d), and Xenophon was at most a young child (if he had been born at all) at the time. Such anachronisms abound throughout Xenophon's writings about Socrates, and they have been well documented; see, for example, Joël, *Der echte und der xenophontische Sokrates*, 2:1080–91. Paul Vander Waerdt has shown how deeply indebted Xenophon's *Apology of Socrates* is to Plato's own *Apology* (and how Xenophon manipulates his Platonic material for his own purposes) in "Socratic Justice and Self-Sufficiency: The Story of the Delphic Oracle in Xenophon's *Apology of Socrates*," paper presented at the Society for Ancient Greek Philosophy, New York City, October 1990.

95. Xenophon's Socrates is not only a good man but also a harmless one. For if, as I will claim in chap. 4 (p. 107), all we possessed today were Xenophon's Socratic writings, we would indeed find it difficult if not impossible to understand why the Athenians put Socrates to death in the first place. That shows how admirably Xenophon succeeded in his goal, which was precisely to make Socrates' execution incomprehensible. As Kierkegaard writes, "it was Xenophon's objective to prove that it was foolishness or an error on the part of the Athenians to condemn Socrates, for Xenophon defends Socrates in such a way that he renders him not only innocent but also altogether innocuous—so much so that we wonder greatly about what kind of daimon must have bewitched the Athenians to such a degree that they were able to see more in him than in any other good-natured, garrulous, droll character who does neither good nor evil, does not stand in anyone's way, and is so fervently well-intentioned toward the whole world if only it will listen to his slipshod nonsense" (*Concept of Irony*, 16–17).

96. See chap. 5, pp. 138–141, below.

97. An interesting discussion of the general ethical background against which the classical Greek philosophers produced their views can be found in K. J. Dover, *Greek Popular Morality in the Time of Plato and Aristotle* (Berkeley: University of California Press, 1974). On some important differences between Homeric and archaic conceptions of justice on the one hand and Platonic ones on the other, see Hugh Lloyd-Jones, *The Justice of Zeus* (Berkeley: University of California Press, 1971), 164: "Plato and the other destroyers of the earlier culture would claim, and many of their modern followers would agree, that they achieved contact with a higher reality than their forbears; but it was not reality in *this* world that was their chief concern."

98. See n. 73 above. The mathematical and metaphysical education that Plato

considers necessary for the philosophic life in the *Republic* is also foreign to Socrates' attitude.

Chapter 4

1. It is worth noting, however, that Xenophon's interests cannot be correctly described as philosophical. John Cooper has argued that our century's complete dismissal of Xenophon as a source for the historical Socrates is due to the idea that his goal is primarily philosophical and that the views Xenophon attributes to Socrates must therefore be directly compared to those of Plato (in relation to which, to say the least, they pale): "Whatever one may ultimately make of Xenophon's claims to historical accuracy, he is not offering to give an account of Socrates as a *philosopher* — of his way of treating philosophical questions as such, of his philosophical theories or opinions, of his conception of what philosophy was and could (or could not) hope to accomplish, and the methods appropriate to its task. It is with Socrates as an educator in the broadest sense that he is concerned" ("Notes on Xenophon's Socrates," in *Reason and Emotion: Essays on Ancient Moral Psychology and Ethical Theory* [Princeton: Princeton University Press, 1998]). Once we realize the great difference in purpose between Xenophon and Plato, Cooper argues, we may well find that Xenophon is reporting on a side of Socrates in which Plato had not been interested but in which Xenophon found his most important and beneficial aspect. Though I am not sure I accept Cooper's qualified conclusion that Xenophon may thus be shown to have considerable historical value concerning Socrates' actual views, I believe the distinction he draws between Plato's and Xenophon's literary purposes is important and needs to be kept in mind. On the virtues and significance of Xenophon as a biographer, and on his influence on the form biography has generally taken, see Arnaldo Momigliano, *The Development of Greek Biography* (Cambridge, Mass.: Harvard University Press, 1971), 45–56.

2. Some of the occasions on which Xenophon claims to have witnessed Socratic conversations are the following: At *Mem.* 1.3.8ff., he is himself a character in a conversation; at 1.4.2, he says he will relate what he heard Socrates himself say to Aristodemus about his *daimonion;* the *Oeconomicus* opens with his statement that he was present at the discussion that follows, though it is clear that the subject of estate management, close to his own heart, was nowhere near Socrates' range of interests; finally, Xenophon begins his *Symposium* with the claim that he was himself part of the company, even though he includes many details that show that the event occurred around 421 BC, when he was not yet ten years old.

3. François Salignac de la Mothe-Fénelon, *Abrégé des vies des anciens philosophes*, in *Oeuvres complètes de Fénelon*, vol. 7 (Paris: J. Leroux et Jouby, 1850), 39–42.

4. The anti-Xenophontic movement reached its culmination with Karl Joël's *Der echte und der xenophontische Sokrates*, 2 vols. (Berlin: R. Gaentner, 1893–1901), and Heinrich Maier's *Sokrates* (Tübingen: J. C. B. Mohr, 1913).

5. Michael Frede, "Euphrates of Tyrus," typescript (Keble College, Oxford University, 1995), 18.

6. Ibid., 40.

7. In *Nietzsche: Life as Literature* (Cambridge, Mass.: Harvard University Press,

1985), I put forward the view that Nietzsche is not interested in such prescriptions but in making something unusual out of himself in a way that others could not imitate (see further chap. 5 below). Tellingly, Robert Solomon asked this question of my interpretation: "Was [Nietzsche] trying to tell us how to live, give us prescriptions and recommendations, and if so, why did he not follow them himself? And if he did not intend to give us prescriptions and recommendations . . . then what is all the fuss about?" ("Nietzsche and Nehamas's Nietzsche," *International Studies in Philosophy* 21 [1989]: 56).

8. Montaigne's lifelong involvement with Socrates prompted Hugo Friedrich to write that "nothing can be found in European writing of the sixteenth century and before which compares with the rebirth of Socrates in the *Essais*" (Hugo Friedrich, *Montaigne*, ed. Philippe Desan, trans. Dawn Eng [Berkeley: University of California Press, 1991], 53).

9. Michel de Montaigne, "To the reader," 3; 2F. I refer to Montaigne's essays in the following manner. I first give the title of the essay and then the page number from Pierre Villey's edition, *Les Essais de Michel de Montaigne*, new ed., 3 vols. (Paris: Presses Universitaires de France, 1965). Each of the three volumes of Villey's edition contains one of the original three books of the essays. The second page reference, followed by "F," is to Donald M. Frame's English translation of the *Essays*, in *The Complete Works of Montaigne* (Stanford: Stanford University Press, 1942). Montaigne added considerable material to the essays during his lifetime, and the various layers of his additions sometimes need to be noted. When that is the case, I will follow common practice and use the letters "A," "B," and "C" to indicate, respectively, the text published before 1588, the text of 1588, and the additions made after 1588.

10. Montaigne, "Of the art of discussion," 942; 720F.

11. Montaigne, "Of giving the lie," 665; 504F.

12. Friedrich, *Montaigne*, 2. See also Philip P. Hallie, *The Scar of Montaigne* (Middletown, Conn.: Wesleyan University Press, 1966), 68: "His is a personal philosophy in three respects: it is frankly the portrait of a particular person named Michel de Montaigne; it talks about the human mind as an instrument, not for finding objective impersonal Truth, but for preserving a given person's own health and life; and it talks to individual persons who may wish to know this particular man."

13. It applies to everyone without exception in Kant, on the grounds of our common nature as rational beings. It applies to everyone, though in different degrees depending on each one's abilities, in Plato, Aristotle, and perhaps in Stoicism. Michel Foucault, whose views we shall examine in detail in chap. 6, attributed to the Stoics an individualist "aesthetics of existence" (see, for example, his discussion in *The Care of the Self*, vol. 3 of *The History of Sexuality*, trans. Robert Hurley [New York: Random House, 1986], 42–46). Pierre Hadot has objected, however, that Foucault's own individualist project caused him to underemphasize the Stoics' desire to live according to the dictates of universal reason, which connects their approach more with those of Plato and Aristotle than with the Socratic attitude I am examining in this book ("Reflections of the Notion of 'The Cultivation of the Self,'" in Timothy J. Armstrong, trans., *Michel Foucault, Philosopher* [New York: Routledge, 1992], 225–32).

14. See Pierre Villey's great work *Les Sources et l'évolution des Essais de Mon-*

taigne, vol. 2 (Paris: Hachette, 1908), 423. A slightly different (and as far as I can tell inaccurate) count is given by Elaine Limbrick, "Montaigne and Socrates," *Renaissance and Reformation* 9 (1973): 46.

15. Montaigne, "Of practice," 378; 273F.

16. Montaigne, "Of repentance," 804; 610F.

17. Some authors tend to underemphasize Montaigne's reliance on Plato. See, for example, John O'Neill, *Essaying Montaigne: A Study of the Renaissance Institution of Reading and Writing* (London: Routledge and Kegan Paul, 1982), 109: "Montaigne's view of Socrates owes very little to Plato, whose influence he largely avoided." O'Neill, though, himself attributes to Montaigne a Platonic reading of Socrates when he writes that Montaigne was attracted to Socrates because, "above all, Socrates left us no teaching, at least, not directly. Socrates conducted his inquiries by means of a conversational art which depended upon the dialogical presence of others" (132). That Montaigne thought of this as a feature of Plato's Socrates becomes apparent from the passage from the "Apology for Raymond Sebond" quoted in n. 53 below. Floyd Gray, "Montaigne and the *Memorabilia*," *Studies in Philology* 58 (1961): 130–39, also emphasizes Montaigne's reliance on Xenophon: Montaigne's portrait of Socrates, Gray writes, "in the main, is not based on Plato. . . . The Socrates of Montaigne is the highest example he knows of natural simplicity, of ironic ignorance, or an attitude characterized by a continual search for self-knowledge. This Socrates is primarily the Socrates of Xenophon" (130). But "ironic ignorance" and "continual search for self-knowledge" are (especially the former) crucial features of the Platonic, not the Xenophontic, understanding of Socrates.

18. Montaigne read the *Memorabilia* in Castaillon's 1551 Latin translation. He refers to Castaillon's death and regrets that such an "[A]outstanding personage" died because he was too poor to find food ("Of a lack in our administration," 223; 165F). His great friend Étienne de la Boétie had himself translated the *Oeconomicus* in 1562. Having been brought up speaking only Latin, Montaigne was also very familiar with Cicero and Seneca. The nature of his education was decided on by his father, who gave him a German tutor unable to speak French "and very well versed in Latin." See Montaigne, "Of the education of children," 173; 128F. Of Greek, Montaigne writes in the same essay (174; 129F), he had "practically no knowledge at all." Montaigne was also well acquainted with Ficino's great Latin Plato and with Amyot's French rendering of Plutarch's *Moralia*. In addition to Ficino's Plato, Montaigne must also have been familiar with the numerous anthologies of Plato, such as *Les plus illustres et plus notables sentences, receuillies de Platon*, published by A. Brière after a French translation of the *Symposium* in Paris in 1556. See Margaret M. McGowan, *Montaigne's Deceits: The Art of Persuasion in the "Essais"* (London: University of London Press, 1974), 189 n. 2. A good discussion of Montaigne's attitude toward, and use of, Plato can be found in Frederick Kellerman, "Montaigne, Reader of Plato," *Comparative Literature* 8 (1956): 307–22. Kellerman shows that Montaigne, despite the many differences between his approach to philosophy and Plato's, quotes Plato extensively and constantly emphasizes what he took to be the skeptical side of the Greek philosopher. A very good example of Montaigne's reading of Plato can be found in the "Apology for Raymond Sebond" (509; 377F): "Some have considered Plato a dogmatist, others a doubter; others, in certain things the one, in certain things the

other. [C]The leader of his dialogues, Socrates, is always asking questions and stirring up discussion, never concluding, never satisfying; and says he has no other knowledge than that of opposing. Homer, their author, laid the foundations equally for all schools of philosophy, to show how indifferent he was about which way we went. From Plato arose ten different sects, they say. And indeed, in my opinion, never was teaching wavering and noncommittal if his is not." For Montaigne's sources, though not necessarily on the exact course of his development, the fundamental work still remains Pierre Villey's *Les Sources et l'évolution des "Essais" de Montaigne*. See also Donald M. Frame, "Pierre Villey (1879–1933): An Assessment," *Oeuvres et critiques* 8 (1983): 29–43.

19. Cicero, *Tusc. disp.* 5.4.10; cf. *Acad.* 1.4.15

20. Socrates, of course, is not the main speaker of the *Timaeus*. But he expresses a keen interest in the cosmology that the character after whom the dialogue is named expounds in its course.

21. See A. A. Long, "Socrates in Hellenistic Philosophy," *Classical Quarterly* 38 (1988): 153.

22. Plato, *Ap.* 20e–23c. In the *Phaedrus* (229e–230a), Socrates claims that the injunction to know oneself has turned him away from activities like the interpretation of traditional myths. Instead, he devotes himself to a self-examination in order to determine "whether he may not himself be a beast worse than the mythical Typhon"—that is, in order to understand the nature of his own soul. It is an interesting point that Plato makes Socrates use a further mythological image while he is having him describe his reasons for neglecting mythology.

23. Montaigne, "Of vanity," 1001; 766F.

24. See Timothy Hampton, "Montaigne and the Body of Socrates: Narrative and Exemplarity in the *Essais*," *MLN* 104 (1989): 890 with n. 12.

25. Montaigne, "Of three kinds of association," 820; 622F.

26. The classic statement of Montaigne's skepticism is to be found in the "Apology for Raymond Sebond," but the view permeates the whole of the *Essays*, from the earliest to the latest. A central thesis of Villey's *Les Sources et l'évolution des "Essais" de Montaigne* is that Montaigne went through three distinct developmental phases, which he characterized as "Stoical," "Skeptical," and "Epicurean." Influential as this view has been, it needs to be qualified, especially since Villey's understanding of skepticism implies that it is impossible to follow it and live a human life and that Montaigne was therefore obliged to give it up. But that view of skepticism is no longer uncontroversial. See Hallie, *Scar of Montaigne*, chap. 2, and the debate between M. F. Burnyeat, "Can the Skeptic Live His Skepticism?" in Malcolm Schofield, Myles Burnyeat, and Jonathan Barnes, eds., *Doubt and Dogmatism: Studies in Hellenistic Epistemology* (Oxford: Clarendon Press, 1980), and Michael Frede, "The Sceptic's Two Kinds of Assent and the Question of the Possibility of Knowledge," in Richard Rorty, J. B. Schneewind, and Quentin Skinner, eds., *Philosophy in History* (Cambridge: Cambridge University Press, 1984).

27. The expression Montaigne inscribed is "Mentre si puo." On Montaigne and Xenophon more generally, see Gray, "Montaigne and the *Memorabilia*." As I argued in n. 17 above, however, I am not sure I can agree with Gray in considering "ironic ignorance" and "a continual search for self-knowledge" (130) as primarily features of the Xenophontic Socrates. See also Limbrick, "Montaigne and

Socrates," 46 (cf. 47): "Montaigne inclines more towards Xenophon's assessment of Socrates since he stressed the practical morality that Socrates taught." But, to repeat, the Socrates of Plato's early works satisfies that description as well. In addition, he has less to say to others than Xenophon's version, and that feature is surely crucial for Montaigne's individualist project. The discussion in Friedrich, *Montaigne*, 52–55, is worth consulting.

28. See, however, *Mem.* 1.2.3, which, it must be admitted, is not consistent with many other statements in the rest of the work: "And yet not once did he [Socrates] profess to be a teacher of *aretê;* still, being himself so obviously virtuous, he made those who spent time with him hope that by acting like him they too would become virtuous." This is the one occasion when Xenophon seems to agree with Plato's portrait of a reserved character who made no claims for his ability to improve others. In most other cases, Xenophon's Socrates shows no hesitation to advise others and thus to present himself as their teacher.

29. Still, Xenophon's Socrates is not totally without irony. Apart from the example discussed in Gregory Vlastos, *Socrates: Ironist and Moral Philosopher* (Cambridge: Cambridge University Press, 1991), 30 (*Mem.* 3.11.16), we should also note 4.2.3 and 4.2.9, where he is being ironical toward Euthydemus. But his irony is not as pointed as that of his Platonic counterpart; more important, it is not a weapon in his ethical interaction with others.

30. Søren Kierkegaard, *The Concept of Irony with Continual Reference to Socrates*, ed. and trans. Howard V. Hong and Edna H. Hong (Princeton: Princeton University Press, 1989), 16. The same point is made by Gregory Vlastos, "The Paradox of Socrates," in *The Philosophy of Socrates: A Collection of Critical Essays* (Garden City, N.Y.: Doubleday, 1971), 3. Donald Morrison, in "On Professor Vlastos' Xenophon," *Ancient Philosophy* 7 (1987): 19, has replied that "it is a tribute to Xenophon's greatness as a writer that he fooled Professor Vlastos into thinking that his Socrates was too conventionally pious to have been indicted. The *Memorabilia* is a defense speech, and Xenophon knows his audience. The aspects of Socrates which will appeal to conventional Athenian attitudes are skillfully stressed, and the controversial aspects correspondingly deemphasized." Morrison is right. But that does not imply, as Morrison infers, that Xenophon's Socrates "rings true." It does imply that, given Xenophon's purpose, the *Memorabilia* is a success. That is all.

31. Xenophon, *Mem.* 1.1.1, in Xenophon, *Conversations of Socrates*, trans. Hugh Tredennick and Robin Waterfield (London: Penguin, 1990).

32. Montaigne, "Of custom," 118; 86F. Socrates' pervasive emphasis on the importance of taking care of oneself is a central feature of Plato's early works. The opening chapters of the first book of the *Memorabilia* are full of claims concerning the conventional aspects of Socrates' behavior. Plato's *Crito* is Montaigne's source for Socrates' attitude toward the laws of the city, an attitude that, though it is based on the radical new principle that injustice should never be repaid, results in his determination to obey the dictates of the court. Both Plato (*Ap.* 34a2–31) and Xenophon (*Mem.* 1.2.31–35) discuss Socrates' disobedience of the Thirty Tyrants.

33. See Xenophon's *Apology of Socrates*, 14–18.

34. Montaigne, "Apology for Raymond Sebond," 498; 368F.

35. But see Marianne S. Meijer, "Guesswork or Facts: Connections between Montaigne's Last Three Chapters (III:11, 12 and 13)," *Yale French Studies* 64 (1983): 167–79.

36. See, among others, Michaël Baraz, *L'Être et la connaissance selon Montaigne* (Paris: Corti, 1968), 185. On the notion of "face" or "appearance" in Montaigne, with a discussion of the essay on physiognomy, see François Rigolot, "Les 'Visages' de Montaigne," in Marguerite Soulie, ed., *La Littérature de la Renaissance: Mélanges offerts à Henri Weber* (Geneva: Slatkine, 1984), 357–70. See also Steven Rendall, *Distinguo: Reading Montaigne Differently* (Oxford: Clarendon Press, 1992), chap. 6, "Faces."

37. Montaigne, "Of physiognomy," 1037; 792F. In what follows, I will give references to this essay parenthetically in the main text, citing the page numbers both in the Villey and in the Frame edition.

38. See Desiderius Erasmus, *Sileni Alcibiadis*, in *Desiderii Erasmi Roterodami opera omnia*, vol. 2, pt. 5, ed. Felix Heinimann and Emanuel Kienzle (Amsterdam: North Holland, 1981), 159–90. Erasmus also describes the Cynic Diogenes, Epictetus, John the Baptist, and the Apostles as Silenuslike. The image, which ultimately goes back to Plato, *Symp.* 215a–b, is also referred by Erasmus to Xenophon (*Symposium*, 4.19, 7.7) and to Athenaeus (*Deipnosophistai*, 5.188d). A brief discussion of the history of the image can be found in the editorial note to the adage on pp. 159–61 of volume 2, part 5, of the collected works cited here. More information is in R. Marcel, "Saint Socrate, patron de l'humanisme," *Revue internationale de philosophie* 5 (1951): 135–43. An English version of adage 2201 is given by Margaret Mann Phillips, *Erasmus on His Times: A Shortened Version of the "Adages" of Erasmus* (Cambridge: Cambridge University Press, 1967), 77–97.

39. Desiderius Erasmus, *Convivium religiosum*, in *Desiderii Erasmi Roterodami opera omnia*, vol. 1, pt. 3, ed. L.-E. Halkin, F. Bierlaire, and R. Hoven (Amsterdam: North Holland, 1972), 254. The parallels Erasmus finds between Socrates and St. Paul, particularly regarding the idea that the body is the soul's tomb, are drawn from Plato's *Phaedo*.

40. François Rabelais, *Gargantua and Pantagruel*, trans. Burton Raffel (New York: Norton, 1990), 7, 8.

41. See, for example, Joshua Scodel, "The Affirmation of Paradox: A Reading of Montaigne's *Essays*," *Yale French Studies* 64 (1983): 211. Raymond B. Waddington, "Socrates in Montaigne's 'Traicté de la phisionomie,'" *Modern Language Quarterly* 41 (1980): 328–45, expresses a similar view, following Baraz, *L'Être et la connaissance selon Montaigne*, 198 n. 44.

42. See the excellent discussion of the function of the adjective "vyle" in this context in Raymond C. La Charité, "Montaigne's Silenic Text: 'De la phisionomie,'" *Le Parcours des "Essais": Montaigne 1588–1988* (Paris: Aux Amateurs de livres, 1989), 63. La Charité connects the term with its Latin etymology and argues that, just like Socrates himself in Montaigne's view, it carries the implication of being "found in great quantities, abundant, common."

43. Plato, *Symp.* 221d–222e. The idea that Socrates always used commonplace examples can also be found in Plato, *G.* 491a–b, and Xenophon, *Mem.* 1.2.37.

44. The quotation is from Alexander Nehamas and Paul Woodruff, trans., *Plato: "Symposium"* (Indianapolis: Hackett, 1989).

45. Xenophon, *Mem.* 4.2.14–15. We should also note that though Xenophon himself used the Silenus motif, he did not develop it in Plato's manner: See *Symp.* 4.19, 7.7.

46. Montaigne, "Of repentance," 80; 614F.

47. Xenophon, *Mem.* 4.1.1. The greatest part of *Mem.* 4 is, in fact, an effort to demonstrate how ὠφέλιμος ("useful") Socrates was to his friends. References to ὠφέλιμος and its cognates as well as to τὸ συμφέρον ("the useful, the expedient") are ubiquitous.

48. Kierkegaard, *Concept of Irony*, 24–25.

49. The reference to "a gentle and ordinary pace" may be a reference to Xenophon's *Apology of Socrates*, 27: "He left, blithe in his look, in his deportment, in his pace." On "blithe" (φαιδρός), see below, n. 62.

It is worth remarking that Montaigne, who is at this point interested in distinguishing Socrates' simplicity from Cato's grandeur, actually illustrates his description of Socrates as a "[B]man who did not propose to himself any idle fancies; his aim was to furnish us with things and precepts that see life really and more closely" and who was not, like Cato, "[B]always mounted on his high horse" (1037; 793F) with a quotation from Lucan's *Pharsalia* (2.381), "Servare modum, finemque tenere, / Naturámque sequi" ("To keep the mean, to hold our aim in view, / And follow nature"), which Lucan had used to describe none other than Cato himself! This is a case of Montaigne's practice of "hiding" his borrowings, "[C]disguising and altering [them] for a new service" (1056; 809F), to which we shall return below.

50. Rendall, *Distinguo*, suggests that this passage, which suggests that Socrates is a character we know well, conflicts with the image of Socrates as Silenus, which implies that his inner aspects are radically different from his outer ones. Rendall goes on to claim that Montaigne ultimately affirms "the physiognomic principle," according to which inside and outside correspond to one another, and "treat[s] Socrates as an exception to the general rule" (103). The situation, as Rendall admits, is complex, and we shall examine it in detail as we proceed.

51. The contrast between health and disease is as important to this essay as it is to Montaigne's work in general; see, for example, 1038 (793F), 1039 (794F), 1041 (796F), 1043 (797F), 1049 (803F). Here, in particular, Montaigne insists on the idea that what we take to be a beneficial medicine turns out to be poison instead, and he applies it both to learning and to the civil war. For an extended discussion of this passage of Plato's *Protagoras*, see chap. 3, pp. 79–81.

52. See Scodel, "Affirmation of Paradox," 230. Scodel believes that Montaigne's criticism of the *Tusculan Disputations* implies a criticism of Socrates' way of following nature, leaving Montaigne himself as the only person who follows nature correctly. He concludes that in this essay Socrates really is Montaigne's opponent. In my discussion, I will try to show that Montaigne's attitude toward Socrates is considerably more positive.

53. See, for example, Montaigne's question, "[A]What good can we suppose it did Varro and Aristotle to know so many things? Did it exempt them from human discomforts?" (487; 358F). And though some of the skepticism of the "Apology for Raymond Sebond" may be directed against the Socratic view that knowledge is virtue ("[A]I do not believe . . . that knowledge is the mother of all virtue, and that all vice is produced by ignorance"), Montaigne's comment regarding this thesis, "[A]if that is true, it is subject to a long interpretation" (438; 319F; cf. 488; 359F), suggests that by "knowledge" here he means school learning and not the self-knowledge for which he praises Socrates consistently throughout this work (cf. 498; 368F, and 501; 370F: "[A]The wisest man who ever was, when they asked him what he knew, answered that he knew this much, that he knew nothing").

54. See Montaigne, "On some verses of Virgil," 875; 667F: "[B]Now I have an aping and imitative nature. . . . Anyone I regard with attention easily imprints on me something of himself. What I consider, I usurp: a foolish countenance, an unpleasant grimace, a ridiculous way of speaking. Vices even more: once they prick me, they stick to me and will not go away without shaking."

55. An interesting account of the gradual genesis of the text, suggesting that the material on the civil war was interpolated about a year after the essay's initial composition in 1586, is given by A. Tournon, *Montaigne: La Glose et l'essai* (Lyon: Presses Universitaires de Lyon, 1983), 274–75. Tournon is driven to his view because he is unable to connect the different parts of the essay, particularly the discussion of the civil war, together. In what follows, I offer a hypothesis that does in fact connect them. That does not show that Montaigne composed the essay at one time. But it does show that all the essay's disparate parts, not unlike the essays themselves in all their colorful variety, are woven together into a common pattern.

56. "[B]The situation of my house, and my acquaintance with men in my neighborhood, presented me in one aspect, my life and my actions in another" (1044; 798F). Montaigne often refers to the many sides of his personality, which sometimes come close to inconsistency, and to his intention of showing himself in all his complexity. See, for example, "Of the art of discussion": "[B]Even our wisdom and deliberation for the most part follow the lead of chance. My will and my reasoning are moved now in one way, now in another, and there are many of these movements that are directed without me. My reason has accidental impulsions that change from day to day" (934; 713F). Also: "[C]I present myself standing and lying down, front and rear, on the right and the left, and in all my natural postures" (943; 721F). Needless to say, the fact that Montaigne describes himself as multifaceted and sometimes even inconsistent does not prevent his portrait from being itself consistent and coherent. His "vices" do not obscure his "virtues"; on the contrary, they give them greater value, more vivacity, in the way Nietzsche was to envisage in regard to the great composers: "*To deploy one's weakness as an artist.* — If we are bound to have weaknesses and are also bound in the end to recognize them as a law set over us, then I would wish that everyone had at any rate sufficient artistic power to set off his weaknesses against his virtues and through his weaknesses make us desire his virtues: the power possessed in so exceptional a degree by the great composers. How frequently there is in Beethoven's music a coarse, obstinate, impatient tone, in Mozart's a joviality of humble fellows who have to be content with little, in Richard Wagner's a convulsive and importunate recklessness at which even the most patient listener begins to lose his composure: at *that* point, however, he reasserts his power, and so with the others; by means of their weaknesses they have all produced in us a ravenous hunger for their virtues and a ten times more sensitive palate for every drop of musical spirit, musical beauty, musical goodness" (*Daybreak: Thoughts on the Prejudices of Morality*, trans. R. J. Hollingdale [Cambridge: Cambridge University Press, 1982], 218; *Sämtliche Werke: Kritische Studienausgabe*, 15 vols., ed. Georgio Colli and Mazzino Montinari [Berlin: De Gruyter, 1980], 3:193–94). See also the good discussion by Françoise Joukovsky, "Qui parle dans le livre III des *Essais?*," *Revue d'histoire littéraire de la France* 88 (1988): 813–27.

57. Xenophon, *Mem.* 4.8.9: "If I die unjustly," Socrates says, "this will prove

shameful to those who put me to death without justice. For if being unjust is shameful, how could doing anything unjustly not be itself shameful?" It is more likely, however, that Montaigne is alluding to Euthyphro's statement: "If [anyone] should try to indict me, I think I would find his weak spots and the talk in court would be about him rather than about me" (5b7–c3; translation from G. M. A. Grube, trans., *Plato: Five Dialogues* [Indianapolis: Hackett, 1981]).

58. In "Of experience," Montaigne contrasts Socrates' understanding of nature with that of the Academics, the Peripatetics, and the Stoics, who have caused us to confuse nature's "[B]footprints" with "[B]artificial tracks" (1113–14; 855F).

59. The final additions Montaigne made to that passage mostly concern frankness, truthfulness, and naturalness.

60. Diogenes Laertius, *Life of Socrates*, 2.2.40.

61. Xenophon, *Apology of Socrates* 1, 5–9.

62. Ibid., 27: "After this speech he was led away; his features, the way he held himself and the way he walked were all cheerful, which was in keeping, of course, with what he'd said." This version is from Xenophon, *Conversations of Socrates*, trans. Tredennick and Waterfield, 47–48.

63. "J'ayme une sagesse gaye et civile" (844; 641F).

64. "La vertue est qualité plaisante et gaye" (845; 641F).

65. Voltaire, in a letter dated 21 August 1746, undertook to defend Montaigne against this common charge. Montaigne, Voltaire wrote, did not simply quote and comment on the ancients. He cited them to use them for his own purposes, to fight and engage with them, with his readers, and with himself. See *Essais de Michel de Montaigne*, ed. Villey, 1197. Similarly, Claude Blum argues that Montaigne consistently uses his borrowings, allusions, and quotations in the *Essays* to undermine the authority of the past and not to perpetuate it; see "La Fonction du 'déjà dit' dans les *Essais*: Emprunter, alleguer, citer," *Cahiers de l'Association Internationale des Études Françaises* 33 (1981): 35–51.

66. One such quotation may be found in a passage from the "Apology for Raymond Sebond" (499–500; 369F), where Montaigne does not indicate clearly that he is paraphrasing extensively from Cicero, *De natura deorum* 1.17.

67. Montaigne refers to his essay as the "[B]treatise on physiognomy" ("le traicté de la phisionomie") on 1056; 808F.

68. Cicero, *Tusc. disp.* 4.37.80; cf. *De fato* 5.10. A [C] addition here reads as follows: "But in saying this I hold that he was jesting according to his wont. So excellent a soul was never self-made." I believe that Waddington, "Socrates in Montaigne's 'Traicté de phisionomie,'" 338, is right when he claims that when Montaigne writes that art cannot teach Socrates' perfection, he "clearly means *art* in the sense he has defined through the essay, art as artifice; in more conventional usage, he is describing the great exemplar of naturalness as having perfected the supreme and most exacting art of self-creation." In his very interesting discussion of the essay on physiognomy and the essay "Of cruelty," Timothy Hampton ("Montaigne and the Body of Socrates: Nature and Exemplarity in the *Essais*," *MLN* 104 [1989]: 880–98) argues that Montaigne's different treatments of the relationship between Socrates' soul and body "lead to paradoxical formulations" (892) and that "Montaigne refuses to resolve the issue. It is in fact impossible to decide which version of Socrates' life holds authority" (894). I am greatly indebted to Hampton's essay, though I suspect that Montaigne finally develops

a unified account of Socrates and of his own relationship to him. We should note, by the way, that Montaigne's statement that "[C]In saying [that he had corrected his nature by training] I hold that [Socrates] was jesting according to his wont. So excellent a soul was never self-made" (1058; 810F), added after 1588, is counterbalanced by another statement, also added at that time (and quoted more fully in the main text below): "[C]This reason, which straightens Socrates from his inclination to vice . . . " (1059; 811F). See also Rendall, *Distinguo*, 102–10.

69. Montaigne's attitude toward Socrates' decision not to escape from jail while he still had the opportunity to do so is rather equivocal. While in "Of custom" (118; 86F) he writes that "[A]the great and good Socrates refused to save his life by disobedience to the magistrate, even to a very unjust and very iniquitous magistrate," in "Of the useful and the honorable" (796; 604F), where he draws a contrast between universal and national justice, he cites with approval the view of "[B]the sage Dardamys, [who] hearing tell of the lives of Socrates, Pythagoras, and Diogenes, judged them to be great men in every other respect, but too enslaved to reverence for the laws, to authorize and support which true virtue has to give up much of its original vigor."

70. "Mon mestier et mon art, c'est vivre"; Montaigne, "Of practice" 379; 274F.

71. Montaigne, "Of the affection of fathers for their children" (385; 278F). On the importance of melancholy to Montaigne in general, see M. A. Screech, *Montaigne and Melancholy: The Wisdom of the "Essays"* (London: Penguin, 1991). In particular, see the discussion of this passage on p. 65. Screech argues that Frame's translation of "resverie" as "daydream" is too weak. The word, he argues, here "means not vague dreaming but mad frenzy. . . . Under the influence of melancholy adust, peculiarly dangerous to a man newly plunged into a life of retirement, Montaigne conceived the idea of portraying himself, of assaying himself. It was the kind of notion that might have occurred to a lunatic." In his own translation of the *Essays*, Screech renders "resverie" as "raving concern": see *Michel de Montaigne: The Complete Essays*, trans. M. A. Screech (London: Penguin, 1991), 333. See also the passages I quoted on p. 104 above.

72. Jean Starobinski, *Montaigne in Motion*, trans. Arthur Goldhammer (Chicago: University of Chicago Press, 1985), 35; italics in the original.

73. On Montaigne's metaphor of drawing his portrait in writing, see "Of presumption": "One day at Bar-le-Duc I saw King Francis II presented, in remembrance of René, king of Sicily, with a portrait that this king had made of himself. Why is it not permissible in the same way for each man to portray himself with the pen, as he portrayed himself with a pencil?" (653; 496F).

74. "This last is the story of the horrible end of the accusers of Socrates" (1054; 807F). See Plutarch, *De invidia et odio* 3, perhaps an exaggeration of Xenophon, *Ap. Soc.* 31.

75. See n. 68 above.

76. Terence Cave, *The Cornucopian Text: Problems of Writing in the French Renaissance* (Oxford: Clarendon Press, 1979), 306.

77. Cave, I should note, proceeds to discuss this issue himself, and his discussion is well worth consulting. "The only chance of rewriting Socrates, or—better still—of rewriting nature," he claims, "is to accept deviation as a second nature" (ibid., 307). I take it that this is another way of putting the point that the

only way to be like Socrates is to be unlike him, though I am not sure Cave would accept my interpretation.

78. Scodel, "Affirmation of Paradox," 217–18. Italics in the original.

79. Even the characterization of Socrates as "a creature of tradition" is problematic, since there is no single tradition that establishes his real nature.

80. Starobinski, *Montaigne in Motion*, 4, 32. To Montaigne's question, "Why is it not permissible . . . for each man to portray himself with the pen?" ("Of presumption," 653; 496F), Virginia Woolf's answer is worth recalling, an answer that connects Montaigne's self-portraiture with its private purpose and exhibits its difficulty: "Off-hand, one might reply, not only is it lawful [permissible], but nothing could be easier. Other people may evade us, but our own features are almost too familiar. Let us begin. And then, when we attempt the task, the pen falls from our fingers; it is a matter of profound, mysterious, and overwhelming difficulty" ("Montaigne," in *The Common Reader: First Series* [New York: Harcourt Brace, 1984], 58).

81. The peasants Montaigne discusses may be an exception to this rule, but their example is not one the educated can any longer follow. Montaigne is not preaching a silly return to nature, a project of shedding one's learning, education, and social self to recapture an innocence that has been lost forever.

82. Montaigne, "Of three kinds of association," 823; 625F.

83. "Il n'est rien si beau et legitime que de faire bien l'homme et deuëment, ny science si ardue que de bien et naturellement sçavoir vivre cette vie" ("Of experience," 1110; 852F; the italics are mine). The addition of "naturally" after 1588 shows that Montaigne is clearly thinking of nature as the product of "play" and "acquisition"—ideas that he may not have seen so clearly in his first version of the essay.

84. "Je n'enseigne poinct, je raconte" (Montaigne, "Of repentance," 806; 612F).

85. Montaigne, "Of vanity," 952; 726F.

86. Montaigne, "Of giving the lie," 665; 504F.

87. Montaigne, "Of repentance," 805; 610–11F. Montaigne also applies a similar description of his mode of traveling to his life as a whole: "[B]My plan is everywhere divisible; it is not based on great hopes; each day's journey forms an end, and the journey of my life is conducted in the same way" ("Of vanity," 978; 747F). Tony Long has pointed out to me that Montaigne may well be referring here to Seneca's view that time runs in concentric circles (*Epistulae morales* 12.6). In general, Seneca had a profound influence on Montaigne, not least through his conception of philosophy, which he too saw as the art of living (*artifex vitae*, 14.2).

88. Montaigne, "Of experience," 1088; 834F.

89. Starobinski, *Montaigne in Motion*, 18.

90. Montaigne, "Of the art of discussion," 922; 703F.

Chapter 5

1. Friedrich Nietzsche, *Schopenhauer as Educator*, in *Unmodern Observations*, ed. and trans. William Arrowsmith (New Haven: Yale University Press, 1990), sec. 3, p. 171. In general, I will refer to passages in Nietzsche first by the initials of

the English title of the work, followed by the number of the main division (in roman numerals, where necessary) and the section number (in arabic numerals) in which they appear, and then by the volume and page number in Friedrich Nietzsche, *Sämtliche Werke: Kritische Studienausgabe*, 15 vols., ed. Giorgio Colli and Mazzino Montinari (Berlin: De Gruyter, 1980). In this particular case, the reference is 1:348.

The present passage continues: "Schopenhauer shares with Montaigne another quality besides honesty: genuinely cheering cheerfulness. *Aliis laetus, sibi sapiens.*" Nietzsche actually misunderstands Montaigne's reference to Plutarch, "[C]Je ne le puis si peu racointer que je n'en tire cuisse ou aile" ("On some verses of Virgil," 875; 666F), which Donald Frame translates as "I cannot be with him even a little without taking out a drumstick or a wing," and writes "'kaum habe ich einen Blick auf ihn geworfen, so ist mir ein Bein oder ein Flügel gewachsen.'" See Hugo Friedrich, *Montaigne*, ed. Philippe Desan, trans. Dawn Eng (Berkeley: University of California Press, 1991), 377 n. 1. Friedrich writes that Nietzsche "drastically softened" the statement, but I suspect that he just did not see its point, since to "sprout a leg" seems a rather inept metaphor for the "borrowing" of inspiration to which Montaigne is referring in his text. Arrowsmith (in Nietzsche, *Unmodern Observations*, ed. and trans. Arrowsmith, 171 n. 6) claims that Montaigne's French "has been wrongly rendered . . . ([as] a marginal note in the manuscript indicates) by Nietzsche as 'I spread a leg or a wing.'" That would constitute a second, different misinterpretation.

R. J. Hollingdale, whose translation of this work I will use from now on, renders the last sentence in Nietzsche's passage as "If I were set the task, I could endure to make myself at home in the world with him" (Friedrich Nietzsche, *Untimely Meditations*, trans. R. J. Hollingdale [Cambridge: Cambridge University Press, 1983], 135). This seems to me wrong as a translation of Nietzsche's "Mit ihm würde ich es halten, wenn die Aufgabe gestellt wäre, es sich auf der Erde heimisch zu machen." Subsequent references to the essays in Hollingdale's translation will be made by the initials *UM*, followed by the number of the essay and of the section to which specific reference is being made.

2. "Γένοιο οἷος ἔσσι μαθών": Pindar, *Pyth.* 2.73. See Alexander Nehamas, *Nietzsche: Life as Literature* (Cambridge, Mass.: Harvard University Press, 1985), chap. 6 and p. 250 n. 3.

3. Friedrich Nietzsche, *Ecce Homo* (hereafter *EH*), in *The Basic Writings of Nietzsche*, trans. Walter Kaufmann (New York: Random House, 1968); 6:320. See also ibid.; 6:316–17: "In the *third* and *fourth* Untimely Ones, two images of the hardest self-love, self-discipline are put up against all this, as pointers to a higher concept of culture, to restore the concept of culture—untimely types *par excellence*, full of sovereign contempt for everything around them that was called 'Empire,' 'culture,' 'Christianity,' 'Bismarck,' 'success'—Schopenhauer and Wagner *or, in one word, Nietzsche*." I have italicized the last four words.

4. See Gary Brown's introduction to Arrowsmith's translation of the essay (Nietzsche, *Unmodern Observations*, ed. and trans. Arrowsmith, 229–30) and Ronald Hayman's *Nietzsche: A Critical Life* (New York: Oxford University Press, 1980), 184–86.

5. For Schopenhauer, see among many others, Friedrich Nietzsche, *Beyond Good and Evil* (hereafter *BGE*), in *Basic Writings of Nietzsche*, secs. 16, 19, 186; idem,

On the Genealogy of Morals (hereafter *GM*), also in *Basic Writings of Nietzsche*, esp. III:5–10 (where he is often associated with Wagner). For Wagner, see idem, *The Case of Wagner* (hereafter *CW*) and *Nietzsche Contra Wagner* (hereafter *NCW*), in *Basic Writings of Nietzsche*. The story of Nietzsche's relationship to Wagner is especially complex, and I have nothing to add to the extensive literature on the topic. Ernest Newman's *The Life of Richard Wagner*, 4 vols. (1937; repr., Cambridge: Cambridge University Press, 1980), 4:525, contains invaluable material on the relationship between the two men, though Newman naturally tends to tell the story from Wagner's point of view and to consider that Nietzsche's experience in Bayreuth in 1876 was the decisive factor in the break between them. That Nietzsche detested Bayreuth is beyond doubt, but his break with Wagner was a much more complex affair, with longer roots, and involved a long series of intellectual, personal, and ideological incongruities between Wagner and the once-adoring disciple who decided to make his own mark on the world.

6. Friedrich Nietzsche, *The Will to Power* (hereafter *WP*), trans. Walter Kaufmann and R. J. Hollingdale (New York: Random House, 1967), 366; 12:160.

7. The original German for the three quoted phrases are "ein wirchlicher P h i l o s o p h," *GM* III:5 (5:345); "Aberglaube," *BGE* 16 (5:29); and "Ein Volks-Vorurtheil," *BGE* 19 (5:32).

8. But cf. *EH* II:3; 6:285: "I have in my spirit—who knows? perhaps also in my body—something of Montaigne's sportiveness."

9. Friedrich Nietzsche, *Human, All-Too-Human* (hereafter *HH*), vol. 2, pt. 2, *The Wanderer and His Shadow* (hereafter *WS*), trans. R. J. Hollingdale (Cambridge: Cambridge University Press, 1986), sec. 6; 2:542–43.

10. Montaigne, "Of experience," 1115; 857F.

11. *WS* 6; 2:542–43.

12. The quotation (*Odyssey*, 4.392) is found in Diogenes' life of Socrates (2.21); Diogenes reports that Demetrius of Byzantium was the person who told that story about Socrates.

13. Friedrich Nietzsche, *Twilight of the Idols* (hereafter *TI*), in *The Viking Portable Nietzsche*, ed. and trans. Walter Kaufmann (New York: Viking Press, 1954), IX:50; 6:152. See also *WP* 585; 12:366: "It is a measure of the degree of strength of will to what extent one can do without meaning in things, to what extent one can endure to live in a meaningless world because one organizes a small portion of it oneself." Nietzsche does not mean that what one does with oneself may not have the most far-reaching consequences for the world at large: Socrates himself is a perfect example of that. What he does mean is that the greatest human beings were not those who were directly useful to the state or to society as a whole. That is doubtless an exaggeration and strictly speaking false. But his point that we are too ready to associate greatness with public use is true and well taken.

14. *The Birth of Tragedy* (hereafter *BT*) was published in 1872. The four completed *Untimely Meditations* were published between 1873 and 1876, and the three parts of *Human, All-Too-Human* appeared between 1878 and 1880. *Daybreak*, which also belongs to Nietzsche's middle period, but manifests a new animosity toward Socrates, was published in 1881. It was followed by the first four books of *The Gay Science* (hereafter *GS*) in 1882. The fifth book of *The Gay Science*, which did not appear until 1887, belongs among Nietzsche's late works.

15. *UM* III:6; 1:401; see also *UM* II:6; 1:285–86: "Socrates considered that to

delude oneself that one possesses a virtue one does not possess is an illness bordering on madness: and such a delusion is certainly more dangerous than the opposite illusion of being the victim of a fault or vice. For in the latter case it is at any rate possible one will become better; the former delusion, however, makes a man or an age daily worse." Other positive references to Socrates during this period can be found in *HH* 361; 2:265, *WS* 72; 2:584–85.

16. Friedrich Nietzsche, "We Classicists" ("WC"), trans. William Arrowsmith in *Unmodern Observations*, sec. 193; 8:95.

17. "The Problem of Socrates" is the second part of *Twilight of the Idols*, which appeared in 1888.

18. *TI* II:3; 6:68. The linguistic connection between this passage and the passage from *Beyond Good and Evil* just quoted above is more direct in German than in English. Both passages use the single word *Pöbel* and not two different terms as the English *rabble* and *plebs* suggest.

19. The passage appears in Nietzsche's notes for an unfinished essay, "Wissenschaft und Weisheit im Kampfe," 8:97. An English translation of the notes appears in Friedrich Nietzsche, *Philosophy and Truth: Selections from Nietzsche's Notebooks of the Early 1870s*, ed. and trans. Daniel Brazeale (Atlantic Highlands, N.J.: Humanities Press, 1979), 127–46.

20. *GS* 32; 3:403. The passage continues: "And the other one would make some personal compromise with every cause he represents and thus compromise it; such a disciple I wish my enemy."

21. If that hypothesis is correct, the connection between the "disgruntled" philosopher and Socrates becomes quite important. We will examine that issue as we proceed.

22. Friedrich Nietzsche, *Thus Spoke Zarathustra* (hereafter Z), in *The Viking Portable Nietzsche*, ed. and trans. Kaufmann, I: "On the Gift-Giving Virtue," 3; 4:101. Zarathustra also says in this section: "Now I go alone, my disciples. You too go now, alone. Thus I want it. Verily, I counsel you: go away from me and resist Zarathustra! And even better: be ashamed of him! Perhaps he deceived you. . . . Now I bid you lose me and find yourselves; and only when you have all denied me will I return to you." The idea that only by denying one's model is one likely to establish something that is truly one's own is central to Nietzsche's view of philosophy as the art of living, the fashioning of a radically new personality and mode of life.

23. A very interesting discussion of Nietzsche's view of the contrast between archaic Greece, where people acted as they did simply because to act that way was sanctioned by tradition, and Socrates' radical requirement that those who followed that tradition also offer reasons for doing so can be found in Randall Havas, *Nietzsche's Genealogy: Nihilism and the Will to Knowledge* (Ithaca: Cornell University Press, 1995), chap. 1. Havas's view is engaging and important, though I am not convinced by his general conclusion that Nietzsche wants to reestablish a culture with the authority that, according to him, archaic Greece once possessed. My own position, for which I cannot argue here, is that Nietzsche may have had the goal of establishing such a culture in his early years but that in his later works, particularly the great works of the 1880s, he ceased believing that philosophy could have such a direct influence on culture in general. He turned, instead, to a vastly more individualist project of self-creation, establishing himself as an individual who fash-

ioned a distinctive, perhaps even inimitable mode of life. We shall have more to say about this last issue as we proceed.

On a historical level, we should note that Bernard Williams, despite his deep debt to Nietzsche, has shown that the discontinuity between Homeric and archaic Greek ethical thought on the one hand and later Greek and contemporary views on similar issues on the other is by no means as great as has often been supposed. See his *Shame and Necessity* (Berkeley: University of California Press, 1993), esp. chaps. 2 and 3.

24. That Nietzsche often (though not always) understood morality in such a Kantian manner is well argued in Maudemarie Clark's Ph.D. dissertation, "Nietzsche's Attack on Morality" (University of Wisconsin, 1975).

25. See *BGE* 202; 5:124–26, where Nietzsche explicitly connects Socrates with modern, Christian, or "herd animal" morality, which he describes in explicitly dogmatist terms and the "heir' of which, he claims, is "the democratic movement." Nietzsche's political views have come under intense scrutiny recently. Books worth consulting on the issue are Tracy Strong, *Friedrich Nietzsche and the Politics of Transfiguration*, exp. ed. (Berkeley: University of California Press, 1988); Mark Warren, *Nietzsche and Political Thought*, (Cambridge, Mass.: MIT Press, 1988); Bruce Detweiler, *Nietzsche and the Politics of Aristocratic Radicalism* (Chicago: University of Chicago Press, 1990); Peter Bergmann, *Nietzsche: "The Last Antipolitical German"* (Bloomington: Indiana University Press, 1987); Leslie Paul Thiele, *Friedrich Nietzsche and the Politics of the Soul* (Princeton: Princeton University Press, 1990); and, particularly in regard to the connections between Nietzsche and democratic thought, Lawrence J. Hatab, *A Nietzschean Defense of Democracy* (Chicago: Open Court, 1995).

26. *BT* 11–15; 1:75–102.

27. For a concise, balanced, and on the whole positive assessment of Nietzsche's treatment of the Greeks, see Hugh Lloyd-Jones, "Nietzsche and the Study of the Ancient World," in James C. O'Flaherty, Timothy F. Sellner, and Robert M. Helm, eds., *Studies in Nietzsche and the Classical Tradition* (Chapel Hill: University of North Carolina Press, 1979), 1–15.

28. By this Nietzsche means the nature of the world itself, of which he thinks in strikingly, sometimes embarrassingly anthropomorphic terms throughout this book.

29. "Consider the consequences of the Socratic maxims: 'Virtue is knowledge; man sins only from ignorance; he who is virtuous is happy.' In these three basic forms of optimism lies the death of tragedy. For now the virtuous hero must be a dialectician; now there must be a necessary, visible connection between virtue and knowledge, faith and morality; now the transcendental justice of Aeschylus is degraded to the superficial and insolent principle of 'poetic justice' with its customary *deus ex machina*" (*BT* 14; 1:94–95).

30. *HH* 126; 2:122. It is interesting to compare Nietzsche's evaluation of Socrates' *daimonion* with Montaigne's: "[B]The daemon of Socrates was perhaps a certain impulse of the will that came to him without awaiting the advice of his reason. In a well-purified soul such as his, prepared by a continual exercise of wisdom and virtue, it is likely that these inclinations, although instinctive and undigested, were always important and worth following" ("Of prognostications," 44; 29–30F). Montaigne here distinguishes between Socrates' rational decisions and

his more instinctive impulses. We shall see that Socrates' rationality is itself not as unequivocal as Nietzsche generally makes it appear.

31. In what follows, I will refer to "The Problem of Socrates" only by means of its section numbers and by the page number in volume 6 of the *Kritische Studienausgabe*.

32. Plato, *Phd*. 118a7–8. Actually, Socrates says not that "*I*" but that "*we* owe a rooster to Asclepius." This will become a central issue in the next chapter.

33. A detailed discussion of "decadence" in connection with Socrates can be found in Daniel R. Ahern, *Nietzsche as Cultural Physician* (University Park: Pennsylvania State University Press, 1995), chap. 3. According to Ahern, "the symptoms of decadence Nietzsche identified with Socrates [include] Socrates' rationality (*TI* 3:10), his role in destroying tragic art (*BT* 12), his moralizing (*WP* 433), and his failure as a physician of culture (*TI* 3:11) " (58). Ahern's examination of the issue is valuable, though I have serious reservations about his view, which is not unrelated to the view of Havas in *Nietzsche's Genealogy*, that Nietzsche considered the role of philosophy to be the construction and articulation of a "healthy" general alternative to contemporary culture.

34. Nietzsche's views on the importance of the ἀγών to Greek culture in general are expressed in an early unpublished essay, recently included, as "Homer on Competition," in Friedrich Nietzsche, *On the Genealogy of Morality*, trans. Carol Diethe (Cambridge: Cambridge University Press, 1994), 187–94. The original text, entitled "Homers Wettkampf," is included in the *Kritische Studienausgabe*, 1:783–92.

35. *GM* II:12; 5:313–15. Cf. *GS* 353; 3:589–90, where Nietzsche argues that the most important part of the founding of a new religion is to locate a way of life that was already there, to "see it," "select it," and "guess" for the first time "to what use it can be put, how it can be interpreted." That is, founders of religions do not generally invent new modes of life; they only bring to the fore and reinterpret, for their own purposes, forms that already existed before them. In general, despite his emphasis on creation and on leaving the past behind, Nietzsche is acutely aware of the necessity of depending on material that is always already there. I discuss this issue in some detail in "Nietzsche, Aestheticism, Modernity," in Bernd Magnus and Kathleen M. Higgins, eds., *The Cambridge Companion to Nietzsche* (Cambridge: Cambridge University Press, 1996).

36. Nietzsche often suggests that Socrates did not simply "destroy" the tragic culture of the Greeks: the culture itself, he claims, was already falling apart, and Socrates hastened its end. If that is so, he never quite explains why Greek culture began to fall into the decadence he finds personified in Socrates. See, for example, *BGE* 212; 5:145–47, which we shall discuss in more detail below, and Ahern, *Nietzsche as Cultural Physician*, 71–77.

37. It seems to me that Nietzsche chooses his words here very carefully indeed. When he describes Socrates as "a cave of bad appetites" ("eine Höhle aller schlimmen Begierden"), he is almost certainly alluding to Plato's most famous metaphor: the metaphor of everyday, passion- and illusion-ridden human life as an unknowing imprisonment in a cave from which only the philosopher, who is of course modeled on Socrates, can ever escape. By means of his description, Nietzsche is implying that Socrates is even more a prisoner in Plato's cave than the common people whose life Plato thought he was describing (*Rep*. 514a1–517c6).

I am grateful to Duncan Large, who, by questioning the accuracy of the English translation of this passage, helped me realize how important it is.

38. *TI* V:2; 6:83. Nietzsche had already written in the previous section that "the church fights passion with excision in every sense: its practice, its 'cure,' is *castratism*. . . . It has at all times laid the stress of discipline on extirpation (of sensuality, of pride, of the lust to rule, of avarice, of vengefulness)." But, as he had already argued in *GM* I, esp. secs. 13–15 (5:278–85), such a practice preserves what it wants to eliminate because it needs to use the very impulses it disavows in order to destroy them (see also Nehamas, *Nietzsche: Life as Literature*, 211–12). Montaigne, too, had a similar thought: "There is no hostility that excels Christian hostility. Our zeal does wonders when it is seconding our leaning toward hatred, cruelty, ambition, avarice, detraction, rebellion. . . . Our religion is made to extirpate vices; it covers them, fosters them, incites them" ("Apology for Raymond Sebond," II:444; 324F).

39. *GS* 290; 3:530–31. I have discussed this passage and the whole issue addressed here in more detail in *Nietzsche: Life as Literature*, 184–99.

40. In the preface to *Beyond Good and Evil*, Nietzsche famously refers to Christianity as "Platonism 'for the people.'" Needless to say, his view of Socrates' and Plato's view of the soul is much too simple. Though it is true that in the *Phaedo* Plato attributes every lower impulse to the body and identifies the soul with reason, the tripartite division of the *Republic* considers not only reason but also emotion and even the lower passions as parts of the human soul. Nevertheless, Plato indicates very strongly that what is most characteristically human is reason, the "ruling element" of the soul.

41. He has been accused of being both by Jürgen Habermas, in *The Philosophical Discourse of Modernity*, trans. Frederick Lawrence (Cambridge, Mass.: MIT Press, 1987), chap. 2. Habermas attributes those views to Nietzsche as a whole on the basis of what I consider a flawed reading of *The Birth of Tragedy*. See Nehamas, "Nietzsche, Aestheticism, Modernity," 228–30 as well as idem, "The Ends of Philosophy," *New Republic*, 30 May 1988, 32–36.

42. *WP* 430; 13:288. The note continues: "What, then, is the significance of the reaction of Socrates, who recommended dialectics as the road to virtue and made mock when morality did not know how to justify itself logically? . . . [M]oral judgments are torn from their conditionality, in which they have grown and alone possess any meaning, from their Greek and Greek-political ground and soil, to be denaturalized under the pretense of sublimation . . . one *invents* a world where they are at home, where they originate."

43. The claims that follow form the central idea of, and are argued for in detail in, Nehamas, *Nietzsche: Life as Literature*.

44. Here I disagree with the radical distinction between the "private" project of self-creation and the "public" task of affecting society in general, a distinction that Richard Rorty draws in *Contingency, Irony, and Solidarity* (Cambridge: Cambridge University Press, 1989), esp. chap. 5. I have given some reasons for rejecting Rorty's view in "Nietzsche, Aestheticism, Modernity," 236–38, and in "A Touch of the Poet," *Raritan Quarterly* 10 (1990): 101–25.

45. See Nehamas, *Nietzsche: Life as Literature*, chap. 5.

46. *GS* 255; 3:516. See Walter Kaufmann's note to this passage in his translation (217) for a possible alternative reading, which, he convincingly argues, cannot be right.

47. This is part of the argument of *GM* I:16 and III:13; 5:285–88, 367–72. Nietzsche's metaphor of human beings as herd animals is rich and textured; it deserves more attention than it has been given so far, and much more than I can give it now.

48. Nietzsche's imagery here suggests that he is thinking of "the creator" as a religious figure, particularly as someone who articulates a universal mode of life. But, first, as *The Antichrist* shows, Nietzsche did not think that Jesus articulated such a mode of life; see especially sections 29, 33, 35. Second, as we shall see in detail a little further on, even when Nietzsche speaks of "writing new values on new tablets," we must always be ready to ask for whom those values are intended. The assumption that they must be intended for everyone is unjustified.

49. I have discussed some of the issues surrounding perspectivism in *Nietzsche: Life as Literature*, chap. 2. Maudemarie Clark has presented an alternative interpretation in *Nietzsche on Truth and Philosophy* (Cambridge: Cambridge University Press, 1990). In general, I am dissatisfied with earlier treatments of perspectivism, including mine, because they paid almost exclusive attention to the epistemological issues raised by the view without taking into account the fact that the divergence between truth and value seems to be more important to Nietzsche. That is the issue to which I shall turn next.

50. Arthur C. Danto, *Nietzsche as Philosopher* (New York: Macmillan, 1965), 71, 72; cf. 79, 99. Danto's pragmatist interpretation is not accepted by everyone writing on Nietzsche, but no other view has won more adherents over the last thirty years. Richard Schacht, *Nietzsche* (London: Routledge and Kegan Paul, 1983), chap. 2, attributes to Nietzsche a number of different theories of truth, depending on the kinds of claims that are being evaluated, while Maudemarie Clark, *Nietzsche on Truth and Philosophy*, chap. 2, claims that Nietzsche accepts a "minimal" version of the correspondence theory that makes no serious metaphysical commitments either in regard to the nature of the world or in regard to our ability to know it.

51. The most famous among them comes from *BGE* 4; 5:18: "The falseness of a judgment is not for us necessarily an objection to a judgment; in this respect our new language may sound strangest. The question is to what extent it is life-promoting, life-preserving, species-preserving, perhaps even species-cultivating." We can make two comments on this. First, even here Nietzsche need not be rejecting falsehood altogether as a reason for objecting to a judgment. His qualification "noch" (which Kaufmann translates, a little too strongly, as "necessarily") suggests that he is not saying that falsehood is *never* a reason for refusing to accept a judgment. Nietzsche's pragmatism is therefore itself qualified. Second, a strict pragmatist identifies truth with utility and falsehood with uselessness. There can be no question of a judgment that is both false and "life-preserving" at the same time, since to be false is to be of no use and to be life-preserving is to be true. The passage cannot therefore support a strict pragmatist interpretation of Nietzsche.

52. *GS* 121; 3:477–478. See also *HH* 517; 2:323: "*Fundamental insight.*— There is no pre-established harmony between the pursuit of truth and the welfare of mankind."

53. *GS* 344; 3:575. Nietzsche makes similar claims in *BGE* 1; 5:15 and *GM* III:23–27; 5:395–411.

54. *GS* 354; 3:593: "We 'know' (or believe or imagine) just as much as may be *useful* in the interests of the human herd, the species; and even what is here called 'utility' is ultimately also a mere belief, something imaginary, and perhaps precisely that most calamitous stupidity of which we shall perish some day." This passage makes clear that if Nietzsche is offering a theory of anything here, it is a theory about why we tend to accept certain beliefs as true. But the fact that our hypothesis (that they are useful) can be so wrong shows that the theory cannot explain why any belief that happens to be true is in fact so.

55. *WP* 455; 13:446–47: "How is truth proved? By the feeling of enhanced power . . . by utility—by indispensability—in short, by advantages (namely, presuppositions concerning what truth *ought* to be like for us to recognize it). But that is a prejudice: a sign that truth is not involved at all."

56. The term was first used by Peter Geach, who believes that Socrates did commit that fallacy, in his "Plato's *Euthyphro*: An Analysis and Commentary," *Monist* 50 (1966): 369–82. For discussion, see John Beversluis, "Does Socrates Commit the Socratic Fallacy?" *American Philosophical Quarterly* 24 (1987): 211–23, and my "Confusing Universals and Particulars in Plato's Early Dialogues," *Review of Metaphysics* 29 (1975): 287–306.

57. In "The Folly of Trying to Define Truth" (*Journal of Philosophy* 93 [1996]: 263–87), Donald Davidson argues, beginning with a parallel between contemporary efforts to define truth and Plato's attempt to offer definitions of the virtues (and, in the *Theaetetus*, of knowledge), that truth is "an indefinable concept. But this does not mean," Davidson continues, "that we can say nothing revealing about it: we can, by relating it to other concepts like belief, desire, cause, and action. Nor does the indefinability of truth imply that the concept is mysterious, ambiguous, or untrustworthy" (265). That is roughly the position I am here attributing to Nietzsche.

58. Danto, *Nietzsche as Philosopher*, 80. The objection is very common; I have tried to address it in *Nietzsche: Life as Literature*, 65–67.

59. I can, of course, pretend to believe it, or act as if I do, for particular purposes. What I cannot do is actually believe something in the knowledge that it is false. I can also hold a particular view even though I know it is not in my interest to do so. But I cannot decide that, because it is not in my interest, that view is false.

60. The persistence of the confusion between perspectivism and relativism is what accounts for the conviction that perspectivism, like relativism, undermines its own truth.

61. What Nietzsche calls "nihilism," the conviction that there are no values at all and that all courses of action are either arbitrary or not worth taking at all, comes from the realization that the objective values posited by Christianity and guaranteed by God do not exist. "The death of God" leaves an empty space where secure values were previously thought to exist. There can be two reactions to that realization. One can think that the opportunity is now open for the creation of new values or that (if one still needs values that are given independently of oneself) there are no values at all. Nietzsche's views on this set of issues are complex, and it is not possible to examine them here. But it is worth noting that Montaigne had had a similar idea: "The common herd, not having the faculty of judging things in themselves, let themselves be carried away by chance and appear-

ance, when once they have been given the temerity to despise and judge the opinions they had held in extreme reverence, such as those in which their salvation is concerned. And when some articles of their religion have been set in doubt and upon the balance, they will soon after cast easily into like uncertainty all the other parts of the belief, which had no more authority or foundation in them than those that have been shaken" ("Apology for Raymond Sebond," 439; 320F). Montaigne officially disapproves of the "execrable atheism" the temptation to which this passage analyzes and attributes it to the stupidity of "the common herd." But the phenomenon he describes is precisely what Nietzsche meant by "the death of God." And where Montaigne discerns stupidity, Nietzsche characteristically finds weakness.

62. Truth derives its unconditional value, according to *GS* 344, not out of *prudential* considerations to the effect that it is always bad to be deceived, which is clearly false, but, Nietzsche claims, from the *moral* commitment "I will not deceive, not even myself." Given that life aims "at semblance, meaning error, deception, simulation, delusion, self-delusion . . . charitably interpreted, such a resolve might perhaps be a quixotism, a minor slightly mad enthusiasm; but it might also be something more serious, namely, a principle that is hostile to life and destructive." Our efforts to differentiate ourselves from the rest of nature, according to Nietzsche, are doomed to fail. But in engendering the notion that we are radically different beings from everything else, morality is for Nietzsche "hostile to life."

63. That is the view of Clark, *Nietzsche on Truth and Philosophy*, 160, 162, and Arthur Danto, "Some Remarks on *The Genealogy of Morals*," in Robert C. Solomon and Kathleen M. Higgins, eds., *Reading Nietzsche* (New York: Oxford University Press, 1988), 13–28.

64. Clark, *Nietzsche on Truth and Philosophy*, 163.

65. Ibid., 202.

66. See *WP* 441, quoted on p. 150.

67. In *BGE* 211; 5:144–45, Nietzsche has already rejected Kant and Hegel, whom he disparages as mere "philosophical laborers," unable to create new values and content with codifying the values that already existed in their world.

68. For a fuller discussion of this passage and the many issues it raises, see my "Who Are 'the Philosophers of the Future'?: A Reading of *Beyond Good and Evil*," in Solomon and Higgins, eds., *Reading Nietzsche*, 46–67.

69. Ahern, *Nietzsche as Cultural Physician*, chap. 3, makes an interesting argument to the effect that Nietzsche can recognize Socrates as a great philosopher but still reject him on account of his "decadence." According to Ahern, "in a healthy organism the combined power of its drives is harnessed toward growth. In decadence, the situation is reversed: the instinct of preservation becomes dominant [and everything functions] for the sake of stability" (63). Ahern defines ultimate stability as death itself and thus accuses Socrates of leading Greek culture to "embrace death" (61). But Socrates was still a great figure because he "revealed the genuine task of the philosopher to be that of a cultural physician. But this great model of the philosopher for the succeeding millennia necessarily promoted the illness he understood himself to be fighting" (76). Socrates, Ahern concludes, "demonstrates that there are times when, confronted with illness, the physician's only 'cure' is a lethal injection" (77–78). This is in a variety of ways an attractive

interpretation, and I agree with many of Ahern's ideas. But I still have serious doubts about whether Nietzsche continued to believe that the philosophers' task is to be "cultural physicians" in the sense of offering a set of views and values — a "cure" — for their culture as a whole. My own position is that Nietzsche retreated to a much more individualist position in his later works and took his task to be the articulation of his own mode of life — a mode that may or (probably) may not be appropriate for the rest of his world.

70. Xenophon, *Symp.* 5.5.

71. For a detailed presentation of the means Nietzsche employed for that purpose, see Nehamas, *Nietzsche: Life as Literature*, chapter 1.

72. The first term is Walter Kaufmann's, in *Nietzsche: Philosopher, Psychologist, Antichrist*, 4th ed. (Princeton: Princeton University Press, 1974), 391. The second is Werner Dannhauser's, in *Nietzsche's View of Socrates* (Ithaca: Cornell University Press, 1974), 272. Despite my disagreement with Dannhauser's final view, I found his book very helpful in pointing out and discussing the "truce" between Nietzsche and Socrates during the works of Nietzsche's middle period.

73. My treatment of Socrates and Nietzsche has been of course far from complete. The most exhaustive, almost encyclopaedic investigation of the topic, and an extensive bibliography, can be found in Hermann-Josef Schmidt, *Nietzsche und Sokrates: Philosophische Untersuchungen zu Nietzsches Sokratesbild* (Meisenheim: Hain, 1969).

74. Nietzsche writes this in an unpublished note (11:440). He claims that Socrates' magic consisted in having "one soul, and another one behind that, and another one behind that." Xenophon, he says, "lay to sleep" in Socrates' first soul, Plato in the second, and in the third it was Plato again, but with his own second soul.

75. *WS* 86; 2:591–92. The passage continues: "Socrates excels the founder of Christianity in being able to be serious cheerfully and in possessing that wisdom full of roguishness that constitutes the finest state of the human soul. And he also possessed the finer intellect." Nietzsche, who writes here that Socrates possesses "die fröliche Art des Ernstes," may have remembered that Montaigne had once attributed to Socrates "a gay and sociable wisdom" (844; 64F).

Chapter 6

1. See Glenn W. Most, "A Cock for Asclepius," *Classical Quarterly* 43 (1993): 96–111, which I discuss in detail below.

2. Foucault died on 21 June 1984. He lectured on Socrates and on the Cynics at the Collège de France between 29 February and 28 March 1984. Those were the last lectures he gave. For more information, see the following note.

3. Michel Foucault, Lecture at the Collège de France, 15 February 1984, 40. The lecture concerns the *Apology*, the *Crito*, and the *Phaedo*. On 22 February 1984, Foucault lectured on the *Laches*. The former, to which I will refer hereafter simply by page number, is the main text I will be discussing in this chapter. References to the second lecture will be given by the page number preceded by the Latin numeral II. The lectures have not been published yet, and I am grateful to James Miller for making the typescripts made from the original tapes available to

me. The translations from these two lectures, rough as they are, are all my own. A general account of the lectures is given by Thomas Flynn, "Foucault as Parrhesiast: His Last Course at the Collège de France," in James Bernauer and David Rasmussen, eds., *The Final Foucault* (Cambridge, Mass.: MIT Press, 1994), 102–18. See also Gary Alan Scott, "Games of Truth: Foucault's Analysis of the Transformation of Political to Ethical *Parrhêsia* and the Disagreement between Socrates and Alcibiades over Truth-telling," typescript (Department of Philosophy, Whittier College, 1996).

4. See Georges Dumézil, " . . . *Le Moyne noir et gris dedans Varennes": Sotie nostradamique suivie d'un divertissement sur les dernieres paroles de Socrate* (Paris: Gallimard, 1984). Dumézil discusses Plato's line on p. 140.

5. Foucault correctly rejects (54–55) Ulrich von Wilamowitz-Moellendorff's conjecture (in his *Platon*, 2d ed., 2 vols. [Berlin: Weidmann, 1920], 1:178 n. 1) that Socrates is referring to a disease perhaps of Xanthippe, perhaps of one of his own children, which he had forgotten to mention while his family was still there. Foucault actually takes Wilamowitz to think that Socrates is referring to an earlier disease of his own, but Wilamowitz's case is weak in any case: the dramatic implausibility of having Socrates forget what becomes his last concern before his death provides an insuperable difficulty to that interpretation.

6. See *GS* 340: 3:569: "O Kriton, ich bin dem Asklepios einen Hahn schuldig." The version in "The Problem of Socrates" is similar: "Ich bin dem Heilande Asklepios einen Hahn schuldig" (Friedrich Nietzsche, *Sämtliche Werke: Kritische Studienausgabe*, 15 vols., ed. Giorgio Colli and Mazzino Montinari [Berlin: De Gruyter, 1980], 6:67).

7. Plato, *Cr.* 47a6–48a1. The point is clear, though the word ψυχή (psyche, soul) is not used in this passage.

8. See Plato, *Laws*, 720d, where the term refers explicitly to taking care of the sick (οἱ κάμνοντες) and Sextus Empiricus, *Pyr. Hyp.* 2.240. Other medical uses of the term can be found, for example, in *De arte*, 9.3, where people with certain symptoms are said to need to take care of themselves; *De articulis*, 11, 61, refers to the care (ἐπιμέλεια) of wounds; Vectiarius, 21.72, writes that patients get better if they are taken care of (ἐπιμέλεια).

9. An extended effort to offer a radically new interpretation of Socrates' last words was recently made by Most, "A Cock for Asclepius." Most provides an exhaustive overview of the secondary literature on this issue, and his article is very valuable. Most disagrees with all previous interpretations of Socrates' final words, including the Nietzschean approach I am adopting here. His own positive proposal is that Socrates, in a moment of clairvoyance just before his death, realizes that Plato, who has made a point of writing that he could not attend Socrates' last day because he was sick (*Phd.* 59b10), has been cured of the disease that had kept him at home. Socrates then asks for the sacrifice on Plato's behalf!

Most's arguments against the traditional view are divided into three groups. The first group consists of four points (pp. 101–2). First, Most asserts that nowhere in the *Phaedo* does Plato claim that life is a disease or that death is its cure. But Plato, as we have seen, does write, twice, that philosophy is a preparation for death, and that the ἀρετή of "the lovers of the body" has nothing "healthy" about it. Second, according to Most, Plato's idea (67a2–6, 83d7–10) that we should not "remain full" (ἀναπίμπλασθαι) of the body but should remain "pure" (καθαροί) from it shows that the connection between soul and body is not medical but religious; the metaphor is not that of infection but of pollution. But it is well known that medical and religious vocabulary often merge together, especially in connection with the notion of κάθαρσις (catharsis), as the debates surrounding the interpretation of that term in Aristotle's *Poetics*, which are too well known to rehearse here, amply show. In addition, the contrast Most invokes in n. 32 between ἀναπεπλημένος ("full") and μεμολυσμένος ("contaminated") preserves exactly the same ambiguity. Third, Most argues, Plato never uses a medical metaphor for the relation of soul and body. But the σῶμα/σῆμα metaphor, which we discuss in the text above, shows that this is not true. Fourth, Most points out, no other parallels for the idea that life is a disease exist in classical Greek literature. But this just testifies to the radical nature of Plato's metaphor and to how difficult it is to accept such a disturbingly otherworldly view.

Most's second argument (103) is that at 95c9–d4 Socrates attributes the view that life is a disease to Cebes and rejects it himself. But though part of the view that Socrates attributes to Cebes here is in fact the idea that life is a disease, the difference is still immense. For Socrates says that Cebes, who denies that the soul is immortal, believes that life is the beginning of the soul's destruction, which is completed at death, as disease is the beginning of the destruction of the body. But Socrates himself, who believes in the immortality of the soul, thinks of life as a disease with a cure. What he rejects is not Cebes' view that life is a disease but that it cannot be cured and that the soul perishes at death.

Third, Most claims (103–4) that the verb ὀφείλειν ("to owe") generally denotes previous and not impending obligations. Socrates then, in saying that "we owe Asclepius a rooster," must be referring to a disease already cured, like Plato's, and not to his own alleged liberation from the body. But Socrates' death, once he has taken the poison, is a *fait accompli*, and even if the sense of ὀφείλειν were as clear as Most claims it is it does not follow that Socrates' impending death, which is certain, cannot constitute a debt that has been already incurred. In addition, according to Most, "whether the god had aided Socrates at the moment of his death or not could only be known after Socrates had already died—to utter thanks beforehand would be impertinent, if not impious" (104). But the whole philosophical point of the dialogue has been to prove that death is a benefit, a liberation, a transition to a better place for which Socrates can be, if his proofs are right, absolutely grateful at this point.

Most also argues (105–6), like Dumézil (though independently of him), that the "we owe" and the other two verbs of Socrates' final sentence show that we must take his words to be genuine plurals and thus to refer not to a personal debt but to a debt incurred by the group gathered round him as a whole. But apart from the arguments I have appealed to in the main text, it is important to note that in the *Phaedrus* Socrates uses the plural εἰς ἡμετέραν δύναμιν ("to the extent of our power," 257a3) to refer to himself *in contrast to Phaedrus*—and that shows that the incidence of the plural is not by itself sufficient to show that two or more people must be referred to by its means. In any case, it seems to me, Socrates can certainly ask all his friends together to sacrifice on his behalf, even to suppose that the debt to Asclepius is collective: for, as Plato was fond of saying, κοινὰ τὰ τῶν φίλων ("Friends have everything in common," *Phdr.* 279c6–7).

On the positive side, Most argues that the Greeks often believed that those who were near death were granted clairvoyant powers. But the Platonic parallels he cites in connection with Socrates are not convincing (108–9). At *Ap.* 39c1–d8, after Socrates has been sentenced to death, he claims that he can prophesy (χρησμῳδεῖν) that the Athenians will be attacked viciously for their decision. But on Most's own grounds, that is too early for Socrates to have acquired clairvoyant powers: Most's argument depends seriously on the idea that Socrates can have become aware of Plato's cure only after he has already drunk the poison and is "at the very threshold of death" (108). The other parallel concerns Socrates' likening himself to Apollo's swans, who sing in joy when they have a premonition of their own death (*Phd.* 85d4–7). But the swan acquires mantic powers only regarding its own death, not regarding the health or illness of others. Further, the traditional view can account for this passage without any trouble: Socrates' whole last discourse, throughout the dialogue, is itself, like the swan's song, an extreme expression of joy; that is just what the otherworldly interpretation of his final words implies.

For all these reasons, I cannot in the end accept Most's interpretation. But his article is well worth consulting, especially for its exhaustive survey of the bibliography on this topic.

10. Plato's view that the good life involves an ascetic separation from the body and that such a separation is an early form of death is in the background of much of what we saw Nietzsche write about the connection between Socrates, morality, and "the will to death" in the previous chapter.

11. Socrates is made to say "I would have been destroyed a long time ago and would not have been of any use either to you or to myself" (πάλαι ἂν ἀπολώλη καὶ οὔτ᾽ ἂν ὑμᾶς ὠφελήκη οὐδὲν οὔτ᾽ ἂν ἐμαυτόν, 31d8–9). The inclusion of "myself" is important for me, since it supports the individualist reading of Socrates I have been trying to give here. Foucault, whose reading of Socrates is more other-directed than my own, tends to underplay such references.

12. Nietzsche, too, was tempted to see Socrates as a "divine missionary" (*Sämtliche Werke: Kritische Studienausgabe,* 2:584–85) but was much less sure than Foucault about how seriously we should take Socrates' self-description.

13. Apart from his lectures on Socrates and on the Cynics at the Collège de France, Foucault gave a course at the University of California at Berkeley in the fall of 1983 entitled *Discourse and Truth: The Problematization of Parrhêsia.* His lectures were taped and transcribed by Joseph Pearson, to whom I am very grateful for making them available to me.

14. See the essays of Pierre Hadot published as *Philosophy as a Way of Life: Spiritual Exercises from Socrates to Foucault,* trans. Michael Chase (Oxford: Blackwell, 1995), as well as his recent *Qu'est-ce que la philosophie antique?* (Paris: Gallimard, 1995).

15. See Hadot, *Qu'est-ce que la philosophie antique?* 18, which seems to me to overstate the prevalence of schools, especially during the beginnings of philosophy in the late fifth century BC, and "Forms of Life and Forms of Discourse" in *Philosophy as a Way of Life,* 59.

16. See Plato, *La.* 178a5, 179c1, 189a1, and Foucault, II.10–11, 28–29. See also Foucault, *Discourse and Truth,* 57.

17. On the *Ion,* see Foucault, *Discourse and Truth,* 18–34.

18. Though I agree with Foucault that Socrates opposes the oracle, and that

he even suggests that he is aiming to refute it (see 21c1–2: "Here, if anywhere, I would refute [ἐλέγξων] the oracle and reply to it, 'This man here is wiser than I, though you said I was the one'"), I am not sure that Socrates' reaction is totally unrelated to interpretation, a notion of which Foucault was suspicious throughout his life. For, in a manner not entirely consistent with the passage I just quoted, his first reaction to the oracle is to ask, "What is the god saying? What is he hinting at? . . . He certainly can't be lying, for that would not be proper to him" (21b3–7). These questions suggest that Socrates is actually trying to understand what the oracle means. His own reaction is uncharacteristic of traditional reactions to oracles because he seems to envisage at least the possibility that the god may actually be wrong.

In this connection, a passage from Nietzsche, with which Foucault may or may not have been familiar, is particularly intriguing: "*Divine Missionaries*. — Socrates too feels himself to be a divine missionary: but even here there is perceptible I know not what touch of Attic irony and sense of humour through which that unfortunate and presumptuous concept is ameliorated. He speaks of it without unction: his images, of the brake and the horse, are simple and unpriestly, and the actual religious task to which he feels himself called, that of *putting the god to the test in a hundred ways* to see *whether* he has told the truth, permits us to imagine that here the missionary steps to his god with a bold and candid deportment. This putting of the god to the test is one of the subtlest compromises between piety and freedom of spirit that has ever been devised. — Nowadays we no longer have need even of this compromise" (*WS* 72; 2:584–85).

19. Foucault, 23–24. See also II.51–52 and *Discourse and Truth*, 62–63.

20. But see W. R. Connor, "The Other 399: Religion and the Trial of Socrates," *Bulletin of the Institute of Classical Studies* 58 (1991): Supplement, 49–56. Connor argues that there is some evidence to suggest that religious trials (which, officially, is what Socrates' own trial was) were rather common in that period and that Socrates' religious practices (without reference to the elenchus) might have been unusual enough to bring him to court. Plato, of course, could have used Socrates' trial, whatever the reasons for which it was originally instituted, for his own purposes. See also M. F. Burnyeat, "The Impiety of Socrates," *Ancient Philosophy* 27 (1997): 1–12.

21. Foucault (7–8, 27) contrasts Socrates and Solon, on the basis of a story, reported by Diogenes Laertius, 1.2.3 (whom he does not cite), according to which Solon, when Pisistratus established a personal military guard for himself, appeared in public fully armed in order to suggest that if the tyrant thought of the Athenians as his enemies it was only fair for the Athenians to be ready to fight back.

22. The effect of this identification must have been must stronger during the lectures themselves, since Foucault, within that oral context, would shift from quotation to paraphrase presumably without indicating that he was doing so.

23. For example, in the decision of Lysimachus and Melesias to address Nicias and Laches in the first place (*La.* 178a–180a5), in Nicias' and Laches' willingness to submit to Socrates' questioning, though Nicias, at least, knows how serious an enterprise that is (187e–188c), and in the decision of the company to continue their own education since they have realized that they are ignorant of the nature of courage and ἀρετή (*aretê*) in general (200e–201c). See Foucault, II.15–19. Foucault also discusses the *Laches* in *Discourse and Truth*, 57–69.

24. "One misunderstands great human beings if one views them from the miserable perspective of some public use. That one cannot put them to any use, that in itself may belong to greatness" (*TI* 9.50; 6:152).

25. Foucault's reliance on Xenophon for a number of Socratic views is evident in *The Use of Pleasure*, vol. 2 of *History of Sexuality*, trans. Robert Hurley (New York: Random House, 1985), esp. chap. 1 and part 5.

26. Michel Foucault, "Interview: Sex, Power, and the Politics of Identity," in *Foucault Live: Collected Interviews, 1961–1984*, ed. Sylvère Lotringer (New York: Semiotext(e), 1989), 27.

27. Michel Foucault, *Madness and Civilization: A History of Insanity in the Age of Reason*, trans. Richard Howard (New York: Random House, 1965), 241.

28. Michel Foucault, *Discipline and Punish: The Birth of the Prison*, trans. Alan Sheridan (New York: Random House, 1977), 30.

29. A starting point for the criticism of Foucault, though ill tempered and partisan, is J. G. Merquior's *Foucault* (Berkeley: University of California Press, 1985). An exemplary critical discussion, on a very specific issue (Foucault's interpretation of the Stoics' notion of the art of living) is provided by Pierre Hadot, "Reflections on the Notion of 'The Cultivation of the Self,'" in Timothy J. Armstrong, trans., *Michel Foucault, Philosopher* (New York: Routledge, 1992), 225–31 (also reprinted in Hadot's *Philosophy as a Way of Life*, 206–13).

30. See Michel Foucault, "Truth and Power," in *Power/Knowledge: Selected Interviews and Other Writings, 1972–1977*, ed. Colin Gordon (New York: Random House, 1980), 123.

31. Sartre's best-known statement of his position is his lecture "Existentialism Is a Humanism," in Walter Kaufmann, ed., *Existentialism from Dostoevsky to Sartre* (New York: World, 1956).

32. Michel Foucault, quoted by Didier Eribon, *Michel Foucault*, trans. Betsy Wing (Cambridge, Mass.: Harvard University Press, 1991), 280.

33. Sartre, "Existentialism Is a Humanism," 295.

34. Michel Foucault, *The Order of Things: An Archaeology of the Human Sciences* (New York: Random House, 1973), 387.

35. Michel Foucault, "What Is an Author?" in Josué V. Harari, ed., *Textual Strategies: Perspectives in Post-Structuralist Principles* (Ithaca: Cornell University Press, 1979), 159. A similar view, though without Foucault's theoretical and historical documentation, was presented by Roland Barthes, "The Death of the Author," in his *Image-Music-Text*, trans. Stephen Heath (New York: Hill and Wang, 1997), 142–48. I have discussed Foucault's view in detail in "Writer, Text, Work, Author," in Anthony J. Cascardi, ed., *Literature and the Question of Philosophy* (Baltimore: Johns Hopkins University Press, 1987), 267–91. My claim is that Foucault's demonstration that the idea that texts have authors, with all its implications, is a historical fact and not a natural given does not imply that authorship can be used only in the oppressive manner he outlines in his essay.

36. Foucault, "What Is an Author?' 159.

37. Michel Foucault, "Prison Talk," in *Power/Knowledge*, 52.

38. Foucault, *Discipline and Punish*, 27.

39. Nietzsche, *GM*, II.3; 5:297.

40. A good account of the different stages of Foucault's development, and also of the continuities among them, is given in Arnold I. Davidson's "Archae-

ology, Genealogy, Ethics," in David Couzens Hoy, ed., *Foucault: A Critical Reader* (Oxford: Blackwell, 1986), 221–34.

41. Foucault's method in those early works was exhaustively descriptive, avoiding all suggestion of alternatives. But his point of view created a serious problem for itself. Since history is itself a human science, how could he claim that his own position regarding the human sciences was correct? If his own analysis was true, then the human sciences might be able to reach the truth after all; and if it was false, why should we bother to believe what he wrote?

This problem, commonly seen as a symptom of Foucault's "nihilism," is exactly parallel to the difficulties we discussed in connection with Nietzsche's perspectivism in the previous chapter. It can be solved by seeing that Foucault placed himself within the domain he was investigating. The issue is not whether there is a general criterion for separating, in all cases, the true from the false, but whether a particular theory or interpretation is or is not better than its alternatives. This, of course, may seem to beg the question. For, one may ask, what are the criteria by which we can determine whether one interpretation is better than another? The answer, again, is that there are no such general criteria. Criteria of evaluation are not immune to dispute, even though it is less likely that people will disagree about general principles than about particular claims of truth or falsehood. Foucault offered his views for evaluation and criticism. His style, it is true, sometimes assumed such magisterial heights that it was difficult to believe that he would welcome discussion. But nothing in the substance of his writing precluded it, and few authors have been as willing to discuss their views and rethink their positions as he was: "As to those for whom to work hard, to begin and begin again, to attempt and be mistaken, to go back and rework everything from top to bottom, and still find reason to hesitate from one step to the next—as to those, in short, for whom to work in the midst of uncertainty and apprehension is tantamount to failure, all I can say is that clearly we are from another planet" (*The Use of Pleasure*, 7).

42. See, for example, Foucault, *Discipline and Punish*, 74: the "need for punishment without torture was first formulated as a cry from the heart or from an outraged nature. In the worst of murderers, there is one thing, at least, to be respected when one punishes: his 'humanity.' The day was to come, in the nineteenth century, when this 'man,' discovered in the criminal, would become the target of penal intervention, the object that it claimed to correct and transform, the domain of a whole series of 'criminological' sciences and strange 'penitentiary' practices."

43. Maurice Blanchot, *Foucault as I Imagine Him*, in *Foucault/Blanchot*, trans. Jeffrey Mehlman and Brian Massumi (New York: Zone Books, 1987), 74. Foucault's *Archaeology of Knowledge* is an extended effort to articulate the methodological principles that underlie his work up to and including *The Order of Things*.

44. Michel Serres, "Géométrie de la folie," in *Hermès ou la communication*, 176, quoted by Eribon, *Michel Foucault*, 117. *Folie et déraison: Histoire de la folie à l'âge classique* (Paris: Plon, 1961) is the original of which the radically abridged *Madness and Civilization* is the English version.

45. This is obvious, for example, in the manifesto Foucault composed for the Group on Prison Information (French, GIP), which aimed to expose the conditions under which the inmates of the French penal system were forced to live:

"The GIP does not propose to speak in the name of the prisoners in various prisons; it proposes, on the contrary, to provide them with the possibility of speaking themselves and telling what goes on in prisons. The GIP does not have reformist goals; we do not dream of an ideal prison. . . . [Our] investigations are not intended to ameliorate, alleviate, or make an oppressive system more bearable. They are intended to attack it in places where it is called something else — justice, technique, knowledge, objectivity" (quoted by Eribon, *Michel Foucault*, 227).

46. Michel Foucault, *The History of Sexuality*, vol. 1, *An Introduction*, trans. Robert Hurley (New York: Random House, 1978), 8–9.

47. Foucault once again proved himself a master of reversing received pictures: "The child's 'vice' was not so much an enemy as a support; it may have been designated as the evil to be eliminated, but the extraordinary effort that went into the task that was bound to fail leads one to suspect that what was demanded of it was to persevere, to proliferate to the limits of the visible and the invisible, rather than to disappear for good" (ibid., 42).

48. Michel Foucault, "What Is Enlightenment?" in *The Foucault Reader*, ed. Paul Rabinow (New York: Random House, 1984), 45.

49. Ibid., 46.

50. Blanchot, *Foucault as I Imagine Him*, 76.

51. Michel Foucault, "On the Genealogy of Ethics: An Overview of Work in Progress," in *Foucault Reader*, Rabinow, ed., 350. See also idem, "The Ethics of the Concern for Self as a Practice of Freedom" and "An Aesthetics of Existence," in *Foucault Live*, 432–49, 450–54.

52. Foucault's evolving attitudes toward that issue are well documented in James Miller's biography, *The Passion of Michel Foucault* (New York: Simon and Schuster, 1993). I am deeply indebted to Miller's book, and to Miller himself, for many of my own views of Foucault. I discuss his book, which met with a generally uncomprehending reception, in "Subject and Abject: The Examined Life of Michel Foucault," *New Republic*, 15 February 1993, 27–36; part of the material of that essay is reproduced here.

53. Foucault addresses these issues in *The Use of Pleasure* and in *The Care of the Self*, vol. 3 of *The History of Sexuality*, trans. Robert Hurley (New York: Random House, 1986).

54. This is obvious in a discussion in *The Use of Pleasure*. In classical Greek practice, especially in Plato, Foucault argued, coming to terms with one's pleasures and becoming able to moderate them was not a process of discovery, "it never took the form of a decipherment of the self by the self, never that of a hermeneutics of desire. . . . [I]t was never an epistemological condition enabling the individual to recognize himself in his singularity as a desiring subject and to purify himself of the desire that was thus brought to light." On the contrary, this effort "did on the other hand open onto an aesthetics of existence. And what I mean by this is a way of life whose moral value did not depend either on one's being in conformity with a code of behavior, or on an effort of purification, but on certain formal principles in the use of pleasures, in the way one distributed them, in the limits one observed, in the hierarchy one respected" (89). Foucault's readings of his ancient sources were not always definitive, and his views have often been dismissed on purely interpretative grounds. A model of how interpre-

tative disagreement can be combined with philosophical understanding is provided, as I have already remarked, by Pierre Hadot's "Reflections on the Notion of 'The Cultivation of the Self.'" See also Arnold I. Davidson, "Ethics as Ascetics: Foucault, the History of Ethics, and Ancient Thought," in Gary Gutting, ed., *The Cambridge Companion to Foucault* (Cambridge: Cambridge University Press, 1994), 115–40, esp. p. 116.

55. Foucault, "On the Genealogy of Ethics," 341.

56. Many such exercises — especially those he calls "spiritual" — have been studied by Pierre Hadot, both in *Philosophy as a Way of Life* and in *Qu'est-que la philosophie antique?* Foucault frequently expressed his debt to Hadot's work.

57. Nietzsche's contrast between philosophical and priestly asceticism in the Third Essay of *On the Genealogy of Morals* comes immediately to mind here. So does his writing (*TI*, V.1; 6:83) that "the church fights passion with excision in every sense: its practice, its 'cure,' is *castratism*. It never asks: 'How can one spiritualize, beautify, deify a craving?' [That may well have been Plato's question, in the *Symposium* as well as in the *Phaedrus*.] It has at all times laid the stress of discipline on extirpation (of sensuality, of pride, of the lust to rule, of avarice, of vengefulness)." Needless to say, both Nietzsche's claim and mine are much too stark and simple. A deeply erotic streak runs at least through one tradition of Christian art, encompassing both poets who are Christians, like Milton, and Christians who are poets, like St. John of the Cross. I am grateful to P. Adams Sitney for suggesting I make this qualification.

58. Foucault investigated four aspects of "ethics" so conceived. First, the issue of "the ethical substance," that is, those aspects of the self, or the individual, that are relevant to ethical reflection — the aspects of the individual that constitute it as a moral or ethical entity. For example, one's sexuality may be part of one's ethical substance while one's athletic ability may not (though such categorizations often change with time: engaging in athletic exercise, "for your health," has almost become an ethical category today). Second, "the mode of subjection," which is to say, the ways in which people come to recognize their moral obligations to themselves (*The Use of Pleasure*, 26) and to others: Foucault does not draw a hard and fast distinction between the two (28). People can accept moral obligations because they believe they are sanctioned by divine law, or because of their allegiance to a specific group that accepts such obligations, or because they consider such practices as manifesting "brilliance, beauty, nobility, or perfection" (27). Third, "the elaboration of ethical work," the various ways one employs in order to bring one's conduct into compliance with a rule and to transform oneself into the right sort of ethical agent ("ethical substance"). This is where the various spiritual exercises we have already mentioned play their most important role (27). Fourth, and final, "the *telos*" of the ethical subject, the sort of person one wants to become through ethical behavior: "A moral action," Foucault writes, "tends towards its own accomplishment; but it also aims beyond the latter, to the establishing of a moral conduct that commits an individual not only to other actions always in conformity with values and rules, but to a certain mode of being, a mode of being characteristic of the ethical subject" (28). Needless to say, both the *telos* of the ethical subject and the ways in which moral actions contribute to it are themselves historically variable. The purpose of *The History of Sexuality* was to document a number of these different conceptions of and methods for con-

structing moral agents over the centuries. Foucault gives a shorter presentation of these ideas in "On the Genealogy of Ethics." Arnold I. Davidson has discussed them well in "Archaeology, Genealogy, Ethics," 227–30, and has offered a more general reading of Foucault's ethical project in "Ethics as Ascetics."

59. One of the reasons for which, according to Foucault, Socrates is given the authority to examine Nicias and Laches, who are his social superiors, in the *Laches* is precisely the fact that his views about courage harmonize with his courageous acts, in war as in peace (II.58).

60. Miller's *Passion of Michel Foucault* has been broadly attacked on the grounds that its approach, concentrating as it does on the personal aspects of Foucault's life, is not true to Foucault's own view that authors are not the objects of criticism and because he mixes the public and the private in an unjustified manner. I have defended Miller against those charges in "Subject and Abject." Didier Eribon, in *Michel Foucault et ses contemporains*, launched a major attack against Miller's book (and a minor one against my review), arguing again (as he had done first during a conference at Berkeley in May 1993) that Miller reduces Foucault's ideas to the events of his life (on which see n. 62 below) and insisting that Miller makes numerous factual mistakes. But his examples of such mistakes (for example, that Dumézil was elected to the Collège de France in 1949 and not in 1968 [37]) are most often irrelevant to the issue of interpreting Foucault's thought. In general, Eribon's book, like his earlier biography, provides a large number of facts without integrating them into a reasonable interpretation. An excellent observer, Eribon is not precisely a philosopher.

61. See Foucault, "Interview: Sex, Power, and the Politics of Identity," 384–88.

62. To defuse the accusation that such an approach confuses the public and the private, I would call into question the very distinction between "private events" and "public ideas." Are Socrates' poverty, for example, his prodigious ability to drink without getting drunk, his unwillingness to leave the city for the country, his walking about barefoot, his attraction to boys — are all those private events in his life or part and parcel of the philosophical figure with which we now contend? The answer is that this depends on whether we can give an interpretation of Socrates that takes such elements into account. The distinction between the private and the public, at least in the case of the philosophers we are discussing, is always relative to an interpretation of their thought. The private is that which cannot be integrated into such an interpretation, not what our moral or sexual attitudes move us to classify as what must not to be discussed in polite society.

We must not be seduced into thinking that biographical events are subject to causal laws and therefore independent of choice while ideas are products of choice and therefore independent of causation. This would lead us to think that the facts of our lives are independently given to us and that the only way of coming to terms with them is by producing ideas that justify them in our own eyes and perhaps in the eyes of our audience, that those "facts" are what the ideas are about. But ideas are as much part of life and among the "facts" that constitute it, as everything else. Neither sort of fact is prior to the other, and both can be exploited, changed, and taken in charge of so as to become elements of a coherent whole.

63. Plato, *Ap.* 36c1–d2. Alcibiades says that Socrates made the same point to him at *Symp.* 216a4–6. That is also the central idea of *Alcibiades I*, on which Fou-

cault lectured at the University of California at Berkeley in the spring of 1983. In his second lecture on Socrates, Foucault makes an interesting distinction between the *Alcibiades* and the *Laches* (II.19–24). The former, he argues, identifies philosophy, conceived as the care of the self, with concern for the soul, while the latter identifies it, more broadly, with concern with life as a whole (βίος) and is thus the founding text of the conception of philosophy as the art of living. I am not quite sure about the textual basis of Foucault's view, but it is clear that the concerns of the *Alcibiades* are considerably more otherworldly than those of the *Laches*. Though scholars are not generally agreed whether *Alcibiades I* is or is not a genuine work of Plato's, the issue is not directly relevant to our topic. We are interested in its position within a general philosophical tradition, which generally, as a matter of fact, did consider it Plato's own work.

64. Cf. Aristotle, *Politics*, 7.13, 1132a.

65. Hadot, *Qu'est-que la philosophie antique?* 66–69, argues that the care of the self is not opposed to the care of the city. He bases his conclusion on the fact that Socrates, as presented both by Alcibiades in the *Symposium* and by Xenophon, participates fully in the affairs of the city. That may be true in regard to Xenophon. But the Platonic Socrates participates in the life of the city to the extent that he is "an almost ordinary, everyday man, with a wife and children, who engages in discussion with everyone, in the streets, in shops, in the gymnasium, a *bon vivant* who can drink more than everyone else without getting drunk, a soldier of courage and endurance" (67). To conclude from this, however, that Socrates participated in political life is to equivocate. For though it is true that the care of the self is not opposed to living *within* the city (that is, after all, one of the main points the personified Laws make in their argument with Socrates at *Cr.* 50c4–54d1; cf. *Phdr.* 230d2–5), it is opposed to occupying oneself with the *affairs* of the city, with politics (which Socrates himself says in the *Apology* we should address only after we have tended to ourselves).

An interesting account of the relationship between Socratic philosophy and the life of the city, arguing that there are ways in which the former is compatible with the latter, is offered by Hannah Arendt in "Philosophy and Politics," *Social Research* 57 (1990): 73–103. My general reaction to Arendt's view is that she reaches her conclusion by relying on a rather broad interpretation of what constitutes political discourse and political life, both of which she describes as a "dialogue between friends" and to which, so understood, Socratic dialectic may indeed be very important (82). But I still doubt that a general devotion to dialectic is compatible with political life if that is taken, as it should be, to include the practical activities involved in making sure that the life of the city is operating smoothly and fairly.

66. The only school that refused to see Socrates as its originator was the school of Epicurus. But, even so, the Epicurean ideal of an "untroubled life" and its emphasis on self-sufficiency is influenced by the example of Socrates. See, in particular, A. A. Long, "Hellenistic Ethics and Philosophical Power," in Peter Green, ed., *Hellenistic Culture and Society* (Berkeley: University of California Press, 1993), 138–56, esp. 141–51 (but also the comments of Paul Woodruff in the same volume, 157–62), and idem, "History of Western Ethics," in *Encyclopaedia of Ethics*, ed. Lawrence Becker (New York: Garland, 1992), 468–69.

67. On the idea that philosophy as a way of life combines living with discourse and is not therefore a purely "practical" enterprise, see Hadot, *Qu'est-que la philosophie antique?* 19, 21, 48, 77–81, 109–22.

68. Friedrich Nietzsche, *Gesammelte Werke*, vol. 16 (Munich: Musarion, 1926), 6.

69. A similar reading of the *Antichrist*, attributing to Nietzsche the view that Jesus provided, as it were, a wall on which Christians were enabled to scribble their own views, has been offered by Gary Shapiro, "Nietzsche's Graffito: A Reading of the *Antichrist*," *boundary 2*, vols. 9 and 10 (1981): 119–40.

70. Montaigne, "Of physiognomy," 1037–38; 793F.

71. Diogenes Laertius, "Life of Archelaus," 2.4.16.

72. Diogenes Laertius, "Life of Socrates," 2.5.18–19, 20–21.

73. Montaigne, "Of experience," 1067; 817F.

Bibliography

Adam, J., ed. *Platonis "Euthyphro."* Cambridge: Cambridge University Press, 1890.

Ahern, Daniel R. *Nietzsche as Cultural Physician*. University Park: Pennsylvania State University Press, 1995.

Allen, R. E. *Plato's "Euthyphro" and the Earlier Theory of Forms*. London: Routledge and Kegan Paul, 1970.

———. *Socrates and Legal Obligation*. Minneapolis: University of Minnesota Press, 1980.

Amory, Frederic. "*Eirón* and *Eiróneia*." *Classica et mediaevalia* 33 (1981–82): 49–80.

Arendt, Hannah. "Philosophy and Politics." *Social Research* 57 (1990): 73–103.

Arieti, James A. *Interpreting Plato: The Dialogues as Drama*. Savage, Md.: Rowman and Littlefield, 1991.

Armstrong, Timothy J., trans. *Michel Foucault, Philosopher*. New York: Routledge, 1992.

Baraz, Michaël. *L'Être et la connaissance selon Montaigne*. Paris: Corti, 1968.

Barnes, Jonathan, ed. *The Revised Oxford Translation of the Complete Works of Aristotle*. Princeton: Princeton University Press, 1984.

Barthes, Roland. "The Death of the Author." In *Image-Music-Text*, translated by Stephen Heath. New York: Hill and Wang, 1977.

Benson, Hugh H., ed. *Essays on the Philosophy of Socrates*. New York: Oxford University Press, 1992.

Bergmann, Peter. *Nietzsche: "The Last Antipolitical German."* Bloomington: Indiana University Press, 1987.

Beversluis, John. "Does Socrates Commit the Socratic Fallacy?" *American Philosophical Quarterly* 24 (1987): 211–23.

Blanchot, Maurice. *Foucault as I Imagine Him*. In *Foucault/Blanchot*, translated by Jeffrey Mehlman and Brian Massumi. New York: Zone Books, 1987.

Bloom, Allan, trans. *The "Republic" of Plato*. New York: Basic Books, 1968.

Bluck, Richard S. *Plato's "Sophist": A Commentary.* Manchester: Manchester University Press, 1975.

Blum, Claude. "La Fonction du 'déjà dit' dans les *Essais*: Emprunter, alleguer, citer." *Cahiers de l'Association Internationale des Études Françaises* 33 (1981): 35–51.

Böhm, Benno. *Sokrates im achtzehnten Jahrhundert.* Leipzig: Quelle und Meyer, 1929.

Bolotin, David. *Plato's Dialogue on Friendship: An Interpretation of the "Lysis" with a New Translation.* Ithaca: Cornell University Press, 1979.

Booth, Wayne. *A Rhetoric of Irony.* Chicago: University of Chicago Press, 1974.

Brandwood, Leonard. *A Word Index to Plato.* Leeds: W. S. Maney and Son, 1976.

Brickhouse, Thomas C., and Nicholas D. Smith. *Plato's Socrates.* New York: Oxford University Press, 1994.

———. *Socrates on Trial.* Princeton: Princeton University Press, 1989.

Brucker, J. *Historia critica philosophiae.* Leipzig, 1767.

Büchner, W. "Über den Begriff der Eironeia." *Hermes* 76 (1941): 339–58.

Bulhof, Francis. *Transpersonalismus und Synchronizität: Wiederholung als Strukturelement in Thomas Manns "Zauberberg."* Groningen: Drukkerij van Denderen, 1966.

Burford, Alison. *Craftsmen in Greek and Roman Society.* Ithaca: Cornell University Press, 1972.

Burger, Ronna L. *Plato's "Phaedrus": A Defense of a Philosophic Art of Writing.* Birmingham: University of Alabama Press, 1980.

Burnet, John, ed. *Plato's "Euthyphro," "Apology of Socrates," and "Crito."* Oxford: Clarendon Press, 1924.

Burnyeat, M. F. "Can the Skeptic Live His Skepticism?" In Malcolm Schofield, Myles Burnyeat, and Jonathan Barnes, eds., *Doubt and Dogmatism: Studies in Hellenistic Epistemology.* Oxford: Clarendon Press, 1980.

———. "The Impiety of Socrates." *Ancient Philosophy* 17 (1997): 1–12.

Campbell, Lewis. *The "Sophistes" and "Politicus" of Plato.* 1867. Reprint, New York: Arno Press, 1973.

Cave, Terence. *The Cornucopian Text: Problems of Writing in the French Renaissance.* Oxford: Clarendon Press, 1979.

Charpentier, François. *Memorabilia: Les Choses mémorables de Xenophon.* Amsterdam, 1699. (Translated into English as *The Memorable Things of Socrates, Written by Xenophon, in Five Books . . . To which are prefixed the Life of Socrates from the French Academy; and the Life of Xenophon.* London, 1712. Translated into German by Christian Thomasius as *Das ebenbild eines wahren und ohnpedantischen philosophi; oder, Das leben Socratis; aus dem frantzösishen-des des herrn Charpentier ins teutsche übersetzt von Christian Thomas.* Halle, 1693, 1720.)

Clark, Maudemarie. *Nietzsche on Truth and Philosophy.* Cambridge: Cambridge University Press, 1990.

———. "Nietzsche's Attack on Morality." Ph.D. diss., University of Wisconsin, 1975.

Cobb, William, trans. *Plato's "Sophist."* Savage, Md.: Rowman and Littlefield, 1990.

Connor, W. R. "The Other 399: Religion and the Trial of Socrates." *Bulletin of the Institute of Classical Studies* 58 (1991): Supplement, 49–56.

Cooper, John M. "Notes on Xenophon's Socrates." In *Reason and Emotion: Essays on Ancient Moral Psychology and Ethical Theory*. Princeton: Princeton University Press, 1998.

Cooper, John M., ed. *Plato: Complete Works*. Indianapolis: Hackett, 1997.

Cooper, Lane. *Plato on the Trial and Death of Socrates*. Ithaca: Cornell University Press, 1941.

Corbett, P. J. *Classical Rhetoric for the Modern Student*. 3d ed. New York: Oxford University Press, 1990.

Cornford, Francis M. *Plato's Theory of Knowledge*. Indianapolis: Bobbs-Merrill, 1957.

Cousin, Jean. *Études sur Quintilien*. 2 vols. Paris: Boivin, 1936.

Croiset, Maurice, ed. *Platon: Oeuvres complètes*. Vol. 1. Paris: Les Belles Lettres, 1920.

Daele, Hilaire van., trans. *Aristophane*. 5 vols. Edited by Victor Coulon. Paris: Les Belles Lettres, 1928–40.

Dane, Joseph A. *The Critical Mythology of Irony*. Athens: University of Georgia Press, 1991.

Dannhauser, Werner. *Nietzsche's View of Socrates*. Ithaca: Cornell University Press, 1974.

Danto, Arthur C. *Nietzsche as Philosopher*. New York: Macmillan, 1965.

———. "Philosophy as/and/of Literature." In *The Philosophical Disenfranchisement of Art*. New York: Columbia University Press, 1986.

———. "Some Remarks on *The Genealogy of Morals*." In Robert C. Solomon and Kathleen M. Higgins, eds., *Reading Nietzsche*. New York: Oxford University Press, 1988.

Davidson, Arnold I. "Archaeology, Genealogy, Ethics." In David Couzens Hoy, ed., *Foucault: A Critical Reader*. Oxford: Blackwell, 1986.

———. "Ethics as Ascetics: Foucault, the History of Ethics, and Ancient Thought." In Gary Gutting, ed., *The Cambridge Companion to Foucault*. Cambridge: Cambridge University Press, 1994.

Davidson, Donald. "The Folly of Trying to Define Truth." *Journal of Philosophy* 93 (1996): 263–87.

Detweiler, Bruce. *Nietzsche and the Politics of Aristocratic Radicalism*. Chicago: University of Chicago Press, 1990.

Dittmar, Heinrich. *Aischines von Sphettos: Studien zur Literaturgeschichte der Sokratiker*. Berlin: Weidmann, 1912.

Dover, K. J. *Greek Popular Morality in the Time of Plato and Aristotle*. Berkeley: University of California Press, 1974.

Dover, K. J., ed. *Aristophanes: "Clouds."* Oxford: Clarendon Press, 1968.

———. *Plato: "Symposium."* Cambridge: Cambridge University Press, 1980.

Dreyfus, Hubert L., and Paul Rabinow. *Michel Foucault: Beyond Structuralism and Hermeneutics*. Chicago: University of Chicago Press, 1983.

Dumézil, Georges. " . . . *Le Moyne noir et gris dedans Varennes*": *Sotie nostradamique suivie d'un divertissement sur les dernieres paroles de Socrate*. Paris: Gallimard, 1984.

Enright, D. J. *The Alluring Problem: An Essay on Irony*. New York: Oxford University Press, 1986.

Erasmus, Desiderius. *Convivium religiosum*. In *Desiderii Erasmi Roterodami opera omnia*. Vol. 1, pt. 3, edited by L.-E. Halkin, F. Bierlaire, and R. Hoven. Amsterdam: North Holland, 1972.

———. *Sileni Alcibiadis*. In *Desiderii Erasmi Roterodami opera omnia*. Vol. 2, pt. 5, edited by Felix Heinimann and Emanuel Kienzle. Amsterdam: North Holland, 1981.

Eribon, Didier. *Michel Foucault*. Translated by Betsy Wing. Cambridge, Mass.: Harvard University Press, 1991.

———. *Michel Foucault et ses contemporains*. Paris: Fayard, 1994.

Fénelon, François Salignac de la Mothe. *Abrégé des vies des anciens philosophes*. In *Oeuvres complètes de Fénelon*. Vol. 7. Paris: J. Leroux et Jouby, 1850.

Ferguson, John. *Socrates: A Source Book*. London: Macmillan, 1970.

Fish, Stanley. "Short People Got No Reason to Live: Reading Irony." In *Doing What Comes Naturally*. Durham, N.C.: Duke University Press, 1989.

FitzPatrick, P. J. "The Legacy of Socrates." In Barry S. Gower and Michael C. Stokes, eds., *Socratic Questions: The Philosophy of Socrates and Its Significance*. London: Routledge, 1992.

Flynn, Thomas. "Foucault as Parrhesiast: His Last Course at the Collège de France." In James Bernauer and David Rasmussen, eds., *The Final Foucault*. Cambridge, Mass.: MIT Press, 1994.

Foucault, Michel. "An Aesthetics of Existence." In *Foucault Live: Collected Interviews, 1961–1984*, edited by Sylvère Lotringer. New York: Semiotext(e), 1989.

———. *The Archaeology of Knowledge*. Translated by A. M. Sheridan Smith. New York: Harper and Row, 1972.

———. *The Birth of the Clinic: An Archaeology of Medical Perception*. Translated by A. M. Sheridan Smith. New York: Random House, 1973.

———. *The Care of the Self*. Vol. 3 of *The History of Sexuality*, translated by Robert Hurley. New York: Random House, 1986.

———. *Discipline and Punish: The Birth of the Prison*. Translated by Alan Sheridan. New York: Random House: 1977.

———. "The Ethics of the Concern for Self as a Practice of Freedom." In *Foucault Live: Collected Interviews, 1961–1984*, edited by Sylvère Lotringer. New York: Semiotext(e), 1989.

———. *The History of Sexuality*. Vol. 1, *An Introduction*. Translated by Robert Hurley. New York: Random House, 1978.

———. "Interview: Sex, Power, and the Politics of Identity." In *Foucault Live: Collected Interviews, 1961–1984*, edited by Sylvère Lotringer. New York: Semiotext(e), 1989.

———. Lectures on Socrates at the Collège de France, 15 and 22 February 1984.

———. *Madness and Civilization: A History of Insanity in the Age of Reason*. Translated by Richard Howard. New York: Random House, 1965.

———. "On the Genealogy of Ethics: Overview of Work in Progress." In *The Foucault Reader*, edited by Paul Rabinow. New York: Random House, 1984.

———. *The Order of Things: An Archaeology of the Human Sciences*. New York: Random House, 1973.

———. "Prison Talk." In *Power/Knowledge: Selected Interviews and Other Writings, 1972–1977*, edited by Colin Gordon. New York: Random House, 1980.

———. "Truth and Power." In *Power/Knowledge: Selected Interviews and Other Writings, 1972–1977*, edited by Colin Gordon. New York: Random House, 1980.

———. *The Use of Pleasure*. Vol. 2 of *The History of Sexuality*, translated by Robert Hurley. New York: Random House, 1985.

———. "What Is an Author?" In Josué V. Harari, ed., *Textual Strategies: Perspectives in Post-Structuralist Criticism*. Ithaca: Cornell University Press, 1979.

———. "What Is Enlightenment?" In *The Foucault Reader*, edited by Paul Rabinow. New York: Random House, 1984.

Fowler, H. W. *A Dictionary of Modern English Usage*. 2d ed., revised and edited by Sir Ernest Gowers. New York: Oxford University Press, 1965.

Frame, Donald M. "Pierre Villey (1879–1933): An Assessment." *Oeuvres et critiques* 8 (1983): 29–43.

Frede, Michael. "Euphrates of Tyrus." Typescript. Keble College, Oxford University, 1995.

———. "Philosophy and Medicine in Antiquity." In *Essays on Ancient Philosophy*. Minneapolis: University of Minnesota Press, 1987.

———. "Plato's Arguments and the Dialogue Form." In James C. Klagge and Nicholas D. Smith, eds., *Methods of Interpreting Plato and His Dialogues*. *Oxford Studies in Ancient Philosophy* 10 (1992): Supplement, 201–19.

———. "The Sceptic's Two Kinds of Assent and the Question of the Possibility of Knowledge." In Richard Rorty, J. B. Schneewind, and Quentin Skinner, eds., *Philosophy in History*. Cambridge: Cambridge University Press, 1984.

Friedländer, Paul. *Plato*. Translated by Hans Meyerhoff. 2d ed. 3 vols. Princeton: Princeton University Press, 1969.

Friedrich, Hugo. *Montaigne*. Edited by Philippe Desan. Translated by Dawn Eng. Berkeley: University of California Press, 1991.

Furley, William D. "The Figure of Euthyphro in Plato's Dialogue." *Phronesis* 30 (1985): 201–8.

Geach, Peter. "Plato's *Euthyphro*: An Analysis and Commentary." *Monist* 50 (1966): 369–82.

Giannantoni, Carlo. *Socratis et Socraticorum reliquiae*. Rome: Bibliopolis, 1990.

Gigon, Olof. *Sokrates: Sein Bild in Dichtung und Geschichte*. 2d ed. Bern: A. Francke, 1970.

Glenos, Demetres. *Platona "Sophistis."* Edited by Giannes Kordatos. 1940. Reprint, Greek-European Youth Movement, 1971.

Gombrich, E. H. *Meditations on a Hobby-Horse*. London: Phaidon, 1963.

Gooch, P. W. "Socratic Irony and Aristotle's *Eirôn*: Some Puzzles." *Phoenix* 41 (1987): 95–104.

Gray, Floyd. "Montaigne and the *Memorabilia*." *Studies in Philology* 58 (1961): 130–39.

Grice, Paul. *Studies in the Way of Words*. Cambridge, Mass.: Harvard University Press, 1989.

Griffin, M. T., and E. M. Atkins, eds. *Cicero: "On Duties."* Cambridge: Cambridge University Press, 1991.

Griswold, Charles L. Jr., ed. *Platonic Writings/Platonic Readings.* New York: Routledge, 1988.

Griswold, Charles L. Jr. *Self-Knowledge in Plato's "Phaedrus."* New Haven: Yale University Press, 1986.

Groden, Suzy Q, trans. *The "Symposium" of Plato.* Edited by J. A. Brentlinger. Amherst: University of Massachusetts Press, 1970.

Gross, Barry, ed. *Great Thinkers on Plato.* New York: Capricorn Books, 1969.

Grote, George. *Plato and the Other Companions of Sokrates.* 3 vols. London: Russell, 1865.

Grube, G. M. A., trans. *Plato: Five Dialogues.* Indianapolis: Hackett, 1981.

———. *Plato: "Republic."* Revised by C. D. C. Reeve. Indianapolis: Hackett, 1992.

Gulley, Norman. *The Philosophy of Socrates.* London: Macmillan, 1968.

Guthrie, W. K. C. *A History of Greek Philosophy.* 6 vols. Cambridge: Cambridge University Press, 1962–81.

Habermas, Jürgen. *The Philosophical Discourse of Modernity.* Translated by Frederick Lawrence. Cambridge, Mass.: MIT Press, 1987.

Hadot, Pierre. *Philosophy as a Way of Life.* Edited by Arnold I. Davidson. Translated by Michael Chase. Oxford: Blackwell, 1995.

———. *Qu'est-ce que la philosophie antique?* Paris: Gallimard, 1995.

———. "Reflections of the Notion of 'The Cultivation of the Self.'" In Timothy J. Armstrong, trans., *Michel Foucault, Philosopher.* New York: Routledge, 1992.

Hallie, Philip P. *The Scar of Montaigne.* Middletown, Conn.: Wesleyan University Press, 1966.

Hamilton, William, trans. *Plato: "Symposium."* Baltimore: Penguin, 1951.

Hampton, Timothy. "Montaigne and the Body of Socrates: Narrative and Exemplarity in the *Essais.*" *MLN* 104 (1989): 880–98.

Hatab, Lawrence J. *A Nietzschean Defense of Democracy.* Chicago: Open Court, 1995.

Havas, Randall. *Nietzsche's Genealogy: Nihilism and the Will to Knowledge.* Ithaca: Cornell University Press, 1995.

Hayman, Ronald. *Nietzsche: A Critical Life.* New York: Oxford University Press, 1980.

Hegel, G. W. F. *Lectures on the History of Philosophy.* Translated by E. S. Haldane. 3 vols. 1892. Reprint, London: Routledge and Kegan Paul, 1962.

———. *Philosophy of Fine Art.* Translated by F. P. B. Gemaston. 1920. Reprint, New York: Hacker Art Books, 1975.

———. *Sämtliche Werke: Jubiläumsausgabe.* Edited by Hermann Glockner. 26 vols. Stuttgart: Fr. Fromann, 1927–40.

———. *Vorlesungen über die Geschichte der Philosophie.* 3 vols. Leiden: A. H. Adriani, 1908.

Hippocrates. *Hippocrate: L'Ancienne médecine.* Edited by A.-J. Festugière. 1948. Reprint, New York: Arno Press, 1979.

Homer. *The Iliad.* Translated by Robert Fagles. New York: Viking Penguin, 1990.

Irwin, T. H. *Plato's Ethics*. New York: Oxford University Press, 1995.

——. *Plato's Moral Theory*. New York: Oxford University Press, 1977.

Irwin, T. H., trans. *Aristotle: "Nicomachean Ethics."* Indianapolis: Hackett, 1985.

Isocrates. *Antidosis*. Edited and translated by Georges Mathieu. Paris: Les Belles Lettres, 1942.

——. *Contra Sophistas*. Edited and translated by George Norlin. Loeb Classical Library, vol. 3. Cambridge, Mass.: Harvard University Press, 1928.

Japp, Uwe. *Theorie der Ironie*. Frankfurt: Klostermann, 1983.

Joël, Karl. *Der echte und der xenophontische Sokrates*. 2 vols. Berlin: R. Gaentner, 1893–1901.

Johnston, Mark. "Self-Deception and the Nature of Mind." In Brian McLaughlin and Amélie Oksenberg Rorty, eds., *Perspectives on Self-Deception*. Berkeley: University of California Press, 1988.

Joukovsky, Françoise. "Qui parle dans le livre III des *Essais?*" *Revue d'histoire littéraire de la France* 88 (1988): 813–27.

Kahn, Charles H. "The Methodology of Plato in the *Laches*." *Revue internationale de philosophie* 40 (1986): 7–21.

——. "On the Relative Date of the *Gorgias* and the *Protagoras*." *Oxford Studies in Ancient Philosophy* 6 (1988): 69–102.

——. *Plato and the Socratic Dialogue: The Philosophical Use of a Literary Form*. Cambridge: Cambridge University Press, 1996.

——. "Plato's *Charmides* and the Proleptic Reading of Socratic Dialogues." *Journal of the History of Philosophy* 85 (1988): 541–49.

Kaufmann, Walter. *Nietzsche: Philosopher, Psychologist, Antichrist*. 4th ed. Princeton: Princeton University Press, 1974.

Kerferd, George. *The Sophistic Movement*. Cambridge: Cambridge University Press, 1981.

Kierkegaard, Søren. *The Concept of Irony with Continual Reference to Socrates*. Edited and translated by Howard V. Hong and Edna H. Hong. Princeton: Princeton University Press, 1989.

——. *The Point of View for My Work as an Author*. Translated by Walter Lowrie. New York: Harper and Row, 1962.

Klein, Jacob. *Plato's Trilogy: "Theaetetus," the "Sophist," and the "Statesman."* Chicago: University of Chicago Press, 1977.

Klonoski, Richard J. "The Portico of the Archon Basileus: On the Significance of the Setting of Plato's *Euthyphro*." *Classical Journal* 81 (1986): 130–37.

Kowalik, Jill Anne. "Sympathy with Death: Hans Castorp's Nietzschean Resentment." *German Quarterly* 58 (1985): 27–48.

Kraut, Richard. "Comments on Gregory Vlastos, 'The Socratic Elenchus.'" *Oxford Studies in Ancient Philosophy* 1 (1983): 59–70.

Kraut, Richard, ed. *The Cambridge Companion to Plato*. New York: Cambridge University Press, 1992.

La Charité, Raymond C. "Montaigne's Silenic Text: 'De la phisionomie.'" In *Le Parcours des "Essais": Montaigne 1588–1988*. Paris: Aux Amateurs de livres, 1989.

Limbrick, Elaine. "Montaigne and Socrates." *Renaissance and Reformation* 9 (1973): 46–57.

Lloyd-Jones, Hugh. *The Justice of Zeus*. Berkeley: University of California Press, 1971.

———. "Nietzsche and the Study of the Ancient World." In James C. O'Flaherty, Timothy F. Sellner and Robert M. Helm, eds., *Studies in Nietzsche and the Classical Tradition*. Chapel Hill: University of North Carolina Press, 1979.

Long, A. A. "Hellenistic Ethics and Philosophical Power." In Peter Green, ed., *Hellenistic History and Culture*. Berkeley: University of California Press, 1993.

———. "History of Western Ethics: Hellenistic." In *The Encyclopaedia of Ethics*, edited by Lawrence Becker. New York: Garland, 1992.

———. "Plato's Apologies and Socrates." In Jyl Gentzler, ed., *Method in Ancient Philosophy*. Oxford: Oxford University Press, 1997.

———. "Socrates in Hellenistic Philosophy." *Classical Quarterly* 38 (1988): 150–71.

MacDowell, Douglas M., ed. *Aristophanes: "Wasps."* Oxford: Clarendon Press, 1971.

Magalhâes-Vilhena, V. de. *Le Problème de Socrate: Le Socrate historique et le Socrate de Platon*. Paris: Presses Universitaires de France, 1952.

Maier, Heinrich. *Sokrates*. Tübingen: J. C. B. Mohr, 1913.

Mann, Thomas. *Fragment über das Religiöse*. In *Gesammelte Werke*. Vol. 11. Frankfurt: Fischer, 1960.

———. *The Magic Mountain*. Translated by H. T. Lowe-Porter. New York: Alfred A. Knopf, 1927.

———. *The Magic Mountain*. Translated by John E. Woods. New York: Alfred A. Knopf, 1995.

———. *Der Zauberberg*. Frankfurt: Fischer, 1952.

Marcel, R. "Saint Socrate, patron de l'humanisme." *Revue internationale de philosophie* 5 (1951): 135–43.

McGowan, Margaret M. *Montaigne's Deceits: The Art of Persuasion in the "Essais."* London: University of London Press, 1974.

Meijer, Marianne S. "Guesswork or Facts: Connections between Montaigne's Last Three Chapters (III:11, 12 and 13)." *Yale French Studies* 64 (1983): 167–79.

Merquior, J. G. *Foucault*. Berkeley: University of California Press, 1985.

Miller, James. *The Passion of Michel Foucault*. New York: Simon and Schuster, 1993.

Momigliano, Arnaldo. *The Development of Greek Biography*. Cambridge, Mass.: Harvard University Press, 1971.

Montaigne, Michel de. *The Complete Works of Montaigne*. Translated by Donald M. Frame. Stanford: Stanford University Press, 1942.

———. *Les Essais de Michel de Montaigne*. Edited by Pierre Villey. New ed. 3 vols. Paris: Librairie Félix Alcan, 1965.

———. *Michel de Montaigne: The Complete Essays*. Translated by M. A. Screech. London: Penguin Press, 1991.

Montuori, Mario. *De Socrate iuste damnato: The Rise of the Socratic Problem in the Eighteenth Century*. Amsterdam: J. C. Gieben, 1981.

———. *Socrates, Physiology of a Myth*. London Studies of Classical Philology 6, 1981.

Morrison, Donald. "On Professor Vlastos' Xenophon." *Ancient Philosophy* 7 (1987): 9–22.

———. "Xenophon's Socrates on the Just and the Lawful." *Ancient Philosophy* 15 (1995): 329–48.

Most, Glenn W. "A Cock for Asclepius." *Classical Quarterly* 43 (1993): 96–111.

Muecke, D. C. *The Compass of Irony.* London: Methuen, 1969.

Navarre, M. O., ed. *Charactères de Théophraste.* Paris: Les Belles Lettres, 1924.

Navia, Luis E., and Ellen L. Katz. *Socrates: An Annotated Bibliography.* New York: Garland, 1988.

Nehamas, Alexander. "Confusing Universals and Particulars in Plato's Early Dialogues." *Review of Metaphysics* 29 (1975): 287–306.

———. "The Ends of Philosophy." Review of Jürgen Habermas, *The Philosophical Discourse of Modernity. New Republic,* 30 May 1988, 32–36.

———. "Eristic, Antilogic, Sophistic, Dialectic." *History of Philosophy Quarterly* 5 (1990): 3–16.

———. "Getting Used to Not Getting Used to It: Nietzsche in *The Magic Mountain.*" *Philosophy and Literature* 5 (1981): 73–89.

———. "Meno's Paradox and Socrates as a Teacher." *Oxford Studies in Ancient Philosophy* 3 (1985): 1–30.

———. "Nietzsche, Aestheticism, Modernity." In Bernd Magnus and Kathleen M. Higgins, eds., *The Cambridge Companion to Nietzsche.* Cambridge: Cambridge University Press, 1996.

———. *Nietzsche: Life as Literature.* Cambridge, Mass.: Harvard University Press, 1985.

———. "Socratic Intellectualism." In John J. Cleary, ed., *Proceedings of the Boston Colloquium in Ancient Philosophy.* Vol. 2. Lanham, Md.: University Press of America, 1987.

———. "Subject and Abject: The Examined Life of Michel Foucault." *New Republic,* 15 February 1993, 27–36.

———. "A Touch of the Poet." *Raritan Quarterly* 10 (1990): 101–25.

———. "Voices of Silence: On Gregory Vlastos' Socrates." *Arion,* 3d ser., vol. 2 (1992): 156–86.

———. "What Did Socrates Teach and to Whom Did He Teach It?" *Review of Metaphysics* 46 (1992): 270–306.

———. "Writer, Text, Work, Author." In Anthony J. Cascardi, ed., *Literature and the Question of Philosophy.* Baltimore: Johns Hopkins University Press, 1987.

Nehamas, Alexander, and Paul Woodruff, trans. *Plato: "Symposium."* Indianapolis: Hackett, 1989.

Newman, Ernest. *The Life of Richard Wagner.* Vol. 4. 1937. Reprint, Cambridge: Cambridge University Press, 1980.

Nietzsche, Friedrich. *Beyond Good and Evil.* In *The Basic Writings of Nietzsche,* translated by Walter Kaufmann. New York: Random House, 1968.

———. *The Birth of Tragedy.* In *The Basic Writings of Nietzsche,* translated by Walter Kaufmann. New York: Random House, 1968.

———. *Daybreak: Thoughts on the Prejudices of Morality.* Translated by R. J. Hollingdale. Cambridge: Cambridge University Press, 1982.

———. *Ecce Homo.* In *The Basic Writings of Nietzsche,* translated by Walter Kaufmann. New York: Random House, 1968.

——. *The Gay Science*. Translated by Walter Kaufmann. New York: Random House, 1974.

——. *Gesammelte Werke*. 23 vols. Munich: Musarion, 1920–29.

——. "Homer on Competition." In *On the Genealogy of Morality*, translated by Carol Diethe. Cambridge: Cambridge University Press, 1994.

——. *Human, All-Too-Human*. Translated by R. J. Hollingdale. Cambridge: Cambridge University Press, 1986.

——. *On the Genealogy of Morals*. In *The Basic Writings of Nietzsche*, translated by Walter Kaufmann. New York: Random House, 1968.

——. *Philosophy and Truth: Selections from Nietzsche's Notebooks of the Early 1870s*. Edited and translated by Daniel Brazeale. Atlantic Highlands, N.J.: Humanities Press, 1979.

——. *Sämtliche Werke: Kritische Studienausgabe*. 15 vols. Edited by Giorgio Colli and Mazzino Montinari. Berlin: De Gruyter, 1980.

——. *Schopenhauer as Educator*. In *Unmodern Observations*, edited and translated by William Arrowsmith. New Haven: Yale University Press, 1990.

——. *Schopenhauer as Educator*. In *Untimely Meditations*, translated by R. J. Hollingdale. Cambridge: Cambridge University Press, 1983.

——. *Thus Spoke Zarathustra*. In *The Viking Portable Nietzsche*, edited and translated by Walter Kaufmann. New York: Viking Press, 1954.

——. *Twilight of the Idols*. In *The Viking Portable Nietzsche*, edited and translated by Walter Kaufmann. New York: Viking Press, 1954.

——. *The Will to Power*. Translated by Walter Kaufmann and R. J. Hollingdale. New York: Random House, 1967.

O'Neill, John. *Essaying Montaigne: A Study of the Renaissance Institution of Reading and Writing*. London: Routledge and Kegan Paul, 1982.

Peek, Werner. *Griechische Versinschriften*. Vol. 1. Berlin: Akademie, 1955.

Phillips, Margaret Mann. *Erasmus on His Times: A Shortened Version of the "Adages" of Erasmus*. Cambridge: Cambridge University Press, 1967.

Platnauer, Maurice, ed. *Aristophanes: "Peace."* Oxford: Clarendon Press, 1964.

Plato. *The Dialogues of Plato*. Translated by Benjamin Jowett. Oxford: Oxford University Press, 1953.

Pope, Maurice. *The Ancient Greeks: How They Lived and Worked*. London: David and Charles, 1976.

Press, Gerald A. *Plato's Dialogues: New Studies and Interpretations*. Lanham, Md.: Rowman and Littlefield, 1993.

Rabelais, François. *Gargantua and Pantagruel*. Translated by Burton Raffel. New York: Norton, 1990.

Rabinowitz, W. G. "Platonic Piety: An Essay towards the Solution of an Enigma." *Phronesis* 3 (1958): 108–20.

Reed, C. J. *Thomas Mann: The Uses of Tradition*. Oxford: Clarendon Press, 1974.

Reeve, C. D. C. *Socrates in the "Apology."* Indianapolis: Hackett, 1989.

Rendall, Steven. *Distinguo: Reading Montaigne Differently*. Oxford: Clarendon Press, 1992.

Ribbeck, Otto. "Über den Begriff des *Eiron*." *Rheinisches Museum* 31 (1876): 381–400.

Rieckman, Jens. *"Der Zauberberg": Eine geistige Autobiographie Thomas Manns*. Stuttgart: Heinz, 1977.

Rigolot, François. "Les 'Visages' de Montaigne." In Marguerite Soulie, ed., *La Littérature de la Renaissance: Mélanges offerts à Henri Weber*. Geneva: Slatkine, 1984.

Robin, Léon, *Platon: Oeuvres complètes*. 2 vols. Paris: Gallimard, 1950.

Robinson, Richard. *Plato's Earlier Dialectic*. 2d ed. Oxford: Clarendon Press, 1953.

Robinson, T. M. *Contrasting Arguments: An Edition of the "Dissoi logoi."* New York: Arno Press, 1979.

Roloff, Dietrich. *Platonische Ironie*. Heidelberg: C. Winter, 1975.

Roochnik, David. "Plato's Use of the Techne-Analogy." *Journal of the History of Philosophy* 24 (1986): 295–310.

———. *The Tragedy of Reason: Toward a Platonic Conception of the Logos*. New York: Routledge, 1990.

Rorty, Amélie Oksenberg. "A Literary Postscript: Characters, Persons, Selves, Individuals." In *The Identities of Persons*. Berkeley: University of California Press, 1976.

Rorty, Richard. *Consequences of Pragmatism: Essays, 1972–1980*. Minneapolis: University of Minnesota Press, 1982.

———. *Contingency, Irony, and Solidarity*. Cambridge: Cambridge University Press, 1989.

Rosen, Frederick. "Piety and Justice: Plato's *Euthyphro*." *Philosophy* 43 (1968): 105–16.

Rosen, Stanley. *Plato's "Symposium."* New Haven: Yale University Press, 1968.

Rowe, Christopher. "Platonic Irony." *Nova Tellus* 5 (1987): 83–101.

Rutherford, R. B. *The Art of Plato: Ten Essays in Platonic Interpretation*. Cambridge, Mass.: Harvard University Press, 1995.

Salkever, Stephen G. Review of James C. Klagge and Nicholas D. Smith, eds., *Methods of Interpreting Plato and His Dialogues*. *Oxford Studies in Ancient Philosophy* 10 (1992)-Supplement. In *Bryn Mawr Classical Review* (Electronic Edition, 1992).

Sartre, Jean-Paul. "Existentialism Is a Humanism." In Walter Kaufmann, ed., *Existentialism from Dostoevsky to Sartre*. New York: World, 1956.

Schacht, Richard. *Nietzsche*. London: Routledge and Kegan Paul, 1983.

Scharfschwerdt, Jürgen. *Thomas Mann und der deutsche Bildungsroman*. Stuttgart: Kohlhammer, 1967.

Schlegel, Friedrich von. *Friedrich Schlegel's "Lucinde" and the Fragments*. Translated by Peter Firchow. Minneapolis: University of Minnesota Press, 1971.

———. *Kritische Friedrich-Schlegel-Ausgabe*. 19 vols. Edited by Ernst Behler et al. Munich and Padenborn: Schöningh, 1956–.

———. *Kritische Schriften*. Munich: Carl Hanser, 1938.

Schleiermacher, Friedrich. "Über den Werth des Sokrates als Philosophen." In *Sämtliche Werke*. Vol. 2. Berlin, 1838.

Schmidt, Hermann-Josef. *Nietzsche und Sokrates: Philosophische Untersuchungen zu Nietzsches Sokratesbild*. Meisenheim: Hain, 1969.

Scodel, Joshua. "The Affirmation of Paradox: A Reading of Montaigne's *Essays*." *Yale French Studies* 64 (1983): 209–37.

Scott, Gary Alan. "Games of Truth: Foucault's Analysis of the Transformation of Political to Ethical *Parrhésia* and the Disagreement between Socrates and

Alcibiades over Truth-telling." Typescript. Department of Philosophy, Whittier College, 1996.

Screech, M. A. *Montaigne and Melancholy: The Wisdom of the "Essays."* London: Penguin, 1991.

Sedgewick, G. G. *Of Irony, Especially in Drama.* Toronto: University of Toronto Press, 1948.

Seeskin, Kenneth. *Dialogue and Discovery: A Study in Socratic Method.* Albany: State University of New York Press, 1987.

Serres, Michel. "Géométrie de la folie." In *Hermès ou la communication.* Paris: Minuit, 1968.

Shapiro, Gary. "Nietzsche's Graffito: A Reading of the *Antichrist." boundary 2,* vols. 9 and 10 (1981): 119–40.

Solomon, Robert C. "Nietzsche and Nehamas's Nietzsche." *International Studies in Philosophy* 21 (1989): 55–62.

Starobinski, Jean. *Montaigne in Motion.* Translated by Arthur Goldhammer. Chicago: University of Chicago Press, 1985.

Stock, Irving. *"The Magic Mountain." Modern Fiction Studies* 32 (1986): 487–520.

Stone, I. F. *The Trial of Socrates.* Boston: Beacon Press, 1988.

Strauss, Leo. *The City and Man.* Chicago: University of Chicago Press, 1964.

Strong, Tracy. *Friedrich Nietzsche and the Politics of Transfiguration.* Exp. ed. Berkeley: University of California Press, 1988.

Swearingen, C. Jan. "Dialogue and Dialectic: The Logic of Conversation and the Interpretation of Logic." In Tullio Maranhão, ed., *The Interpretation of Dialogue.* Chicago: University of Chicago Press, 1990.

Taylor, A. E. "Aeschines of Sphettos." In *Philosophical Studies.* London: Macmillan, 1934.

Thesleff, Holger. "Platonic Chronology." *Phronesis* 34 (1989): 1–26.

———. *Studies in Platonic Chronology.* Commentationes humanarum litterarum 70. Helsinki: Societas Scientiarium Fennica, 1982.

Thiele, Leslie Paul. *Friedrich Nietzsche and the Politics of the Soul.* Princeton: Princeton University Press, 1990.

Thomson, J. A. K. *Irony.* London: Allen and Unwin, 1926.

Tiles, J. E. *"Technê* and Moral Expertise." *Philosophy* 59 (1984): 49–66.

Tournon, A. *Montaigne: La Glose et l'essai.* Lyon: Presses Universitaires de Lyon, 1983.

Trilling, Lionel. *Sincerity and Authenticity.* Cambridge, Mass.: Harvard University Press, 1971.

Ussher, R. Glenn, ed. *The Characters of Theophrastus.* London: Macmillan, 1960.

Vander Waerdt, Paul. "Socratic Justice and Self-Sufficiency: The Story of the Delphic Oracle in Xenophon's *Apology of Socrates.*" Paper presented at the Society for Ancient Greek Philosophy, New York City, October 1990.

Vander Waerdt, Paul, ed. *The Socratic Movement.* Ithaca: Cornell University Press, 1994.

Versenyi, Laszlo. *Socratic Humanism.* New Haven: Yale University Press, 1963.

Villey, Pierre. *Les Sources et l'évolution des "Essais" de Montaigne.* 2 vols. Paris: Hachette, 1908.

Vlastos, Gregory. "Introduction." In *Plato: "Protagoras,"* translated by
 Benjamin Jowett, revised by Martin Ostwald. Indianapolis: Bobbs-Merrill,
 1956.

———. "The Paradox of Socrates." In *The Philosophy of Socrates: A Collection
 of Critical Essays*. Garden City, N.Y.: Doubleday, 1971.

———. Review of Thomas C. Brickhouse and Nicholas D. Smith, *Socrates on
 Trial*. *Times Literary Supplement*, 15–21 December 1989, 1393.

———. *Socrates: Ironist and Moral Philosopher*. Cambridge: Cambridge
 University Press, 1991.

———. *Socratic Studies*. Edited by Myles Burnyeat. Cambridge: Cambridge
 University Press, 1994.

Völker, Ludwig. "'Experiment,' 'Abenteuer,' 'Traum' in Thomas Manns
 Roman *Der Zauberberg*: Struktur-Idee-Tradition." In Heinz Saueressig, ed.,
 Besichtigung des Zauberbergs. Biberach: Wege und Gestalten, 1974.

Waddington, Raymond B. "Socrates in Montaigne's 'Traicté de la
 phisionomie.'" *Modern Language Quarterly* 41 (1980): 328–45.

Warren, Mark. *Nietzsche and Political Thought*. Cambridge, Mass.: MIT Press,
 1988.

Weigand, Hermann J. *"The Magic Mountain": A Study of Thomas Mann's Novel*.
 1933. Reprint, Chapel Hill: University of North Carolina Press, 1965.

Weiss, Roslyn. "Euthyphro's Failure." *Journal of the History of Philosophy* 24
 (1986): 437–53.

Weiss, Walther. *Thomas Manns Kunst der sprachlichen und thematischen
 Integration*. Hefte zur Zeitschrift *Wirkendes Wort* 13. Düsseldorf: Schwann,
 1964.

Weissenborn, H. *De Xenophontis in commentariis scribendis fide historica*. Jena:
 G. Nevenhahni, 1910.

West, Thomas G., and Grace Starry West. *Four Texts on Socrates*. Ithaca: Cornell
 University Press, 1984.

Whiston, Robert. *Demosthenes, with an English Commentary*. London:
 Whittaker, 1959.

White, Nicholas P., trans. *Plato: "Sophist."* Indianapolis: Hackett, 1993.

Wilamowitz-Moellendorff, Ulrich von. *Platon*. 2d ed. 2 vols. Berlin:
 Weidmann, 1920.

Williams, Bernard. *Shame and Necessity*. Berkeley: University of California
 Press, 1993.

Williams, C. E. "Not an Inn, but a Hospital." In Harold Bloom, ed., *Thomas
 Mann's "The Magic Mountain": Modern Critical Interpretations*. New
 Haven: Chelsea, 1986.

Woodruff, Paul. "Plato's Debt to Protagoras." Typescript. Department of
 Philosophy, University of Texas, 1993.

———. "Plato's Early Theory of Knowledge." In Stephen Everson, ed.,
 Epistemology. Cambridge: Cambridge University Press, 1990.

———. "Response to A. A. Long." In Peter Green, ed., *Hellenistic History and
 Culture*. Berkeley: University of California Press, 1993.

Woodruff, Paul, trans. *Plato: "Hippias Major."* Indianapolis: Hackett, 1982.

Woolf, Virginia. "Montaigne." In *The Common Reader: First Series*. New York:
 Harcourt Brace, 1984.

Xenophon. *Conversations of Socrates.* Translated by Hugh Tredennick and Robin Waterfield. London: Penguin, 1990.

Young, Charles M. "Plato and Computer Dating." *Oxford Studies in Ancient Philosophy* 12 (1994): 227–50.

Zeitlin, Froma. "Playing the Other: Theater, Theatricality, and the Feminine in Greek Drama." In *Playing the Other: Gender and Society in Classical Greek Literature* (Chicago: University of Chicago Press, 1995).

Zeller Eduard. *Die Philosophie der Griechen*, vol. II.1, 4th ed. (Leipzig: Fues's Verlag, 1889).

———. *Socrates and the Socratic Schools,* translated by Oswald J. Reichel (New York: Russell & Russell, 1962).

Ziolkowski, Theodore. *Dimensions of the Modern Novel* (Princeton: Princeton University Press, 1971).

Index

Designer:	Ina Clausen
Compositor:	Integrated Composition Systems
Text:	10/13 Galliard
Display:	Galliard
Printer:	Data Reproductions
Binder:	Data Reproductions